Spahn

THE TEMPERING YEARS

Books by Edwin P. Hoyt

THE TEMPERING YEARS

THE VANDERBILTS AND THEIR FORTUNES

JUMBOS AND JACKASSES

THE
TEMPERING
YEARS

by
Edwin P. Hoyt

Charles Scribner's Sons
New York

For my wife and all the other children of the depression who may have forgotten or who may never have known how near our nation came to failure in the 1930's, in the hope that they will be persuaded through these pages to accept national responsibilities cheerfully and to draw the cloak of freedom close.

CONTENTS

THE GLORIOUS AUTUMN

CHAPTER ONE

THE UNITED STATES had never been busier, more purposeful, more filled with energy and love of life than it appeared to visitors in October, 1929. Americans were proud of their country and pleased with themselves. They looked forward to a brilliant future in which there would be two cars in every garage and each man could tune in Amos 'n Andy, the blackface comedians, on his own eight-tube radio set. With the confidence of men who knew they lived in a golden age, sociologists predicted that by 1960 New York City, America's largest metropolis and capital of the financial world, would be a city of twenty-one million people. The nation's optimism was unalloyed. That was not odd; Americans had long been optimists who blessed the forefathers who came to this best of all possible lands, on the most serene of all continents, far from the turmoil and intrigues of Europe.

It was fall, the season that belongs to New York City in the way that spring belongs to Paris and the cold austerity of winter belongs to Moscow. It was October, the finest month of autumn. The breath of Indian summer lingered in the air, touched with the winter chill. The days were brisk. It was a joy to be alive and to be American.

All but a handful of Americans were convinced that the national prosperity was indefatigable, and that they had created a society of perpetual abundance. Rugged individualists were earning fortunes almost overnight in oil, in motorcar manufacture, in the infant airlines industry, in chemicals, in radio, in advertising, and a hundred other areas. Business was ripe for the conquering, as every college boy knew. Most attractive of all was the financial world of New York's Wall Street, itself a compendium of a hundred dizzy little vortexes, each moving more rapidly one month than the next, spewing forth new millionaires who had gone into the market place with only a few dollars. It seemed that an investor could not lose in the spiralling market as prices of stocks went up and up and up.

A minor setback had been felt on the stock market during the previous March when many stock prices tumbled. For a few days, some of the new millionaires were reduced to speculating furiously to recoup their paper losses. A handful of sober spokesmen pleaded for saner ways. President Hoover was one who warned often, although indirectly and usually *sotto voce*, that the current tendency to rash speculation in common stocks must eventually end in a break in the market. Roger W. Babson, a cautious stock analyst, was convinced that the market was due for a serious break. He had predicted the earlier drop in March—almost to the moment. But for every sober head there were ten thousand men and women who were intoxicated by the lure of stock market gambling. From Maine to California the best-read pages of the newspapers were not the comics, but the market reports. To offset Babson's gloomy predictions there was the optimism of Professor Irving Fisher, head of Yale University's economics department. Professor Fisher, an eminently respectable economist, was called upon to address banquets of the largest and most important business conventions, to talk on the subject which fascinated the entire nation—that greatest gamble in the American world, the stock market. Professor Fisher advised that the productivity of the nation had increased so much in postwar years that ever-rising stock prices still had not brought stocks to their true values in dollars. The boom would go on indefinitely, he predicted.

Few men in the business world questioned the acuity of that judgment—more than a million Americans were engaged in stock speculation in the autumn of 1929. Most of the speculators bought stocks on margin, which meant they actually pledged only between 25 and 50 per cent of the amount of money required to buy a share of stock. Brokers were willing—even eager—to carry such margin accounts. They felt protected against price declines by a 25 per cent cash payment. The brokers earned more money from margin accounts than from outright stock sales, and they were willing to borrow money at 25 per cent interest, if need be, to back their customers. A few men like Joseph P. Kennedy, the Boston millionaire, had become distrustful of the market and had gone out of it altogether, into real estate and other investment. Others, like Jesse Livermore, financier and acknowledged king of the "bears," played the stock game with another purpose. The "bears" formed investment pools to manipulate the price of stocks and force them down. They created millions of dollars in profit by the strange reverse technique known as short selling, in which the short seller promised to deliver a stock to another person at a given price—say 100—and then forced the price down to 75, bought the stock, and cleared twenty-five dollars on each share.

Still, the vast majority of the men and women in the market— bankers and bellboys, telephone operators and brokers—were on the bull side, buying stocks on margin, sure that the stocks would rise in price in a few days or even in a few hours. For months, until a ragged September, this had been the road to fortune. On Professor Fisher's stock exchange index, where 100 represented the average figure of the 215 most important stocks on the New York Stock Exchange in 1926, the figure rose in October, 1929 to 200. There seemed to be every reason for brokers to continue their heavy borrowings from banks to support customer margin buying and their own speculation. In the week that began on October 21, brokers' loans stood at an all-time high of $6,804,000,000, despite the Federal Reserve Bank's high-discount policy. The high discount represented federal disapproval of the atmosphere of easy money and easy speculation. But although the Federal Reserve showed disapproval, few private bankers shared that conservatism. Charles E. Mitchell, chairman of the board of the National City Bank of New York, and a member of the governing board of the New York Federal Reserve Bank, defiantly offered the public $25,000,000 in speculative money on the heels of the Federal Reserve announcement. The giants among manufacturing companies opened their cash reserves to make loans to brokers. The lure of 15 per cent and 20 per cent interest on short-term loans was great, and the risk seemed slight, based on the upward surge of the market for more than two years. Conservative bankers, among them George Whitney, a Morgan partner, were deep in the market. Wall Street brokers, among them George Whitney's brother, Richard Whitney, were in even deeper. Some members of the inside group of the financial world, the brokers of the New York Stock Exchange, organized pools which manipulated stock prices in violation of common morality. Richard Whitney, a broker's broker, was a particularly active plunger, and not a very adept one. Even on a rising market, and carrying about half the Morgan bond brokerage business as he did, and handling 10 per cent of all the bond transactions of the New York

Stock Exchange, Richard Whitney was constantly in financial trouble. He had been in trouble off and on since 1925, when he first began playing the market on his own account.

The term "broker's broker," when applied to Richard Whitney, carried more than the usual meaning in Wall Street jargon. Primarily Whitney was so termed because he carried very few personal accounts, almost none on margin. His business consisted largely of the handling of stocks and bonds for other brokerage houses.

In still another way, Richard Whitney typified the inner circle of Wall Street. He was the epitome of what a broker ought to be, from the tip of his snap-brim fedora hat to the laces of his well-shined, imported shoes. He was a son of the Boston Whitneys, not to be confused with the Whitneys of New York. The New York Whitneys had produced a cabinet minister and had married into the Vanderbilt family, but they had not come across on the *Arabella*, the ship which followed the *Mayflower* across the Atlantic to the Massachusetts colony.

Richard Whitney had been educated at Groton preparatory school, where he played center on the football team and was captain of the baseball team. At Harvard College he rowed stroke oar in the first varsity crew. He was elected to Harvard's Porcellian Club, and he completed the four-year course in three years.

Following graduation, Richard Whitney joined his brother George in New York. With the help of his father, a Boston banker, Richard purchased a seat on the New York Stock Exchange in 1916, after a few years of apprenticeship in Wall Street as a clerk with Kidder Peabody and Company. That same year he became engaged to Gertrude Sands, the daughter of George R. Sheldon, an old J. P. Morgan associate. Sheldon was a member of the Republican National Committee, and a former president of the Union League Club.

It was a good match for both families. Richard Whitney held memberships in the Knickerbocker, Piping Rock, Racquet, and Tennis clubs. Any one of these memberships was sufficient to guarantee him entrée into the highest society. Although Richard Whitney was only twenty-eight years old in 1916, he was already accepted as a member of the inner circle of Wall Street, a position supported by the importance of his brother as a Morgan partner, and cemented by the wedding.

Four years later, in 1920, Whitney became head of his own firm, Richard Whitney and Company. The Morgan Guaranty Trust Company began to send young Whitney much of their extensive bond business. Had the young broker been less of a gambler, his personal fortune would have been assured by the Morgan bankers and he would have become a rich man.

But Richard Whitney was not built that way. From the beginning he invested his patrimony and his income in high living and brash forays in the business world. By 1925 he had taken actions that were questionable, although unquestioned. In the following year— although no one knew it then—Whitney had committed a serious breach: In 1926 he misused securities which were part of a trust fund set aside by George Sheldon for Mrs. Whitney. Richard had pledged his wife's securities for a personal loan at a New York bank. Had that action been discovered, Richard Whitney's position in the financial world would have been destroyed. Since this action was not known he was regarded in Wall Street as a coming young man, although reckless. But in the 1920's recklessness was not regarded in Wall Street with more than a casual eye.

In the fall of 1929, Richard Whitney was forty-one years old. He had grown heavy but was none the less handsome, six-feet tall, with smooth, rectangular face and carefully groomed hair. He carried his well-tailored figure with the air of a gentleman among gentlemen, and he gave the impression of a completely successful, self-satisfied man. Richard Whitney looked forward with reason to becoming the most important man in the New York Stock Exchange. He lived in a $200,-000 town house on East 73rd Street in New York City, he maintained an estate of several hundred acres at Far Hills, New Jersey, on the bank of the Raritan River, where he was President of the Essex Foxhounds Hunt Club.

Whitney had made enemies among the men of Wall Street, for he was self-contained and reserved. He could be sarcastic, and he ignored those who were not so fortunate as to be members of the inner circle. He was often brusque with the commission agents who

did business with the public, particularly if these men had not enjoyed
the advantages of an education at Harvard or one of the other important schools of the eastern United States. Yet even among his
enemies, Whitney was regarded as the ideal Wall Street man. Youngsters copied his mannerisms and inquired the name of his tailor. Even
those who knew Richard Whitney as an inveterate borrower of large
sums of money trusted him completely. There was no word of scandal
or disrespect about him, even among those whom he snubbed regularly. This man, then vice-president of the New York Stock Exchange,
was being groomed for the presidency to succeed President E. H. Simmons, who had chosen October, 1929 to marry and leave the city for
a honeymoon in Hawaii. For all practical purposes in this week Richard Whitney was already president of the exchange. At least he had
the operating responsibility, if not title and authority.

As usual, Richard Whitney was skating along thin ice in his own
affairs. He had spent one hundred thousand dollars the previous year
on personal living. He had borrowed half a million dollars from his
brother George to cover some investments that autumn, and had
lost a million dollars, on paper at least, in a short-selling maneuver
which went astray as the prices of common stocks continued to climb.

Whitney's personal expenditures and obligations had increased
a great deal in the last few years. He had taken up yachting as well as
hunting. He had been elected an officer of the New York Yacht Club,
and he had begun spending parts of each winter in Florida, where he
was intrigued enough by real estate development and the talk of a
Florida industrial boom to invest money in several wild schemes.

Richard Whitney was as "heavy on margin," personally, as any
speculator on the street that year. By October 21, 1929, he was deeply
immersed in a round of loans and financial manipulations that kept
him as busy as juggler W. C. Fields, although Whitney's juggling involved borrowing from one bank to pay another, and borrowing from
acquaintances to continue his speculations. It was possible for him to
juggle and manipulate without interference because the rules of the
New York Stock Exchange required financial statements only from
brokers who dealt in margin accounts, and Whitney's firm did not,
so he was not asked to certify his financial condition. Those in Wall

Street who knew of Richard Whitney's financial problems would not mention them, at any rate. In 1929 the code of honor among Wall Street men precluded informing anyone in the outside world of inside activities of those "in the club"—a code of silence carefully respected in the market place.

Nor did any government body in the nation take an active interest in the stock exchanges. Historically, the exchanges always governed themselves. In New York this meant the New York Stock Exchange and the lesser New York Curb Exchange. Outside New York it meant flourishing markets in Boston, Chicago, Philadelphia, and San Francisco. Only a handful of malcontents proposed any other system, for the stock exchanges around the country were recognized as free markets, parts of the mechanism of a sovereign business community. Since that business community had served the nation well enough to bring it the world's highest standard of living and the greatest period of prosperity in history, it was generally conceded that only radicals or fools would suggest drastic change.

Yet signs existed—in America and outside—of an impending crisis in the American business community.

President Hoover was concerned, largely because he knew of the changes which had been taking place in trade and foreign relations in the past few years. Herbert Clark Hoover had been inaugurated as President amid a splash of promises about prosperity only six months before, but he had served as Secretary of Commerce under President Harding and under Calvin Coolidge. He was eight years in the Commerce post altogether, an eight years in which his punctilious engineer's mind had neatly sorted out and pigeonholed the financial facts of world affairs.

The President was aware of the dangerous condition of the stock market that existed on Monday morning, October 21. He had argued as early as 1925 against the inflation of credit by the Federal Reserve Board. But Hoover's arguments as Secretary of Commerce had been to no avail because pressure had been brought on the Federal Reserve by the three great debtor nations of World War I: Great Britain, Germany, and France. The German Reichsbank's Hjalmar Schacht had been influential in persuading the American Treasury Department to a policy of easy credit since Germany was in serious economic trouble and she needed help if her economy—and thus an important American market—was not to collapse.

By 1928 Germany, France, Great Britain, Canada, Holland, Sweden, and Japan were all suffering business recessions, the outgrowth of inflation and overproduction in the postwar years. After the faltering of the American stock markets in March, 1929, British investors sensed from afar that an end was coming to the years of prosperity in Wall Street.

For several weeks European investors had been quietly withdrawing their money from America, in the belief that the boom was over and that the long-range trend of American securities would be downward.

The President was aware of this change. His method of combatting the dangers of speculation was quiet and indirect, for Mr. Hoover had the mind of a businessman and technician, not that of a politician. Further, he was a thoroughgoing believer in rugged individualism and he detested government control of any kind. He saw his function as Chief Executive, in this case, to be persuasive, not coercive. Consequently, six weeks after his inauguration, Mr. Hoover began an anti-inflation campaign which was monumental in its ineffectiveness. He met with the editors of major newspapers and magazines and asked them to write strong editorials against speculation. Most of the editors complied with the President's request, but their readers were too intrigued by newspaper market pages to read the editorial pages. The educational campaign produced little but yawns.

The President asked Andrew Mellon, his Secretary of the Treasury, to make strong statements in favor of caution. Mellon did so. The statements bored even financial editors.

President Hoover then called in bankers from all over the country and lectured them about the dangers of speculation. The bankers scoffed, and went right back to their short-term moneylending at 15 and 20 per cent interest. Thomas Lamont, a Morgan partner, wrote the President a detailed letter, proving to Lamont's own satisfaction that the financial world was firmly established on the soundest basis possible. The bankers reminded the President that this was his "New Era" of continual prosperity. Depression had been banished, along with the enemies of democracy, who had been vanquished in mortal combat in Flanders fields and at the Meuse-Argonne. The Presidential pleas for financial sobriety had no more effect than beer laws on a bootlegger.

The President was in a strange position, even had he not seemed determined to make his own office ineffectual. He had been elected on the coattails of prosperity; he and the Republican publicists had concentrated on that theme for three months before the election of 1928. It would be unseemly for him to turn around a few weeks after he took office to declare that the prosperity he had promised to make permanent was threatened—and threatened by what? There was little on which anyone could lay a finger, except the physical law which declares that what goes up must come down. In the campaign his own party claimed it had repealed that law with the election of Warren Harding to the Presidency. The Republicans said the administrations of Calvin Coolidge had made prosperity secure and that under Herbert Hoover every American town would become a little Eden.

The immediate problem was no more readily visible from Pennsylvania Avenue than from Wall Street so it was not odd that neither President Hoover nor anyone else seemed to recognize what was happening. American steel production had fallen off 5 per cent at the end of summer. Steel mills produced at only 80 per cent of capacity. Gradually, almost unnoticed, the uses of steel had changed over the past few years. Steel and other basic commodities were used more for production of luxury goods, and less to make necessities. The economy of the United States had changed, subtly but significantly. The nation was not building dams or bridges or highways in quantity.

President Hoover had, on October 1, embarked on an inspection tour of the new Ohio River development, but he was convinced that federal meddling in the affairs of the states should end with the deepening of the river channel to make it navigable. He was fighting opponents in Congress who wanted federal development of the Muscle Shoals Dam which would be the keystone of the Tennessee Valley power system. Equally important to the national morale, the President and Mrs. Hoover travelled that day to Dearborn, Michigan, to participate in ceremonies honoring Thomas Alva Edison on the fiftieth anniversary of his invention of the incandescent electric bulb. In a gesture consonant with the times Henry Ford had recreated the Edison laboratory at his private museum in Dearborn, and now the old inventor was coming to re-enact the scene of his great discovery on a coast-to-coast radio hookup. Hoover, Edison, Ford, and the newspapers took this charade quite seriously. There seemed a need to indulge in such luxuries and little time for concentration on necessities.

The New York career girls who made their ways to offices and counters in Wall Street on that morning of October 21 wore cloche hats, long-waisted dresses with V-necks, fur-trimmed overcoats, and silken hose. One telephone operator in one of the city's larger hotels wore a new sealskin coat. Her spending was typical. She was playing the stock market on a broker's margin account, and boasted neither a bank savings account, insurance, nor a penny in the world except what she earned from week to week. But would she take her profits and convert them to bonds, as President Hoover wanted her and all Americans to do? She would not even consider it, for the gambling fever had her, as it had a million other Americans. The fever held her and them in red-cheeked, bright-eyed frenzy.

To be sure, E. I. du Pont de Nemours and Co. had informed the press a few days before that the company's income had increased by a million dollars a month, a direct result of a policy of diversification. But what were the products that brought the increase? They were cellophane and rayon—substitutes, not necessities.

There were other trouble signals on the business horizon. The amount of wheat in storage had reached a new high: 393,000,000 bushels lay in elevators in the United States and Canada; 125,000,000 more than in 1928. Worse, the European wheat market was closed to the United States for all practical purposes. Argentina, blessed that year with a bumper wheat crop, was shipping five million bushels of wheat a week to Europe and selling it at dumping prices. Yet the United States Government's Federal Farm Board was at that moment putting the final touches on an agreement to lend a half-million dollars to the Cooperative Wheat Growers' Association of Kansas City. The Kansas City association would turn around and lend the money to its members, to finance their production of more wheat for the coming year. As grain piled up and prices dropped, farmers turned to their traditional method of maintaining their income: they produced more.

Industrial production had increased since 1925, but not as much as most people believed. In 1929 production fell off. Production had to fall off. In the shoe industry, alone, American factories had built an annual plant capacity of 900,000,000 pairs, but they could only sell 300,000,000 pairs of shoes to consumers each year. While millions of dollars were being made on the stock market, on the farms and in the tenements of the cities even casual observers could see that there were hungry people in America. The average family income, in this New Era, was $2,000 a year. The number of farm foreclosures had increased alarmingly. Not only shoemakers, but thousands of steelworkers and other skilled laborers were unemployed.

The plight of the poor disturbed the men of the federal government, yet the federal government would not recognize its own jurisdiction over this area of life. Mr. Hoover's Republicans stood staunchly for free enterprise and against federal intervention in the problems of the states. The succor of the unemployed was first a personal problem, second a concern of organized private charity, and finally a problem for local and state government, but never, never, within the fiat of the national government in Washington. Reformers, soft-eyed social workers such as the gangling young Harry Hopkins at Christadora House on New York's lower East Side, might insist that social responsibility included the problems of the poor and that in a national society these were at least partially national problems. Such arguments were not understood in Washington.

The attitude was different in Albany, the capital of New York, where in 1929 Franklin Delano Roosevelt had come to be chief executive officer of the state. Roosevelt, a Democrat elected by a margin of twenty-five thousand votes in a Republican election year all over the rest of the country, was acclaimed by some Democrats in Washington as the great hope of their party for 1932.

Governor Roosevelt was pushing former Governor Al Smith's program for public power development on the St. Lawrence River on October 21, 1929, while a statewide economic congress of businessmen recommended that the water power problem be removed from politics and put in the hands of "unbiased business interests." There, certainly, was a clue to vastly different attitudes.

Roosevelt had no call to concern himself with the larger problems of the nation, and in his attack on the problems of New York State he had not shown himself to be always either forthright, farseeing, or effective. Yet Roosevelt was building around himself a corps of assistants and consultants who had already stamped their personalities on the state administration. One of these men was Samuel Rosenman, the governor's counsel in Albany and his favorite speech writer. Another was Louis McHenry Howe, a tough fifty-eight-year-old newspaperman whose fingers were yellowed with cigarette stains, whose unkempt appearance caused his friends to liken him to Heywood Broun's "unmade bed," and who at first aroused repugnance in the sensitive Eleanor Roosevelt. Still another, a woman, was Frances Perkins, a former social worker in New York City's Hull House who had become the chief social welfare adviser to the state of New York as Industrial Commissioner. This *was* a change—employment of social workers in such key positions brought a different atmosphere to the government of New York. Roosevelt was an admirer of intellectuals, if too practical himself to be one, so intellectuals inevitably found their way into his government circle. They came in odd ways. Raymond Moley, professor of public law at Columbia University, was brought into the Roosevelt sphere by Louis Howe, the cynical newspaperman. Their communality of interest was the administration of justice, which interested Howe as an old police reporter, and interested Moley as a teacher and writer. In 1928 Professor Moley had encountered Roosevelt, introduced by Howe. After election to the governorship, Roosevelt began to ask Moley to help draft speeches, practical speeches, conservative in tone, for Moley called himself a practical, conservative man.

Practicality and conservatism were virtues. Radicalism was a vice, and yet radicalism was felt, and feared, all across the nation, from the home-grown radicalism of the farm states of the upper Middle West to the imported brand purveyed by the Communist International from Moscow. Norman Thomas, the minister turned socialist, was running for mayor of New York, but he took time out from his campaign this October week to don one of his other hats, that of executive director

of the League for Industrial Democracy, to appeal to a vastly uninterested labor movement to organize the Negroes and whites who worked
in southern textile mills. The Thomas plea was typical and appropri-
ate. At that moment a half-dozen textile mill strikers were on trial in
Gastonia, North Carolina, accused of using and inciting violence in a
bloody labor dispute. The strikers were unquestionably led by communists, but the position of Norman Thomas was that the answer to
most labor problems was useful, loyal labor organization. Organized
labor, however, was no more free from race prejudice than organized
capital, and besides, American labor was then organized on a craft
basis, not on industrial lincs.

The conservatism of the American Federation of Labor and the
conservatism of business leaders had combined to give rise to company unions, which claimed nearly two million members of the working force. Neither company union nor the AF of L type of organization
appealed to a young philosophical socialist named Walter Reuther.
He had left the South and moved, with his brother Victor, from the
family home in West Virginia to Detroit. Walter had taken a "swing
shift" job at the Ford motor plant, and enrolled in Wayne University,
while Victor stayed home and kept their tiny house. The Reuther
brothers were preparing themselves for places in a new labor movement.

The South was beset by labor problems, and race problems, but
also by a problem southerners recognized as legitimate; even in times
of prosperity there was no ease for the sharecroppers, Negro and
white. This year their problems were serious after the prices of cotton
and corn slumped. One southern leader, Governor Huey Long, had his
own way of dealing with such unrest. He built a political organization
on the foundation of the dole. He acquired the title of Kingfish, and
he ran his state with the personal authority of a Japanese shogun.

Disarmament, a fiery tariff debate in the Congress, and international monetary problems all related to foreign affairs but Americans
were only dimly conscious of the reasons for the revolt of Feng Yu-
Hsiang, the Christian general, against the Nanking government of
Chiang Kai-shek, or the stalling of European nations in organization
of a Bank for International Settlements. The League of Nations, of
which the United States would have no part, was trying in this week

to organize a Permanent Court of International Justice at The Hague. In welcome to fifty members of the Institute of International Law at Princeton, the university's president, John Grier Hibben, expressed hope that America would show more sense of responsibility in such matters.

Would it do so? The average American was far more concerned about the new talking pictures. Talkies were bringing a revolution to the movie industry; just that week the be-spectacled Harold Lloyd had appeared in *Welcome Danger,* and the movie-going public was aghast to hear, for the first time, Lloyd's high, piping voice. Another comedian named Charlie Chaplin faced a decision: should he talk or not talk in his forthcoming movie, *City Lights?*

Paul Robeson, the Negro singer, was in London, angry because he had been refused entrance to the grill room of his hotel, and Alfred P. Sloan, Jr., president of General Motors Corporation, was in London, too, conferring with Anthony Fokker, the Dutch aircraft designer. General Motors had just purchased 40 per cent of the Fokker Aircraft Company's stock. Because of the General Motors financial interests in Germany, Sloan was concerned, but only mildly, by the news that 235,000 more German workers were unemployed this year than at the same time in 1928. Sloan should have been worried to learn that American automobile production for the year was only 415,332 units—just 18 more cars produced than the year before. The incidence of instalment purchases was rising sharply. What had happened to the unparalleled prosperity of America? As far as Mr. Sloan could see—nothing.

On Sunday, October 20, millions of churchgoers across America were exposed to a theme which had been spreading among the God-fearing: the moral decline of the nation. One minister noted that on picking up his daily newspaper he had found five of eight columns on the front page devoted to revelations of fraud or other business dishonesty. Dr. Harry Emerson Fosdick, the prominent Baptist minister, referred to his "money-mad generation." Both statements were easily documented. The national experiment prohibiting indulgence by Americans in their inherited taste for alcoholic liquor had given birth to an entire new class of criminals—the bootleggers. In 1921, the first year the law was enforced, the federal government had brought 29,000 prohibition cases; in 1929, the government had already begun action in 56,000 cases, and the heavy drinking season was yet to come.

To the concern of moralists, disrespect for the law was not confined to liquor. Amateur smugglers were running the Treasury's customs agents ragged. Mrs. Frank Vance Storrs, the wife of a prominent New York real estate man, had been nabbed aboard the *Berengaria* on her return from Europe along with her daughters Carolyn and Anna, with $70,000 in jewelry and $15,000 worth of clothing. The customs agents did not say that all this amount was smuggled, but they accused Mrs. Storrs of breaking the laws, and allowed the ladies to go to their apartment at the Ritz-Carlton hotel wearing only the clothes they stood in, and carrying their dressing cases.

James F. McConnochie, the chief of special agents of the Treasury, said the government had finally become exasperated and was cracking down. Mrs. Storrs said it was an outrage. Mr. Storrs made his way to the customs house on lower Manhattan Island to try to straighten the matter out with customs officials. Philip Elting, collector of customs for the port of New York, was inclined to be sympathetic. No criminal charges would be filed, he said, but the ladies would have to pay a fine.

Personal smuggling was a minor part of the lawlessness. The former Secretary of Interior, Albert B. Fall, was on trial for taking a $100,000 bribe in the Teapot Dome oil scandal. Frank H. Warder, former superintendent of banks in New York, was on trial charged with accepting a $10,000 bribe to hold off state banking examination of the books of the City Trust Company. A neat, if criminal, business in using the bankruptcy laws for huge profits flourished. The auditor of Salt Lake City awaited arraignment on charges of misusing public funds.

What upset the moralists was the national attitude towards these peccadilloes. The Salt Lake City auditor, accused of criminality, that October week outdistanced all his rivals in the primary elections which were expected to choose a more honorable candidate to succeed him. The Carnegie Foundation for the Advancement of Teaching had investigated college athletics earlier in the year and found them to be the same across the country—"sodden with commercialism." Of 112 schools investigated, only 28 did not offer improper subsidies to athletes. But instead of hanging their heads in shame, many colleges defended their athletic activities. A Brown University professor attacked the foundation for meddling. A Bucknell professor accused the foundation of breach of faith in naming names. The Big Ten's commissioner of athletics defended the practice of buying college players.

Wild stock market speculation, while bemoaned by the ministers from their pulpits and by the President from his chair in the White House, was exactly in the spirit of the day. The bribetakers, misappropriators, bootleg whiskey buyers and amateur smugglers did not believe they would be caught by the authorities. Market speculators did not believe they could possibly lose, so certain were they of national prosperity and so assured were they of the continued strength of the stock market.

In this easy atmosphere which pervaded almost all of America except on Sundays, Richard Whitney suffered few twinges of conscience when he "borrowed" his wife's securities to pledge them against bank loans. From boyhood, Richard Whitney had made his own rules, and as he said himself he believed firmly in his right to do anything he wanted to do. His elder brother George, the Morgan banker, would not have approved of such "borrowing," so Richard did not inform him. But in any serious problem, Richard knew he could count on his millionaire brother to rescue him from financial difficulty. Nor were the free and easy bankers he knew inclined to question Richard's sources of security, knowing the family. Those were Richard Whitney's hedges against trouble in these days of unparalleled prosperity and license. Such hedges were not uncommon among the businessmen of that time.

In retrospect, it might seem apparent that Richard Whitney and a million other dabblers in Wall Street would have comported themselves quite differently had they been able to see into the future, but events of the next few weeks, and even the next few months, seem to belie the hope that the majority of men were able to absorb contemporary experience, separate reality from illusion, and draw sharp conclusions about the future.

THUNDER ON THE FLOOR

CHAPTER TWO

ON OCTOBER 21, 1929, when the New York Stock Exchange opened trading on the last stroke of ten o'clock, the financial world rested confident and serene. During the previous week the market had dropped, causing some men who were given to comparisons to recall the "rich men's panic" of 1903. In that year "undigested" new securities carried on brokers' credit had suddenly flooded the market to the point of depression. But the comparison was generally regarded as useless since in 1903 the financial community had not been protected by requirements for brokers' loan reports and regular financial statements of brokers who dealt with the public on margin (as the public seemed surely protected in 1929). In September, 1929, the output of new securities was the highest of the year, but that happy statistic was regarded as just another reflection of continued and unbridled prosperity.

The Monday morning edition of the *Wall Street Journal* noted that the professionals in Wall Street were as "bearish" as they had been at any time in the year, but "bearishness" did not extend to many amateurs. Later that Monday stocks slumped sharply in the heaviest trading day on record. Nearly 6,100,000 shares changed hands. On the New York Stock Exchange the trading was so intense that the stock ticker fell behind at the end of the first ten minutes and the end of the day saw the ticker one hundred minutes behind the market. This lapse did not paralyze the brokers on the floor of the exchange since they could move readily from one trading point to another to keep abreast of price changes, but the delay in reports caused consternation in the markets of Denver, St. Louis, and San Francisco, which relied on telegraphic reports to keep posted on movements in Wall Street.

Some stocks broke sharply. Commercial Solvents, for one, dropped 145 points that day, and there was noticeable "distress selling" on the Curb Exchange, which meant brokers were unloading stocks held on narrow margins when their margin calls had gone unanswered by customers over the weekend.

By nightfall the professionals had recovered their aplomb. None of them were seriously worried, although they expressed sympathy to the losers among their customers. It was easy to find plausible reasons for the decline, from announced suspicion that a "bear" pool of wealthy investors had combined forces to drive down the price of stocks, to presumed worry by stockholders who had amassed large paper profits and were willing to lose part of those profits to protect the remainder and get out of the market for a few days. There was no real concern on Wall Street, except by a few Cassandras like Roger Babson.

One reason for broker serenity was the recovery of U.S. Steel that day. Steel had opened at 212, dropped to 205½, but by the end of the day had picked up to 210½, and since Steel was regarded as the bellwether of the market the brokers went home to dinner in good humor on Monday evening. In Washington, U.S. Treasury officials pronounced the situation "sound." Wall Street's bankers, at the close of trading, had made their daily telephone checks around the financial community and they saw no reason for alarm, although common stocks were selling at an average of thirteen times their annual earnings, and some of the heavily traded stocks represented companies which had shown no earnings at all. Professor Fisher of Yale repeated his customary statement that the prices of stocks had not caught up with values, and he attributed the decline to the "shaking out of the lunatic fringe that attempts to speculate on margin."

On Tuesday the professor's words seemed to be borne out by fact. The market rallied. U.S. Steel went to 216½, although it closed lower at 212⅛. Roger Babson frantically advised his followers to sell their stocks and buy good bonds, but Charles Mitchell of the National City Bank said he saw nothing to worry about. Mitchell had arrived home that day by steamer after a month in Europe but he had not been out of touch with the market on his trip across the Atlantic on the *Majestic*. Every passenger steamer carried its own brokerage office in the fall of 1929 so passengers could play the market from their deck chairs. Ships' news reporters asked Mitchell, as head of New York's largest bank, what he thought of the talk about "undigested securities" and the huge amount of money outstanding in "brokers' loans," which financed customer margin accounts. That was not the point at all, the banker said. The increase in brokers' loans simply represented a shift by stockbrokers, from long-term to short-term financing. In effect it was just another registration of confidence in the current business scene. The general public, Mitchell said, was suffering from "brokers' loanitis," an annoying, if harmless disease, akin to myopia.

Charles Mitchell was an optimist. He had backed the stock market boom against the policy of the Federal Reserve Board. He had helped boom his own bank's stock to an all-time high of $585 a share. In order to promote the sale of National City Bank stock, he had made shares available to employees on very easy payment plans. His bank was carrying a loan to one employee for $345,000 worth of stock. Mitchell was not worried. Neither was Richard Whitney, presiding over the Stock Exchange in the absence of President Simmons on his honeymoon. Whitney did not even feel impelled to make a statement on the condition of the market on that Tuesday.

Wednesday, October 23, was an evil day on stock markets all over America and the end of the day was notable for significant changes in tone of the statements made by business leaders. Literally thousands of small investors were wiped out when they failed to supply cash to back their stocks and replace their share of the four billion dollars in paper losses suffered that day. Official Washington expressed surprise that the market remained so negative. Professor Fisher, speaking before the District of Columbia Bankers' Association, noted that the stock slump was surely "temporary." Bankers and brokers began discussing "support" of a market that had not seemed to need any support twenty-four hours earlier.

Support could come in several ways: by heavy investment in stocks by large investment trusts, which were reported to have cash reserves of at least a billion dollars, by a lowering of the rediscount rate on loans—an action by which the Federal Reserve Bank could make money easier to borrow, or by outright banker support, which meant the banks themselves would buy stocks in quantity.

In Chicago that Tuesday night Alexander Legge, chairman of the Federal Farm Board, warned the national convention of meat packers that the condition of American farmers was becoming serious. Mr. Legge said he was concerned because farmers must realize that four bushels of grain sold at $1.50 a bushel was a better investment for the farmer than five bushels sold at $1. Mr. Legge's comparison caught the eye of the nation because on the Chicago grain market wheat futures fell to $1.24⅞, a thirty-three cent drop in price in less than three months. Still, it was a rare man who added the figures of rising unemployment, falling production of staples, falling farm prices, and rising farm foreclosures, and connected the sum with the condition of the stock market. For a hundred years Wall Street men had maintained that the market place was an entity in itself, an exchange for buyers and sellers which was made possible by the existence of producing industry, but which neither controlled nor responded directly to the factors which brought about industrial prosperity or industrial depression. Secure in this belief, Wall Street's bankers still were not worried about the national economy. Their concern extended no further than their own investments.

After another poor day, on Wednesday night the atmosphere in Wall Street changed markedly. On Thursday morning when the big clock on the west wall above the floor of the New York Stock Exchange struck ten and Superintendent William B. Crawford struck the gong to announce the opening of trading, brokers surged to the trading stations, clutching handfuls of orders from customers—orders to sell. These were not usual "sell" orders. Kennecott Copper opened with a lot of 20,000 shares, General Motors the same; with such volume the ticker fell behind immediately. This was "dumping." As the extent of dumping became known the sell orders multiplied, along with rumors. The worst hour came between eleven fifteen and twelve fifteen, as investors across the country panicked and ordered their brokers to "sell at the market"—sell as quickly as possible before prices dropped further.

Prices were dropping five, ten, even fifteen points a minute. Auburn Motors plunged from 260 to 190, Montgomery Ward from 84 to 50. Usually, 750 or 800 brokers occupied the floor during a day's trading, but this day 1,100 brokers and a thousand assistants crowded around the trading stations, shouting and gesticulating to catch the eyes of the trading specialists.

The public gallery, seldom crowded, was jammed to overflowing. Winston Churchill, former British Chancellor of the Exchequer, dropped in for a few moments to view the confusion on the floor, then went on his way uptown to prepare for an important speech he was to make that evening. Other watchers stayed on, fascinated by the roar of the excited market place. It was the worst crash in history, so severe that by twelve thirty, Acting President Richard Whitney ordered the exchange's visitors' gallery closed to cut down the noise and help end the unceasing flow of rumors which said, erroneously, that the Chicago and Buffalo stock exchanges had been forced to close their doors in the flood of selling.

By noon that day a crowd had gathered on the steps of the U.S. sub-treasury building, eyes fixed on the entrance to the J. P. Morgan bank. A platoon of reporters and photographers stood there, waiting impatiently for developments. Inside the building, five of the most important bankers in the United States discussed the week's events. Outside, the crowd continued to wait for a report of the meeting.

The bankers conferred for twenty minutes, then four of them walked outside dolefully, leaving Thomas W. Lamont, senior partner of J. P. Morgan and Company to speak to the press. J. P. Morgan was in Europe, so Lamont was the spokesman for the Morgan bank. Five minutes later Lamont came out to hold an impromptu press conference at the entrance.

"There has been a little distress selling on the Stock Exchange," the banker began, in what eventually may be adjudged the financial understatement of the century. That was the closest Lamont came to recognizing the existence of panic. He went on to say that no financial houses were in trouble, that brokers reported margins were being maintained satisfactorily, and that the little bit of distress was caused by a "technical condition" which none but the professionals could be expected to understand. At that moment, Burton Rascoe later wrote, every bank in the country was probably technically insolvent because of the plunge in value of stocks that secure outstanding loans.

Skimpy and unrealistic as Lamont's statement was, it caused an immediate revival of optimism on the floor of the New York Stock Exchange, not because of what Lamont had said, but because it was known that the most important bankers of all had met together. Brokers, investors, and speculators forced themselves to believe that the bankers had agreed to support the market. In fact the bankers had done so and the proof of it came an hour later when Richard Whitney appeared on the floor of the exchange, walked over to post No. 12, the station where U.S. Steel was traded, and began buying steel, with an initial bid of 205. The stock had slumped during the morning to 193½.

Here was a master stroke, both in timing and in selection of the man to do the buying, a man known as a "Morgan broker," a dignified, imposing figure in his own right, who exuded an air of confidence and well-being. Whitney did not stop to explain what he was doing. He walked purposefully from one trading station to another, ordering stocks in lots of ten and twenty thousand shares, not ostentatiously, not jumping the price above the last quotation, but buying at the last previous quotation.

In half an hour, Whitney had ordered two hundred thousand shares of various stocks, representing more than twenty million dollars worth of purchases. Richard Whitney did not have to comment, it was apparent to Wall Street that a bankers' pool had come to the rescue of the market.

Wall Street hoped, that afternoon, that the Federal Reserve Board would come to the assistance of the financial community by lowering the rediscount rate on loans, and in Washington the board met twice, the second time with Treasury Secretary Andrew Mellon. By the time the board held its second meeting, the action of the New York bankers was known. The board members decided the market was under control so no action was taken. The board was true to its principle: interfere with business only when there seemed to be no other course.

On the floor of the stock exchange there were some indications of rallying. Some stocks moved upward during the last hour of trading but others moved down. It was late in the day and there was no sense to be made of the pattern, and at three o'clock, when Superintendent Crawford gavelled the gong three times to announce the end of the trading day, the sweating brokers, collars torn open, hands full of orders that would have to wait, breathed a collective gasp of relief and began to file back to their offices for a night of work.

On Thursday night fifty thousand Wall Street employees worked late, sending out calls to customers for more margin to cover losses, entering records of sales and purchases, assessing the positions of the brokerage houses at the end of a day in which nearly thirteen million shares of stock had changed hands on the New York Stock Exchange.

Nearly half as many shares had been sold on the smaller Curb Exchange that day. Thousands of accounts, most of them in the $1,000 to $10,000 range (which represented amateur investors) were closed out, and hundreds of thousands of shares of stock were earmarked for sale the following day when calls for margin remained unanswered by stunned speculators around the country.

The pattern was the same all over the nation, and beyond. Lights burned late in the brokerage houses in Boston and Philadelphia, in Atlanta and Los Angeles. Despite the lag of the stock ticker, which had fallen four hours behind the market by closing time, Broker M. J. Meehan aboard the Cunard Liner *Berengaria* had traded twenty thousand shares. One woman passenger had lost $160,000 in the morning, but had recouped all but $40,000 in the afternoon by vigorous trading. She had done well, for billions of dollars were lost that day, including those of the young telephone operator in the New York hotel who had invested everything she owned in her sealskin coat and in a margin account on the stock exchange. A hotel resident, unable to complete a telephone call that night, had gone to the switchboard himself, to overhear her talking to her broker, her voice breaking and eyes bathed in tears. All the telephone operator had left at the end of this Black Thursday was her sealskin coat and her job.

That night the relatives of Abraham Germansky, a wealthy real estate man who lived in Mount Vernon, New York, put in a frantic call to police to help them find Germansky. He had last been seen late Thursday on Wall Street, tearing up ticker tape and scattering it along the sidewalk.

Later on that night of Black Thursday, October 24, the brokerage and banking houses registered cautious optimism, once again sure that the worst was over and that the market would begin to rise. On the demand of Charles Merrill, who had removed himself from the market, Merrill Lynch and Company advised its customers to keep their margins high without formal request, but also noted that it was a good time for investors with ready cash to buy stocks outright. Thirty-five of the largest brokerage houses on the New York Stock Exchange (who did 70 per cent of all the business on the exchange) wired clients all over the country predicting quick recovery of the market. The house of Hornblower and Weeks prepared advertise-

ments which would run in eighty-five newspapers recommending purchase of "sound securities."

The next day, Friday, U.S. Steel opened at 207, and the big
bankers said everything was under control. There was an implicit
promise that they would not allow affairs to get out of control again.
The original group in the bank coalition was reinforced. Altogether the
bankers represented pledges of more than a quarter of a billion dollars
to support the market. President Hoover issued a reassuring statement
to the effect that fundamentally business was on a sound and prosperous basis. Banker Lamont, in a telling slip, had asked reporters on
Thursday if they knew of the failure of any financial houses. This next
day he had taken pains to reassure himself that "the street" was sound.

The street—Wall Street—was anything but sound. It was under-
going the most spectacular disaster of all time—but no one could
call the turn from one day to the next. So long had the financial
world steeped itself in optimism that no one appeared to be able to
recognize the earmarks of disaster. Governor Franklin D. Roosevelt,
who might have stepped in to regulate the New York stock exchanges,
criticized speculators in general but expressed his confidence in the
improvement of business and political morality. Alfred P. Sloan, returning from Europe, remarked that the slump was "healthy" for the
business world. Senator Carter Glass of Virginia, a conservative who
frowned on speculation, argued on the floor of the Senate in favor of
a 5 per cent tax on stock held less than sixty days. Senator Glass was
trying to combat speculation, which Senator King of Utah characterized as a "national disease." Senator King proposed an investigation
of the Federal Reserve System to discover why the Treasury had not
caught the downward trend and had not stopped it in time to save
millions of dollars in losses.

These were all indications of the national feeling that the worst
was over, a belief that persisted through the weekend of October 26
and October 27. The stricken speculators cried themselves to sleep or
drowned their woes in bathtub gin or, like Arthur Bathein, an officer
of the Northern Pacific Finance Company of Seattle, shot themselves
to death in the privacy of offices that no longer meant wealth or position, but ruin. Some continued to be listed among the missing, among
them Abraham Germansky.

The worst had not yet come. On Monday, October 28, stock prices plunged another fourteen billion dollars, and stocks which had resisted the earlier disaster fell hard and fast. Eastman Kodak dropped 40 points. General Motors went down only 6¾ points, but so large was the volume of General Motors stock sold that this spread meant a loss in values of nearly $350,000,000.

In this second week the disaster took a new turn: those who had been wiped out in the market began to withdraw their savings from the banks. The stock of New York's First National Bank dropped $500 a share that day. The banker coalition, surprisingly, did nothing. The Federal Reserve Board met again in Washington, but took no action.

On Tuesday, October 29, the market collapsed in a splash of trading which involved sixteen and a half million shares, and while several industrial giants announced extra dividends to be paid on their stocks in an effort to stimulate confidence, the confidence was gone. Bank stocks began to fall off. The value of New York's First National Bank dropped from $6,800 a share to $5,200 and the first broker's failure was announced: John J. Bell Company of the Curb Exchange suspended activity, wiped out. There was only one bright spot in the entire dismal picture, if one could call it that. The state of New York, which levied a stock transfer tax of two cents per $100 on stocks, had collected $1,500,000 from six days of stock market trading.

The bankers had shown their inability to understand what was happening or to stop it. So had the United States Treasury Department. So had Governor Roosevelt in Albany. New York City Mayor James Walker displayed his understanding of high finance when he spoke to the group of motion-picture exhibitors at the Astor Hotel and advised them to refrain from showing newsreels which pictured the run on the market.

On the American side of the Atlantic Ocean, there was no understanding of either the course of events or of the portents for the future. The American philosophy made no provision for the collapse of the nation's economic system. Americans from President Hoover to Roger Babson predicted that a turning point was just around the corner.

In the city of London, however, financial men were far enough removed from events and from the fatal optimism of New York to realize what was happening in America. The first cries of "I told you so" gave way at the end of the first week of collapse to sober consideration of the effects of the American disaster on the rest of the world. "We are watching the complete disorganization of a complex market by an assault upon it of a leaderless and panic-stricken mob," said the London *Daily Mail*'s financial editor, who looked on from afar in awe. Depression was bound to strike America, the British said. The British were concerned lest the American depression be so deep and so extended that it would cut American purchase of British imports.

America still did not know it had suffered disaster. Then the American failures began to pile up. At first they were the predictable kind of failures: David Korn, a Providence coal distributor, dropped dead in his broker's office, watching the falling stock ticker. A Kansas City insurance man named John G. Schwitzgebel fired two shots into his chest in a Kansas City club, after he had lost his fortune. Anthony Schneider, president of the Webster Eisenlohr cigar company fell to his death from an apartment window in mid-town New York after his company's stock had dropped from 113 to 4.

Brokers in New York, in Santiago, Chile, in Worcester, Massachusetts, and in scores of other cities closed their doors. The happiest failure in the world was a member of the Byrd Expedition to Antarctica who announced cheerfully that he had been wiped out but could not think of a better place to be when it happened.

On October 31, Richard Whitney consulted the board of governors of the New York Stock Exchange. After that meeting he closed the exchange for the remainder of the week, ostensibly to give the brokerage houses a chance to catch up on their work. Actually, the situation was desperate. The exchange was failing in its basic purpose: to provide buyers for stocks at all times. Some stocks, in the last few days of panic selling, had been offered for sale at times when no buyers could be found at any price. This, perhaps, was the "technical condition" of the market to which Thomas Lamont had referred in his statement on Black Thursday. It was technical, to be sure, but it was also fatal.

The bankers continued to meet each day and were joined by Owen P. Young, chairman of the General Electric Corporation. But the bankers had supported stocks for a long enough period on Black

Thursday to bail out their own investments. No medals for courage or charity are bestowed on Wall Street, and the bankers' concern at this point was to maintain the semblance of a market. They would prevent total destruction of the financial community if they could, for that was in their own interest, but they would not step in further until sure the patient was on his deathbed.

Richard Whitney had not only ordered closure of the stock exchange on Friday and Saturday, giving the brokers a three-day respite, but on Thursday trading was reduced to three hours, from 12:00 to 3:00 P.M. Pressure was thus cut down in two ways: the selling time was slashed almost in half, and by delaying the opening until noon, commission brokers and stock specialists were given two or three hours before market time to be sure there *was* a market for a stock which was expected to be dumped in quantity.

These were emergency measures. Whitney and the governors of the exchange did not resolve any of the problems of the financial world but they did make sure that a market of some kind would be maintained for stocks listed on the exchange.

Preparing for the new week, the business community again rallied its deep-seated optimism. The Federal Reserve Board had finally taken action—cutting the rate of bank interest from 6 per cent to 5 per cent. Stuart Chase, the economist, predicted that national prosperity would last for at least three more years. *The New York Times* financial writers proclaimed that a new chapter in national financial sanity had been opened with the readjustment of the market, and the elimination of the horde of margin speculators. Alfred P. Sloan, Jr. announced that he was more bullish than ever. General Motors' Opel auto plant in Germany, he said, was producing cars at the rate of 50,000 a year, but within five years he expected Opel to produce 200,000 automobiles each year.

Mr. Sloan did not say who was going to buy these automobiles or the ones his company manufactured in the United States for that matter. Therein was the crux of the problem, for the *important* capital which had been wiped out in the avalanche was not the big money of the business community. The disastrous losses were the cash reserves of small companies and the thousands and tens of thousands of dollars of middle-class savings which had been diverted from banks, bonds, insurance, and actual ownership of homes and automobiles while the public bought goods on the instalment plan and sank savings into the speculative market.

While the business world talked of sanity, banks began to merge all over America, merging at this point not to inflate bank stocks and create huge capital gains for the owners, but for their own salvation. The flood of deposit withdrawals, plus the losses the bankers had suffered in their own unwise investments, made combination necessary. In Philadelphia there was a call for a six months moratorium on first mortgages in view of the increase in foreclosures of small home-owners. In Minneapolis, that weekend, the $20,000,000 utilities holding company of Wilbur B. Foshay failed, wiping out the savings of small investors in thirty states. The people ruined here were not margin speculators but investors who had been steered by investment counsellors to outright purchase of "safe" utilities stocks—the ill, the retired, the widows, and the orphans.

On Monday, November 2, the stock markets opened in a resurge of optimism, but that day the important City State Bank of Chicago failed. On Wednesday, November 3, stocks sagged again all over the country, and now Richard Whitney and the governors of the New York Stock Exchange made the three-hour trading sessions permanent and exchanges across the country followed. The Bankers' Capital Corporation—a huge investment trust—failed on Wednesday, and a respected broker was arrested when he issued a $21,000 check on an overdrawn bank account. On that third weekend, Abraham Germansky was finally located, safe in a sanitarium, but Mabel Walker, the former secretary of Senator Edwards of New Jersey, was found dead, a suicide, in her Washington apartment. Miss Walker was just thirty years old, but all her savings had been wiped out, and the optimism of Mr. Sloan and the other business leaders had somehow failed to impress her.

The sudden pessimism of the public worried and angered the leaders of business. Newspapers and magazines began to devote full pages to reassuring advertisements of their own. In the first week of November the editors of *The Saturday Evening Post* announced that they were putting to press the largest issue of their magazine in history, carrying the greatest amount of advertising ever placed in a magazine. The *Post* advertisement was a fitting ending to the boom. It explained the continuation of big business optimism when the confidence of the nation was gone. Most of those *Post* advertisements had been ordered months before, when the nation appeared to be speeding ahead on sixteen cylinders.

Advertising agencies, which claimed to be at least as sensitive to the currents of public opinion as magazine editors, began to have their worries. The agencies responded to the public pessimism confidently, then pleadingly, and sometimes even in bad temper. Erwin Wasey and Company purchased a full page in *The New York Times* to chide the man who "hurls himself from a high window with complete disregard for the busy people who are really going somewhere on the sidewalks below."

On November 6, 1929, the opening phase of the great change in the United States had ended. For the first time in weeks the stock market story was moved off the front pages of the newspapers, moved back to the financial sections where it normally belonged.

Businessmen were still confident in November, 1929. The president of New York's Best and Company said he was looking forward optimistically to the holiday trade. Manufacturers felt the loss of sales, slashed production, and laid off workers, but the moguls of big business announced that mass layoffs would only delay the recovery they fully expected, so layoffs were delayed. President Hoover said the country would be back to normal in sixty days, and businessmen, if not the American public, believed the man the American communists called "the Pope of American business." Dr. A. H. Giannini, president of California's Bank of America, said the crash would have little effect on business.

In those strained, frightening weeks of the crash Richard Whitney had comported himself with the magnetism and assurance of a born leader. Ready for the job of president of the New York Stock Exchange, he had been thrown into command during the most trying period in the history of the exchange, when all that saved the market from outright collapse was the confidence he and a few others were able to instill in the nervous community of the moneyed. He had appeared on the floor daily, immaculate, the brim of his expensive hat turned up rakishly. He exuded confidence, smiling and waving to acquaintances while others cursed among the flood of torn memo paper and lost opportunities that cascaded to the floor. Whitney had not panicked once, nor had he lost his air of optimism, although his personal losses were more severe than those of many other brokers. (He was reported to have lost $2,000,000 in the crash.)

Richard Whitney had been virtually unknown outside the tight little Wall Street community before Black Thursday, but afterwards the newspapers christened him the "white knight" of Wall Street. If there had been any doubts about the ability of this forty-one-year-old broker to assume the leadership of the most important stock exchange in America, the doubts were erased by the events of late October and November, 1929.

On the second Monday in January, 1930, the members of the stock exchange assembled on the floor and elected the nominators, who in turn would choose a candidate or candidates for the presidency of the exchange. It was known at that moment that the nominators would select Richard Whitney. They would make a pretense of deliberation until the second Monday in April, but then would offer him as their only choice for the highest office in the American financial world. Whitney was nominated in April, as expected, and on May 12, 1930, he was elected president of the exchange, the youngest man to occupy that position since a group of colonial traders had met at the tip of Manhattan Island one hundred and fifty years before and agreed to favor one another in business.

Richard Whitney moved his headquarters from the office of his company at 15 Broad Street into the heavily carpeted room of the president of the stock exchange. He occupied a room whose windows gave a view of the city and harbor below. It was a pleasant office. Portraits of George Washington, Benjamin Franklin, and Thomas Jefferson hung above a stock ticker, symbolizing honesty, conservatism, vision, and impeccable business ethics.

As chief executive of the New York Stock Exchange, Richard Whitney was to be responsible for the Wall Street community's relations with the public and with government. Early in 1930, when the apparent recovery of the stock market was halted by a series of slumps, President Hoover was convinced that John J. Raskob, chairman of the Democratic National Committee, and other speculators were conducting "bear raids" on the market to embarrass the Republican administration. Hoover was a firm believer in the ability of the business community to recover without government interference, but he was annoyed by reports that the Democrats were using the stock market in politics. Characteristically, he turned the tips over to his Secretary of Commerce, Robert P. Lamont, who in turn consulted President Whitney.

Whitney denied that short selling had any harmful effect on the stock market but he did supply the administration with weekly reports of short sales. By April, 1932, when Hoover's predictions of national recovery had begun to arouse groans from the public, the first-term President of the United States demanded that the third-term president of the New York Stock Exchange put an end to short selling. Hoover could be rasping when he wished, but so could Whitney, who detested any kind of interference with his activities. The discussion ended in heat, Hoover picked up the telephone, and within the week the United States Senate Banking and Currency Committee began an investigation of the stock market.

Whitney then was called upon to defend the activities of the stock exchange and its members, a task he undertook with thoroughness and dispatch. He spoke in Boston of the work of the New York Stock Exchange in quieting the panic of 1929. He spoke before the Merchants' Association of New York on trade depressions and stock panics. He asked to testify fully before the Senate committee, and when he had done so once, he asked to appear again to refute charges that exchange practices were responsible for the growing depression. The committee would not hear him this second time, so he published his testimony for the benefit of the members of the exchange. The belated federal investigation produced no significant changes in stock exchange practices but it did separate opinion on the stock exchange itself. The old guard, led by Whitney, stoutly denied the right of any outside agency to regulate or interfere with the exchange's practices or to change the time-honored system. Others, especially the commission brokers who dealt with the general public, began to believe there was room for improvement in the system, but the old guard was both in majority in the board of governors and in control of important committees of the exchange. Nothing was done.

In the fall of 1932, it was apparent that three years of continuous responsibility and crisis had weighed heavily on Richard Whitney. His clear eyes were no longer so clear, his high forehead was slashed with wrinkles, touches of gray had appeared on his temples, his solid face had grown heavy and sagged, and his oarsman's figure had begun to bulge with fat.

Richard Whitney's friends were grateful for his unyielding resistance to the hand of government and they were concerned for him, but their concern was lest he wear himself out in behalf of the common good. Few suspected that the causes of Whitney's rapid aging were to be found in his personal business affairs.

After he had moved from the Broad Street office of Richard Whitney and Company, the president of the stock exchange spent very little time attending to the affairs of his own company. There was little need for close attention—two competent junior partners and a number of trusted employees handled the normal business of the company. Richard Whitney and Company dealt heavily in bonds, not stocks, and the over-the-transom business from the Morgan bank still provided the largest share of the company's income. The junior partners did not see Whitney from one month to the next, nor were they cognizant of his personal business activities.

For three years, from 1926 to 1929, those securities belonging to Mrs. Whitney's trust fund had been pledged to secure a loan to Richard Whitney and Company. Finally, Whitney had paid the loan and rescued the collateral but he used it again from time to time for his own purposes. Whitney was treasurer of the New York Yacht Club, and shortly after his election to the presidency of the exchange in 1930 he had begun pledging yacht club securities against personal loans. In 1931, he had negotiated an unsecured loan for half a million dollars from the Corn Exchange Bank, an unethical and unwise move, since he was a director of the bank. When partners of the Morgan bank heard of this action, they quietly paid off the Corn loan and lent the money to Whitney on George Whitney's account.

These were not impeccable business practices. In the following year, 1933, Richard Whitney proved that he was neither conservative nor visionary, either. When the manufacture and sale of liquor was again legalized in America that year, Whitney bought heavily in

stock of the Distilled Liquors Corporation, a firm established to produce applejack liquor. He bought stock at $45 a share, but immedi-
ately the stock fell, and he needed money to protect his investment by
purchasing more stock to hold up the value of his earlier purchases.
Whitney borrowed $750,000 from his brother George in 1933, largely
for that purpose. As time went on, Richard Whitney became involved
in a number of Florida speculations. He sank $1,250,000 in the Florida
Humous Company, which failed: he invested $200,000 in the Colloidal
Products Corporation of America, a firm which planned to mine and
sell mineral colloids. That company failed, too. In 1933, although no
onc on Wall Street knew it, the Richard Whitney brokerage firm was
insolvent. Whitney kept the business afloat only by negotiating one
large loan after another, paying uncounted thousands of dollars in
interest every year, to give the president of the New York Stock Exchange a chance to recoup his losses.

Under the Hoover administration the New York Stock Exchange
had managed to keep government at bay. When the Roosevelt administration took power, part of its New Deal involved a thorough
investigation of the financial structure of American business. The
new administration intended to draft new laws to prevent repeat of the
stock frauds which had cost American investors millions of dollars in
the decade just past.

By the middle of 1933 the purposes of the Roosevelt administration had become apparent to the old guard of the stock exchange.
The exchange committed itself to do everything possible to sidetrack
the investigation and to avoid federal regulation of the securities
market. Ferdinand Pecora, the new counsel of the Senate Banking
and Currency Committee, was equally determined that the investigation would not be sidetracked.

In the beginning, Franklin Roosevelt considered the flotation and
marketing of securities as entirely separate business ventures. The administration began by drawing a law which would establish a Securities
and Exchange Commission to oversee the issuance of securities. Professor Raymond Moley of Columbia University had helped plan
Roosevelt's campaign in 1932, and later as head of the group of intellectuals known as the "brain trust," Moley picked on Thomas G.
Corcoran and Benjamin V. Cohen to prepare that particular law.

Pecora, Corcoran, and Cohen needed information about the stock market to draft the proposed law, and they applied to Richard Whitney, asking him to circulate a questionnaire among members of the stock exchange. In October, 1933, Pecora sent David Schenker and financial writer John T. Flynn to New York, to seek Whitney's help, perhaps not knowing that the sight of Flynn would make Whitney turn purple with anger, for Flynn had long been caustic in his attitude toward Whitney and the old guard of the stock exchange.

Whitney did turn purple—so purple that he walked out of the office to compose himself as Flynn arrived. When he returned, he flatly refused to assist the government.

The result was a barefisted conflict, in which the stock exchange, for the first time, split openly into two groups. One group was led by Whitney, and one was shepherded in the beginning by Paul Vincent Shields, a commission broker who had contributed to the Democratic party during the presidential campaign. Shields was one of the few brokers in Wall Street who favored cooperation with the federal government in reform of the stock exchange.

Richard Whitney's vigor in attempting to block any federal regulation of securities was anything but disinterested. His situation at this time was so precarious that he could not stand investigation of Richard Whitney and Company or of his personal financial affairs. It was logical for Whitney to suspect that if the federal government once set foot inside the securities market, the stock exchange would next come under scrutiny, and the field of this new regulatory body would be extended to the sale as well as issuance of securities.

So Whitney marshalled the forces of the exchange, and moved his headquarters temporarily to a house in Washington to lobby and argue and try to defeat the administration bill. He was certain enough that he had won the fight by the first of May, 1934 that he wagered that the bill would never pass, but on May 14, the bill passed the Senate by a large majority, and proceeded through the House and Executive branch to become a law.

The first chairman of the Securities and Exchange Commission was Joseph P. Kennedy. Kennedy was a Wall Street man but he was also a tough, profane Massachusetts Democrat who knew politics as well as the tricks of the financial trade.

It did not take long for the Roosevelt administration to realize that it was impossible to regulate the issuance of new securities and still keep its hands completely off the sale of securities in the market, particularly when the largest stock exchange in the country resisted government supervision with every weapon it could find or invent. As Whitney and the old guard fought the federal government, the split within the stock exchange membership widened. Richard Whitney was elected president of the exchange for the fifth time in the spring of 1934, but in the spring of 1935 disaffection with his administration led even the old guard to decide that he must give up the presidency to a man less obviously opposed to the federal administration.

Whitney resisted stoutly. He was a proud man, and by now he was also frightened. He believed the stock exchange was his personal barony, the thought of relinquishing his title appalled him, and already he suspected or knew the pressures which would be exerted on the exchange for self-regulation.

Richard Whitney and Company had never filed a financial statement with the stock exchange, and by 1935 Richard Whitney could not possibly have filed an honest financial statement without being subjected to suspension and charges by the exchange.

When the nominating committee argued that he must step down, Whitney threatened to run as an independent. He was dissuaded from this move by his brother George and by Thomas Lamont, who wanted no open split among the old guard. Richard Whitney stepped down in favor of Charles R. Gay, a compromise candidate who represented the conservatives but was not detested by their opponents.

Richard Whitney had his small satisfaction in the election. He ran for the board of governors. President Gay was elected by 1,131 votes, while Richard Whitney received 1,146 votes for the governor's post.

This victory assuaged Whitney's pride, and it also maintained him in a position of importance within the exchange administration. Therein he hoped to continue the fight against federal interference with stock exchange practices.

President Gay was persuaded to continue the struggle against the SEC during 1936, blocking every avenue of information and lobbying continually with friendly legislators to undermine the regulatory agency. The second chairman of the SEC, James M. Landis, was not inclined to pursue the search for authority. Under Landis the regulatory commission languished, neither doing its job properly nor pleasing the administration or the financial world.

There was talk in Washington of abolishing the commission as ineffectual, until, in the fall of 1937, a young transplanted western lawyer named William O. Douglas was appointed chairman to succeed Landis. Douglas was a New Dealer who took the philosophy of government regulation seriously, so seriously that he was not content to be just a member of a weak commission. He was in Washington, with his bag packed and train reservations for New Haven, where he had been chosen dean of the law school, when Roosevelt, sparked by Joseph Kennedy, appointed him to head the commission. After a lazy summer basking on the sand at Cape Cod Douglas returned to Washington determined to force the New York Stock Exchange to clean its own house, or failing that, to bring in the Securities and Exchange Commission to regulate stock market activities.

The latter prospect sent shivers of terror down the spines of the most liberal-minded exchange members. For a hundred and fifty years the stock exchange had maintained absolute authority over its membership. Stock exchange seats had sold for as much as $600,000 in the boom years—and for as little as $100,000 in the depths of the depression—but the purchase of a seat was not a sinecure. A member must obey the rules implicitly or be ejected and never again allowed the license of the exchange, which was worth a fortune.

It was apparent in 1937, as it had been for ten years, that some members of the exchange manipulated stocks to suit their own purposes. Richard Whitney had consistently denied any knowledge of the existence of manipulating pools on the floor of the exchange, but brokers who had no reason to be loyal to Whitney had reported instances in which Whitney himself had led groups in rigging the market —a practice known in Wall Street as a "jiggle."

"It takes a snoop to catch a jiggle," SEC chairman Douglas remarked one day, a revealing wisecrack which indicated his philosophy of regulation. If the exchange would undertake the snooping all would be well; if the exchange would not, then the SEC would snoop.

Pressed by Whitney and the old guard, President Gay stalled and squirmed. He met with President Roosevelt at Hyde Park. Douglas was there, too.

The meeting occurred in the morning. As Douglas recalled it later the two men spent about an hour with the President. But Roosevelt employed a tactic at which he was expert: he controlled the conversation, talking about traffic conditions in upstate New York during the entire meeting. Finally, before Gay had a chance to say anything about the stock market, Secretary Missy Le Hand walked in and told the President that his next appointment was due.

The pressure grew more intense instead of slackening. Gay issued a president's report so derogatory to the SEC that it aroused doubts as to the effectiveness of the regulating body. Paul Shields and E. A. Pierce, leaders of the exchange minority who sought peace with the government, went to Douglas to seek a way out.

They saw Douglas on October 16, 1937. Two days later the bottom dropped out of the stock market, a crash almost as resounding as that of 1929. James Roosevelt later said he suggested that the stock exchange be closed. But President Roosevelt did not follow this radical course, which at that moment would have destroyed the financial community, and no matter what happened would have placed the blame for the crash squarely on the administration. Roosevelt did not interfere with Douglas in this matter.

President Gay began telephoning Washington. Douglas recalled that he had telephoned "about every hour on the hour" saying the situation was hopeless and that Douglas would have to close the stock market, which he had power to do under the 1934 SEC law.

If Douglas had closed the market then, it would have proved the point Gay was never able to make to Roosevelt—that federal intervention and regulation made the market unworkable.

Douglas passed the responsibility for closing—if that was what Gay wanted—directly back to the board of governors of the stock exchange.

Slowly, dragging their feet every step of the way, the governors of the stock exchange were forced to yield to federal pressure. Chairman Douglas angrily informed Gay that if he continued to delay reform, Douglas would take over the exchange. If such a drastic move became necessary, Douglas said, all he wanted to know was where they kept the paper and pencils—there would be nothing left of the old system of self-regulation once he finished his job.

The battle lasted for a month, with the old guard of the stock exchange hoping the stock market slump could be blamed on the SEC, and that the commission would be dumped or so completely reorganized as to be ineffectual. Douglas worried over this possibility and increased his efforts to secure a victory which would take the commission out of the spotlight of public criticism, while Richard Whitney and the Wall Street bankers did everything they could to give the impression that this crash came as a direct result of government meddling in business.

Neither the administration nor the Wall Street old guard knew at this moment that the same pressures working on them—reduced stock values and a short money supply—were bringing the career of Richard Whitney to a climax which would upset the entire financial world.

On Monday, November 22, 1937, Chairman Douglas terminated negotiations with the representatives of the stock exchange, accusing them of bad faith. President Gay gave a newspaperman an exclusive story, indicating that Douglas was trying to make the exchange the goat for the market collapse. Douglas responded with a statement to the press that he was ready to take control of the exchange. After reading that indicative statement, Gay began to discuss the specific regulatory changes the SEC demanded with the law committee of the exchange's board of governors.

On the same day, in a meeting of the board of trustees of the Stock Exchange Gratuity Fund it was revealed that Richard Whitney was in possession of $1,125,000 in securities which belonged to the fund. Whitney had not attended this particular meeting, so George Lutes, a clerk, took the opportunity to tell the attending members something he had been afraid to mention for months: Whitney had never returned $375,000 in securities he had been asked to deliver a year before. Whitney's predecessor as president, now the chairman of the trustees—E. H. H. Simmons—telephoned Whitney's office and left word that the securities were to be returned immediately.

Whitney was not in his Broad Street office when that fateful call was received. He was in Wall Street, trying to borrow money to shore up a position which had gone from desperate to hopeless in the month past. When Whitney learned what was required, he informed the exchange that the securities would be returned the following day—an admission that he did not have them in his possession.

For so much money there was only one source to which Richard Whitney could turn—his brother George. He went to the House of Morgan, borrowed more than a million dollars, paid off the loan involving these securities and returned the securities. Again he had misused the funds of others, and this time his speculation could not be kept secret. His brother knew—and others suspected.

On Thursday, November 25—Thanksgiving Day—Richard Whitney spent most of the holiday at the home of his brother on Long Island, answering searching questions about his financial condition. Richard Whitney insisted that he was solvent. At the end of the conference George Whitney accepted his brother's assurances but told Richard he would have to liquidate Richard Whitney and Company, and retire from the securities business in the interest of the family name.

Richard Whitney then began his last attempts to escape the trap that lay before him: approval of the SEC changes by the stock exchange. In committees, Whitney fought the changes in rules, item by item, no longer hoping to win, but stalling for a few more weeks of precious time. Outside the meeting rooms Whitney trudged up and down Wall Street, negotiating no less than 111 different loans, some of them secured by almost worthless stock he owned, some secured by stock entrusted to him by customers, a surprising number of them secured by nothing at all.

Whitney delayed his personal reckoning for two months, borrowing from one man to pay another, and at the same time he led the old guard in stalling the exchange's acceptance of the SEC changes in the rules.

Chairman Douglas was nettled by the stalling, which was transparent. A study by the SEC made during the last months of 1937 revealed that short selling had been an important factor in the market slump. Short selling had not caused the market recession—announcement of a cutback in federal spending had been enough to make the market fall. It was a decline which "the short sellers picked up and turned into a fury," Douglas said.

Douglas was puzzled as to what kind of rule the commission should make to control short selling. He, too, believed that the practice served a useful function in controlling the market. He wanted only to control the abuse.

At the suggestion of James Forrestal of Dillon, Reed and Company, Douglas went to New York one Sunday night in January to visit with Clarence Dillon in the privacy of Dillon's apartment. Douglas handed Dillon three proposed short-selling rules. Dillon studied them silently for about twenty minutes, then handed them back, saying that the one he had marked Number One would do the job Douglas wanted done. The next day the rule was promulgated. Thereafter no one could sell short for less than one-eighth above the last sale price, a move which stopped the vicious practice of running a stock up in price and then dumping it to make the price fall.

The rule served another purpose, to remind the stock exchange of the SEC's impatience with its delays. That same month, John B. Shethar, a specialist in Greyhound stock, noted distress selling in Greyhound shares. Someone was unloading at a loss. He suspected Richard Whitney (wrongly as it turned out) and informed a member of the stock exchange board of governors of his suspicions. It was common knowledge that Whitney was borrowing heavily—suddenly even more heavily than he had been borrowing for the past five years.

To propitiate the SEC, the exchange had agreed to send out requests for financial statements to all members. In the normal course of events, Richard Whitney's firm, which had never filed before, would be well down on the list, but on learning this news the chairman of the Business Conduct Committee told a clerk to put Whitney's name at the top of the list.

Richard Whitney now had thirty days more grace.

On February 21, 1938, Richard Whitney replied to the request for a financial statement, having first tried unsuccessfully to delay filing the statement. That same day the stock exchange controller examined the Whitney statement, found indications of a shortage of working capital, and sent accountants to the office of Richard

Whitney and Company. If he was to avoid disaster, Richard Whitney must find more money, but where?

George Whitney was vacationing in Florida, so Richard called on Francis Bartow, another Morgan partner, seeking a loan of $280,000, and confessed that the loan was necessary to prevent his bankruptcy. Bartow would not make the loan until he first conferred with J. P. Morgan. Bartow and Morgan consulted their attorney, who informed them that in making the loan they might be participating in a crime, and they refused to act.

Whitney went everywhere in Wall Street seeking money. In the past four months he had borrowed $27,000,000, trying to stave off disaster. In this last week he visited old friends and even old enemies, but it was too late. He had already mortgaged his five-hundred-acre estate in New Jersey—although for face-saving purposes he had persuaded the bank not to register the mortgage. He had sold and borrowed money wherever he could; but it was not enough.

On Saturday afternoon, March 5, Richard Whitney visited the president's office in the stock exchange, the office he had occupied for so long, and he told President Gay the truth. It was a last, desperate clutch at safety. He, Richard Whitney, epitomized the stock exchange to millions of Americans; the exchange could not afford to let him go under, Whitney told Gay.

The exchange could and would let him go under, Gay said. Those words ended the meeting.

Such news could not be kept secret long. It reached Washington, and on the evening of Monday, March 7, President Gay made a hurried trip to Washington to see SEC Chairman Douglas, to tell him of the defalcations of Richard Whitney, and to agree, at last, to the need for overall reform of the stock exchange.

When Gay left Douglas that night, the SEC chairman called his New York office and directed the subpoena of all files relating to the Whitney matter. He wanted to forestall seizure of the files by New York District Attorney Thomas E. Dewey, who was informed of the defalcations that same night. The SEC men did get the files, and on March 8 the commission issued an order for the investigation of the whole affair.

That same morning, when stock exchange trading opened at

ten o'clock, President Gay went to the floor and tightly announced the suspension of Richard Whitney and Company for misconduct.

The shock was felt in Wall Street, in Washington, over most of the United States. Whitney had been correct in one respect: he *was* the stock exchange to millions of Americans, the symbol of wealth and propriety and big business. His defilement meant the end of the stock exchange as it had always been constituted. If Richard Whitney's honesty was in question, then who in the financial world could be trusted?

Richard Whitney was arrested, a tall, drawn figure in velvet-collared coat and pearl-gray hat, and taken to the Elizabeth Street police station to stand among Bowery derelicts charged with drunkenness and vagrancy. Even then the magic was not yet totally lost.

"Mr. Whitney, I'm sorry to see you in this trouble, and wish you good luck," said the arresting officer, Lieutenant Breen of the New York police.

But Whitney was arraigned, on two indictments of grand larceny, and his luck deserted him. He pleaded guilty but District Attorney Dewey demanded a "substantial and punitive sentence." On April 11, he was sentenced to serve from five to ten years in the New York state penitentiary.

Perhaps on the day of his sentence some members of the Philadelphia Chamber of Commerce recalled a speech Whitney had made to them in 1931, as president of the stock exchange. Then Richard Whitney said: "The fraudulent security criminal is a coward. Like all other criminals what he fears most is punishment, and the weapon which will cure the evil is the prison sentence."

The Whitney sentence seemed harsh to some, but Richard Whitney had gone bankrupt owing $5,500,000. His default outraged a trusting public, and the young prosecuting attorney, Thomas E. Dewey, demanded retribution in the name of the public. Once Whitney was convicted, however, District Attorney Dewey believed the matter was ended. He telephoned SEC Chairman Douglas and said as much.

Douglas disagreed. The investigation was just beginning, he said. The public was to learn not only what had happened, but why and how in the hearings conducted by Gerhard Gesell during the next three months.

When the facts were exposed, Wall Street men and the public realized that Richard Whitney had been engaged in criminal activities during all the time he was serving as president of the New York Stock Exchange. Contrary to their belief, the exchange's system of self-government did not provide protection either to the public or to the knowing professionals of the financial world. Instead, the system, the Wall Street "code of silence," and the atmosphere of an exclusive private club which existed in the stock exchange served neither business nor the public.

It had been common practice on Wall Street, said New York Assistant Attorney-General Ambrose V. McCall, for brokers to use their customers' securities from time to time to avoid a financial pinch. Perhaps it was common practice, but until this day no insider in Wall Street had ever admitted so much to the public.

Chairman Douglas and the SEC had demanded a reorganization which would call for annual independent audits of all firms which did any business with the public, total segregation of brokerage and speculative moneys by Wall Street firms, reports and restrictions on brokers' loans, establishment of a central trust to hold securities, and election of a professional executive as president of the exchange, a man who would not be a broker, or a member of the exchange.

Suddenly Wall Street men realized that any one of these restrictions would have unmasked the activities of Richard Whitney years before or, passed soon enough, might even have protected him. All the old protestations were stilled. On March 17, 1938, the very day that Richard Whitney was formally expelled from the New York Stock Exchange, the members voted for the reorganization the administration demanded. There were 1,013 votes in favor of the motion, only 22 against.

THE SHIP OF STATE THAT SANK

CHAPTER THREE

IN THE FALL OF 1928 nearly sixty per cent of the voters of the United States had chosen Herbert Hoover as their candidate for President. Theirs was a handsome vote of confidence in the national steward-ship the Republican party had exercised over nearly eight contented years. It was also an expression of faith in the ability of this tall, cherubfaced Californian to produce prosperity and progress.

Herbert Clark Hoover was an ideal Republican candidate. He was born in a one-storey cottage across an alley from his father's blacksmith shop in West Branch, Iowa. He moved to a green valley in Oregon to exchange his boy's labor for an early education. He graduated as a mining engineer from Stanford University after the struggle of working his own way. He proved himself adept in his profession in the hard-rock mines of the West. He was befriended by a powerful man who recognized the youth's courage and abilities. He searched for the great chance in the infant mining industries of far-off lands. He converted opportunities into a personal fortune, then turned to apolitical public service in 1914, feeding the sick and hungry of war-torn Europe, and in this work he earned a reputation as statesman, administrator, and economist.

Until his forty-sixth year, Herbert Hoover had shown no interest in partisan politics. He had lived most of his adult life abroad. But so great was the reputation he gained in administering the relief of postwar Europe that both major parties tried to claim Hoover's allegiance before the election of 1920. It was almost inevitable that Hoover should choose to become a Republican, when he finally became interested in politics. West Branch, his boyhood home, was a center of cornbelt individualism. More to the point, Herbert Hoover's career was proof of the Republican belief that given foresight, ability, and the willingness to work hard an American could climb to the top. Hoover believed in "progressive individualism." Here was a personal political creed whose major point was equality of opportunity for all. Hoover believed that government must always be kept at arm's length from business. American business, the production and distribution of commodities and services, was the machine which would create a near-perfect social system if left alone.

Hoover was neither blind, nor stupid, nor reactionary. He was a product of the *laissez faire* system. He did not believe in the inviolability or the omniscience of business, but he did believe in keeping business free from controls he considered excessive and in exercising government's influence through persuasion rather than coercion.

Hoover enthusiasts had made an unsuccessful bid in his favor for the Republican Presidential nomination in 1920. When President Harding took office, Hoover was given a chance to prove his business theories as Secretary of Commerce, and so well did he lead business through the recession of 1921 that he remained in office during Calvin Coolidge's caretaker administration, and was reappointed to the Coolidge administration of 1924.

In 1928 Herbert Hoover was the leading Republican candidate for the Presidency. He was regarded, then, as a solid rock of a man. His personal integrity had not been questioned when cabinet officers and lesser officials were falling all around him in the shambles of the puerile Harding years.

When he took office as President of the United States on March 4, 1929, Herbert Hoover undoubtedly knew more about foreign affairs and international finance than any other man in the American government. He knew also that the economies of nearly all the countries of Europe were near collapse. He was certain that the speculative boom in the stock markets of America must come to an end—which meant a fall in the prices of stocks.

President Hoover hoped from the first day of his administration to pad the fall and prevent a plunge. His method was to inform, to persuade, and only as a last resort to threaten direct action. Any other course would have meant betrayal of his own individualism and his own faith in the unique sanity of the American economic system.

When the crash came in Wall Street in October, 1929, Hoover was not unduly worried. Like millions of others the President believed that "readjustment," while bound to deal harshly with some people's livelihood and fortunes, was one of the perpetual realities of American economic life. By mid-December, 1929, however, Hoover was of two minds. He held one public view and one private view. They were not the same.

The President's public view of the business crisis was wildly optimistic, given the serious doubts in his private mind. Publicly, President Hoover looked upon the volume of Christmas business reported by the retail stores in the year of 1929 and pronounced the economy sound. Business was returning to normality, he said.

Privately, Mr. Hoover was holding one conference after another with business leaders, trying to persuade them to take action to stabilize an economy Mr. Hoover knew was very weak indeed. On November 19, the President of the nation met with the presidents of the major eastern railroads to ask them to continue and expand their construction programs to assure work to more men. The railroads agreed to cooperate.

President Hoover had already asked Treasury Secretary Mellon to propose that Congress increase the federal public works program. Secretary Mellon was to request an extra expenditure of $423,000,000. Two days after the meeting with the railroaders, President Hoover called in other leaders of American business to discover how much help they could and would give. Several of the important business leaders said they thought the problem was only temporary, but all agreed to help the administration if labor would cooperate.

That same day the President called labor's leaders in to secure their cooperation. The next day he met with a selected group of builders and promoters, to shore up the private construction business. It is an indication of Hoover's philosophy of government that only when business leaders had been called to a meeting did the President ask the governors of the states—by telegram—for help to avoid a national collapse.

The state officials responded quickly to the President's call. Even Democrats pledged full cooperation. The leaders of business stoically accepted President Hoover's contention that profits must give way before wages. Labor leaders agreed to temper their current demands. Nearly every responsible person in industry, in labor, in business, in public utilities, in farm federations, and in state and local government agreed to do anything possible to stave off disaster. If it were true, as Richard Whitney had held, that the stock market was not a reflection of the condition of American business, or if it were true, as the administration held, that the American business economy was as sound as a dollar, then the combined efforts of Henry Ford, Alfred P. Sloan, Pierre Du Pont, Samuel Insull, William Green, Governor Franklin Roosevelt and all the hundreds of others would logically have brought a return to prosperity.

Yet in the face of this program of cooperation, the economy of the United States continued to decline. The President knew the nation was staggering, but Mr. Hoover believed so thoroughly in the prevailing system, and he was so sure that the solution to the problem lay largely in confidence, that he was less than open in the statements he made to the American people. Then Mr. Hoover made a serious mistake. A few days after the stock market crash, Mr. Hoover alienated a number of working reporters when he lost his temper over reports of his secret meetings with business leaders. He ordered an investigation of the leak. That act marked the end of his short honeymoon with working newspapermen.

Nearly all Americans, including reporters, exhibited a healthy respect for President Hoover in the abstract. In personal meetings, the favorable impression was often reversed, for the President had an unfortunate habit of displaying impassivity. His face might have been carved from stone. He sat stiffly in his chair, a high round collar torturing his neck, and he spoke in a mild and faraway voice, looking at his shoes, at the ceiling, everywhere but at his questioners. This personal impression of coldness and loftiness began to find its way into the pages of the press.

Needing exercise to control his robust figure and to reduce his weight from two hundred pounds the President had invented a modified volleyball, played with a four-pound "medicine ball," and had formed a "medicine ball cabinet." The nation was accustomed to such informal gatherings of the influential; Teddy Roosevelt had his tennis cabinet and Warren Harding had his highball and poker society, but the country found it ridiculous that the President took his exercise at seven o'clock in the morning, because that was the only time of the day Mr. Hoover felt he could spare from official duties.

The timing of his daily exercise was typical of Herbert Hoover. It was an intellectual decision made by the strong mind of a man who planned his life carefully.

Herbert Hoover maintained a schedule that might have killed a weaker man, particularly after the crash and its consequences began tumbling down upon him. One typical day he conferred with a dozen men in the morning, spent the precious moments between meetings on the telephone, moved out to the White House lawn to have his picture taken with one delegation of visiting citizens after another, ate lunch, returned to conferences in the afternoon until six, retired for a short nap, dined at eight, and went back to his office at ten for another two hours of work before going to bed.

Wall Street's Bernard Baruch said Hoover's mind absorbed facts as a sponge absorbs water. There was little doubt that Mr. Hoover was well-prepared, mentally, to be President of the United States; but within nine months of his inauguration it was also apparent that Herbert Hoover was cantankerous, distant, insensitive to people, peculiarly sensitive to even the slightest personal criticism, and unwilling to make the adjustments necessary in the world of politics.

So the Hoover honeymoon with American reporters was short, and the honeymoon with Congress was almost as short. On December 2, 1929, the Seventy-first Congress returned to Washington. In name, it was an overwhelmingly Republican Congress, seating a comfortable majority of a hundred of the President's party in the House of Representatives and a GOP majority of seventeen members of the Senate. Fourteen of those Republican Senators, however, were "Progressive Republicans," hardheaded mavericks who leaned away from individualism and toward increased federal responsibility. They controlled the balance of power and must be wooed if they were to be won to President Hoover's support. The President showed no conception of the manner and no understanding of the need to reach an accommodation with them. Rather, almost from the beginning of the session, President Hoover began to attribute his growing body of troubles to the "reactionaries" and "radicals" of his own party as well as to the Democrats.

The President could muster a convincing argument about Democratic intransigence. In 1929 Democratic National Chairman John J. Raskob had appointed a newspaperman named Charles Michelson to begin a campaign to unseat Herbert Hoover in 1932. Michelson's spirited program included insulting slogans, open attacks, planted rumors, and whispering campaigns which drove the sensitive Hoover from one rage into another, and from exasperated thought to intemperate remark. When the remarks were duly reported back to the Democratic National Committee, they caused a redoubling of the efforts of Charles Michelson and his crew of Democratic propagandists.

Still, Herbert Hoover would stand or fall with the American people on his ability to assess the true condition of the nation and then to take steps necessary to restore progress and prosperity.

Late in the winter of 1930, President Hoover said the trend of unemployment had been reversed. Unemployment had leaped just after the Wall Street crash. It was momentary, the President said.

Not long afterward Mr. Hoover predicted that serious unemployment would be ended in sixty days.

Generally speaking, newspaper editorial writers greeted the President's remarks gladly, but in April, 1930, the editors of the monthly magazine of New York City's Guaranty Trust Company said they could see no signs of comeback. Another month later President Hoover noted for the first time publicly, that a serious national crisis had occurred—but he said it was all over. It was May, 1930. The President said the future looked bright.

Nine days later the stock market slumped again. From this point on, many newspaper writers adopted a wait-and-see attitude toward Mr. Hoover's hopeful predictions. The general public, less understanding, began to look upon the Hooverian statements with outright suspicion.

The public suspicion of the President was a normal American reaction. In the election campaign of 1928 Hoover had been presented as a super-economist. The Republicans had taken full credit for national prosperity. Now they must accept responsibility. As early as February, 1930, first in Congress, then in the streets of the cities and the lanes of the country towns, came discernible cries for Hoover to exhibit the superb qualities of leadership the Republicans had attributed to the President during the campaign of 1928. In the East Mr.

Hoover was already unpopular, for the industrial East sensed early that Mr. Hoover was not bringing the country out of the slump, nor did the public see where he was exerting the leadership expected. In the farm states of the Middle West and the far West opinion was slower to crystallize and slower to change. There the President was still given the benefit of the doubt, but dissatisfaction was growing, even among Republicans.

Senator Arthur Capper, the wily organization Republican from Kansas, called Hoover's handling of the nation "masterly," but blunt Senator William Borah of Idaho, one of the "radical" Republicans did not agree. In February, 1930, Borah further annoyed the administration by instituting personal correspondence with the Bolshevik government in Moscow. Senator Robert La Follette, another sharp-tongued "radical"—and from the Middle West—announced in March that the Hoover administration was a failure. Senator La Follette addressed himself to the slowness of the administration to offer measures to reduce unemployment. Progressive Republicans and Democrats did not like Mr. Hoover's government by indirection.

Hoover supporters assessed the President's first year as successful because he had pushed through a bill which gave some relief to beleaguered farmers, because he had made progress in negotiations for international naval disarmament, and because he had *warned* about the pending crash months before it occurred. But Professor Paul H. Douglas of the Department of Economics of the University of Chicago scoffed, and accused the President of "attempting to cure economic evils by the practice of mental healing." Governor Franklin Roosevelt accused Mr. Hoover of trying to scrap the law of supply and demand and replace it with high-pressure sales campaigns.

The President paid no heed. One grim month slipped into the next, and the recovery promised by the party of peace and prosperity did not materialize. President Hoover knew of one deep canker in the American scene: the weakness of the American banking system, a structural weakness accelerated by selfishness and the optimism which had marked the last years of the twenties.

In the spring of 1930 it was revealed that the bankers' coalition which had shored up the market on Black Friday had not acted altogether altruistically, that the Morgan bank and the others had joined forces primarily to protect themselves. The banks had created a market for securities in which they held heavy investment but less than a week after the crash the bankers had sold their securities at a profit, and having done so they had retired from the stock market. The public found these facts unpalatable. The administration did not forget them.

A year after the stock market crash, even President Hoover had been forced to admit that the economy had sunk low. He was hoping, but not hopeful, that a Republican Congress would be elected in 1930, hoping that somehow a new Congress would do something for him that the old had not done. Hoover was almost certain, however, that the Congress returning would be Democratic.

In that summer of 1930 a new disaster, in the form of drouth, struck the overburdened farming community. The President had persuaded much of industry to keep workers on the payrolls although production was falling and the national income had slipped from $83.3 billion in 1929 to $68.9 billion in 1930. The farm crisis resulted in reduced farm buying, and the downward spiral quickened. Mr. Hoover's response to the drouth was immediate, and typical. He called upon the railroads to haul feed to drouth areas at half-rates; the railroads cooperated. The President called on governors to help plan for farm relief; the governors came to Washington and pledged their assistance. The Red Cross and the Federal Farm Board doubled their efforts to avert disaster. Mr. Hoover directed that federal highway funds be diverted to the drouth states to give employment to farmers. This, too, was done.

But it took money to buy feed, even at half-rates. Thousands of farms were already mortgaged to the maximum. The Red Cross could not be everywhere, and highway funds diverted to drouth states left financial vacuums in other states.

In October, 1930, the President realized that the coming winter would bring real want all over the nation.

On Wall Street, stock market firms began to fail. Hoover called in Richard Whitney and issued the warning that if the New York Stock Exchange did not police itself, the federal government would step in. Thus were aligned the forces in the financial world that were to battle for the next eight years.

Hoping he had resolved the problems of the stock market with his warning, Mr. Hoover turned to the economy at large. He appointed Colonel Arthur Woods, who had helped him with unemployment relief in 1921, to organize a special President's Committee for Unemployment Relief. He was grateful when the response from business leaders was immediate and enthusiastic, and he hoped that here he had plugged another dike.

Business did cooperate in its fashion. The Beneficial Industrial Loan Corporation, for example, set aside $100,000 for small non-interest bearing loans in the 200 cities in which Beneficial maintained offices. It was a handsome gesture, reported widely in the press, but with no explanation that $100,000 divided among 200 cities would mean only an allocation of $500 for each city, or loans of $1.00 each for 500 people in each community.

The national radio networks gave free time to Colonel Woods and his local committees. In New York the volunteer committee took over the entire forty-third floor of the new Bank of Manhattan building in Wall Street and hundreds of people volunteered their services.

New York, the American metropolis, was already in serious trouble by October, 1930. The City Department of Hospitals, at the call of Mayor Walker, pledged $10,000 a month from its budget to help the poor. The sheriff's office found another $1,000 a month. But what use was this? More than twenty-four thousand men were idle in the city's five boroughs. Some of them had been out of work for an entire year. All of the city's agencies hustled to find jobs for these men, but most of the jobless were sent to work in the city parks at $3.00 a day. They were glad to take the work, for they were willing to do anything at all to earn money. Even so, there were not enough jobs to go around. On October 29, Magistrate Murphy of the New York City Tombs Court sentenced twenty-three men to thirty days in jail for vagrancy. The men had been arrested in the Pennsylvania Railroad ferry terminal on Cortlandt Street, where they had sought shelter from the cold and rain. Fifteen others who were picked up in the same place were set free, but only because each could produce a few nickels and dimes from his pockets. The twenty-three men sentenced had not a penny among them.

That same day, principals of the public schools of the city were taking names of children and families known to be in distress, to forward them to the volunteer relief committee. A dozen food stations of the Salvation Army fed 7,263 persons in twenty-four hours, and the Army enlisted Grover Whalen to lead a million-dollar fund drive to help the poor. The money would not be enough, and the Salvation Army officers knew it. Winter had not yet come, but at the end of the season's first cold drizzly day the requests for help had already doubled. On the night of October 28 the Salvation Army shelter on West 48th Street had accommodated seventy sleepers; the next night 140 applied. By the end of the week, the Army hoped to increase the capacity of this place to accommodate four hundred persons a night.

As the weather worsened, the poor flocked to the bread lines. These were not just homeless men, but women and children too. St. Vincent's Hospital opened a bread line, and served breakfast to 350 people on October 29. By lunchtime the word was out, and 1,000 persons came to the hospital for a meal. At the Salvation Army soup kitchen on the Bowery, 350 men, 22 women, and 5 children stood for two hours in the rain, waiting for handouts of bread, soup, and coffee.

New York was the largest of the cities. New York's problems were no worse than those of others, but New York's situation was indicative: the city was unprepared to house and feed a growing army of hungry unemployed.

What answers did other urban areas find to their problems?

In Boston, the Volunteer Employment Committee made a number of specific recommendations:

1. Employers should stretch their production to give employment for a few more months, at least.
2. Those whose incomes had not been reduced should go on spending as usual.
3. Christmas shopping should be done early.
4. Property owners should make their spring repairs that fall.
5. The city should increase its construction program.

Chicago's acting police commissioner proposed to hire five thousand more policemen and 840 more firemen to reduce crime and property destruction and to "speed prosperity." The New Jersey Civil Service Commission recommended a cut in the work week, to five or even to three days, rather than lay off workers. A Dallas furniture dealer called on one hundred of his business acquaintances to spend $25,000 each on construction during that winter.

Although wholeheartedly applied, these palliative measures did not touch the real problems of the nation. In scores of cities block committees were established to canvass the needs of the poor and to dredge contributions from the wealthy, the well-to-do, and those who were still employed. One anonymous donor was able to donate fifteen hundred sit-down Thanksgiving dinners to the Salvation Army in New York.

But private charity did not solve the problems of the nation. Edgar S. Bloom, president of the Western Electric company, was forced to announce just before the elections that his company was following President Hoover's recommendation: instead of laying off men, Western Electric was cutting the work week, and already half its men and women were working less than full time. Neither, it seemed, could industry solve its own problems.

President Hoover had already taken steps to limit immigration into the United States, but any help in the reduction in the potential work force was more than met by the negative results of the Hawley-Smoot Tariff which had been passed earlier in the year. The new law had increased tariff rates on 890 items, and it affected nearly every country in the world. Mexico announced that it would reduce imports from the United States by $25,000,000 a year to counter the tariff. Switzerland, which had been shipping $11,000,000 worth of watches to America each year, was so sorely hurt that many of her watch factories closed—and Switzerland had been buying $45,000,000 annually in goods from the United States.

Just before the elections of 1930, business leaders in conference at the University of Chicago predicted that a trade revival would begin in 1931. But just then the German government announced an increase on its tariff on tobacco—from $19 to $95 per kilogram. High tariffs begot high tariffs. Former President Coolidge emerged from retirement to defend the high American tariff, but in Tiffin, Ohio,

James M. Cox, the 1920 Democratic Presidential candidate, called the tariff an act of "moral and mental decadence." Other countries raised their tariffs. Trade showed no signs of reviving.

Consistently, the political tide ran against the Republicans that fall. While President Hoover had called for an increase in public works, the Republican Congress appropriated $26,000,000 less in 1930 than in the previous year. Although Mr. Hoover had talked about spending $3,000,000 for construction of Veterans Hospitals, and about the start of the vast Colorado River project known as Hoover Dam, building had not yet begun.

How many men were unemployed by this time—a year after the crash? It seemed to be anyone's guess: the official figures showed three million five hundred thousand unemployed, but an Antioch College professor said seven million men were out of work, and the British claimed that if the U.S. used their method of calculating, American unemployment would reach a figure of twelve million persons. Nor did any of these estimates take into account the thousands of family budgets which were reduced sharply as company after company followed President Hoover's call to reduce the work week—and take-home pay—but keep as many men as possible on the payroll.

When the 1930 elections were over, the alignment of Congress had been reversed. In name, there were forty-eight Republicans in the Senate, but Hoover could count on only thirty-six of them to support his programs. In the House, the Democrats were in control.

It had become apparent that no matter what might happen, President Hoover would be held personally responsible for the paralyzing depression which gripped the United States. No matter what he might do, or how much he knew about the causes and course of the decline, his uncandid public statements had indicated undue optimism for months after the crash of 1929 and the beginning of the business slump.

Governor Franklin Roosevelt, running for his second term in New York, had campaigned that year on what might be national issues: increased executive responsibility, public power, and a state program of relief. All these were programs antithetical to Herbert Hoover's beliefs. He considered them socialist in theory and thus dangerous to liberty.

Roosevelt, however, had again won election while most Hoover supporters of rugged individualism were sent back to their businesses or
law practices.

Although he would be faced with a hostile Congress, the President
in no way slackened his efforts to stop the depression in the traditional
American way, but now he was on the defensive. In the winter of 1931,
Hoover sought and secured huge contributions to the Red Cross, to
the Community Chests of the nation. He continued his efforts to find
useful public works for the unemployed. But the 130 Community
Chests in America found that while they had 14 per cent more funds
in 1931 than in 1930, the demands on them had grown by 300 or 400
per cent, and not all the Community Chest funds went for relief. The
Red Cross did its best, achieving in the end a $20,000,000 relief fund,
but in the cities and on the farms people were burning their furniture
to keep warm. In January, Senator Robinson of Arkansas, the Democratic majority leader, sponsored a resolution for direct federal relief.
The measure passed the Senate, but bogged down in the House.
Hoover did everything possible to kill the measure, then was accused
of not caring if people went hungry and cold in the United States. He
defended his way as the American way; if the federal government
stepped in to give direct relief to the American people, the President
said, the first blow would be struck at the roots of self-government. He
would not strike that blow.

The President argued and explained and pleaded for understanding of the "American road." He made forty-six speeches in his first
twenty-seven months in office, compared to President Coolidge's thirty-
seven speeches in seven years. He appointed one committee after another to "get the facts." He became the best-informed President in
history, working sixteen or eighteen hours a day, every day, every week,
every month. Most businessmen continued to back the President, and
the system they had respected for so long. The Erwin Wasey advertising company paid tribute to the system of rugged individualism in
full-page newspaper advertisements, praising that advertising man who
measured his efforts "neither by the dollar nor the clock." But in that
same fortnight, the New York *World*, once a highly successful newspaper, was sold to the Scripps-Howard publishing company, and most
employees of the *World* were thrown out of work. With two weeks'

When Black Friday came, in the middle of that marvelous autumn of 1929, the euphoria that had lasted four long years suddenly vanished and was replaced by tears, shock, and silence. WIDE WORLD PHOTO

Even in disgrace, Richard Whitney was in every way a distinguished man, from the careful part in his fine hair to the tips of his shoes. WIDE WORLD PHOTO

The Bonus Army marched on Washington in shirt-sleeves and campaign hats, and arrived at the steps of the Capitol where the army's leaders demanded relief for the fighting men. WIDE WORLD PHOTO

When the disastrous depression hit the nation, Herbert Hoover's plan was to push industry into solving the problems without interference by the Federal government. One of his advisers was Walter S. Gifford, president of the American Telephone and Telegraph Company. They talked and talked and talked. . . . WIDE WORLD PHOTO

pay in their pockets, they were pushed into the lines of the unemployed, to practice their "rugged individualism" in looking for jobs that did not exist.

Congress passed a bill which would give soldiers of the First World War a bonus, claiming it would cost the government only $700,000. Hoover, who knew his figures, said it would cost nearly twice as much, and vetoed the legislation. Congress passed the law over his veto. Matters worsened between Executive and Legislative when the Senate adjourned in March; it quit Washington without the traditional courtesy of notifying the President of the United States, so low had Mr. Hoover's prestige fallen among the senators.

In April, 1931, President Hoover said that despite all opposition his measures had begun to take effect. (Studies made during the later years of the succeeding administration proved him correct.) Hard as the American pocketbook had been hit, the natural business cycle was still in motion, and there were some signs that meant recovery to the President.

The signs went unnoticed, nevertheless, because in April the varied economics of Europe began to collapse. To Americans, financial failures in Europe meant a sharp decrease in European buying of U.S. goods, default in payments of money owed in this country, and the withdrawal of European capital which had been invested in the United States. The American business economy could rebound from an internal crash, but it could not withstand another, equally shattering bump within two years. Instead of improving, the depression in the United States grew worse.

In the autumn, farm income fell below that of the disastrous year 1921. The largest wheat crop in history had been grown by farmers in 1931, as they tried to recoup losses in the old way—by growing more when the price was low. The price of wheat fell to thirty-six cents a bushel, a decrease of twenty-nine cents a bushel in a single year. Hoover refused to interfere.

The Democrats, and especially Franklin Roosevelt, openly referred to President Hoover now as "reactionary." His enemies said Hoover policies were half a century behind the times. Even in business circles there was talk of need for "planned economy," the anathema President Hoover had fought for two years. Walter Lippmann called for a reorganization of American society. Bishop William T. Manning of the Protestant Episcopal Church talked from his pulpit about need for drastic economic reforms and fairer distribution of the national wealth.

Other critics were less restrained. As Hoover talked of self-help, the Communists heralded the imminent collapse of the capitalist system in America. Where the Communists and the socialists and radical splinter groups had spoken to thousands before, hundreds of thousands of Americans began to listen.

A thousand people attended a dinner given by the *New Leader* to hear Morris Hillquit, national chairman of the Socialist party, denounce Herbert Hoover's total lack of social vision and to assert that relief of the distressed was a function of government, not of private charity. The audience also heard approving telegrams from scientist Albert Einstein and film star Charlie Chaplin.

Two hundred thousand people deserted the cities for the countryside in 1931. Without work they returned to their homes, or, if they had no homes, they established some kind of dwelling place on the land in the hope that they could at least eat if they went back to the farm.

Thousands of the farms were owned by the banks, but the American banking system was near collapse, money was short and unemployment was growing again. In that year twenty-three hundred banks failed, nearly twice as many as had failed in 1930, nearly four times as many as had failed in 1929.

Early in 1931, Herbert Hoover had said that "no one is going hungry, and no one need go hungry or cold"; but if that was truth in February, there was no semblance of truth in that claim in December.

Businessmen began to turn away from Hoover under the crippling blows of 1931. In the bank crisis, he tried to mobilize the private financial agencies to protect one another, but the bankers were in business to stay in business, and they told the President he was asking them to do government's job. This manner of refusal of the bankers to combine for the common good represented the first important break by businessmen with the theory of rugged individualism and private self-help. Herbert Hoover responded by taking on the job of rebuilding the world economy, too. He declared a one-year moratorium on the payment of Europe's war debts in order to stimulate Europe's recovery. In domestic affairs, while he held out against direct federal relief to the unemployed, the President pushed Congress into establishing the Reconstruction Finance Corporation early in 1932. The new agency would do the job private business had refused to do for itself— strengthen the weakest links in the chain of the American business economy. The President's critics called RFC a relief agency for big business. Hoover found this RFC idea so distasteful that he hoped to scuttle the agency within a year or two, when the emergency was past. Philosophically, the President had breached his own barrier, but what recourse did he have? Faced with the flat refusal of the stronger banks, most of them in the East, to commit their resources to the common good, the President had no alternative—unless he wished to see the entire banking system collapse.

He also strengthened the federal program of farm mortgage support, to keep local banks from foreclosing on mortgages they could not afford to hold, and thus acquire property they could not sell.

These exercises of federal strength helped the economy, but their effect on the President was to confuse the cool logic with which he had been able to define the differences between "the American road" and collectivism, in the past. In his own words—if the "deadline between our system and socialism" was that "government must keep out of production and distribution of commodities and services"—he had led the nation across the deadline.

The President's logic failed here, too. In defending a ninety million dollar loan by the RFC to the failing Central Republic Bank and Trust Company of Chicago, Mr. Hoover said that Central Republic served 122,000 depositors and was associated with 755 other banks in fifteen states which served 6,500,000 depositors, and that these in turn were associated with other banks who served twenty million people. By extending his logic a step or two further, undoubtedly he could have proved that the salvation of the Central Republic Bank affected calculably, if indirectly, half the people of the United States.

Few Americans would have quarrelled with such an assertion by the President; most Americans were less concerned with the abandonment of the old system than with the immediate effects the physical breakdown of the economy was exerting on their own lives.

The President could not see that the system had broken down, but it became apparent to others who began to become painfully aware of gross inequities in the distribution of the nation's wealth.

At that time the Brookings Institution later reported, 1 per cent of the people of America owned 59 per cent of the national wealth. Another 12 per cent of the people owned 33 per cent of the wealth. The vast majority of 87 per cent owned only 8 per cent of the wealth. Or to put it to extremes: 92 per cent of all American families had annual incomes of $2,500 or less, and 36,000 families shared $9,800,-000,000 a year, more than $2,500,000 per family—a thousand times as much.

The system was not only inequitable financially, it was inequitable in every way. The justice given the rich was not the justice given the poor. William Kissam Vanderbilt III could terrorize the countryside in a fast car, but when an eighteen-year-old student pilot named August Lauer zoomed low over the J. P. Morgan estate on Long Island one day in the winter of 1931, he was first reprimanded for low flying; when Department of Commerce officials heard *whom* he had disturbed, they recommended a fine and stiffer punishment for the offense.

In May, as the first contingent of the Bonus Expeditionary Force had set out from Portland, Oregon, Mrs. Marshall Field gave a dinner for six hundred at Camsett, her splendid Long Island estate. It was a dinner under the stars. At Newport, the Clambake Club celebrated the pleasant May weather with a sumptuous party at Bailey's Beach.

Despite such exhibition of the privileges and power of wealth, President Hoover was shocked and infuriated by allusions to classes within the society of the American republic. The politicians were only just beginning to recognize what the very rich had claimed for years —American society was stratified even if it could not be so neatly categorized as that of England, and if Mr. Hoover stoutly maintained that the United States had a classless society, both Norman Thomas (the socialist) and Grace Vanderbilt (the socialite) were ready to dispute him.

Before spring came to the United States in 1932, it was also obvious that the "voluntary" relief programs had failed, both abroad and at home.

Abroad Hoover had been abandoned by those he tried to help. France had dragged its heels in every way and continued to do so. In Italy Benito Mussolini called on all Europe to renounce further reparations from Germany and demand cancellation of the debts to the United States. Hoover could expect no help for America from abroad.

In the United States, the personal relief program had fared no better. Unemployed men lived in jerry-built shacks in the shadows of the hotels. Hoover had taken America out of the poorhouse and put it onto the bread lines, Washington reporter Robert S. Allen said. Most of the cities and states in America had exhausted their funds for relief; in New York relief seemed destined to end entirely, for the city was out of funds. The New York City board of education deferred appointment of six hundred needed teachers in January, because the board could not afford to pay them. Yet the President, although he looked twenty years older than he had in 1928, did not give up his efforts for "the American way."

He took the American Legion, the AF of L and the Association of National Advertisers into a voluntary "war-against-depression" campaign, which was dedicated to finding one million jobs. Had the campaign been totally successful it was too little, for there were now twelve million unemployed persons in America.

The volunteer relief organization sent its collectors in search of funds, to secure hundreds of thousands of dollars where tens of millions of dollars were needed. In New York the women's division of the relief committee publicized needy cases such as the typical one of Number 701, a man who had been employed by one company for twenty-two years before he was laid off in 1931. Number 701 had exhausted his savings. He had borrowed $375 from his sister-in-law, and could borrow no more. The sole income of his family of three was a pension of $2.50 a week.

Another case was that of a white-collar worker whose wife was ill, suffering from malnutrition, while her husband sat by her bedside and watched her life slip away—without money, without a job, without relief.

The block canvasses were successful enough, by their own standards, but when in New York the campaign raised a million dollars, that was still a half million dollars short of enough to give five thousand men work for even twenty weeks of the winter, the dangerous time of year.

Edward F. McGrady, a spokesman of the AF of L told the Senate Manufactures Committee that if something was not done and "starvation" continued, "the doors to revolution would be thrown wide open."

The national situation was indeed desperate. President Hoover responded by denials that people were starving in the United States. He vetoed another veterans' pension bill, and he vetoed a bill that would let civilians employed by the army secure medical treatment in military hospitals. When a ragged band of veterans appeared in Washington calling themselves the "bonus army," they were first officially ignored, and finally fired upon by American troops. Hoover would not see them or deal with them.

America fell into an ugly mood that spring. The President recognized it, at least enough to plan "national unity meetings" and to talk of "sane" fiscal policies. The hungry who lived in the open were not interested in "sane policies."

In New York, Governor Roosevelt sensed the feeling of the nation and the need. Roosevelt had not solved the problems of the depression in his own state. He had failed to regulate the stock market as he might have done before the 1929 Wall Street crash. He had misread as many economic signs as anyone else, but by 1932 Roosevelt at least realized that the old ways had failed. He was searching for new ways to combat the depression, and he gathered around him a group of men who were capable of improvising policies.

Yet even as he and they planned, the crisis grew.

In May, Fred J. Keegan, fifty-five, an unemployed millinery salesman jumped into Madison Avenue from a thirteenth-floor window. A few days later, G. Grenville Hunter, forty, a socially prominent advertising man who was facing a cut in income, left his wife and family for a stag weekend on the New Jersey shore. Hunter tried to drown himself off the beach, and after he was restrained, he finished the job with a shotgun.

J. P. Morgan was heard on radio for the first time in his life. He broadcast to help the Emergency Unemployment Relief Committee, convinced that at any moment private and local government relief funds would be exhausted. But J. P. Morgan did not pay a dollar of income tax that year. Robert R. McCormick, owner of the *Chicago Tribune,* demanded editorially that all citizens pay their full taxes, paid a personal property tax of only fifteen hundred dollars himself.

Colonel McCormick was one of the few Chicago rich men who paid any of the tax willingly. Even University of Chicago professors cavilled, and finally made a group settlement with their city government, to preserve the amenities.

Obviously it was hard to judge a nation by the actions of individuals. There were fools among the wealthy and fools among the poor.

That spring and summer of 1932 President Hoover plodded on to the Republican nomination that could hardly be denied him, and Governor Roosevelt stormed the Democratic convention to win a nomination many wished he could be denied. In the campaign that followed Roosevelt belittled his adversary, heaped scorn upon him and upon the Hoover policies, and offered reforms. The President read and analyzed his opponent's speeches, and declared that if Roosevelt were elected, the New Deal he promised in his acceptance of the Democratic nomination would destroy the very foundations of the American nation.

But how sturdy were those foundations by 1932? Scarcely a week before the election a hysterical crowd of thirty thousand outside Madison Square Garden tried to rush a police cordon, heads were smashed, and the crowd was dispersed only by force. Inside, President Hoover was insisting that his road was the only road to salvation. Elsewhere that day the bankers of New York City refused the city government a loan of $25,000,000 for relief, because the city was not a good credit risk. In Chicago, a mob of ten thousand people chanted "we want bread," booed when speakers mentioned the words "public officials," cheered the Red flag, and cried for "revolution."

The suicide rate in the United States had risen so high it upset the insurance actuarial tables, and the insurance agencies studied a drastic plan to raise insurance premium rates. In New York City the number of known suicides, a matter of no concern before 1929, had risen to 734 in 1932, and the number of concealed suicides might have been two or three times as high. New York's rate was low. Madison, Sacramento, Cedar Rapids had rates of suicide twice as high.

President Hoover threatened that if Roosevelt was elected the grass would grow in the streets of a hundred cities and that weeds would overrun the fields of millions of farms. But the grass was already growing between the cobblestones of the factories and warehouses in cities, and in upstate New York a farmer cried as he turned his pigs loose in fields of potatoes he could not afford to harvest, or if he harvested them, he could not sell.

Mr. Hoover's warnings held no sting for such men.

On election day nearly sixteen million Americans registered their approval of the traditional American way, and their belief that Herbert Hoover's program would lead the United States away from the brink of chaos. They voted for a modified business economy. President Hoover had, perforce, interjected the federal government more deeply in the affairs of local communities than ever before in history. Yet Hoover, his supporters knew, stood as a spokesman for the old business society, a man with a deep respect for the right of the individual to make his own way.

That same day nearly twenty-three million Americans voted for Franklin Delano Roosevelt. They chose a program whose goals and whose road no one knew—least of all Roosevelt. They voted in protest against hunger, against the indignity of the private dole. They voted against a system which allowed grain elevators to spill their precious harvest while in the shadows of the elevators men marched and children cried for bread. They voted for promises of relief, of work, and finally of the dream of a future prosperity.

Herbert Hoover represented the finest mind in the old American system. He was courageous and public-spirited to begin with, and in four years of almost total agony he had turned himself into a slave of the American people, refusing the course that would have been so easy in the crisis: to take power and make of himself a dictator.

Yet the majority turned him out of office that November certain that he had failed. And Hoover had failed, even by his own standards.

In 1919, having gone to Russia to survey the holocaust of the Russian revolution, Hoover had seen the Bolsheviks floundering. He sensed that the Russian leaders had failed to realize that the processes of production and distribution could not be broken down in any country if freedom was to survive. In 1932, if those processes had not yet broken down in the United States, they were close enough to breakdown that the majority of the people feared total collapse, feared for their very lives and the lives of their children. They voted for drastic change.

GIVE THEM A NEW DEAL

CHAPTER FOUR

NEWSPAPERMEN AND MAGAZINE WRITERS are the catalysts of American politics, and it might be said that sometimes they help set overall political trends in American government. If this influence was ever felt, it was felt in the emergence of the name and trend of "the new deal," a term coined to describe the economic and social revolution Franklin Delano Roosevelt brought to the American people in 1933.

The best-known historian of the Roosevelt era, Arthur M. Schlesinger, Jr., has speculated that the term was picked up by a speech writer leafing through a contemporary article by economist Stuart Chase in the *New Republic*—"A New Deal for America." At any rate, once Franklin Roosevelt had uttered his pledge of "a new deal for the American people" in his address accepting the Democratic Presidential nomination of 1933, the headline writers had a short, pithy, and descriptive phrase which quickened the imagination of a people struggling against moral and physical disaster. The term "New Deal" spread across the United States like a prairie-grass fire, and caught the public imagination. The words suggested that someone had a plan for the future of the country.

In fact, Franklin Delano Roosevelt and his advisers had nearly no plans at all, except to elect Governor Roosevelt President of the United States. Herbert Hoover knew that, and he saw, as the election campaign of 1932 progressed, that the government of Franklin Roosevelt would be frankly experimental, with extremely heavy emphasis on Executive leadership. "Collectivism," Hoover called it then, in his predictions of national disaster. Later he was to call the program and Roosevelt by harsher names.

From the day of the election it was obvious that Franklin Roosevelt felt a sense of destiny, even if he was, as Justice Charles Evans Hughes noted, possessed of only a "second class mentality." President Hoover called on Roosevelt to make joint policies in the interim period between election and the transfer of power to the new administration on March 4, 1933. Roosevelt, sensing disaster in any connection of his New Deal with the discarded past, flatly refused to accept the responsibility. He would not commit himself to any policies laid down by his late, and perhaps future, political opponent, lest he either be forced to carry these policies out after March 4, or be forced to assume the responsibility for letting such programs die.

It had often been the same with Presidents before. In particular, the signet of authority had passed twice between Cleveland and Harrison in times of national economic emergency. Neither had asked the other for advice or help. It was a mark of the desperate situation of America that in 1932 an embittered President Hoover would call for joint effort with the victorious rival for whom Hoover had such vigorous distaste.

In February, the banks of Detroit closed, reducing the people of the Motor City to confusion and a system of barter that might have come from the Middle Ages. Three weeks later, on the eve of the Presidential inauguration, the entire banking system of the nation collapsed. Franklin Delano Roosevelt was sworn into office on a gusty March day in an atmosphere made solemn by the enormity of the disaster: on March 4, 1933, all the banks of the nation were closed. Almost none of them had the cash to meet the demands of their depositors.

On that day, neither Franklin Delano Roosevelt nor anyone else could predict what would happen next, but strangely, the drastic action of suspending the nation's economy was greeted by the public with favor and a sense of relief. It showed, as Washington correspondent Barnet Nover later put it, "that the new administration was prepared to act promptly and urgently."

The banks, for their part, made plans to issue scrip for the public to use instead of money. Where was the money? Much of it was gone, shipped abroad during past months in gold coins and gold certificates. The shippers were wealthy foreigners who had investments in America and did not know what might happen to their wealth, and wealthy Americans who had lost faith in their own nation. On the day the bank crisis began, space had been engaged by clients of several New York banks to ship $9,000,000 in gold to Europe aboard the liner *Paris*. The shipment was stopped only because the banks were closed and the gold could not be loaded aboard the liner, but tens, scores, hundreds of similar shipments had been made in the months before.

No one knew how much of America's gold and gold currency remained on the American shores; but the bankers did know that not enough money remained in the country to carry on normal business.

Luckily for the new President, Inauguration Day fell at the end of the week, and he had the weekend to improvise a policy to carry the nation through this crisis.

On the weekend, as Franklin Roosevelt pondered this problem, the clearing house associations across the country prepared their scrip. In New York, the presses of the American Bank Note Company ran night and day, printing scrip for New York, Philadelphia, and Chicago banks. All across the country banks made similar preparations. Some medium of exchange *must* be available the next week. The country could not exist without some kind of money.

Just a single day of bank closure showed how frightening the situation could become. Many shops refused to change even five-dollar bills. A Brooklyn lawyer who had collected two one-hundred dollar bills for a fee could not change them until he went to a U.S. Postal Savings Bank and managed to secure two fifty-dollar bills for one of his hundreds. Then he found that he could not change either of the fifty-dollar bills into smaller currency.

In Washington, sightseers who had come for the inauguration found themselves unable to pay their hotel bills, and the hotels refused to take checks. The offices of the two telegraph systems were deluged with wires for money. Western Union and Postal Telegraph both limited wires for money to one hundred dollars. In Pasadena, millionaire clothing manufacturer L. B. Kuppenheimer used stage money in the dining room of a resort hotel. In New York, the president of a watch manufacturing company traded a valuable watch for a pair of riding boots so he could keep a date on horseback in Central Park.

Ten thousand people marched in New York's Union Square on Saturday, March 5, demanding unemployment insurance and more relief. They were led, openly, by the Communists. At 2:00 P.M. Carl Winter, a rising young man in the party, shepherded a delegation of twenty-five marchers to the offices of Harry L. Hopkins, New York State's relief director, to make a protest. Hopkins was not there. Winter raised his voice, claiming he had an appointment for one-thirty, but Hopkins's aides noted the appointment had been for twelve-thirty. The administrator had waited, they said, but he had left to keep a two o'clock appointment with Governor Lehman to discuss the manner of payment of relief funds all over the state during the bank holiday.

New York State's relief organization, two years ahead of the rest of the nation in meeting the problems of poverty, had fewer problems than almost any similar body in America. The state relief program was well-planned and well-executed. Hopkins's single concession to the financial disaster was to issue relief checks in small denominations— making them as good as currency. Thus, a man who might be entitled to twelve dollars for a week of labor under the "work relief" program which had partly supplanted the dole in New York, would be given three checks of four dollars each.

The Atlantic and Pacific Tea Company suggested that books of coupons be given out by employers and government agencies, coupons which could be redeemed for food in grocery stores. Hopkins, slight but vigorous, refused flatly to countenance any such handouts. Privately, he detested the idea of payment of relief in kind; publicly, he noted simply that the law insisted that payment be made in money— which in the case of the state meant by check.

But such was the temper of the nation on the weekend of March 5 and March 6, 1933 that thousands of employers were turning to scrip, to other kinds of "funny money," and to barter. The Louisville *Courier Journal* paid its employees in scrip that next week. Steamship and air lines advertised in the newspapers that they would accept scrip for passages, and the railroads, which always ran a little behind, came along with the same approach a few days later. Jesse Isidor Straus, the first director of relief for New York and head of Macy's department store, announced full confidence in President Roosevelt's ability to solve the problem of money, and also announced that he was paying the eight thousand Macy employees in cash, on Tuesday morning. He felt the matter important enough to take a full page advertisement in *The New York Times* to tell this news. It *was* news.

At the end of the weekend, President Roosevelt announced the continuation of the bank holiday for at least four more days, and the emergency plans of banks and business were put into effect.

No one did any more business than necessary, but some transactions had to be completed. Food must be bought by stores, by restaurants, and by householders. In the virtual absence of cash, those with gold or paper money could buy the cream of the crop in whatever quantities they chose. Some people began to hoard food, and the price of foodstuffs jumped everywhere, in produce market and in grocery store. This evidence of human penury increased both the sense of unreality and the tension in the land.

The crisis continued until March 8, when President Roosevelt finally secured a pledge from Congress that would enable him to authorize the printing of two billion dollars more in paper money. The money could be rushed to the banks, they could open their doors once again, and disaster could be staved off.

It was not a solution to the basic economic problem, but there was no time for solution—the President was simply reinforcing the levee against black waters that threatened the nation as it had never been threatened before. John Dewey, the philosopher, noted that a single banking system for the United States was the solution. Roosevelt and his advisers agreed, and practically speaking, a single national banking system emerged from the crisis. But that was to take time, and time had to be purchased.

The people in America who were best equipped to face the banking crisis of March, 1933 were the very poor. They had no money and they knew the ways of finding a bit of food or a warm overcoat without the use of cash. In number, the very poor were legion. Industrial production, given a par of 100, had dropped to a new all-time low: 56. In New York State, where Harry Hopkins had carried out Franklin Roosevelt's relief policies for two years, the number of factory workers had fallen from 1,100,000 in 1929 to 733,000 in 1933. Wages fell further, from $1,650,000,000 to $754,000,000. A third of the workers in New York State were unemployed, and another quarter were working part-time. New York was hard hit, not as hard, for example, as Pennsylvania, but perhaps that was only because New York had begun a state relief program two years before.

The first effort in state relief had been made by Governor Roosevelt five months after the Wall Street crash. Roosevelt was not acute enough to stem the crash by reforming the ways of Wall Street overnight, as his critics have suggested *ad nauseam*. He did have a sense of responsibility for human beings as individuals, a sense of *noblesse oblige* inculcated in him as a boy. He was one of the new patroons of the Hudson River valley, the landholders who took care of their own. As governor, Roosevelt felt that same fatherly responsibility for the people of New York State, and after the crash he began a five-point program to deal with unemployment. He ordered a census of the unemployed, he began to coordinate various relief agencies, he pushed for local public works, he began campaigning for new jobs, and he established free employment agencies as a state responsibility.

Here, basically, was a blueprint for a federal program for relief of the unemployed. But while New York's effort equaled that of the federal government under Hoover in scope, it was only the beginning of the Roosevelt relief work for New York State.

In 1930, besides the emergency relief program of the state, and the volunteer program pushed by President Hoover across the nation, the towns and cities in New York, as everywhere, had tried to shoulder a part of the burden of joblessness. Rochester was the first city to put its unemployed to work. But by the summer of 1931 the job had been proved too great for the local governments. Governor Roosevelt had realized the state must step in, and in August, 1931, New York State did begin a state relief program, optimistically called the Temporary Emergency Relief Administration, although it was to continue for nearly seven years.

Jesse Straus was the first chairman, but actual administration was under Harry Hopkins. Hopkins had been brought to Roosevelt's attention by Frances Perkins. This was Hopkins's first departure from the traditional role of worker in private charity, but the change was easy enough to accept since he believed wholeheartedly in the responsibility of government for the welfare of the people.

Hopkins liked to refer to himself as "the son of a harness maker," a statement which was true enough, if slightly idealized. His father had made harnesses in Harry Hopkins's native Iowa, but had failed to secure the family's fortunes, and the Hopkinses of Iowa had lived constantly on the edge of poverty. In 1901, Harry's father had moved the family to Grinnell, and there Anna Hopkins, Harry's mother, had decided they would stay. Grinnell was a university town, and here at least she knew her children could secure a college education.

Harry was a bright, inquisitive child, who stuttered his way through grammar school. By the time he reached high school he was a politician. When he reached the Freshman class of Grinnell College, he won election to a group called "the Institute," which usually took in only upper classmen. He also represented the Freshman class on the college council. Here, he entered social work, as chairman of the local YMCA—but without the slightest thought of becoming a full-time social worker. Hopkins intended, in fact, to become a newspaperman, and after graduation from Grinnell, with honors in political economy, he found a job on a newspaper in Montana.

He was not, however, to go to Montana. He was persuaded to spend the final summer of his college days supervising young people at a camp for the underprivileged New York slum children maintained by Christodora House at Bound Brook in New Jersey.

Harry Hopkins liked this work. He liked the bright lights of the eastern cities, too, and when fall came, he persuaded himself to join Christodora House as a staff member, and began work among the immigrants of the lower East Side of New York. It was 1912.

During the years that followed, Harry Hopkins showed a remarkable ability in relief administration. He moved through the ranks by a combination of hard work, intelligence, easy personal grace, and the good fortune of making friends in high places. He worked for the Association for Improving the Condition of the Poor, one of the favorite charities of such wealthy families as the Vanderbilts. He moved to the Board of Child Welfare, at a salary of three thousand dollars, when he was twenty-five years old. That year he married Ethel Gross, a fellow social worker.

Thereafter, Harry Hopkins's rise was steady in the unspectacular world of private charity. In later years he moved to the suburbs, walked in the woods, and collected fungi. He liked to drink and eat well. He was addicted to what Damon Runyon and others called "the bangtails"—Hopkins was an inveterate patron of the two-dollar parimutuel window all his adult life. He spent some of his happiest evenings in night clubs, and if he had money, which was seldom, he spent it cheerfully on entertainment.

In World War I, Hopkins would have enlisted in the army, but was kept out by defective vision in one eye. Instead he went to New Orleans as head of the Gulf of Mexico division of the Red Cross. From there he moved to Atlanta as chief of the entire southern division of the Red Cross.

Seeing the Deep South, he acquired an insight into every facet of American poverty, in the cities, in the towns, in the hill country, and in the share-cropping farms of the black belt.

In 1921 Hopkins was appointed director of the public health division of the AICP. In 1924 he became executive director of the New York Tuberculosis Association, where he spent more money than he took in, but expanded the activities and prestige of the association so greatly that no one cared. He made up much of the association's deficit, too, by successfully promoting the sale of Christmas seals for holiday mail.

In these years Hopkins was a chain-smoker and a chain coffee drinker. He changed his shirt only when reminded, and he usually shaved his black beard at the office. Officially, he spent money as though he had an unlimited supply, and he usually achieved the results he wanted. He hated red tape, and the "normal procedures" which careful workers used to protect themselves. Hopkins assumed that there would always be a certain amount of cheating in charity. He was cynical about human nature, but he was optimistic, too, and daring enough to follow his convictions.

When Roosevelt and Jesse Straus chose Hopkins to head the New York State relief organization, Hopkins realized that he was being asked to participate in a radical departure from normal charity, and he embraced the chance. In the first ten months of the program he spent $48,000,000, but he helped a million and a half people. For a lesser administrator, it might have taken half that time just to get organized for action.

In 1932, Harry Hopkins succeeded Straus as chairman of the state relief organization, and began to draw one of the highest salaries of his entire life: $11,500 a year. In two years he had spent $140,000,-000 of state money, but was just getting started in his expansion of the idea that the state owed men and women relief—not the dole but work relief, which kept them from starvation but also gave them the satisfaction of working for their own support. If the work was raking leaves, which it often was, at least the men doing the raking were not on the dole. They kept their self-respect.

How successful was Hopkins in areas other than spending money?

Hopkins was successful enough as a relief administrator so that at the end of 1931 eight states had followed the lead of New York in the establishment of state relief organizations. By the end of 1932 four more states had copied the New York plan. Thirteen of forty-eight states could not carry on the national relief job alone, however, and in the states where relief was sorely needed the state governments were too poor to afford such programs.

By the spring of 1933 one of every six families in America was actually suffering in poverty. The national income, which had hit eighty-one billion dollars in 1929, fell to thirty-nine billion dollars in 1932. The nation was ready for revolution. The hope that the revolution might be peaceful rested on the ability of the new federal administration to feed the seeds of self-respect before they could be crowded out by the weeds of fear and hatred.

States and municipalities, by 1933, had almost exhausted their resources in dealing with relief. They could not meet the need. New York, by straining her resources, might muster an adequate relief program for her people. But how could the poorer states of Georgia, Mississippi, or Nevada do the same?

Outside doctrinaire Republican circles, the Roosevelt idea of federal relief was accepted with remarkably little objection, even from captains of industry. In the ranks of the National Association of Manufacturers and the National Chamber of Commerce could be found strong adherents of the new approach. Even some industrialists who had voted for Hoover in November indicated that if they had it to do over again they would vote for Roosevelt.

Roosevelt laid his plans to spend money to get the nation back on its feet, but he was sufficiently imbued with traditional economic and financial views to plan for a balanced budget. Since living costs had declined in the past four years by 23 per cent, Roosevelt planned to cut the pay of federal workers by 15 per cent. He spoke in those early days about the need for a few hundred million dollars for relief and he planned cuts of $900,000,000 in the other areas of government to balance the federal budget.

And who was to administer this relief? It was a knotty problem, and one that must be solved very quickly.

When Roosevelt arrived in Washington, another bonus army was on the march. Had the new President greeted this army with federal troops and gunfire, treated the men as a mob, as Hoover had treated the first group, bloody revolution might have begun then and there. But Roosevelt treated the new bonus marchers with courtesy. He opened an army camp to house them. He sent the Marine band to play for them. He made sure they were fed. And he dispatched his wife as an emissary to visit them and hear their woes.

Concurrently, Roosevelt sent to Congress his first relief measure —a bill authorizing the establishment of a Civilian Conservation Corps to employ men in the forests of the nation. Among the quarter million men who went into the CCC were 2,600 bonus marchers, who went straight from Washington, trading misery for food, a dollar a day, and a sense of belonging to society once again.

Roosevelt's relief program came none too soon. Even in New York, where the state had taken hold of the problem of relief, Harry Hopkins's efforts were not enough. Private industry, too, was doing its best to prevent a swelling of the relief rolls. The New York Telephone Company admitted it was keeping nine thousand more employees on its payroll than were needed. All fifty thousand workers, from the president of the company down to switchboard operators, worked on a part-time basis, and the company officially encouraged resignations in an offer of a "dismissal wage" that amounted to a week for each year of service.

Mrs. August Belmont's volunteer relief workers continued to press their "adopt a family" campaign and at the end of March, 1933, were still seeking a thousand new jobs for needy workers.

It took twenty-seven days for Roosevelt to establish the Civilian Conservation Corps. That was only the first step in federal relief of the needy. Other steps were to come.

Representative John Taber of New York grumbled that Roosevelt's policies would further extend government invasion of private industry's domain, and he voted against the CCC, but he was running against the tide. The nation and the Congress cheered Roosevelt and the bright-eyed, eager men who had flocked to Washington to help shape this New Deal. Washington buzzed with a renewed optimism in these first days. The old order of affairs had passed and would nevermore return, said Harold Ickes, Secretary of the Interior.

"We are going back to the faith," said Professor Raymond Moley, now Assistant Secretary of State for public affairs. The "faith," to Moley, then meant re-establishment of a nation of equals. Henry Morgenthau, Jr., the head of the Farm Credit Administration, talked of a new sense of interdependence. Rexford G. Tugwell, Assistant Secretary of Agriculture, spoke of the "orderly" revolution of 1932, and predicted the frankly experimental course of the administration without apology. Senator Robert Wagner talked of national planning.

The planning, hastily conceived as it had to be to meet the overlapping series of crises, was hailed at first in every part of the nation, in every segment of society, except by those guardians of huge capital whose interests would be hurt by any form of government intervention in business and industrial affairs. In the first famous one hundred days, the form of the New Deal took shape, and then the nation stood back a little to look it over.

Indeed, a revolution had been accomplished. The banking system had been turned upside down, stratified, regulated, and the deposits of average citizens guaranteed. Agriculture had been placed under a supported, regulated system. Public power had been established in the Tennessee Valley Authority. The gold standard had been abandoned. The beginnings had been laid for stock market regulation. All industry and business was under regulation in a code system established under the National Industrial Recovery Act, and a federal relief system was in effect, and working under Harry Hopkins.

Hopkins, the man whom business was later to hate as the most dangerous radical in the New Deal, came to Washington late in the one hundred days in May, 1933. He was greeted as he arrived on the national scene with the greatest cordiality. Even Herbert Hoover praised him. Perhaps this was not so strange, for Hopkins, like Hoover, was a poor Iowa boy. Hopkins, like Hoover, had spent his life in relief work, although Hopkins had never taken time out to earn a personal fortune as had the former President. Moreover, Hopkins, when he came to Washington to administer the federal relief program, an-

nounced that he intended to eliminate the dole at the earliest possible moment. He was greeted as one of the "soundest" among the
men surrounding the new President.

Hopkins had jumped at the chance to come to Washington, although it meant he took a personal pay cut of three thousand dollars a
year at a time when he could not well afford it.

He had been divorced by his first wife, who had taken custody of
their three children, and had married again, a Michigan girl named
Barbara Duncan whom he had met when she worked in the office of
the Tuberculosis Association, and in 1932 a daughter, Diana, was born
to them. His financial responsibilities were heavy, and his means, at
best, were not great.

In May, Harry Hopkins moved into a four-and-a-half-room apartment in Washington, and moved his offices into a shabby building
sprayed regularly with a disinfectant that gave the place an institu-
tional—some said "barnyard"—air.

The original Federal Emergency Relief Act of May 12, 1933, provided for an appropriation of $500,000,000—half of it to be given as
grants to the states, on the basis of one federal dollar for every three
state dollars spent. On the first day, from his musty office, Harry
Hopkins stopped the work of organizing a staff long enough to allocate
five million dollars to seven states where relief organizations existed,
nearly bankrupt as they were. The other $250,000,000 was to be spent
to avert personal disasters, where the joint machinery moved too
slowly, or in states which had failed or refused to establish their own
relief organizations. Hopkins did not start from scratch. The Hoover
administration had sponsored an emergency relief act in 1932 which
had made available $300,000,000 in federal funds on a loan basis, and
an organization had been established to handle the funds. Harry
Hopkins's job, however, was not simply to dispense funds, but to find
the areas of need, and make relief available to individuals. This was
the Roosevelt philosophy, enunciated in his term as governor of New
York; when applied on a national scale, as it was to be applied, it
marked a basic change in the political philosophy of federal government.

The federal relief program, as with so much else, was not a result
of any single long-term plan. It was a series of immediate programs,

one leading into the next, and each extending the area of responsibility of the federal government in the field of public welfare.

Before Roosevelt and Hopkins, federal authorities had conceived of "relief" as meaning the provision of food for hungry people. Plans for public works were carefully scrutinized, to make sure that these projects did not conflict with private industry. Neither Roosevelt nor Hopkins felt any compunction about interfering with private industry, if in their opinions it best served the interest of the people to let government step in.

Less than a month after he took office, Hopkins told the National Conference of Social Work in Detroit that the federal government had an obligation to extend relief directly, without funneling the money through private agencies or even state governments. Then, in order to distribute relief money effectively, Hopkins hired a group of investigators who were actually hard, slogging reporters, although their reports were made by letter to Hopkins himself.

By October, 1933, although each month Secretary of Labor Frances Perkins duly reported gains in the return of workers to their jobs, the economy was not yet back to the payroll level of October, 1931. Hopkins, through his own investigators, knew the nation's sixteen million needy faced a long, hard winter. He had discovered anew that the vast majority of those forced to accept relief wanted work, not a handout of food, or coupons, or even of money.

Work relief was not universally favored by the states, for it was more expensive to administer and more trouble to control. In the field of public projects, the states were lagging, even where money was available. Secretary Ickes was disturbed because while New York had let out 67 per cent of the highway contracts agreed upon to reduce unemployment, the state of Georgia had done nothing at all.

That fall, Lorena Hickok, one of Hopkins's investigators, reported ghastly conditions all over the country. In September, when the state of Kentucky failed to put up its share of relief funds, federal relief officials in Kentucky stopped the flow of money to the people. Miss Hickok, visiting Pineville, in the mountain country, discovered cases of actual starvation.

In September, she told of one woman, a miner's widow with six children, who had nothing at all to eat in her shack, and no prospects of getting anything. Relief had been discontinued three weeks before. Most families in the area were down to two meals a day. Some were living on green corn and string beans. Up one little creek bed outside Pineville, Miss Hickok said, she heard that five babies had starved to death in the previous ten days. When the mountain men passed one particular cabin near the settlement, they averted their eyes: the women in that family had no clothes at all to wear, not even rags.

After three weeks in which nothing happened, the local relief administrator, a woman, could stand it no longer. She put up ten dollars of her own money to start a fund with which storekeepers prepared food packages, worth eighty-five cents each, which would carry a family for a week. What was in the packages? A little corn meal, a little lard, a bit of sugar and some coffee. That was all, but it was hope.

In the cities it was not much better. The welfare commissioner of New York asked for $10,000,000 a month. In Newark, New Jersey, teachers and city employees did not receive the pay checks due them on October 1 until October 17.

Obviously, the Federal Emergency Relief Administration was not the last answer, although Hopkins siphoned funds, wherever possible, from the dole to work relief all over the country. The dole neither solved the problem, nor even worked effectively as a palliative for long. Hopkins wanted a giant program of work relief, and he wanted it for the winter of 1933–34.

By the first of November, Hopkins had taken his proposal to the President, armed with a precedent—a statement made some thirty-five years before by Samuel Gompers of the American Federation of Labor in favor of a program of work relief in time of crisis. Hopkins hoped to provide four million jobs before the first of the year, a figure Roosevelt estimated would cost about $400,000,000. The President, further, knew where the money could be found—in Secretary Ickes's public works fund which was moving more slowly than Roosevelt had hoped. The President did not criticize Ickes for his way of setting public works in motion; Ickes insisted on sound projects which would give taxpayers the benefit of their dollar's worth. But to Hopkins, the miners' widows and sick children near Pineville were more important than the taxpayer. Hopkins insisted that hunger was not debatable.

With Roosevelt's preliminary approval, Hopkins and his assistants went to work over a weekend in a Washington hotel, and emerged, exhausted, but with a plan for the Civil Works Administration. A week later, on November 9, Hopkins was made Civil Works Administrator.

On November 15 the President explained his new program to allot $100,000,000 a month for four months to move men off the relief rolls and back to work. Before a month had passed, CWA had, astoundingly, cut through red tape to put the four million to work. America began to pulse a little faster.

The Roosevelt administration was nine months old that November. Some of FDR's earliest adherents were beginning to have doubts about the direction of the New Deal, and the worst fears of the old-dealers were being confirmed. It *was* a revolution as reporter Ernest K. Lindley declared in his book, *The Roosevelt Revolution*. Lindley's report, rushed to the bookstores in November to document the first months of the revolution, was sold next to stacks of 100,000,000 *Guinea Pigs*, the shocking exposé of food and drug and commodity misrepresentation by Arthur Kallet and F. J. Schlink. The literary uplift of the season was provided by *Life Begins at 40*, by Walter B. Pitkin, one of the first declarations that the future of America's old people was not as bleak as it then seemed. Less serious readers buried themselves in *Anthony Adverse* and *Oil for the Lamps of China* which led the best-seller lists and provided escape from the realities of approaching winter.

It was an odd year in many ways. History was to show that while some people went hungry, and some actually starved, the income of corporations rose 35 per cent in 1933 over the previous year, to $654,-000,000. Individual incomes, however, dropped $340,000,000 in that same period. Even in this decrease, the rich seemed to grow richer, while the poor languished. The number of people who earned $25,000 or more in 1933 *increased*, and their incomes increased, but those who earned less than $25,000 saw their incomes shrink, drastically and steadily. The number of persons who reported incomes of $1,000,000 or more jumped from twenty to forty-six, and one man (unnamed) reported an income of $5,000,000, a huge sum for an individual, but only enough money to solve New York City's relief problems for two weeks.

These income figures were not to be made known to the public for nearly a year, but businessmen sensed that on the business level, the affairs of the nation were improving. With improvement, they grew critical of the new administration's heavy spending, and the statements of some administration officials.

Henry Wallace, struggling to avert an incipient revolt against crop controls in the Middle West, said he foresaw control by federal government of all American farm lands, and "the rational resettlement" of America. "If the New Deal means anything, it means the subordination of capital rights and property rights to human rights," Wallace declared in a speech in Muncie, Indiana. "Do you want to go back to the vomit of capitalism?" he asked his listeners.

These were strong words, and they made businessmen and industrialists uneasy. Roosevelt had been portrayed as the saviour of the capitalistic system in America. Businessmen were now not so sure this was true. In Chicago, where Henry Wallace talked about "control," a group of businessmen, including Sewell Avery, Alexander Legge, and the advertising man Albert Lasker set up a committee on national monetary policy, in outright opposition to the trend of the New Deal.

These men were not ready to condemn Roosevelt yet, but they demanded an end to experimentation with the national currency. They wanted an end to *all* experimentation in fact, sensing the gulf that had already begun to separate this new America from the old. They wanted a return to the gold standard, and a return to the business economy of the twenties, the economy whose public benefits Henry Wallace regarded as so much "vomit."

Republican Representative Hamilton Fish, Jr. of New York came out flatly to call the New Deal "Socialist." Senator Thomas D. Schall, Republican of Minnesota, attacked Franklin Roosevelt and the NRA in a speech in Minneapolis. Senator Schall was talking before a student audience at the University of Minnesota, and was booed loudly for his sentiments by youth who believed in Roosevelt.

In social, economic, industrial, political affairs, and even in the internal affairs of the Democratic party, the gulfs were widening and the lines were hardening perceptibly before the first year of the New Deal was out.

WORK IN PROGRESS

CHAPTER FIVE

THANKS TO THE AUDACIOUS BEHAVIOR of Harry Hopkins and Franklin Roosevelt, the winter of 1933–34 was not as painful as it might otherwise have been, but it was bad enough. Between fifteen and sixteen million Americans lived in desperation, but in one way or another most of them got some relief.

From an average sum of fifty cents per family of four, relief assistance increased to an average of sixty cents a day—the federal government furnishing sixty-five cents of every relief dollar dispensed in the country.

The rise seems insignificant—and it was. The difference lay in the change in the source of relief, and the manner in which relief was given. Relief ceased to be a question of charity. It became a matter of national survival, quite aside from the sensibilities involved, and it was so recognized, even in Wall Street. Cities, towns, and private charity could not have carried the program necessary to prevent wholesale starvation in America during that winter, and most of the government bodies, at least, admitted it frankly.

Business was showing a contrary kind of progress that winter. The NRA reported newspaper advertising was on the increase. (Newspaper advertising was always a barometer of business confidence, if nothing else.) Betterment had not yet translated itself onto the consumer level, however. In Alabama one hundred thousand people subsisted on relief funds. More than a third of these people lived in the industrial area around Birmingham. But in Alabama, as elsewhere, the relief rolls did not tell the entire story. Some people were too proud to ask for assistance, and some people were simply too remote from cities and news centers to know that relief was available, or did not know how to go about asking for assistance. That winter a feeling of despair crept across the country, a hangover from the previous year of inaction. The feeling crept as quietly as a caterpillar. It was a debilitating feeling that many men and women seemed unable to shake off even when they saw and heard and read the signs of hope in work relief and the growing number of government building projects.

In many people despair showed itself as a form of personal guilt, the guilt of a person who felt that somehow he had failed.

One young Alabama schoolteacher had been fired from her job after the Wall Street crash although she had held a teaching job for eight years. After layoff, this girl was forced to seek government relief from time to time in the next few years, although she never took aid when she could find any work at all—even work as a servant. In the winter of 1933 the young teacher worked for a few weeks as a housemaid. She quit finally, because her employers gave her only room and board for her full-time labor. Later, for a few weeks the teacher found a job in a convalescent home, which paid her three dollars a week plus board and room. That job ended, the home a victim of the hard times. Then—nothing.

When a caseworker tried to cheer the teacher, the girl would not be cheered.

"If with all the advantages I've had I can't make a living," she said, "I'm just no good, I guess."

Relief—christened by its enemies as "the dole"—created serious new problems in American society. Until Harry Hopkins entered federal government almost all relief was awarded after a means test. A family was forced to admit its entire shame to a relief caseworker. Direct relief could be given no other way, but the baring of family confidences hurt the morale of all recipients. Envy and antagonism developed, too, particularly in such careworn areas as Delaware, where fully half the people in the state suffered, but where most families had not become destitute—able to qualify for relief from the federal government.

By the spring of 1934, when more than a half-billion federal dollars had been disbursed, Hopkins's official reporters sensed a renewal of hope in the national attitude.

They reported that in the town of Florence, Alabama, men on work relief virtually changed the face of the town by the addition of a single feature, a spacious and attractive town park.

In 1933 workmen had flocked to the edge of the Tennessee River basin, in hope of finding work at Muscle Shoals Dam, the federal power project authorized so reluctantly by Herbert Hoover in the last days of his administration. When Roosevelt came into office, the new President learned that Hoover had planned to build a low dam which would not have the capacity to use all the water power available. Since once the dam was built the site would be ruined forever, Roosevelt stopped construction of the Muscle Shoals project for replanning. This action slashed a little more into the scanty federal employment level of that moment. Most workmen who had flocked to the area were without resource. They remained in Florence, to become public charges and a nuisance to the townspeople.

When CWA began, the attitude of Alabamans changed. CWA officials brought an unemployed landscape architect from Birmingham to work as superintendent of a construction gang. A thousand of the transient workers were employed to create a park on a large plot of barren land within the town. This plot had been set aside by the town fathers of Florence for a park 120 years before, but for one reason or another Florence had never built the park.

In a few months, the CWA workmen built a large park for the people of Florence. They built a municipal swimming pool, barbecue pits, and several picnic areas, a complete drainage system, curved walks, and bridle paths. The citizens of Florence would never have afforded such a park had it not been for the expenditure of federal funds—and they knew it.

Was this a boondoggle? The word was used time and again to describe such projects bought with taxpayers' money. Or was it social progress?

The Florence project was certainly no more wasteful than the raking of leaves, jobs to which New York City put its symphony violinists when they came straggling into the city relief offices, begging for any kind of manual labor before federal relief began. The Florence Park represented no more boondoggling than the cleared campgrounds and rustic furniture that graced the Oregon coastline at Ecola Park, near Cannon Beach, courtesy of the taxpayers and the young men of the Civilian Conservation Corps. Was it not better that taxpayers' money be spent for public projects than that men either starve or live on handouts without work?

In the CCC, the PWA, and the CWA, critics could always find waste and examples of foolishness. Still, in Florence, conditions would have been desperate except for the park project. Families lived wherever they could. One family lived in an abandoned trolley car and paid eight dollars a month rent for the privilege. A torture to the soul of the social workers was the shack-town built up in Florence in a gulch along the railroad tracks—a new slum, made of corrugated iron and boards, a town without sanitation, without a water supply.

But what could be done?

Lorena Hickok came to Florence, and described conditions there in a series of detailed letters to Harry Hopkins.

She reported on the successes of CWA and FERA—and the failures. She told of conversations with friends of the administration and of talks with enemies of Roosevelt and of the changes that were taking place.

As Miss Hickok travelled, the enormity of the problem and the despair and weariness of the country were reflected in her letters. From Florence, she noted that CWA money was being spent to erect a handsome amphitheater for future college theatricals (except in rain), while on the other side of the town a hundred families were living in misery in their shacks.

"It all seems sort of silly, doesn't it?" Miss Hickok asked her chief.

There were many such reports from a half-dozen skillful observers in the field. These men and women were Harry Hopkins's eyes and ears. Harry Hopkins soon saw the need for action in matters greater than simple work relief.

By summer, 1934, Hopkins realized that work relief, public works, and all other government and private help had not stopped or stayed American poverty. In Houston, a federal relief worker donned old clothes and joined the ranks of the "reliefers" to see how they were getting along. Wandering in one of the tough sections of Houston he was accosted by one woman after another. These were young girls, neophyte streetwalkers. In response to one of them who was more insistent than most, he turned out his pockets.

"I can't," he said. "I haven't any money."

She looked at him ruefully. "It doesn't cost much," she answered. "Only a dime."

Looking upon such immorality, Hopkins's reporters were first shocked, then outraged, and finally numbed. They realized how great a levelling influence was despair. The "nice" young women of America, all too often were willing to exchange their favors for a glass of beer, or just an hour or two of human warmth and forgetfulness. Hopkins's reporters were witnesses to the warning signs of the collapse of a society.

Yet there were other, more positive, signs in 1934. Birmingham, despite the fact that thirty thousand people were unemployed, showed a sudden business spurt early in April, after the steelworkers still on the job received a raise in pay. Birmingham's General Motors distributor told Miss Hickok that April 1 had been his biggest business day in five years, bigger than 1929 boom days.

Still, a few months later, from Detroit, CWA investigator Lincoln Colcord wrote Hopkins that in spite of an increase in production in the auto industry, the general economic condition of Detroit was very low. Martha Gellhorn, another of Hopkins's roving investigators, despaired of her own inability to describe the degradation she encountered in Gastonia, North Carolina; Fall River, Massachusetts; Laconia, New Hampshire; Minot, North Dakota; and Klamath Falls, Oregon.

The investigators of Harry Hopkins travelled that year through many different worlds, all of them within the continental boundaries of the United States.

The federal administration, particularly through Harry Hopkins's relief organization, was engaged in a huge social experiment Americans watched, some hopefully, some nervously, while some ignored it, and others never knew about at all.

At this time, Hopkins began to advocate the decentralization of American industry from the old population centers. He wanted to transfer people on farms from submarginal lands to good lands, and even to establish government factories in the wilderness if necessary, to give work to the unemployed. He created a homestead policy under which the government gave farmers a plot of ground and the seed and equipment to farm it. He put other farm families to work canning foods and making mattresses.

The private canning companies objected to government competition. So did the mattress manufacturers. Hopkins replied that work relief was necessary, that neither the small-cottage canning industries nor the home mattress makers interfered with the flow of

American business. The recipients of those homemade mattresses, he said, would have purchased no mattresses otherwise, for they had no money to buy on the open market.

Businessmen had applauded repeated statements by Hopkins that the dole wasted human values, but after a year of Hopkins's work relief many American businessmen were dissatisfied with work relief, too.

They knew that the cost of work relief was 50 per cent greater than that of the dole. In Delaware the National Industrial Conference Board discovered the monthly cost of keeping a man working for his assistance was $109.92—more than three times the cost of the dole in the previous year.

Using the high cost as part of their argument, in December the National Association of Manufacturers called on government to stop competing with industry. By the end of the year, the United States Chamber of Commerce began laying the groundwork for a demand that Roosevelt give up all the emergency powers he had assumed as soon as private enterprise was ready to absorb responsibilities for the American economy. Businessmen, perennial optimists, had regained their faith in the few signs of economic upturn.

The National Chamber of Commerce pondered its best approach to Roosevelt. Real estate men across the country protested against plans of Harold Ickes for slum clearance; they cringed under suggestions from Hopkins that the country needed low-cost housing.

The lower reaches of the American economy had not responded with the bounce of the businessmen, however. In Carlisle, Pennsylvania, a starving man named Elmo Noakes suffocated his three small daughters rather than see *them* starve. If his was not a valid reason, Noakes still had so little hope for the American future that he killed himself, too. The public accepted the incident with none of the outrage or outcry which usually accompanies an unusual anti-social act. The tabloid newspapers had too much of this grist to be interested in another murder-suicide.

Such contradictions continued. English author J. B. Priestley visited the United States, and wrote that on a journey across the country he had seen few signs of real distress. Such a trip was possible. One phenomenon of the American depression was its invisibility to all but the sharpest eyes. But Governor Scholtz of Florida said he was worried about the influx of jobless to his state in the winter of 1934, and the expense they would cause the Florida taxpayers. Upton Sinclair, the visionary, sometimes socialist, who ran for governor of California, was defeated, on a Democratic ticket that promised to end poverty, but a few months later even his victorious Republican opponent, Governor Merriam, had proved so progressive that he frightened California businessmen.

California, beset by an expanding population of job-hunters, learned that it would have to increase its state revenue by ninety million dollars in the next two years to meet expenses.

Where was the money coming from—for California and the rest of the nation? Franklin Roosevelt and his financial advisers worried over the federal aspect of the problem. Harry Hopkins, perhaps alone, did not care. Hopkins was not a financier or a fund raiser. He had always been a spender.

Secretary of Commerce Roper called on each American community to shoulder its own relief burdens. But there was no enthusiasm for that call. Hopkins continued on his way. Federal funds were found, as they had been found in 1933—by borrowing.

This was federal deficit financing—a system which worried conservative budget officers in the government and businessmen and industrial leaders. Roosevelt talked of balancing the budget, but still he faced actual need in every direction. The budget was not balanced. He did not see how it could be balanced. Nor did anyone else offer a positive program for budget-balancing.

Harry Hopkins, by 1934, had risen high in Roosevelt's esteem and belonged to the President's "poker cabinet," a handful of penny-ante gamblers who met primarily to give companionship to Roosevelt—and to talk over politics and policies.

When Hopkins arrived in Washington, with Roosevelt's approval he had tried to keep politics out of relief. Democratic party chairman James Farley was dismayed by this decision, and the Democratic members of Congress were disgusted. A year after Hopkins's arrival the structures of the relief organization and the Civil Works Administration had grown so that the pressure of politics and politicians on Hopkins was continuous. In 1935, when Congress passed the Pres-

On the surface Herbert Hoover and Franklin Roosevelt appeared friendly enough on that raw March day as they rode together to the Capitol for Roosevelt's inauguration ceremonies. WIDE WORLD PHOTO

Raymond Moley saw the delegates to the London Economic Conference off in New York City. They were Rep. Samuel D. McReynolds, chairman of the House Foreign Affairs Committee, Secretary of State Cordell Hull, and Senator Key Pittman. Moley was to see them later. WIDE WORLD PHOTO

Those concerned with relief went to the White House to talk to Roosevelt in the spring of 1935. They were, left to right, Secretary of the Treasury Morgenthau, SEC Chairman Joseph Kennedy, Harry Hopkins, Budget Director Bell, Secretary Harold Ickes, Charles West, the administration's liaison officer with Congress, Rex Tugwell, Undersecretary of Agriculture, and Rear Admiral Peoples, whose job was procurement of supplies for the administration. WIDE WORLD PHOTO

There was little to do in Chicago's Grant Park but read newspapers, and then without hope. PHOTOGRAPH BY FRED G. KORTH, COURTESY CHICAGO HISTORICAL SOCIETY

ident's five billion dollar work relief bill, it became apparent that public assistance would be established as national policy for a number of years to come. Congressmen exerted the final pressure to throw welfare into politics when they amended the original administration bill in order to require Congressional approval of the appointment of any administrator who was paid more than five thousand dollars a year. Politics then moved into relief in a way that made it impossible to treat the program apolitically.

Out of that omnibus relief bill of 1935 was born the WPA, not as the huge government industry it became, but as a part of the reorganized relief program. Harold Ickes, as Secretary of the Interior, was responsible for the federal Public Works Administration.

In a typical effort to resolve frictions, Roosevelt decided that work relief should be placed in the hands of a triumvirate. Frank Walker, an old Roosevelt friend and president of the National Emergency Council, was put in charge of planning relief projects. Ickes was made chairman of the committee which submitted the projects for the President's approval. Hopkins was given the third division—the administration of the projects after their approval. His section was named the Works Progress Administration; the title suggested the limitations on his mandate. The President, however, gave Hopkins outright authority to plan and carry out "small useful projects" all over the nation without consulting the other members of the triumvirate.

As an executive, Roosevelt consistently gave his loyal subordinates as much leeway as possible, trusting in his own authority and ability to settle the differences that were bound to arise among them. Perhaps Roosevelt was led to this course by his ego, perhaps by his warm sympathy for the aspirations of his assistants. Without doubt he knew the executive adage that men make of jobs what they will, and he gave each of these three men opportunity to exert leadership in the relief program.

Ickes was spending much of his time on his own dream—the establishment of a separate department of natural resources. He did what he could to maintain government projects on a useful and paying basis.

Walker, a great conciliator, attempted to keep the peace.

Harry Hopkins, convinced that it was his job to transfer money from the government into the hands of individuals with as little delay and as little administrative expense as possible, made of WPA a kind of super-corporation whose main function seemed to be to keep in constant motion.

Ickes, alone, would not have invested millions of federal dollars in government writers' projects and art projects. Yet, in the end, these projects produced things of value, such as guidebooks to America. WPA workers collated information for libraries and prepared bibliographies and surveys which made the 1930's the most thoroughly documented period in American history. More art for government use was produced in the 1930's than in all the years before. Harry Hopkins had small interest in building dams or changing the courses of rivers; he wanted to put people to work quickly. There was an almost constant butting of heads, between Ickes and Hopkins, but big projects and small ones both flourished before the agonized eyes of businessmen. The businessmen realized, in 1935, that government was becoming bigger than business.

As with direct relief, WPA offered endless opportunities for public criticism. Hopkins was reviled in Republican meetings everywhere, but he pushed ahead, allotting WPA assistance for victims of the southeastern floods in 1935 (over which there was little criticism), ordering extensive murals for public buildings across the country (over which there was criticism twenty years later) and turning down such obviously impolitic requests for WPA employment as that of a down-and-out fan-dancer.

Direct relief was subordinated in 1935 to work relief, once and for all, but direct relief continued to play an important role in the nation. That year 80 per cent of the states still relied on federal funds as their most important source of relief revenue. Some of the states, such as New Jersey, asked that the federal government assume the entire relief burden, but Hopkins refused.

If WPA was subject to business and Republican criticism, direct relief was more so. In New York, one couple was held for relief fraud after investigators discovered that the husband had held a full-time job for several months while on relief. When the investigator came to their apartment, an obliging male neighbor came in to impersonate the husband and make sure the checks continued. But it was not only a federal problem and the federal government was no more inept in administration of aid programs than states and cities. In the Bronx, newspapermen discovered a mosquito control project on which there were nearly as many supervisors as workmen, and the actual payroll of the supervisors was greater than that of the workers. This was supposedly local work relief. Actually it was giant graft.

With 1936, and the prospect of a Presidential election, the Republicans turned a thoughtful if unfriendly eye toward Harry Hopkins. They knew Hopkins had more direct political appeal for more voters than any other man in the administration except President Roosevelt. Even had Hopkins wished to continue to be apolitical it would seem to have been impossible by 1936, for he became a national target of political jibes. Even before 1936 Hopkins had finally yielded to the repeated requests of Jim Farley and the other professional politicians that his relief moneys be dispensed, at least partly, through the Democratic political organization.

Politics in relief made a great change in Hopkins's career. His salty tongue and his direct answer to questions and attacks made Hopkins a favorite with reporters, but their subsequent dispatches raised the blood pressure of red-blooded Republicans.

Hopkins was called "Communist" time and again, and even more often "socialist." Colonel Robert R. McCormick's *Chicago Tribune* termed him the "greatest wastrel" in Washington. But Hopkins was respected and feared, if detested, by Republicans even in Chicago.

As a direct focus of Republican attack, Harry Hopkins became a more important figure in Democratic political circles than anyone would have believed possible three years before. He was no longer just a social worker in deep water, but a powerful politician, all the more powerful because he was a cynical realist with a sense of humor.

At the end of the 1936 campaign, Hopkins and his wife chose to spend the election night with a party that included columnist Dorothy Thompson, in one of Hopkins's favorite haunts, the expensive Iridium Room of New York City's St. Regis Hotel. The St. Regis was a property owned by Vincent Astor, a friend of Roosevelt's and one of the few Democrats among the old families of Society. The hotel was administered by Raymond Moley, a Roosevelt intimate—a fact which gives some indication of the interplay among members of the New

Deal, and also accounts for the frequency with which Hopkins, always a poor man, wined and dined at the St. Regis.

The St. Regis was always known as a fine hotel, an expensive hotel, and a watering place for rich Republicans. Hopkins's presence there on election night must have been prompted, in part, by a puckish sense of humor. When the noise of Roosevelt's landslide had subsided and the results had been announced to the stunned occupants of the Iridium Room late that night, Dorothy Thompson rose and proposed a toast to a man she had not supported—Franklin D. Roosevelt, President of the United States. Thereupon the orchestra leader signalled frantically, the orchestra began to play, and the last of Miss Thompson's words were drowned. Dancing couples began to move across the floor, studiously ignoring Miss Thompson's table. Harry Hopkins looked around the room, and laughed so hard he choked on his champagne.

Hopkins's biographer, Robert Sherwood, noted some signs of Presidential ambitions in Harry Hopkins as early as 1935, but two years later the signs were unmistakable. Hopkins apparently had no idea that Roosevelt might want to run again himself. Nor was Hopkins as sharp an analyst of his own affairs as he was of the politics of others. He had allowed himself to become so controversial a figure in American politics by 1937 that conservative Democrats in the Senate combined with Republicans in a petty move to cut his salary from $12,000 to $10,000 a year. But instead of hurting him, this helped establish Hopkins as a mistreated public servant and as a symbol of Roosevelt's New Deal. That summer, Barbara Hopkins died of cancer; Hopkins went to the Mayo Clinic himself for a cancer operation in which much of his stomach was removed. Yet neither the cancer (which did not recur) nor his awkward marital status as a divorced widower prevented Hopkins and Roosevelt from talking about Hopkins for the Democratic nomination in 1940.

Hopkins had one great advantage as a political figure. He was still at the heart of America's greatest problem.

In 1936 seven million Americans were still unemployed. This decrease from twelve million represented a remarkable recovery from the depths of the depression, but it was not enough progress to make it possible for Roosevelt to eliminate either relief or to make enough cuts in WPA programs to try to balance the national budget.

Thirty-one billion dollars had been spent on relief since the beginning of the Roosevelt administration. If the end seemed in sight in 1936, the following year it again seemed far away, for the business economy fell into a recession that in any other period would have been known as a depression. In the last quarter of 1937 applications for home relief doubled, after seventeen straight months of decline. Until then WPA rolls had been declining too; in the summer of 1937 nineteen thousand WPA workers had been dismissed. Following this cutback, in the summer of 1937 relief needs had declined further, but by winter industrial production had fallen off for reasons that were not readily apparent, the country had been shocked and hurt by a series of strikes and layoffs in industry, and the recession was so serious that Roosevelt, in discussing political prospects, remarked that unless the country showed a remarked degree of recovery, no Democrat could be elected President in 1940.

Hopkins, following his cancer operation, spent much of his time resting in the sun and trying to recover his health, but while the cancer did not recur, his body chemistry seemed to be almost continuously upset, and he found himself ever less able to assimilate many necessary foods.

Despite this weakness in 1938, Hopkins was generally acknowledged as the candidate of Roosevelt for the Presidential nomination in 1940. The preference was recognized by many when Hopkins was appointed Secretary of Commerce just before Christmas, 1938.

If F.D.R. intended all along after 1936 to run for a third term, as some suspected, and Raymond Moley was convinced, the President still gave Hopkins and others the impression that Hopkins was closer to being an heir-apparent than anyone in America.

For a man who had for three years been regarded as the prime enemy of the business community, to be appointed to supervise Commerce seemed to many like asking the wolf to shepherd the flock. Republicans and Republican businessmen snorted in disgust, but Hopkins had a friend in W. Averell Harriman, chairman of the businessmen's advisory committee to the department, and Harriman did what he could to make Hopkins palatable to the business community. Hopkins leased a farm near his hometown of Grinnell, Iowa (because he could not afford to buy one) and set out to re-establish roots as an Iowa citizen. If he could make the roots grow it would contribute mightily to his chances for success in campaigning for the nomination in 1940. By the summer of 1939, however, it was apparent to Harry Hopkins that his health precluded further political ambition. It was also indicated that Franklin Roosevelt, viewing the prospects of war in Europe, was giving every consideration to a third term for himself.

After the election of 1936, the role of Harry Hopkins changed completely. He was no longer an administrator of social work and adviser on the problems of social recovery. Under Roosevelt's grooming he concerned himself with the entire social and political scene. After appointment as Secretary of Commerce, Hopkins ceased to appear publicly in his shirtsleeves in his office, and he seldom cocked his feet on the desk when talking to the press. He was practicing a new dignity.

When Hopkins became Secretary of Commerce, relief and its problems were turned over to Colonel Francis Harrington, a Hopkins deputy who was an active officer in the army, drawing army pay. Yet there were signs that the Works Progress Administration was becoming too permanent for the liking of conservatives in Congress. One such sign was the coming on the scene of WPA's own union, the Workers' Alliance of America. The alliance sought to organize all the three million Americans who still held relief jobs in 1938. Government administrators did not like that much better than congressmen.

By the middle of the following year the national atmosphere had changed markedly. Industrial employment was increasing again. Congress, disturbed by continual deficit spending, time after time scaled down administration requests for appropriations for relief. On June 30, 1939, Congress passed an emergency relief appropriation of a billion and a half dollars to enable WPA to continue its work, but Congress pulled the reins in sharply on WPA. The Federal Theater Project, for one, was cut off entirely. The name of WPA was changed from Works Progress Administration to Works Projects Administration. An eighteen-month limit was fixed for continuous WPA employment.

On the night that the Federal Theater Project died, at New York's Ritz theater, after the curtain had come down on the WPA version of the story of Pinocchio, playwright Yasha Frank went on stage to denounce the abolition of the theater project, and a hundred employees of the project demonstrated, carrying placards from the Ritz theater to Father Duffy Square on Broadway.

CIO President John L. Lewis beetled his eyebrows, and told the nation that all organized labor resented the "starvation period" that would then begin for those who had been employed by WPA for eighteen months.

Harry Hopkins, the man who had begun it all, was not heard. He was summering in 1939 in a quiet old house on the Patuxent River in Maryland, fifty miles southeast of Washington, trying to regain his failing health, eating strained vegetables, dosing himself with hypodermic shots to try to better his digestive powers. Relief, the essence of hope in the early days of the Roosevelt administration, had grown old, and the nation had grown weary of the sameness of it. Harry Hopkins, ill as he was, had also grown beyond his role of social worker, and in a few short years to come was to exercise enormous power and influence on government in the United States. But in 1939 Hopkins had already come far; an unknown social worker had become the czar of all American business. It was one of the strangest changes of the years.

. . . AND SOME FELL OFF THE WAGON

CHAPTER SIX

DURING THE FORMATIVE MONTHS of the New Deal President Franklin Roosevelt appeared to enjoy a high level of confidence and cooperation from every faction in American society except the organized radicals of the right wing and the left.

Even the Republican opposition was quiescent. On the day after the 1932 election Republican leaders in New York vowed to shake the last vestiges of "Hooverism" from their party. Religious leaders, who had favored Hoover overwhelmingly, tempered their criticisms of the New Deal with hope expressed in piety. Most of America's businessmen had backed President Hoover, but once the election was decided, they too looked forward and upward, not backward. On the eve of the election Julius R. Bux, president of the Philadelphia Textile Manufacturers Association, predicted that the election of Hoover would mean eighty thousand more jobs in textile mills while the election of Roosevelt would mean one hundred thousand more layoffs. After election, such extremist talk died out almost overnight. The business community began to look for signs of recovery, and after Inauguration Day when the paralyzation and near-panic of the bank crisis was past, businessmen had begun to recover a degree of optimism, although it was watchful optimism. Something was being done, the leaders of business could see.

Within the Roosevelt administration, however, there were signs of dissent and discomfiture almost from the earliest days in Washington, although many of the signs were not to be known, or understood, by the world outside the administration for a number of years.

The dissenters were not apostate New Dealers for the most part, nor were they discomfited officeholders or office seekers. These dissenters were men who had rallied around Roosevelt in 1932 and before, seeking, through him, to fill what they saw as a vacuum in national administration. They were men of vastly different backgrounds and political philosophies. They shared one hope: that in the Democratic party and in F.D.R. each of them might find a way to exert his own efforts in behalf of change or restraint. The desire for change and a simultaneous restraint were anomalous characteristics of Raymond Moley who was at one time perhaps Roosevelt's closest political adviser. Moley began his national political career as a friend and confidant of Franklin Delano Roosevelt. He became, before the end of the 1930's, a friend and admirer of Herbert Hoover.

As a young man Moley had travelled east to Columbia University and to his political destiny from Ohio. He had undergone a personal experience which planted in him the seeds of conservatism.

Before he was twenty-four years old, Moley contracted tuberculosis. He spent part of a year in the dry climate of New Mexico. The next year he travelled to Denver with $350, hoping to enter the University of Colorado at Boulder and study law. On his second night in Denver, Moley suffered a lung hemorrhage. He spent two months in bed, and in the contemplation of life during his long recuperative period, he nurtured a physical conservatism and restraint which he later said was to color his mature philosophy.

By nature, Raymond Moley was a teacher and a reformer. On his return to Ohio, Moley taught and administered teaching in public schools; later he taught courses in politics at Western Reserve University. Then he became director of the Cleveland Foundation and turned to the study of criminal justice and municipal government with such interest in reform that he was referred to by practical Ohio politicians as Cleveland's "bookkeeping inspector."

Originally, Raymond Moley went to the East Coast to earn his Ph.D. at Columbia University. When his studies were completed, he left, then returned to Columbia as a professor, and there, in the late 1920's he encountered Louis Howe, Roosevelt's leg-man and unofficial assistant in many matters.

Louis Howe was living in Roosevelt's house in New York City. Howe drew a salary for part-time work for a voluntary national crime commission, and in this work he sought Moley's assistance. In 1928 Howe brought Moley to see Roosevelt, then running for his first term as governor. Moley's initiation into the Roosevelt circle came with his assistance to the candidate in preparation of a speech on judicial reform.

In 1930 it seemed to those around Roosevelt that the Governor of New York was seeking the Presidency of the United States. Moley was one of those around Roosevelt, although he worked on the outer fringes of the circle in the gubernatorial years, and his major contact with Roosevelt came through Moley's appointment as research director of the Commission on the Administration of Justice. Roosevelt respected Moley as an expert in public law, and Moley, for his part, had some opportunity to see Roosevelt, the politician, in action. Moley was favorably impressed with the Rooseveltian agility and with Roosevelt's open search for new ideas. In 1931, President Hoover made the flat assertion that all laws on the books must be enforced. Moley, a student in this field, knew that governments have a careless habit of disregarding outmoded laws instead of repealing them and said such blunderbuss enforcement was impossible. It was apparent, in 1931, that Raymond Moley's sympathies were with his friend, the Governor of New York State.

And why should not a basically conservative Moley have been inclined toward Roosevelt? By family history, by background, by education, Franklin Roosevelt was a member of the most naturally conservative group in American society—the landed gentry—no matter what they were called. As a politician, Roosevelt's appeal in New York had been to the rural districts. Running first for the state legislature, Roosevelt had gone racing up and down the bank of the Hudson River in a red Stutz automobile, attracting votes that no Tammany man and few Democrats could ever hope to receive. When Roosevelt rose to the highest office in his state, he had not joined Tammany Hall. The big-city machine had joined him in an uneasy alliance. Tammany Hall never had much regard for "agrarian reformers"—and it was in just this light that Raymond Moley saw Franklin Roosevelt. Moley's Roosevelt was a natural conservative.

In 1932, through association and suggestion by Louis Howe and by Samuel Rosenman, the governor's counsel and one of his advisers, Raymond Moley was brought into the inner circle around Roosevelt. As governor, Roosevelt had learned the arts of government. Among other lessons, he had learned how much he did not know about government of a nation. Roosevelt was eager to learn. He had to learn, and learn quickly, if he was to prepare himself to capture the Democratic nomination, possibly the Presidency, and then to govern. In Roosevelt's need was born the "academic cabinet," an organization also known as the "brain trust." Many men were to be credited—and accused—of holding membership in this inner council. Adolf Berle and Rexford G. Tugwell, both of Columbia University, were members. Rosenman was an occasional consultant. Bernard Baruch was added—after the convention. Many other men of ability were brought in for specific purposes, but the catalyst, executive, and errand boy of the "brain trust" was Raymond Moley. By his own estimate, Moley's value to Roosevelt lay in an ability to help F.D.R. crystallize his own opinions and ideas, to reflect Roosevelt's inclinations accurately and to extend them, and to present them attractively.

And why did Roosevelt choose Moley? A clue can be found in the later appraisal of Moley as Assistant Secretary of State, an appraisal made by a contemporary in the State Department, as reported by Arthur Schlesinger, Jr., in *The Coming of the New Deal*: Moley, said officials of the State Department, had an interested mind, which only partly exposed itself. He did not seek systematic solutions to problems, but caught at ideas and measures. He was prone to asking others to think problems out. He did not do so himself. He was prone to dispose of serious problems with a jest. To another that description might be one of the mind and character of F.D.R.

In the course of his work, naturally Moley presented ideas new to Roosevelt, and yet he never pretended that he spoke for Roosevelt. Roosevelt was his own man, and no one knew it better than Raymond Moley, who was used for his peculiar abilities and who stayed out of the machinery of politics. Moley's concern was the machinery of policy.

The term "revolution" is often used to describe the policies of the New Deal, but the initial effect of the first New Dealers—Roosevelt and most of those around him before F.D.R. won the Democratic nomination in 1932—was directed at winning the nomination and the election and then in reforming the capitalistic society. The differences between the words "reform" and "revolution" seemed to be differences of degree, not so important as the need for drastic change in a nation whose agriculture, industry, and very social structure were being weakened day by day. Change was desirable, it was essential, and neither Roosevelt, Moley, nor many of the rest around them saw anything wrong with drastic ideas if they promised the betterment of the American people. If Moley had a criticism of Roosevelt in this pre-election period, it was the governor's very openness to ideas, his "receptivity" and his naive trust in the truth of what was told to him. But Moley was not a respecter of dogma and information for their own sakes. He had small use for the conservative Herbert Hoover's approach to government.

Far more radical in his approach than Moley was Rexford Tugwell, and yet Moley had been instrumental in bringing Tugwell into the "brain trust" as the chief adviser on agricultural matters. "Radicalism," "Liberalism," "Conservatism"—these were no better words at that time to describe the forces of change than they are now. The first, and sometimes the second, was used by the Republicans to vilify the Roosevelt men. Moley was often characterized as a radical. Such misreading of motivation and character made it a matter of course for the Roosevelt adherents to submerge inquiry and discussion into theory. They were all tarred with the same brush. A factor more in control of their actions was the need for immediate declarations of policy on a hundred matters, before the nominating convention of the Democratic party.

Raymond Moley was the principal architect of the "Forgotten Man" speech of April 8, 1932, in which Roosevelt attacked President Hoover's philosophy as an attempt to rebuild the national economy from the top down, instead of from the bottom up. Roosevelt—and Moley—believed that the farmer must receive immediate assistance. Homeowners must have help. The restrictive tariff policies of the nation must be revised. In this speech was a hint that planned programs would be devised by the Roosevelt forces to put the nation back to work if Roosevelt came to power.

Moley was also the major architect of the speech F.D.R. gave after his dramatic and precedent-breaking flight to Chicago to accept the nomination—a speech in which Roosevelt and all his brain trust had indicated the policies in which the candidate believed. Moley had actually gone to the convention when the speech was finally prepared. So had Louis Howe, who had his own ideas about a proper acceptance speech. Howe sat down in the last few hours after the nomination, before Roosevelt announced that he would break precedent by flying to Chicago to accept the nomination immediately. He wrote a speech of his own, and journeyed to the airport to ride back with Roosevelt and try to persuade him to use that speech. Roosevelt, nearly overwhelmed in the excitement and confusion of the moment, still took a few minutes to glance at the pages of the Howe speech, then deftly substituted the first page of Howe for the first page of his own, and delivered the product of his own brain and that of his brain trust almost intact. That speech was assailed by Republicans as "radical." It was defended by Moley as a "workable program of reconstruction."

During the summer and fall, Raymond Moley maintained policy headquarters in New York City's Roosevelt Hotel, then took to the road with Roosevelt, talking, writing, listening, searching out facts in preparation for policy speeches. His hand was in the speech before the Commonwealth Club of San Francisco in which Roosevelt stated that every man had a right to a comfortable living and to protection of property, that government's relationship to business was to assist in development of an economic declaration of rights, that government would assume economic regulation only if private industry failed. This San Francisco speech was also attacked as radical. It was conservative, said Moley. As the speeches were put together, painfully, painstakingly, they assumed a pattern which was recognized by a few—Herbert Hoover among them—as presaging drastic change. This was radicalism, said Hoover. It was not radicalism, said Moley, but a program of reform and experimentation—the latter needed because the road ahead must be built even as the nation travelled on it.

When the election was won, Moley, as Roosevelt's coordinator of policy during the hectic months of the campaign, knew more about F.D.R.'s plans and general policies for government than any other man. Moley went with Roosevelt to the meetings with Hoover in the White House—but he did not make the decision to remain aloof from Hoover in the "lame duck" period. Roosevelt made the decision against cooperating with the defeated administration.

Nor did Roosevelt consult Moley—or any other single individual —in the formulation of *all* his policies. Sam Rayburn, the pithy Texan, once remarked to Moley that he hoped there would be "no Rasputin" in the Roosevelt administration. There was no Rasputin. Roosevelt made his own decisions, as he had before.

Before the 1932 campaign, Raymond Moley's background and interests had been largely confined to law and government. In the campaign he was forced to learn the nuances of government finance. The settlement of European war debts was an issue of pressing importance on which some decisions or statements of policy must be made by the incoming administration even before it took office. In attacking this, Moley became involved in the problems of international finance, a matter of only passing consequence to him at that time, although it was to be important in his political career a few months later.

Between Election Day and Inauguration Day in March, 1933, one of Moley's principal responsibilities was the approaching and offering of key positions in the new administration to the men Roosevelt selected for the jobs. Moley could make little sense or pattern of the Roosevelt appointments, but he carried out the negotiations skillfully.

In one such negotiation, that for the cabinet post of the Treasury, Moley sensed some of the coming difficulties which the Roosevelt manner and Roosevelt method would bring to the administration. F.D.R.'s first choice for Secretary of the Treasury was Senator Carter Glass of Virginia, perhaps not so much because F.D.R. wanted Glass as because the loyal senatorial contingent and southerners of the party expected Glass to be offered the post. F.D.R. was extremely sensitive to that type of pressure, real but unstated, so Moley was instructed to negotiate with Glass, once the initial offer had been made by Roosevelt, and Glass had stalled for time.

Senator Glass stalled because he wanted assurances that he would be able to appoint his own secondary officials. Roosevelt had appointed Cordell Hull as Secretary of State, but had appointed Undersecretary William Phillips without consulting Hull. Glass was aware of the extreme sensitivity of the Treasury post. Financial affairs, even when they affected foreign relations, were still Treasury matters, and financial affairs in the winter of 1932–33 loomed gigantically on the American horizon, dwarfing all else. Glass was also cognizant of Roosevelt's ebullient nature and of F.D.R.'s eagerness to experiment in searching out the manner of national recovery. Specifically, Glass was afraid that Roosevelt would take the country off the gold standard. Roosevelt never offered Glass any more than casual assurances to the contrary, and the old senator suspected that neither his health nor his political temperament could survive an extended period of argument or inflation of the economy. He turned down the post.

Following a casual suggestion of Moley, made to Louis Howe, Will Woodin was selected for the important Treasury job. Woodin was president of the American Car and Foundry company. He had been valuable to Roosevelt during the campaign. Woodin was a small man, almost painfully shy, to whom Moley had been attracted during the campaign because Woodin was intelligent, helpful, and anything but arrogant.

Woodin, in his turn, admired Moley, and when the serious business of trying to stem the bank landslide arose on the eve of the inauguration, Moley went with Woodin to the Treasury, to work with Secretary Mills and Hoover's Republican staff, during a long and sleepless week in which the Emergency Banking Act was passed. Banks which had closed were reopened, re-supplied with federal money; it was all that saved the nation from going on a scrip basis, as previously noted. The crisis began March 2 when it became apparent that some banks must close their doors; it was partially resolved by March 7, when the banks were reopened, even if tentatively, and by March 9 Roosevelt had a pledge from Congress that new currency would be issued.

As the Roosevelt administration began, Raymond Moley was of two minds. Sometimes he said he was going to stay only about ten minutes in Washington. He told the press that he intended to remain a month after Inauguration Day. Woodin offered Moley the job as Undersecretary of the Treasury, but F.D.R. balked, saying that he wanted Moley to go into the State Department as an Assistant Secretary (a job that carried no specific duties outlined by law). Roosevelt wanted Moley in the State Department so he could use Moley's services as catalyst and speech coordinator.

Now, at this time, a great number of rumors about Moley's position flooded Washington. It was said that he *was* a Rasputin. It was said that he had been moved into the State Department to act as a counterbalance and a Roosevelt agent in the offices of the conservative Secretary Cordell Hull. It was also rumored that Moley aspired to be Secretary of State himself—which seems completely unjustified since

Moley's interests in foreign affairs had been confined almost entirely to monetary and tariff problems. Had Moley aspired to a cabinet post, it is much more likely that he would have wanted to be Secretary of the Treasury and would have pressed to take Woodin's offer. He believed the Treasury was to be the scene of action and the key to recovery—not the State Department.

Moley's background and the loose nature of his duties in the State Department conspired to make his position in Washington unwieldy from the first moment. Anyone as close to Roosevelt as he seemed to be was suspect of innumerable ambitions. Moley's every action in the old Victorian structure across the street from the White House was subjected to microscopic scrutiny. It was remarkable how many imputations could be drawn from a simple Moley trip from his own room to the Secretary's office to deliver a message from Roosevelt.

Nor had Secretary Hull any particular fondness for Moley. No secretary could like the manner in which a confidant of Roosevelt's had been inserted in his department for purposes of F.D.R.'s alone. Publicly, Roosevelt always managed to remain blissfully unaware of the psychological burdens he distributed so generously within his administration by his apparently random placement of men. He made appointment after appointment without regard for the temperaments of men who were to work closely together. A Machiavellian construction was often given to these appointments. Republicans, and later, embittered Democrats, saw them as the skillful maneuvering of a master politician, to keep any individual from gaining too much power. Moley's own documentation of his government career in his book *After Seven Years* indicates that Roosevelt was simply concerned as a geometrician might be: it seemed most useful for F.D.R.'s purposes to place Moley where he did, and any other considerations, personal or political, were to be disregarded with a smile and a wave of the hand.

Certainly, however, Franklin Roosevelt intended to assume strong power over the decisions in the State Department, and in that role, the new President was to function as anything but an internationalist in these early years. Roosevelt's attitude toward foreign affairs was promulgated for all the world to see in the events and policies developed at the London Economic Conference, a meeting at which the political future of Raymond Moley was also decided by the events of a few days.

For several years, President Herbert Hoover had been convinced that the root causes of the American financial crash and the depression lay in Europe, not in America. Before his retirement in 1933, Hoover had laid the groundwork for a massive economic conference between the United States and European nations. Hoover's object was to bring England and Germany back to the gold standard, and to stabilize the positions of France, the other countries, and yes, even of Soviet Russia, which was not yet regarded as a full-fledged member of the community of nations but which was, by its very size, impossible to ignore.

When Roosevelt came to office, the trappings of American policy were the same, but Roosevelt's attitude toward the American economic crisis was nothing like Hoover's. President Hoover had always held that Wall Street crashed because London fell first. Roosevelt saw the cause and cure of the depression as lying within the borders of the United States.

Roosevelt, and the men close to him, were really dedicated to what was later known as isolationism, at least in monetary affairs. They did not accept the view (held by Secretary Cordell Hull) that the United States had responsibility to help stabilize world financial affairs, or that such stabilization would help the United States.

The fact was, however, that the United States was committed to international discussion of the money and trade issues, and there was no avoiding it. So Roosevelt selected an American delegation, a mixed bag if there ever was one, of isolationists, internationalists, high tariff men, silver men. Secretary Hull led the delegation, and basically, he went to London to confer with other nations, hoping to achieve lower tariffs, but without clear instructions from Roosevelt, and with no idea of what might happen from one day to the next.

Before the conference Roosevelt made it clear that the United States would pursue an independent course. (The United States had gone off the gold standard that spring.) He rejected one plan offered by the conference for stabilization of currencies, perhaps only to force his delegates to drive a harder bargain. What was wanted, by all but

F.D.R., was a stabilization between the dollar and the pound. He rejected that, and, in typical Roosevelt fashion, during this vital meeting, he went off on a yachting cruise in New England waters.

Raymond Moley, who had developed a personal, almost fatherly interest in monetary affairs, had been concerned from the beginning of the administration about involvement with European nations in financial dealings. Moley, a party to the formulation of Roosevelt's New Deal policies, felt also that he knew more about this aspect of policy than anyone else. Fearful about the confusion in London, Moley ordered up a navy plane, transferred to a destroyer, and joined Roosevelt to discuss the problem on board the yacht *Amberjack*. Characteristically, Roosevelt insisted that Moley go to London right then, to carry a message. He had decided, the President said, that it was important to do so. If such action was taken the implication seemed to be that the United States would participate in general trade agreement and currency stabilization.

Moley sailed for Europe in late June amid the fanfare which only the American press can create when it seizes upon an individual or an issue. Here it had both: Moley was a controversial and somewhat mysterious character in the administration. There had been much speculation about his icy relationship with Secretary Hull. The London Economic Conference was the greatest international gathering since the Paris Peace Conference at the end of World War I. So the newspapers devoted column after column to the Moley trip. Report, interpretation, speculation, editorialization, and wild, untrammelled rumor appeared in nearly every daily newspaper in the world. Moley was going to take over, said some newspapers. Moley was going to deliver a message of the utmost importance, said others. Moley was going to read the riot act to Hull, to whip the delegation together, for a dozen different reasons, the stories said.

Actually, Moley was going because he had once said he wanted to go and because he had been sent, by a Roosevelt who undoubtedly disregarded any personal matters which might have affected Moley's later thoughts or usefulness in this mission. After a long talk with Senator James F. Byrnes, Moley decided it might be unwise for him to go to London. Oblivious to personal conflicts, Roosevelt sent Moley anyhow, because Moley represented very nearly his own point of view up to that moment, and because Moley, no matter what he said or felt, could hardly bear to stay away. He had booked passage on a steamer even before he went to see Roosevelt. He had always planned to attend the conference, but he would not have gone had Roosevelt said no. Senator Byrnes had heard of the trip. He thought it unwise and persuaded Moley to stay home—but to no avail. The die was cast.

The newspaper reports which seeped into Britain as Moley's ship steamed on did not help matters. Hull's position, as Secretary of State and head of the American delegation, immediately was placed in doubt. Other diplomats, not knowing Roosevelt, but knowing diplomatic protocol too well, drew the immediate conclusion that Hull had been displaced. Roosevelt then and forever after, stoutly denied any such intent.

Moley saw Hull and believed afterward that he had assuaged Hull's injured feelings. He had done nothing of the kind. Hull's impersonal dislike for Moley, the Roosevelt man, had turned into hatred for Moley, the meddler. Moley also, in fact, took over temporary direction of the negotiations whether he thought he was so doing or not.

He was hoping to achieve stabilization of the relationship between the pound and the dollar. He did achieve tentative agreement which promised stabilization of the two currencies later. The entire effort came to nought, and the conference broke up entirely after Roosevelt rejected a formula he had earlier seemed to like.

First in a message to Moley, then in a cable to the delegation, F.D.R. indicated that the United States would pursue its own policies. That was the end of the London Economic Conference. It was also the beginning of the end of Raymond Moley's career in federal government. Moley believed he had been "double-crossed" by Roosevelt, that his position in London had been made ridiculous (even more ridiculous that the manner of his trip had made the position of Hull temporarily) and fruitless by the President's out-of-hand decision which retreated beyond the nationalist attitude Moley had helped to formulate.

Roosevelt's was a radical decision in a way, a flat refusal to become involved in international cooperation, when all the signs pointed to the need for such cooperation.

It was a firm if temporary withdrawal to isolationism, and while Moley was a nationalist, and would not have disagreed so heartily with the decision had he remained in Washington with Roosevelt, by his trip to London he felt that much of his usefulness in government had been impaired.

In the memoirs and histories written about the Roosevelt administration, much attention has been paid to the London Conference and to the parts played by Hull, Moley, and F.D.R.; and dozens of motivations have been attributed to all these principals. One fact is very clear: all of these men were political adolescents in international affairs. None of them, with the possible exception of Secretary Hull, realized how sharply foreign governments watched their every action. None of the others cared.

This London Conference was the first international meeting held in the time of the Roosevelt administration. Not one of the members of the American delegation had ever attended an international meeting before. In the roaring years of the twenties America's attentions were directed almost entirely at national affairs, and there was no concern at all for bi-partisanship in foreign affairs. So any international meetings in the twenties, and these were few, were Republican affairs.

The London Conference left bitter scars, but it also taught the President and members of his administration a lesson in the handling of international relations, and press relations. Thereafter, Roosevelt and his advisers were to be more circumspect; there would be no further flamboyant races by plane and destroyer to the side of the President and subsequent travel of the courier across half the world to do the President's bidding.

Once Roosevelt sent his message to London during the fateful conference, Moley's usefulness in London was ended; his feud with Hull broke into the open, and even Roosevelt could no longer ignore it.

Roosevelt never apologized for wrecking Moley at the conference or even gave cognizance to what he had done. Moley was upset; then began a period of reorientation, in which Moley sought to discover his true position. Meanwhile, Moley ordered his courses on government inserted once again in the Columbia University catalogue—an indication that he planned to return to private life, as he had said he would do after a few weeks in Washington.

Of course that decision could be changed easily, but there seemed to be small reason to do so.

It was apparent that Hull forced the decision to remove Moley from the State Department. In any such open breach, Roosevelt had no choice but to side with Hull and to jettison Moley—or at least to submerge Moley temporarily. For in Hull's case there were political considerations: Hull had been a highly respected senator before he was a cabinet officer, a representative before that, and a man who had been considered as Presidential timber himself. Moley was a technician, valuable but sacrificeable, too.

And that is what happened. Prematurely it was reported that Moley would go off to Hawaii to check on law enforcement problems. Moley refused the assignment when it was offered. Roosevelt made another offer: to detach Moley from the State Department and assign him to the Department of Justice to study possible reforms in administration of criminal law. This post, which might have kept Moley in the administration had it been offered and accepted initially, was now an escape hatch, which made it possible for Moley to retire from government with such honor as could be mustered.

As a prudent man, during the summer of 1933, Moley had begun to establish other lines which would permit his return to private life. He, Vincent Astor, and members of the Harriman family had formulated a plan to purchase the Washington *Post*, with the understanding that Moley would become editor. The group made an offer, but the *Post* was auctioned to Eugene Meyer instead. So the Astor group initiated a weekly public-affairs magazine, which they named *Today*. In September, 1933, after six months in government, Raymond Moley left the Roosevelt administration, personally, but not yet politically, embittered.

The fall of 1933 saw the beginning of defections from the New Deal, but unlike Moley, most of the defectors left for political rather than personal reasons. James P. Warburg, banker, adviser, and friend of Roosevelt, broke with him over monetary policies. So did O. M. W. Sprague, a Treasury official. Treasury Secretary William Woodin resigned when his health failed absolutely following the harrowing experiences of salvaging a moribund banking system in the spring and summer of 1933. Dean Acheson, Undersecretary of the Treasury was forced to resign by Roosevelt, who thought Acheson had betrayed confidences, but the underlying reason was basic differences between Acheson and Roosevelt over Treasury policy. Al Smith, who had at least paid lip-service loyalty to Roosevelt in the last few years, broke irrevocably with the President.

Many Democrats left Roosevelt when it became apparent that the United States was off the gold standard to stay. The dollar had been devalued by 40 per cent. Gold, which had been selling at $20.67 an ounce, had risen to $34.45, and the inflation of the American economy—an attempt to stimulate business—was in progress. Businessmen, generally, did not like it.

Raymond Moley, continuing as Presidential adviser and speechwriter, began to have serious doubts about some Roosevelt policies, but Raymond Moley, the editor of *Today*, was unrestrainedly loyal to the New Deal.

That fall, some conservative businessmen came full circle in their political views: they had opposed Roosevelt with heat before the election. They had discarded Hoover with revulsion afterward. They had embraced the New Deal tentatively. But when Roosevelt inflated the currency, a blow at property, and showed himself to be the strongest executive in recent history, these men went back into opposition.

Charges of "dictatorship" filled the air in October of 1933, charges viewed seriously enough by Editor Moley that he devoted his editorial in the first issue of *Today* to a defense of Roosevelt policy. Roosevelt was not a dictator, he said. ". . . President Roosevelt is merely fulfilling the purpose of the Presidency as the makers of the Constitution intended."

In subsequent issues of *Today* that year, Moley backed recognition of Russia, he forecast a different form for the Democratic party in 1934, and hailed the departure from old party traditions because adherence to those traditions had done little but keep the party out of office for half a century. He defended Roosevelt's gold policy, and the efforts to stabilize credit. He praised the NRA and called for an NRA of finance.

Raymond Moley entered 1934 with high praise for the administration. *Today*, in fact, had all the appearances of a semi-official New Deal journal. It was not that, but Harry Hopkins wrote on relief in

Today's pages. Rex Tugwell wrote on agricultural planning. General Hugh Johnson wrote on the problems and hopes of the NRA. The articles were factual, forceful, and even messianic in tone. Neither writers nor editors feared words like "revolution" or the prospect of drastic change in the nation. Raymond Moley did not ever seem to fear these words either, except that as the year wore along a careful reader might have noted that Moley became ever more defensive about the New Deal, and less positive that the administration was taking the nation in the direction in which he thought America should go.

Moley defended Roosevelt's enormous budget request of 1934 with the note that Congress would not be a "tournament of munificence," and another note that business was finding grounds for temperate optimism. Moley wrote that the United States was headed for government ownership and operation of all the facilities of credit unless some sensible solution to the banking problem was found, a solution in which the government would exercise control. He encouraged Carl Sandburg to write an article comparing Roosevelt to Lincoln, and to liken the Roosevelt "bill of rights" to the Lincoln Emancipation Proclamation. He employed Sherwood Anderson to write poetically, if not particularly repertorially, about the Civilian Conservation Corps, the Civil Works Agency, and the struggle against poverty that was being waged across the country. Moley defended Roosevelt and the New Deal. He defended himself and his publication against scurrilous attacks from a press that might have been jealous of Moley's continued close connection with the administration.

Moley's connection with Roosevelt did continue to be close during 1934. Perhaps not as often as before, but with great frequency, Moley journeyed from New York to Washington, to register quietly at the Mayflower hotel, and then to visit the White House for a talk or an evening or a dinner. These sessions produced many of Roosevelt's messages to the American public.

Throughout 1934, Raymond Moley supported his friend, Roosevelt, although he was not as trustful of Roosevelt the man as he had been before. He was becoming uneasy as he viewed the growing influence of others on Roosevelt.

Conservative that he was, Moley was not frightened when Orville

Wright predicted in an interview that socialism would come to the United States in ten years. Wright faced the prospect, as he said, with neither fear nor hope, except that he had always felt it of doubtful morality for a man to make money with money itself. Moley seemed to agree. He defended Roosevelt against charges made by *The Saturday Evening Post* that Roosevelt was a radical. He called Roosevelt a conservative and compared the *Post* to the Bourbons, who never learned and never forgot. Moley was a conservative, not a reactionary, and perhaps he was not then as conservative as his critics later believed.

In 1934, Al Smith, John J. Raskob, several Du Ponts, William S. Knudsen of General Motors, Sewell Avery, and a number of other business leaders organized the Liberty League, a political pressure group which set out to try to defeat Roosevelt's New Deal in the congressional elections. Moley heaped scorn upon the Liberty Leaguers. He accepted the retirement of Hugh Johnson as chief of the NRA, although he liked the wild man in Johnson. He was annoyed with charges that brain trust members were radicals who were leading Roosevelt down the garden path.

An Indiana educator named Dr. William A. Wirt called the brain trust Communist, and indicated that Roosevelt was the Kerensky of America, who would soon fall before a Bolshevik assault.

Perhaps it was lunatic attacks such as that of Wirt's which kept Moley's loyalty from flagging late in 1934 and even in early 1935. He sensed, all this time, that the radical element around Roosevelt was pressing hard for more drastic changes in the economy and in the philosophy of government. Moley, in meeting these arguments, tended to become more conservative in his own approach, or at least to stop almost at the end of the plans he himself had participated in drawing before the inauguration. Here, Moley said, in NRA, the Agricultural Adjustment Act, and in the banking changes, the establishment of a Securities Exchange Commission, and in PWA and the detested CWA, there was enough for the nation to swallow. He hoped that the administration would stop and declare a breathing spell. His hope was fervently echoed in the circles of business by such men as Malcolm Muir, president of McGraw-Hill Publishing Company, who called in the spring of 1934 for a moratorium on new legislation affecting the business community.

This moratorium on new laws might have come to pass and Moley's counsel might have prevailed, save for the action of the Supreme Court of the United States in outlawing the NRA (and subsequently much else) and the growth of a loose radical alignment of such diverse characters as Father Coughlin, Huey Long, Gerald L. K. Smith, and Dr. Francis E. Townsend.

The NRA demise (in the Schecter "sick chicken" case) shocked Moley and many others in and out of government. Moley had felt the New Deal was complete in May, 1934, with the passage of the SEC law. But what was done had suddenly become undone. The Supreme Court gave every indication that it would continue to outlaw *all* New Deal social legislation. Moley, among others, was not quite sure where to turn. He engaged in a spirited debate with Walter Lippmann over the advisability of a constitutional amendment—a referendum on the New Deal—which would secure the principle of cooperation under government's paternal eye between business and labor.

The truth was that no one knew quite how to meet the challenge suddenly thrown up by the court. Moley, an architect of the policies in question, defended those policies, and was as outraged as the next Roosevelt man at the court's retrogressive interpretations of law.

In New York, Moley spoke over the radio in defense of federal relief. Later he defended Harry Hopkins against attack for employing white-collar workers in research and art projects.

But notwithstanding his public defense, by the summer of 1935 Moley had engaged in a number of policy arguments with Roosevelt, most of them based on the different approaches of the two men to the problem of achieving the original aims of the New Deal. For a time, in the late summer, Moley seemed to have won his major point: after a conference at Hyde Park with Moley, Roosevelt went on to suggest a "breathing spell" for the nation, recognizing the unhealthiness of a furor caused by so many different pieces of New Deal legislation during two years.

But at that moment the political pressures were extreme. Roosevelt's program was in trouble in Congress. The Supreme Court appeared to be increasingly recalcitrant almost week by week. Huey Long had raised real havoc in the American political world with his alliances, temporary or ephemeral as they might be, his proposals for "share the wealth," and his discussions with other pie-in-the-sky leaders. New York City (Bronx) Boss Ed Flynn, whose political advice Roosevelt valued, had suggested that it was time for Roosevelt to concentrate his vote-getting ability on the people who had been flocking into the cities for the past four years.

Moley did not *become* conservative, he maintained. He *was* conservative. Roosevelt, who started out as a conservative, moved sharply to the left in the summer of 1935. Moley continued to hope, he wrote in his editorials, that public relief would disappear with the revival of private business. (He knew as he wrote this that Harry Hopkins had opened the purse strings to the political bosses.) Moley continued to call for a respite in New Deal social legislation, and as late as the fall of 1935 he continued to note that the New Deal was an extension of the Progressive movement which had begun twenty-five years before under Roosevelt's cousin Theodore.

But in 1936, Moley finally broke with Roosevelt, personally and politically. They had quarreled, publicly, at dinner at the White House over something inconsequential early in 1936—inconsequential except that harsh words were spoken which could be smoothed over but not forgotten. Much of Moley's influence had already passed—with his blessing—back to Sam Rosenman, and on to Thomas Corcoran and Ben Cohen.

The final break came over Roosevelt's speech accepting the Democratic nomination of 1936, when Roosevelt, as far as Moley was concerned, declared war on business generally, and took the New Deal into a new and radical phase which Moley could not stomach.

That was the end of it. Raymond Moley saw Roosevelt a few more times, each time with a diminishing sense of participation in F.D.R.'s life. He declined to serve in the 1936 campaign, because he no longer believed. He lunched with Roosevelt one final time at Hyde Park in September, 1936, and the relationship slipped away. After that September day on the river, Raymond Moley never saw Franklin Roosevelt again.

But even after the personal break, the political disengagement from the New Deal was more difficult for Raymond Moley. Moley's editorials in *Today* during the fall of 1936 showed the indecisions of agonizing reappraisals. In 1932 Moley had called Herbert Hoover a reactionary. In 1936 he referred to Republican candidate Landon and Democratic candidate Roosevelt in the same breath. "Both are honorable men," he said. He reviewed his friend Ernest Lindley's second study of the Roosevelt administration, as he had earlier reviewed the first, but, oh, how different was the tone. The best Moley could muster for Lindley's second book was the note that "for those who want to find the best of the arguments for Mr. Roosevelt's re-election, this book is indispensable." And on the eve of the election Moley noted that there was no reason to believe that "President Roosevelt looks ahead to an essentially different America than the one we now have."

After election, when Roosevelt had won in a landslide, *Today* carried the following gratuitous note in its post-election issue:

"A cynical Republican said that 46 states of the American union have rejected the American way of life." It was a meaningless statement, a wisecrack that might have come from anywhere, but its inclusion in *Today*'s post-election issue was an indication of how far Raymond Moley and Franklin Roosevelt had moved apart, and how great had been the change in American government policy in so short a time.

AND IN THIS CORNER . . .

CHAPTER SEVEN

THE PLIGHT OF THE NEGRO in America was always the special concern of white men and women of liberal thought. Liberal whites brought the Negro out of physical slavery. They cajoled and shouted and wrote stirringly of the brotherhood of man. Yet in the third decade of the twentieth century, sixty years after Abraham Lincoln's Emancipation Proclamation, the Negro in America was still all too much a slave in fact. He had even lost the benefit of the single positive attribute of slavery: the responsibility of the slave holder to look after the welfare of his slaves.

In North and South, American Negroes were mistreated and segregated. Manners were different but results were the same. The Negro quarters of southern cities were slums in which thousands of people mingled in such miserable conditions that white Americans in Boston would not believe they existed in the United States. But what of New York's Harlem? That city within a city was a sordid segregated area marked off from the rest of Manhattan as clearly as though the whites had erected a stone wall around a Negro ghetto.

The whites had produced a few national leaders who tried to better the lot of colored Americans but in the twentieth century the Negro's affairs became the special province of the radical political movements in America. Eugene Debs, then Norman Thomas, the leaders of the Socialist party, strained to organize Negro labor in the South, and so did the American branch of the international Communist movement after 1921.

It is something of a wonder that the radical movements in the United States did not attract more American Negroes than they did attract during the 1930's. In both major political parties the Negro was regarded as venal, stupid, or as a clown. The votes of Negro politicians were bought and sold freely by Republicans, and to a lesser extent by Democratic leaders.

Traditionally, the Negro was Republican, for the Republicans had freed him from slavery of one kind. But Negro political affiliation was nominal at best. Actually, a handful of Negro politicians had no trouble delivering votes to both parties because the Negro in Harlem or the Negro in southern states where the colored man was allowed to vote was too downtrodden and too uninterested to worry about theoretical freedom.

Negroes secured a special justice in America—harsher than the justice meted out to whites. They performed the same work alongside white workers, and received less pay for it. They were the last hired and the first fired. Few Negroes took any interest in education or self-improvement because they had learned from painful experience that no matter how much they exercised their brains, there was a low ceiling on accomplishment for Negroes in the white community, and there was no mixed community. Not since the days of reconstruction had there been Negroes in Congress. The Negro who attained a federal job or a clerkship with any arm of government was notable enough to be mentioned prominently in the Negro press.

Many—and some odd—attempts had been made to solve the race problem over the years. Even before the Civil War, well-meaning whites had established an African Colonization Society, which resulted in the creation of the state of Liberia. That was one way to resolve the question: send the Negroes back to Africa.

The movement had its counterparts among the Negroes themselves. Marcus Garvey, an idealist among Negroes, firmly believed that the only solution to the Negro problem could come through the establishment of a Negro republic in the rich lands of the Black Belt. The Communists insisted with astonishing effrontery, that white Americans must get out and turn the land over to the blacks.

Most American Negroes wanted no part of such schemes. Maltreated as they were, all the majority of American Negroes wanted was to be treated as citizens of the country they had helped to form. But was this strange? These American Negroes were far removed from Africa and from Africans. Their blood was not the blood of black men, but a mixture of bloods like those of other Americans.

American Negroes had their own heroes, of course, but few of them were known to the white community. Booker T. Washington's life story was known to whites and it was taught in schools, apparently as a sop to the inquiring and unprejudiced minds of children, who at sometime in their lives had to realize that Americans came in two colors. Nor was Washington's patient hope for limited and gradual equality admired by the Negroes of the North. They agitated for full and immediate freedom. By the 1930's, in the North, Washington was regarded by Negroes as an "Uncle Tom," despised because he had been too ready to settle for less than the whole loaf of liberty.

These agitators wanted liberty, but they still wanted it within the framework of American society. Negroes worked unceasingly to that end. Walter White, who could have passed as a white American, gave up his opportunity to achieve full citizenship thus as unworthy. He chose, instead, to carry on the struggle for Negro freedom as secretary of the National Association for the Advancement of Colored People, an organization for Negroes begun and backed by whites.

A. Philip Randolph, a brilliant Negro leader, chose to make the fight in the labor movement. In the 1920's the Negro in America took a long forward step when Randolph began pressing the American Federation of Labor for equality of Negroes in unions. Randolph first formed the National Association for the Promotion of Labor Unionism Among Negroes. By 1926 this movement had been followed by the establishment of a Colored Housewives' League in Harlem, New York City, New York. The Housewives' League first encouraged Negro women to shop only in stores where they or their men could find work. A year later the Negroes began a boycott against stores that refused to employ Negroes.

By 1928 Randolph had organized the Brotherhood of Sleeping Car Porters and had enlisted 7,300 members. In a strike vote that year, 6,053 members voted to walk out of their jobs with the Pullman company if the union was not recognized as a bargaining agent. Only seventeen men voted against the strike.

That first strike attempt failed even before a strike was called, but in Randolph's militant unionism, unassisted and detested by the white unions, but backed by the Negro communities of the North, it was apparent that Negro labor was on the march.

Some dissatisfied Negroes did gravitate to the radical movements in the 1920's, just as did whites. Paul Robeson, college football star, actor and singer, was incensed by snubs in his own country. When Robeson visited Soviet Russia and discovered that he was not only treated as an equal there but as an honored celebrity, Robeson's conversion must have been complete.

From that time on Paul Robeson supported the Communist movement. While he attempted, thus, to serve his downtrodden people, most of them did not want to be served in that way, and Robeson's radicalism brought more than attention—it brought anxiety and worry to Negro communities of the United States. Other radical Negroes tried to help the Negro in America, too, but their methods appealed neither to the majority of the colored people nor to the whites, who feared Negro radicals even more than white ones.

This fear was bound up in the problems attendant to miscegenation. The word itself has negative and sinful overtones, although it is a meaningless word. As a nation, white America apparently had a guilt complex about this frightful "miscegenation,"—and with reason. They made a negative and unscientific term into a dirty word.

Jack Johnson, one of the greatest heavyweight fighters of all time, caused murderous reprisals against members of his race after he won the heavyweight championship of the world from the white Tommy Burns in 1908. For seven years Johnson was heavyweight champion of the world. When he was not fighting, Johnson spent his time drinking, carousing, and, most objectionable of all to white Americans, roistering with white women.

During those seven years Johnson enhanced the white fear and hatred of Negroes in the North. Sports fans, but not only sports fans, called on heaven for a "white hope" who might destroy Jack Johnson.

After Johnson was defeated by a white man, Jess Willard, the white sporting world breathed easily for the first time in years. Privately, every effort was made to see that Negroes did not again become ascendant in the ring. Publicly the matter was glossed over. There were not any Negro fighters good enough to stand up to the whites, the promoters said publicly. Privately, they shunted colored fighters aside before they achieved enough prominence to be called serious contenders for fame and title.

This was the negative side of Negro life in America. On the positive side, during the 1920's the Negro became established as a full-fledged member of American society on quite a different level. The

Negro might not be able to vote. He might not be able to find a job. He might not have any basis of equality with whites. But the Negro produced the *only* native American folk music that was regarded abroad as of any significance at all. Spirituals were part of it; in the twenties, jazz became the most of it, and jazz took Europe and white America by storm. With the rise of jazz, the Negro became a cultural symbol in America and *of* America. Eugene O'Neill wrote a tragedy based on a Negro theme—*Emperor Jones,* suggested by the sad story of the rise and fall of the tragic Toussaint L'Ouverture, the Emperor of black Haiti. Marc Connelly created *The Green Pastures.* George Gershwin wrote *The Rhapsody in Blue.*

The 1920's, in a way, were years in which the Negro made huge, if hidden progress in his movement for equality. It was slow progress, however, and many Negroes could not recognize progress at all. It was in the following decade that the Negro made real and apparent strides toward achievement of full citizenship—in ways that could not be denied.

In the depression of the 1930's Negroes suffered more than any other group in North or South, even more than any other minority. The Chinese and other small non-white communities had a history of taking care of their own people. But there were twelve million Negroes in the United States, more Negroes in America than there were Greeks in Greece.

Nor was there enough Negro money. Negroes had always faced great difficulty in establishing business enterprises. White bankers usually refused to loan money on Negro property.

The eminent Negro successes occurred in the insurance business (insuring Negroes), in the cosmetics business (cosmetics for Negroes), in the professions (serving Negroes), in Negro banking, and in the underworld. Even in the underworld, however, the Negro was segregated.

World War I had caused thousands of Negroes to move north from cotton fields to work in factories. One youth who came this route was to become the most important symbol of the American Negroes since Booker T. Washington and a great asset to all Americans. His name was Joseph Louis Barrow. His great-great-grandfather was a slave named Anthony. His great-great-great-grandfather was a

The bank crisis really began years before that terrible week in 1933. As early as 1931 the Bank of the United States closed its doors, leaving thousands of depositors without money. UNITED PRESS INTERNATIONAL PHOTO

Harry Hopkins went out into the countryside early in 1937 to see just how much good his Works Progress Administration had accomplished in solving the terrible problem of hunger. WIDE WORLD PHOTO

The beginning of depression lay in those empty furrows. Too much wheat, harvested too many years in a row, sucked the life from the soil and soon the farmers went sadly away.
FSA PHOTOGRAPH BY DOROTHEA LANGE, LIBRARY OF CONGRESS

Hunger was not debatable. FSA PHOTOGRAPH BY DOROTHEA LANGE, LIBRARY OF CONGRESS

white Alabama planter. Joseph Louis Barrow's grandmother was descended from a Cherokee Indian and from a half-breed Negro slave overseer.

This boy's early life was spent in the Negro poverty of the Deep South. He was born on May 13, 1914, just before World War I began. His father, Mun Barlow, was a share-cropping cotton planter who worked a farm outside the little town of Lafayette, Alabama. The farm was not much. It consisted of 120 acres, located on the edge of the foothills of the Buckalow mountains, but who was to measure? The soil was not productive. Mun Barlow never did own the farm, of course. He lived out his life as a tenant farmer, who shared his crop with the owner, and then was cheated by the local white storekeeper who carried him on credit between crops. Cotton share-cropping was viable enough during the First World War, when the American government and its allies bought all the cotton that could be produced on any land. Five years after the boy's birth, however, the bottom fell out of the cotton market. There were eight children then.

The strain, the debt, the worries of life sapped Mun Barrow's strength. Eventually his mind, not his body, fell sick, and he was committed to a state institution. The mother of Joseph Louis stayed on in the house with the children, and the children sporadically attended a one-room school nearby. The school was colored and segregated, of course, but Joseph Louis and the others who were old enough for school learned the rudiments of reading and writing and arithmetic there.

A few years after Mun Barrow's commitment, his wife went to live with another sharecropper named Patrick Brooks. It was not long before Patrick Brooks discovered that it was impossible to feed and clothe so many bodies with the money to be earned in a depressed farm area. Like thousands of other Negroes, Patrick Brooks heard of the jobs to be found in the North. The family pulled up the shallow roots grown in six generations in Alabama and moved to Detroit without a qualm, so little was there in their native land to hold them there. Save for memories of a handful of Negro neighbors there remained in Alabama no trace of the Mun Barrow family after Mun Barrow himself died in the institution a few years later.

Joseph Louis Barrow was in his early teens when the family moved into a crowded tenement on Madison Avenue in the colored district of Detroit. His education had been so neglected that he was enrolled in the third grade. The boy was not brilliant but he completed that grade, and shortly afterward was transferred, to Detroit's Bronson Trade School to learn cabinetmaking.

Joseph Louis Barrow's first job in Detroit was on an ice wagon. He received a dollar a week and tips for lugging twenty-five and fifty-pound cakes of ice up the stairs of the tenements. Joseph Louis Barrow developed huge arm and shoulder muscles, which were later to play an important part in his career.

For a time Joseph Louis worked on a street crew, and for a time after he left the trade school, he worked for the Briggs motor manu-facturing company as a laborer, at twenty-five dollars a week.

Before Joseph Louis left school, he had learned something about boxing. Until he began fighting, first for glory, Joseph Louis had been a shy, retiring boy. He did not belong to any street-gang, although they were common then in Detroit. He spent his free time sleeping or listening to the radio. He attended the Baptist church with his mother and his brothers and sisters. His one vice was an inordinate appetite for fried chicken.

Fighting was Joseph's principal diversion. It cost nothing to go to Brewster's East Side Gymnasium. There he joined a boxing club and began to train for amateur tournaments.

These 1930's were difficult years for the wife and children of Mun Barrow. Joseph Louis's mother was forced to accept public assistance. She received a little more than thirty dollars a month during that one cheerless winter to help her feed her large family.

But in this period of depression Detroit was not the only city in which people suffered, or even where the Negroes suffered more, proportionally, than the whites. The Negroes always suffered more.

In the summer of 1932 conditions had grown so serious for Negroes in Washington, D.C. that 7,200 Negroes lined up to apply for assistance in the newly opened Emergency Relief Bureau—Herbert Hoover's answer to unemployment. Those Negroes represented 80 per cent of the total applicants for relief.

Shortly before the 1932 Presidential election, a survey by the

Baltimore *Afro-American* showed that across the country the Negro population was dependent more on relief in proportion to numbers than any other group of Americans. Few Negroes had savings, because American Negroes had no opportunity to earn enough money to put aside savings.

Negroes had built thirty successful insurance companies in the nation before the crash. After 1929 the number began to dwindle, as families dropped programs or cut their insurance. All Negro business suffered disproportionately except that of the Negro loan-sharks and the racketeers, who preyed on American Negro society in the cities just as other racketeers preyed on the whites.

Nevertheless, when the nation went to the polls in 1932, the Negro vote was delivered, as was traditional, to the Republican party. Except for a handful of malcontents, the Negroes had never seriously considered switching to the Democratic party.

Once the election was over, the Negroes took a second look at Franklin Delano Roosevelt. In the campaign the new President had promised the Negroes of America that they would become first-class citizens if he was elected. His promises had not won him many votes in Harlem, Detroit, or other Negro voting strongholds, but he was nonetheless to be held to account for his views.

Less than a week after the Presidential election the Pittsburgh *Courier* listed its demands on the administration in behalf of American Negroes. Mr. Roosevelt must:

1. End discrimination in Civil Service.
2. End segregation of Negroes in government departments.
3. End Jim Crow in interstate travel.
4. Urge Congress to enforce the 14th and 15th Amendments to the Constitution.
5. Increase the number of Negroes in government jobs.
6. Follow a hands-off policy toward Haiti and Liberia.
7. Recognize the special problems of Negroes and improve their status.
8. Put an end to the breakup of Negro regiments in the army and open the technical branches of the army and the navy to Negroes.

Negroes had heard promises about equality before. They were not quick to leap to the praise of Franklin Roosevelt, no matter what he promised. They would wait and see.

The Negroes of America did not have to wait too long before there were matters of interest for them to consider in the actions of the federal government.

One of Franklin Delano Roosevelt's first Presidential acts indicated that the role of the Negro in American society was going to change during his administration. In March, 1933, when Roosevelt held his first press conference, Edgar G. Brown, the correspondent of the Chicago *Defender*, stood in the room with other American newspaper correspondents and listened to the new President. Brown was the first Negro newspaperman ever to be admitted to a White House conference.

Still, the Negro community waited, seeking the signs that would indicate Bourbonism in a President of the party that, to them, represented southern white dominance. When the National Recovery Administration was formed, Republican Negroes thought they had found an issue. Traditionally, in the South, there were two wage rates: one for white workers and a lesser wage for Negro workers. With NRA, wages were legally standardized by code, but the wage of a steelworker (Negro) in Birmingham's mills was twenty-seven cents an hour. The wage of a steelworker (white) in a Pittsburgh mill was forty cents an hour. The Negroes protested the differential.

They had more than the NRA to protest. One large southern manufacturing firm was soon stuffing the pay envelopes of its Negro workers with threatening literature.

One notice said this: "If the false friends of the colored people do not stop their propaganda about paying the same wages to colored and white employees, this company will be forced to move the factory to a section where the minimum wage will produce the greatest production."

That particular company was paying its Negroes between six and thirteen cents an hour.

There was no quick victory—as the watchers suspected. Industry continued to discriminate against Negroes, in North and South. But in 1933 and 1934 Franklin Roosevelt continued to show sympathy for Negro Americans and concern about their problems.

By the middle of 1934 the Negroes were beginning to accept the idea that they might, for the first time in seventy years, truly have a friend in the White House. Harry Hopkins appointed Negro assistants to administer his relief program. Harold Ickes, once head of the Chicago chapter of the NAACP, appointed Negroes to help him. Walter White was asked to serve on the Virgin Islands advisory board. Another Negro, Henry A. Hunt, of Fort Valley, Virginia, was appointed to administer the farm credit program among Negroes. It was a novelty for a Negro to achieve such high office.

In 1934, the national average of Americans on relief was fixed at around 10 per cent. With Negroes, the figure was far higher. In New York 25 per cent of the Negro population was on the dole. In Florida 36 per cent of Negroes were receiving relief. In some states of the Deep South the number of Negroes was smaller, because the Negroes were refused relief and told by local authorities to "go pick cotton" when they asked for aid. Discrimination in the NRA wage rates continued. Discrimination in AF of L unions continued, too. Negroes were allowed to join the unions but they were not accorded full privileges of membership, and were segregated in local unions or in special units of locals.

Still the Roosevelt administration was finding favor among the Negro people.

Harold Ickes, the Secretary of the Interior, quickly proved himself as good a friend of the Negro as Harry Hopkins was. In October, 1934, Ickes established a subsistence plan, in collaboration with Hopkins. The plan meant a great deal to the poor farmers of the South, Negroes and whites. Three special settlements were established in Alabama. In one type of settlement the farmers were given the use of sixty acres of land, equipment, and training. They were expected to farm full time and to grow cotton, fruit, and dairy products.

A second type of subsistence homestead involved purchase of land farmed by a tenant. The land was then given to the tenant. He was expected to switch from cotton farming to producing dairy products and truck-garden crops.

The third type of homestead was a part-time farm given to an industrial worker who lived on the outskirts of one of the cities. Each of these was a farm of from one to five acres of land. In theory, the worker would earn his basic income from local industry, but would supplement that income with a real income earned from farming.

The new homestead program received the approval of Negroes since it was help they could understand.

Franklin Roosevelt had won over many Negroes with a single one of the impulsive, humane gestures of which he was capable. One day in the spring of 1934, Sylvester Harris, a Negro farmer in Columbus, Mississippi, spent his last ten dollars to call Roosevelt and tell him of his desperate circumstances. The President took the call, and heard the farmer's story. When he put down the telephone, the President ordered that something be done for Harris and for all the farmers in that condition. A week later Harris had been granted a federal loan (which he repaid in time), and a few months later, the nation had been given the subsistence plan. The dividends Roosevelt collected included Harris's support of the Democrats during the 1934 Congressional elections, a Thanksgiving turkey from the Harris farm, and the gratitude of thousands of poor farmers.

Joseph Louis Barrow had been making something of himself in one of the few ways open to a young Negro. Joseph applied himself to boxing and became so adept that by 1933 he was sent to Boston to fight for the light-heavyweight title in the National AAU championships. Joseph lost the title to Max Marek, a Notre Dame football player, but in the ring, at least, Joseph Louis Barrow was on even terms with the white man. Here was one of the areas of life in which a poor, uneducated boy could hope to rise to fame and fortune.

In the year of the AAU championship fight, Joseph Louis Barrow was taken under the promotional wing of John Roxborough, one of the most prominent members of Detroit Negro society. Roxborough was ostensibly engaged in the insurance business. He was a college man, from the University of Michigan. He also had a police record and was suspected of participation in the rackets of Detroit. By Negro standards, however, John Roxborough was considered an honest and admirable man. The Negroes, pressed so far down by the whites, given harsh tastes of white man's justice, possessed a different standard of morality than the whites. To them the underworld was real and understandable. There was no conflict, to Negroes, in a John Roxborough with a police record who asked this new young fighter to promise that he would never do a single thing that would bring discredit on the Negro race.

Having made those statements, Roxborough then sought the participation of Julian Black, a Negro real estate man in Chicago to help share expenses of training the new fighter. He also changed the name of the fighter to Joe Louis.

John Roxborough had no difficulty in persuading Joe Louis to behave. Joe was not an intellectual but he was aware of the problems of the Negro in American society. If he could make the top rung of the boxing ladder, he vowed that he would become "a credit to the race."

In 1934 Joe won the light-heavyweight amateur title in a fight at St. Louis and made the decision to turn professional. Jack Blackburn, a wily old Negro fighter-turned-manager, was persuaded to train the young, raw recruit. Blackburn shook his head at first. He did not want to be associated with a Negro fighter. There was no future in the ring for a Negro as far as he could see. After a few fights had established a reputation, if the Negro fighter would not lie down on cue, the promoters made sure that he got no more bouts. If the fighter followed these rules, after a few years he was a stumblebum or a cripple.

All that argument came before Jack Blackburn saw Joe Louis fight and saw for himself the speed and power in those brawny iceman's shoulders and those heavy laborer's hands. Blackburn changed his mind. He agreed to train Joe Louis.

Blackburn began to teach Louis the facts of ring life. He also began to teach Louis the extra tricks a Negro boxer had to know to succeed. Most important of these was that the Negro need not expect equal treatment, even in the ring. It was best to knock out one's opponent, Blackburn advised. Then there could be no argument about who had won the fight. A harsh judgment? A truthful one.

Louis had won fifty-four of his fifty-eight amateur fights, and forty-three of them by knockout. But amateur boxing and professional fighting were two different games, and Joe Louis still had much to learn to be a true professional.

The best way to learn was to start fighting. In June, 1934, Louis defeated Jack Krachen in Joe's first professional fight. He earned about fifty dollars. In his fifth fight he knocked out Buck Everett, a professional who had fought some fifty times, and won $250 for that fight.

In December, 1934, sports writers rated Joe a "comer" when he was matched with Lee Ramage, a fighter of some reputation in a bout at the Chicago Stadium. Joe Louis won by a technical knockout. This was his first taste of bigger money; the Louis crowd received $2,750 as its share, and, more important, the fight established Joe as a drawing card. He was in the big money class at last.

Early the next year Joe and his backers travelled to the West Coast for a rematch with Ramage in San Francisco. After Joe had beaten Ramage again, he was called to the attention of Mike Jacobs, who had succeeded Tex Rickard as the most important fight promoter in the nation. Jacobs brought two Pullman cars filled with New York sports writers to Detroit in March to see the young Negro fight and when the sports writers arrived they were impressed. Louis was given a number of names; "Shuffling Joe" and "The Brown Bomber" among them. The latter was to become the trademark of the young Negro.

After this acceptance by New York, the key to the boxing world, Louis fought first in the New York area for Mrs. William Randolph Hearst's Milk Fund. In the summer of 1935, he was advanced by Jacobs and was selected to face Primo Carnera, the Italian giant who had held the world championship until he was knocked out by Max Baer. There was more than a little interest in this fight, because Italy was then moving against Ethiopia. Symbolism is the stock-in-trade of sports writers, so many of them built the match into a gladiatorial contest which would, they indicated, somehow portend the course of events being traced in the news pages of their newspapers.

On the eve of the fight, Arthur Brisbane, the Hearst editor and columnist, and Westbrook Pegler, the irascible curmudgeon of the journalistic and sporting world, expressed fear that the Louis-Carnera fight would stir race riots throughout New York. Pegler suggested that Mike Jacobs needed the services of a psychiatrist for having scheduled the fight in Yankee Stadium, a few blocks from the Harlem line. Pegler recalled, vividly, events of a recent race riot over a rumor that a Negro boy had been killed by a white store detective for stealing a cheap pocketknife. There was likely to be a riot after the Louis-Carnera fight, said Pegler, linking Louis indirectly with Negro policy racketeers and other undesirables.

Walter White of the NAACP suggested that Pegler and Brisbane were indulging in Negro-baiting. The attitude of these columnists was strange, particularly since most of the sports writers of the nation were well impressed by Joe Louis and his fighting.

Louis was everything that Jack Johnson had not been. Louis was quiet. He had never dated a girl except his sister until 1934. He did not smoke. He did not drink. He did not chase white women. He had no visible bad habits and he had the strongest punches these writers had ever seen. Louis's left jab, the instrument he used to sound out an opponent, had the strength of some other fighters' major punches. Joe Louis's right hand was the most powerful in the ring.

On the night of June 25 Joe Louis knocked giant Primo Carnera about the ring and then knocked him out. Harlem went wild that night, but not in riot. At the Savoy Ballroom on Lenox Avenue, thirty mounted policemen and twenty motorcyclemen had to be called to clear the floor and the streets around the dance hall but this was not riot—it was exuberance. One girl fainted, and her escort revived her by dousing her with the contents of a bottle of gin. After the fight Bill "Bojangles" Robinson, movie star and the unofficial mayor of Harlem, traced Joe to a quiet apartment in the middle of Harlem, and demanded that he come and show himself in the center of the little city. Joe did not want to go. He was sleepy and he did not see what all the fuss was about.

As time went on, however, Joe became used to his special position as a symbol of the best of what he called "his race." He continued to live the clean life. When he visited night clubs (which he enjoyed) he ordered drinks for the crowd, but Joe Louis's drink was milk. He kept regular hours, he watched his weight, a difficult task for a man who liked fried chicken. By the end of 1935 Joe Louis had made an amazing monetary record: in one year he had risen from virtual anonymity to fame, and he had earned more than $300,000.

Wealth affected Joe Louis in a simple way that white Americans could understand and laugh about with respect, without bitterness.

He bought a house for his mother. He bought a fast car for himself, although he drove too fast and not well enough to please his friends and managers. He bought three dozen new suits, most of them light-colored, and an endless supply of shirts, socks, neckties, and other haberdashery. But his brothers wore his suits and his family and friends spent his money.

Joe was generous. One of his favorite ways of celebrating a victory was to take a half-dozen Detroit neighborhood colored boys to the movies, and afterward to treat them at the local ice-cream parlor. His older friends borrowed money from him and persuaded him to engage in business enterprises which collapsed, one after another.

As time went on Louis was exploited shamelessly by most of those around him, but this did not create feelings of contempt for the young Negro boxer. White boys and colored boys alike could look to him with pride for there were no overtones of racism in him, and he aroused none except in the hearts of the truly vicious. Perhaps one of the secrets of the success of Joe Louis in raising the status of the Negro in America was his own humble attitude.

To some white Americans Louis was a "tough nigger who knew his place," and did not push himself in white society. To others he was a stupid Negro who was born with the animal strength to hit hard with his fists. But to millions, Joe Louis was a great fighter, and because he was so great a fighter, when he fought most Americans forgot for a few moments that he was also a Negro.

Other factors that arose in the American of the middle 1930's gave Joe Louis real significance as a symbol, even in history. In 1933 Adolph Hitler seized control of the German government, and began to build a racist state. The new Germany claimed to have the greatest athletes in the world. Hitler managed to secure the staging of the 1936 Olympic Games in Berlin and two years before the games, the German government began a campaign to train athletes. The games were planned (by Hitler) to be a total victory for Aryanism over the dark and Semitic races of the world.

Adolph Hitler and his propagandists were eager to win every possible advantage in all professional and amateur sport. They encouraged Max Schmeling, a great fighter and certainly the greatest German boxer of all time, to try to win the mythical World Championship in the heavyweight class, which had rested in the United States for so many years. The championship was held by James J. Braddock at that time, but a number of contenders were seeking the attention of promoter Mike Jacobs, the great panjandrum. If Jacobs so willed, there could be a championship fight.

Former champion Max Baer wanted another crack at the title he had lost to Braddock a few days before Louis knocked out Carnera. If Baer was to have a rematch with Champion Braddock, he would have to whip Joe Louis first. Then, probably, the victor of the Louis-Baer fight would meet Max Schmeling.

In the fall of 1935, Joe Louis met Max Baer and knocked him out. That battle had some overtones of racism, although it was a case of a Jew fighting a Negro: Jack Dempsey had offered to train Baer, not because he liked Baer but because he feared Joe Louis would ruin boxing as Jack Johnson had nearly done.

In the following June, when Max Schmeling and Louis were to meet, the German propaganda machine was going full blast. In Yorktown, the German quarter of New York City, Schmeling was regarded as a "white hope." There was similar talk in boxing circles, but there was another kind of talk, too. Louis was not only the symbol of his race, he was a symbol now of those who did not like Adolph Hitler, totalitarianism, and racism.

Going into the Schmeling fight, Louis was overconfident. He had been brought too far, too fast, as his trainer Jack Blackburn had suggested even earlier. Joe Louis was in good physical condition, but he still had things to learn. His confidence was increased, too, by the odds of twenty to one in his favor.

In the fourth round of the fight Schmeling floored Louis with a right hook. Louis went down for a count of three, recovered, and wobbled through the rest of the round. At the end of the fifth, Schmeling caught Louis on the point of the jaw with a right hand, just as the bell sounded and Louis dropped his hands. After that it was disaster; Louis was an automaton, going through the motions dazedly until he was knocked out in the eighth round.

In victory Schmeling became a racist.

"I would not have taken this fight if I did not think I, a white man, could beat a colored man," he said. He also accused Louis of deliberately fouling him, but Louis, when he awakened after the knockout, and was told about the fouls by his seconds, sent John Roxborough to apologize for the fouling.

After the Schmeling fight boxing writers who had backed Louis to win were doubly cautious about him. White supremacists made the flat claim that Louis had laid down because no Negro had "enough guts" to be a great fighter.

Joe Louis said very little, but went into training again. This time he was to meet Jack Sharkey, who had defeated Max Schmeling to hold the heavyweight title himself for a little while. This time the newspapermen picked Sharkey: Joe Louis knocked him out in three rounds.

Having defeated Louis, however, Max Schmeling demanded a try for the title against Braddock. He would have had the try in 1936, except that Braddock developed arthritis and the bout was postponed until the following year. Schmeling contemptuously refused to meet Louis again.

By this time—1937—it had become apparent that Adolph Hitler's plans were neither local nor peaceful. Schmeling's demand for a chance at the heavyweight title aroused religious and anti-discrimination groups in America to oppose the fight, fearing that if Schmeling won the heavyweight championship he would not again give any but an Aryan the opportunity to challenge him, and that a victory for racism would play into Hitler's hands. The Anti-Nazi League announced its intention to boycott and ruin the fight.

Louis got the first chance at the title. He trained hard, and in Chicago, on June 22, 1937, he knocked James Braddock out in eight rounds, to become the heavyweight champion of the world.

Exactly one year later Max Schmeling had his chance at the heavyweight championship of the world, in a bout billed by German Propaganda Minister Joseph Goebbels as the fight in which Aryan supremacy would be established forever. In Manhattan's Yorktown the betting was heavy, but surprisingly enough, a great deal of the German-American money this year was on Joe Louis.

Hitler himself invited Schmeling to luncheon before he sailed for America, and Hermann Goering telegraphed his best wishes. Then, during the fight, Schmeling telegraphed an opening in the first round and Joe Louis knocked him out to settle the matter of Aryan supremacy.

The ascendant years of Joe Louis were good years for the Negroes, not solely because of him, and perhaps hardly at all because of his influence except emotionally. Yet Louis was a symbol of opportunity —the sharecropper boy grown successful; and other Negroes looked on him with pride. They also looked upon their government and the Roosevelt administration with increasing favor as their position in America improved.

John L. Lewis, in forming the CIO, broke the barriers of race in labor organization in 1935. Eleanor Roosevelt entertained Negro girls at the White House in 1936—part of a reception for sixty delinquent girls to call attention to her disapproval of the discrimination at the National Training School for girls in Washington. She made her point, even though the forty-nine Negro girls of the party were segregated. For the moment it was enough that the girls had been invited to the White House at all.

By 1936 the Negroes had been convinced that the Roosevelt administration was actually dispensing relief and government jobs to them on the same terms as to the whites. Roosevelt had received Negro delegations, including a delegation of Negro Elks. When Mrs. Roosevelt visited Howard University she was photographed with a pair of young Negro ROTC cadets wearing snappy army officers' uniforms. Roosevelt, the Negro press reported, had given more jobs to Negroes than the three previous Republican Presidents combined. Roosevelt denounced lynching, and earned the praise of the Chicago *Defender*: "His New Deal has now become a human deal in which all parts of the nation can feel themselves a part." And Negro intellectuals saw the Roosevelt administration as the fourth major change in America, from their point of view: first was the American Revolution; second was the Jackson election and Jackson's extension of freedom to the common white man; third was the Civil War, which freed the slaves; then came Mr. Roosevelt's Revolution. Joe Louis, even though he did not recognize it himself, was a part of that revolution. The Negroes were beginning to stir, getting ready to demand rights as full-fledged Americans.

THE NEW WORLD:
SOCIALIST OR COMMUNIST?

CHAPTER EIGHT

ON THE EVENING of November 27, 1935, twenty thousand enthusiasts of the political left wing assembled in Madison Square Garden to hear a debate between Norman Thomas, the leader of the Socialist party of the United States, and Earl Browder, the general secretary of the Communist party—USA.

The subject of the debate was "Which Road for the American Workers—Communism or Socialism?" but that title was pretentious. The real reason for the debate was the drive of the Communist party for a United Front movement in which the Communists could submerge themselves, yet continue to work for revolution. Yet, in another way the title of that debate was revealing: it showed the dead seriousness of the radicals of America and their confidence in the coming of a radical state on the death of the hated capitalism.

The idea of United Front had suddenly become respectable in Communist circles that very year. The change had come to public attention in the surprising announcement of a Franco-Soviet alliance, in May, 1935. Before, the Communists in Moscow (and thus everywhere else) had expressed nothing but disgust for Social Democrats. After the announcement of the pact between the USSR and the Socialist government of France on May 12, Soviet opposition to Socialism suddenly died. Socialists and Communists had always been brothers under the skin, the Communists now claimed. Did they not both follow the precepts of Karl Marx? Was it not simply a matter of difference in method? Surely, said the Communists the world over, the Socialists and the Communists could be reconciled.

In America the Communist attempt at reconciliation took the form of Communist urging of this series of debates between prominent Socialist leaders and the spokesmen of the Communist party. Chief of the Communist spokesmen was William Z. Foster, fifty-four, an American of Scotch-English-Irish descent, who had grown up in the slums of Philadelphia.

Foster was a radical leader long before Communism came to

America. He joined the Socialist party in 1901. He left Socialism to work for the Industrial Workers of the World, the "wobbly" organization he advised to "bore from within" and thus control trade unionism in America. By 1912, Foster had become disgusted with the IWW, and established his own syndicalist movement. In 1918 he was in the AF of L, and the next year led a violent steel strike, which failed and destroyed his growing power in the native labor movement.

Foster had been brought into the Communist movement by Earl Browder in 1921 after the Communist International had formed an American committee whose members had convinced Browder that he had a great future in the Communist movement. Browder's prestige was established when he was able to bring Foster to Communism, because Foster was an important radical labor leader.

William Foster rose rapidly in the American Communist movement. He became the Communist Presidential candidate in 1932. But while barnstorming across the country that year, Communist candidate Foster had been stricken by a heart attack. It had been months before he could make even the slightest public gesture. Now, in 1935, and for the rest of his life he was to continue as leader of the Communists in America, but as an invalid he must leave the chores of mass rallies and public importunation to others.

As the time of debate drew near, the Communists doubled their efforts to seem agreeable. During the summer and fall of 1935 they had been very careful to refrain from name-calling. Since the Seventh World Congress of the Comintern, held earlier in 1935, the "class struggle" had been played down. Now the international Communist line called for cooperation with the bourgeoisie all over the world. Instead of praising Russia, the Communists praised democracy. Instead of calling on the workers of the world to unite and back Soviet Communism, the American Communists tried to appeal to Americans as nationalists.

The Socialist party was torn. Since the earliest days of Communism, the party nurtured within itself the seeds of destruction. The Old Guard Socialists, most of them Marxists of European birth, held to the original theories of Marxist Socialism. Norman Thomas led the New Guard, which was unorthodox, a native American offshoot of Socialism. An extreme left wing of the Socialist party wavered in its loyalties, unsure of the road, unsure of the depth of distrust the party ought to exercise toward the Communists.

At this debate in Madison Square Garden, Earl Browder was determined to capitalize on these divisions. Like his taller, larger, placid-faced superior, the wiry Browder had an infinite capacity for taking himself seriously and an almost equal optimism that the Communist party would bring about revolution in America. The political assessors of the Comintern, a shrewd group of internationalists, had long since written off the American Communist movement. Foster and Browder had reconvinced some of the men in the Kremlin that the economic collapse of 1929 and 1930 had made the time ripe for revolution. Yet the revolution had never gotten off the ground. President Hoover's use of federal troops to drive the bonus marchers out of Anacostia and the burning of their shacktowns had not brought the workers to the barricades. The failure of the agriculture system had not brought the farmers to the city with guns and pitchforks. Speaking practically, the revolution was further away than ever, and most of the radicals of the United States knew it in 1935. Even the Communists suspected it, as could be seen in their movement toward conspiratorial secrecy and subversive activity.

The Communists were openly eager to please. "I don't recognize myself any more when I read the *Daily Worker*," Norman Thomas joked. But even so old a campaigner as Thomas was not absolutely certain that the Communist change was just a tactical device.

Thomas was suspicious of the Communist aims. He voiced his suspicions loudly and often. He referred publicly and contemptuously to the mudslinging of Browder and others. But he did not say flatly that the Communists were insincere. He did not refuse to debate Browder on the unrealistic subject of the course of labor: Socialist or Communist.

Thomas could not refuse the challenge that was issued to him. His own party, for which he had had the highest hopes in 1930 and 1931, was slipping badly. In 1932 the Socialists had reached their high point in American political life. Thomas had polled nearly 900,000 votes in his campaign for the Presidency. William Z. Foster had polled only 102,000 votes. But since 1933 the course of the Socialists had been downward, and the course of the Communists seemed to be upward. The Communists claimed only 15,000 members in 1932. This year they were strong enough to bring out the vast majority of the crowd of 20,000 which sat expectantly in Madison Square Garden, waiting for the debate to begin.

The Communists were determined to find agreement with the Socialists at almost any price; that much was apparent in their accession to the Socialist demand that the chairman of the evening be a Socialist. Too many times before had Socialist speakers and debaters been muffled and mistreated at Communist-rigged meetings. The Communists did not object when Leo Krzycki, national chairman of the Socialist party, took the chair and began to introduce the topic and the speakers.

It was an historic date, to begin with. Just six years before, the stock market had crashed with a noise heard around the earth. It was the third year of Franklin Roosevelt's New Deal. Ten million men and women were still jobless, but Roosevelt was keeping them from hunger with relief, employing them with federal construction and WPA projects, and giving them hope with his own magnetic personality.

John Llewellyn Lewis, the huge hawk of the American labor movement, had pledged money from his United Mine Workers Union coffers to organize the unorganized laborers of America in what he called the Committee for Industrial Organization. In the spring of the year, Lewis had called on the American Federation of Labor to organize the huge complexes of steel and automobiles along industrial lines. Lewis worried because as long as laborers employed by the steel companies in their mills were unorganized his mineworkers could not organize the coal mines owned by the steel companies. Those non-union mines stood as a silent but constant threat to Lewis's suzerainty in his own field. When the entrenched craft unions of the AF of L refused to break precedent and give up their own specialties within the huge steel and automobile industries for the common good of labor, then Lewis ignored the craft unions and with the help of David Dubinsky, the garment unionist, and a handful of others, Lewis began his own organization drive in what was then the AF of L's Committee for Industrial Organization.

Lewis was to be the revolutionary force in American labor—not this ineffectual pair of radical parties, but they were to play roles of

their own within the CIO. In less than a year Lewis was to bring together five million men in the CIO—more men than belonged to the
entire AF of L. (It was easy for Lewis to organize labor under the
government support of Roosevelt, as opposed to government disapproval and hindrance under three previous Republican administrations.)

While the radical left met to talk about the future course of
American labor, John L. Lewis was beating through the industrial
jungle, mapping his own course, and taking labor along it. Yet Lewis's
plans did not stop him from using the Socialists and the Communists
nor did it stop them from working with Lewis and from planning, too.
With all their divisions, as they met at Madison Square Garden,
Thomas and Browder were agreed on one point: labor must be made
into a potent political force, and labor must somehow achieve political
power if the revolution was to begin.

This agreement that labor should be leftist was the sum total of
their agreement. That one issue provided the only possible basis for
the meeting and debate. It was relatively unimportant what might be
said that evening. It was far more important how the reports of the
debate were received by the Socialists and the independent left which
presumably read Socialist publications.

Following Chairman Krzycki's introduction, Norman Thomas
arose to speak. He was a gangling, powerful man, whose strong voice
and intense masculinity brought many to hear him out of admiration
and curiosity. Thomas could not refrain from needling Browder from
the outset, turning to his shorter opponent, bowing slightly in exaggerated gesture. First he noted that circumstances were far different
that night from those of a few months before. Then the Communists
had come to Madison Square Garden to riot, to attack Socialists and
others meeting there to commemorate the bravery of working-class
Austrian soldiers and martyrs who had risen in the Socialist cause
against tyranny.

Thomas's heavy-handed irony was greeted nervously by the majority of the audience. They had come to support the Communist ploy,
not to hear their Secretary General attacked by the man he was trying
to woo.

The pro-Communist audience was somewhat reassured when the

Socialist leader sensed their restlessness and said he regarded the experiment in Russia as "the one outstanding achievement, the one bright pillar of hope, in the turbulent, confused world of the last few years." The crowd cheered wildly, openly displaying its overwhelmingly pro-Soviet sentiment.

Thomas then sobered, to discuss problems common to all the left-wing Marxists. He lamented and condemned Red-baiting in the American Federation of Labor and outside it. He admitted cheerlessly that the American masses had not accepted Marxism in any form, that it would be necessary, somehow, to find a basis of appeal to farmers, workers, and professional people if Marx's dream of a Socialist society were ever to be realized in America.

Thomas was not stating the case realistically, as far as his own Socialist party was concerned except that it was true enough that the American Socialists had few members who were workers. In 1932 Thomas and the party had managed to persuade a handful of state federation labor leaders to give support to the Socialist ticket. The party appeared on the ballot in all but five states in that election, but labor and farmers had not been interested in it. They never did become interested in Socialism. A German Social Democrat, after attending a mid-western Socialist meeting, observed disgustedly that the American Socialist party seemed to be made up of housewives and college professors.

Where was the mass base which might force the changes the Marxists wanted?

There was no mass base. The whole history of the development of the American Republic had been just enough different from the development of Europe to make it impossible for Marxist techniques to be applied in the new world as they had been applied in the old. American farmers, even poor farmers and sharecroppers, did not regard themselves as members of a peasant class. Nor did laboring men regard themselves as members of a working class. Every farm community, every worker's block in the city had its own story of the man who left the land or the assembly line and "made good" in the business world. Such a record made the task of the Socialists extremely difficult. The Socialist party had fettered itself further in choosing, under the leadership of Norman Thomas, to seek change through the ballot box alone. This was not the position of all who called themselves Socialists, but it was the position of the effective leadership of the party. It was also the greatest single area of difference between the Communists and the Socialists.

Considering the fact that both parties had begun from a common root, and that both hoped to lead Americans to a new life, the differences between the parties were a matter of concern to leaders of both groups.

Thomas, himself, had joined the Socialist party in 1917, two years before the split which occurred in the Chicago convention of 1919, when the Communist party was born. In a way, Thomas represented all that European Socialists found objectionable in the American movement. He was a man of gentle birth. He graduated from Princeton University, where he was class valedictorian. He attended Union Theological Seminary, and he became a Presbyterian minister. As a young man Thomas was assigned to the East Harlem Presbyterian Church. There he became immersed in the problems of the poor and the minorities, to whom the American dream of "making good" was nothing but a dream. He also became interested in pacificism. He was, for a time, Secretary of the Fellowship of Reconciliation, a Christian pacifist organization. And from that approach to life, he was attracted to the pacifism of the Socialist movement, which also promised to better the lot of the poor people Thomas saw in his pastoral rounds.

Eventually, the Reverend Norman Thomas lost his faith in doctrinaire Christianity. He resigned his pastorate and began to devote himself to the causes of peace and the redistribution of wealth through Socialism.

Yet the apostasy of Norman Thomas was never quite complete. "American Protestantism," he wrote, "has been weighed in the balance by our generation and found wanting, if palpably it has failed to meet the needs of a world already caught in the toils of revolution, intellectual as well as social, it did at its best nourish men and women worth loving who faced life and death more bravely for their faith."

Those may be the words of a man who no longer could believe, but they were also the words of a man who honored the Christian ethic.

Yet Thomas had come to be the Socialist party's candidate for President almost by accident.

How?

Eugene Debs, the leader and founder of American Socialism, was dead. Morris Hillquit, who might have succeeded Debs, was unacceptable to the new breed of Socialists, some of them not even Marxist, who had come into the party. Thomas represented an entirely new force—reform, not revolution.

Where reform was needed, Thomas had much support. In 1929, when he ran for mayor of New York City against Jimmy Walker, he was supported by the New York *World* and the New York *Telegram*. The Reverend Harry Emerson Fosdick voted for Thomas that year. But the newspapers and the general support he received did not represent endorsement of Socialism, but respect for an honest and able man.

And what did the Socialists represent?

After the split over the course of the Russian Revolution, the American Socialists were never able to shake the fuzz from their political doctrine. Thomas and others of the new group believed in redistribution of national wealth through government ownership of the basic means of production. They did not face squarely up to the problem of compensation vs. confiscation. Some members of the party held that the wealth of the nation would be seized by the people, once Socialists were elected to power. Others held that the wealth would be seized, but that the capitalist owners of the land and factories would be compensated.

In 1932, the Socialists looked forward with hope to the future and the collapse of capitalism. In the spring of 1933 they organized a Continental Congress to meet in Washington. Four thousand men and women came to the meeting, but instead of the farmers and workers the Socialists had wanted to address, they found themselves talking largely to Socialists once again.

Once the New Deal began, Norman Thomas began to redouble his efforts in behalf of the downtrodden. He harassed the Roosevelt administration with demands for direct payment of relief moneys to sharecroppers under the AAA program. He exerted some influence in securing change by which the tenant farmers were granted direct aid.

But constantly, surely, the ground was being cut from under the Socialist program by the success of the New Deal in appealing to the American people. By 1934, the Socialists were floundering, and at their Detroit convention, they had broken into battle on the floor over the question which faced Norman Thomas and Earl Browder at this Madison Square Garden debate: United Front.

If Thomas, the gentleman and scholar who liked to crack jokes and pun in Latin, was representative of the controlling faction in his Democratic Socialist movement, so was Earl Browder representative of the American Communists.

And who was Browder?

In one way Browder was as much of an anomaly among Communists as Thomas was among Socialists. Browder could trace his American lineage back to pre-Revolutionary days in Virginia. He was born, however, in Kansas, where his father had journeyed in the nineteenth century to settle in a sod hut on the prairie. Earl Browder attended a country grammar school near Wichita for a time, but at the age of nine his schooling ended and he went to work as a cash boy in a department store for a dollar and a half a week to help support the large Browder family.

In later years Browder's enemies within the Communist party were to characterize him as a man with the mind of a bookkeeper. They may not have been so far from the mark—for at the age of twenty-one, Browder was chief bookkeeper of a wholesale house. That was before he began reading the Socialist newspaper *The Appeal to Reason* in earnest, and decided to devote his life to that particular substitute for religion.

Browder became an ardent Socialist, if not one of the greatest admirers of Eugene V. Debs. Browder followed the reasoning of Big Bill Haywood, the extremely radical Socialist who took the position that the revolution would be attained only through violent action by the working man. Haywood struggled within the Socialist party to put power in the hands of an "action" group—before the Bolsheviks were known in America or the Russian revolution had fallen into their hands. And when Haywood broke with the party leadership to form the International Workers of the World, this violent radical movement became Earl Browder's new religion, as it was for a time

William Z. Foster's. Through syndicalism the radicals hoped to achieve revolution in strike and labor agitation.

It was in Kansas City, in the syndicalist movement, that Browder encountered William Z. Foster. The latter was an established figure in radicalism then; Browder was just making a name for himself.

Browder spent most of his early years in politics as an organizer of labor and radical movements in the Middle West. He was a studious man and so, despite a shortage of formal education, he completed law school by taking correspondence courses, although he sneered at that bourgeois institution the American Bar and refused to take the bar examination.

Like Norman Thomas, Earl Browder was opposed to the First World War. He took an active part in fighting against American involvement. In May, 1917, he was arrested for conspiring to defeat the draft law, and also later charged with non-registration himself.

Browder was still a Socialist, but in jail he discovered the Communist revolution. He spent much of the next three years behind bars or out on bail, and there his conversion to the extreme radicalism of Communism began.

In 1919, Browder was freed in the post-war atmosphere of forgiveness. He left Kansas City to take a job as chief bookkeeper for a wholesale house. Theodore Draper, in *The Roots of American Communism*, says that Browder was seriously thinking then of settling down to private life. He joined the new Communist party, and was honored as a charter member for his martyrdom in jail although he was not at the earliest conventions.

There in New York, Browder was approached by the members of the overseer committee of the Communist international movement, the American Agency, when an attempt was made to find an American delegation to attend the first Congress of the Red International of Labor Unions. Promised much, he deserted private life and travelled west, for the fateful second meeting with William Z. Foster. When Browder persuaded Foster to attend the Moscow meeting as an observer, Browder's immediate future as a Communist leader was assured.

In 1927, Browder was given an important assignment by the International. He travelled to China to inspect the work of Mao Tse-tung's Communist movement. Browder arrived in China as Chiang Kai-shek was mopping up Communist resistance to his revolution in the cities and heavily settled areas of the east and south. Browder's dedication and efficiency were shown in the manner in which he approached his China assignment. No railroad ran from Canton, where he entered China, to Hankow, where he was to go. He and a companion covered more than a thousand miles, walking through a strange, wild country ravaged then in the struggle of civil war.

Browder, an American citizen, organized Communist cells within the villages of Kiangsi province, and although he was a citizen of a neutral nation, he set up resistance against the Chiang Kai-shek Nationalist government.

If, on the face of it, these activities of Earl Browder during the 1920's had very little bearing on the debate at hand at Madison Square Garden in 1935, still, the presence of Earl Browder on that platform showed that the Communists were seeking allies. Browder had never failed to practice deceit or to tell untruths in the service of the Communist cause. Norman Thomas suspected that the Communists were not sincere in their announced search for a common and popular front with the remainder of the radical movements, although he could not prove it.

And what were the Communists trying to accomplish?

There was reason for the suspicion of the Socialists at the time of this debate on a fall evening in 1935. Anyone who professed any interest in radical change as the solution to America's problems had read William Z. Foster's blueprint for American Communism. Following the Wall Street crash and the slump of manufacturing, radicalism became as nearly acceptable in the American scene as it had ever been. Many manufacturers and important businessmen like Orville Wright either believed or suspected that the capitalist system had failed. The suspicion was so widespread by 1932 that when the Coward-McCann Publishing Company brought out Foster's book in which he outlined a plan for bringing revolution to America, there was no outcry or general demand for the outlawing of the Communists, as there would have been had the book been published ten years before or ten years afterward.

In this book, with an air of certitude, Foster discussed his plan for a Soviet America: The U.S. would be called the United Soviet States of America. The soviet state would come into being as a result of violent revolution—the uprising of the workers. Foster specified no time or place, but he made it clear enough that the Communists were prepared for a bloodbath.

First the Communists would build soviets before the day of the revolution. The soviets were to be cells which could expand to take over local and state government. They would be the foundation of the worker's state.

When the revolution came, Communist Chairman Foster said, the organization of the soviets would be enforced by the armed Red Guard of workers and peasants. It was unstated but inherent that the cadre of the Red Guard must already be organized, at the very time the book was written and published.

The Red Guard would direct the seizure of American industry through factory committees, and the seizure of agricultural production control through peasants' committees.

Reading these strange words, some Americans could not help but marvel that the Communists had so little sense as to import a foreign vocabulary to describe the coming revolution. Foster and the other leaders of the American branch of the party were later to realize that they must try to seem more American. Yet there was reason for the Communist terminology: the internationalism of the movement.

The Communists of the world saw the problems of the world as parts of one great problem; the peoples of the world as parts of one great machine; the governments of the world as decaying excrescences which would one day be eliminated. International Communism was so contemptuous of national societies everywhere that the Communists translated the directives of the revolution literally. So sure were all Communists that the road of the Comintern was the right road, and would soon be the only road of the world, that they eschewed dissemblance.

Peasants? Proletariat? These were not American words, nor did they fit Americans. Readers shook their heads in disbelief. Was William Z. Foster mad? Were the Communists *all* mad? It was impossible to believe that could be true. It was also impossible to accept this blueprint at its face value. Therefore, those entrusted, and those who entrusted themselves with responsibility for American security began seeking deeper meanings.

Had they been more familiar with Communist method, the anti-Communists need not have sought too far. For the distinguishing characteristic of Foster's work—of the entire American Communist party —was naïveté. By 1932 the world Communist movement had adjusted its philosophy.

Lenin had miscalculated in 1917—he had expected the Bolshevik revolution in Russia to touch off similar successful revolutions in Germany and in other industrial nations. When this did not occur, Lenin realized that the road of the revolution would be long and slow. It served the interest of the Communist movement to maintain a party in America, and it served the interest of the Soviet state to maintain a loyal group of supporters from which could be drawn valuable recruits for Soviet intelligence. Physically weak, faced with the united opposition of the capitalist world, the Soviet government found intelligence to be its chief weapon of survival, and it began to make use of intelligence in a wholesale manner that was matched during the thirties only by the espionage of the Japanese—another nation which faced powerful enemies and relied on its own resources for survival.

There ended the Russian state's immediate concern for the Communist movement in America.

William Z. Foster foresaw the day when the American government would be organized along the Soviet line, with American citizenship denied the old families of wealth. "Capitalists, landlords, clericals and other non-producers will be disfranchised." America would be governed by a Soviet Congress, a Central Executive Committee, a Presidium, and final power would be in the hands of a Council of Commissars, with one party, and one leader—William Z. Foster.

Earl Browder, of course, accepted this view only up to a point. The real leader, he was certain, would eventually be Earl Browder. But that was a matter for infighting within the party, which would be refereed by Joseph Stalin.

The Communists, Browder and Foster among them, were a strange breed of men. They had personal lives—Eugene Dennis's affairs of the heart were a scandal in the party—but their personal lives were always subordinated to the party. Howard Fast, in later years, was to recall that he had never known more sincere, dedicated people than his Communist friends. Their preoccupation with party affairs made it seem that they lived in a ghost-world, although to insiders the struggles and differences that characterize all organizations were apparent.

But one point on which all Communists were agreed, although Socialists could not agree among themselves on this point, was the manner in which control of the American economy would pass from the hands of capitalists into the hands of the "proletariat." The Communists said this would come through outright seizure—confiscation without recourse. Large property owners, the Communists hinted, would be fortunate to escape with their lives.

This Communist contempt for the processes of democracy was not lost on the Socialists who attended the debate between Norman Thomas and Earl Browder. Browder spoke windily about the dangers of totalitarianism of the right. Fascism would come to the United States very soon, Browder warned. He pointed to the growth of the Liberty League, that organization of capitalists and disgruntled Democrats who feared Franklin Roosevelt and hated him as much as did the Communists. He pointed to the Red-baiting of William Randolph Hearst and the anti-Communist rantings of Father Coughlin (whom the Communists had embraced for a short time earlier).

He called for a United Front to preserve democracy.

Thomas spat out his words of doubt about the Communist interest in the ways of democracy.

He saw no withering away of the state or of dictatorship in the USSR, Thomas said. He saw no civil liberties there. In America, he saw only Communist attempts at disruption of the labor movement; not attempts to reform it or lead it to betterment of the laboring man. He saw widespread use of dishonest and immoral tactics. He held up a leaflet distributed by the Communists in an election in Pittsburgh. The leaflet showed a picture of a Negro baseball player, and a picture of Joe Louis, and a picture of a twenty-three year old girl named Carolyn Hart on the front page. Carolyn Hart was the Communist candidate for city councillor of Pittsburgh. The ballplayer and Louis had been put on the cover only for effect. The implication was clear that these two Negroes supported Carolyn Hart and the Communists. (Neither of the Negroes knew anything about this leaflet, of course.)

Here was a new style of Communist propaganda, to which Thomas took particular exception because of its portent. Philosophically, Norman Thomas had no objection to a united farmer-labor movement, in which the Socialists might run the danger of losing their identity. He did fear the Communist potential for disruption and creation of confusion in which only the Communists prospered.

Thomas was cognizant of the Communist record. Since 1930 that record had been clear and intense in disruption of the American social system.

Carl Winter and the other Red leaders had marched at Union Square and then had gone to visit Harry Hopkins that March day in 1932. Two years before the Communists had organized demonstrations of more than a million persons against unemployment. In 1930 they had circulated petitions for unemployment insurances, and had secured a million endorsements. In 1931 they had taken a million workers on a National Hunger March. They had organized a National Committee of Unemployed Councils, and claimed 75,000 members of this group. They had seized control of a number of unions—which they proudly designated "revolutionary unions." These unions included the 35,000 workers of the New York Cloak Union, and 12,000 members of the furworkers union.

The Communists proudly claimed to have arranged and maintained a number of serious strikes. The cloak makers and the furriers struck during the twenties. So did the textile workers of Passaic, New Jersey, in a bloody strike for which the Communists took credit.

The Communists had tried to take control of the United Mine Workers Union. They claimed to have secured 101,000 votes in an election in 1926, a majority, they said. John L. Lewis had not agreed that they pulled nearly so many votes, and he had first broken their power, then driven them underground in the UMW.

The Communists claimed credit for strikes of textile workers in Gastonia, in Lawrence, Massachusetts, and in a dozen other places in New England. Driven from Lewis's union, they had formed their own "revolutionary" National Miner's Union, and claimed 40,000 members by 1931.

Their policy was announcedly to destroy the American economy. Foster called on the party to win workers to Communism during strikes and agitation, and to lead the way to economic disruption of the business system. He had gone to San Francisco during the 1934 general strike, in the hope that he might be able to help destroy the American economy right there.

He wrote later in praise of the general strike in San Francisco, and of the leadership of Harry Bridges of the International Longshoremen's and Warehousemen's Union. Foster said that had the strikers only held out for a few more days, they would have been joined by strikers in Portland, in Seattle, in Los Angeles. It was apparent that Foster regarded the general strike of San Francisco as an opportunity lost—the greatest opportunity of history to destroy the American economic system. Once the whole coast was on strike, Foster could see that the railroad men would spread the strike across the nation; from the disruption of communications would come hunger and chaos. From the chaos would come seizure of control by the one organized revolutionary body. There had been the great opportunity for Communism.

Thomas knew the Communists and their recent history. He made it clear that night in debate that he suspected Earl Browder and his motives.

The Thomas-Browder debate ended on a typical note of confusion, when Thomas could not resist the opportunity, before the Communist-dominated crowd, to bait Browder with the reminder that the Soviet Union—that defender of the downtrodden—had been sending large quantities of oil to Italy, oil that was then being used to fuel Italian tanks and Italian troop-carriers fighting in Ethiopia.

When Thomas was so brave as to denounce the motherland, the Communists booed him loud and long. And on that fitting note of confusion the meeting ended.

The Thomas-Browder debate was not important or politically significant as meetings go. In his history of the Socialist party, David Shannon does not even discuss the debate. The day after it was held, *The New York Times* buried the story where it belonged, under a small headline on page 36.

The debate was a fuzzy, uninspired pair of harangues by two radicals who had no real hope of coming to power in America, although both had important places in the stream of American history;

Thomas to hold a positive place as a great dissenter and goad to liberals; Browder to serve as a central point of focus for the testing of America's strength and pliability in dealing with a subversive, disloyal faction.

At the time of that debate, Norman Thomas was becoming conscious of his true role in America. He had been running for office as a Socialist for nearly ten years. Sometimes he had hopes, or almost-hopes, that he would one day be elected and that the course of America would be shifted by that election. But by 1935 the role of Roosevelt as the bringer of great change was beginning to become apparent, too. Thomas could trace the downward course of the Socialist movement in America in direct proportion to the liberal and radical changes in the social structure made under the Roosevelt administration.

Such a conservative historian as Dexter Perkins has noted that Roosevelt did not truly alter the American system, as his detractors were accusing him of doing, even in 1935. His alterations of the American way of doing things, however, tended to steal the thunder of the left wing. As Roosevelt's strength and popularity grew, the honest left declined.

After that debate with Norman Thomas, Earl Browder went on to become a more important figure. The Communist party grew some, as the Socialists declined late in the 1930's. John L. Lewis made a snowball of the CIO, and within two years it was far larger than the AF of L. Some called it a Red snowball, however, because of the obvious and important influence of the Communists on the CIO. Communists infiltrated the central organization, they infiltrated many important unions and controlled their policies in some cases. They infiltrated the federal government, the National Labor Relations Board, the State Department, and the Department of Agriculture in particular.

The Communists attracted intellectuals. Where the Socialists had gained the support of writers, artists and teachers in the 1920's, in the middle and late 1930's the Communists took their place. John Dos Passos, Granville Hicks, Edmund Wilson, Matthew Josephson—these and scores of others joined the Communist movement or supported it in the late 1930's.

Throughout the world, the Communists worked diligently to

bring about United Fronts with Socialists and labor movements. The United States was no exception. There was a feeling of exultation in the air in the late 1930's, a feeling that Communism represented a wave of the future, that the fate of the ordinary man was somehow tied up with the fate of the Spanish Republic, of the French Popular Front. Communism was linked with anti-Fascism all over the world. It was regarded as the reverse side of the coin.

As the fear and distrust of the Fascist and Nazi governments grew, the fear and distrust of the Communist government of the Soviet Union waned. Communism, in the late 1930's reached its high point of intellectual appeal to Americans. Writers, film personalities such as Charles Chaplin, and educators felt no disgrace in announcing Communist sympathies and in backing Communist causes.

But the end of important Communist influence on the American political scene came in the 1930's too, with the gradual disillusionment of most of the native American radicals who had turned to Communism in their search for a better society.

James Wechsler, later editor of the *New York Post*, who was to be one of those affected, pointed to the great Stalin purge of 1936-38 and the Moscow trials as a turning point. As Dictator Stalin ruthlessly stamped out the lives of hundreds of thousands of men and women who had made the revolution in Russia, young Americans like Wechsler became disillusioned and dropped out of Communist affairs in America.

But the great change, the point at which Communism in America ceased to be a political movement and the Communist party was recognized by millions as the servant of a foreign government, came with the announcement of the Nazi-Soviet pact in August, 1939. For years the Communists of the world had trumpeted against Naziism. Forty-five days before the signing of the alliance, Earl Browder declared that there was no more chance of the Russians siding with Nazi Germany than there was of Earl Browder's being elected president of the Chamber of Commerce.

When the announcement of the alliance was made, the silence of the Communists in America was deadly, if brief. The party and its religious following were able to swallow this renunciation of humanity. Most intellectual adherents to the Communist party were not able to swallow it, and they dropped off the bandwagon by the thousands. In signing the alliance the Russian Communists had affirmed the old doctrine that the end justified any means. Stalin had made it quite clear that the Russians sought destruction of the western world and placed the interests of Soviet nationalism above all else.

The Communist party in America never recovered. Socialism was dying in the middle 1930's and was effectively dead by the end of the decade. Communism was to have another brief spurt during the uneasy alliance of the Second World War, but having revealed itself in the Nazi-Soviet pact it was never again to delude any but those in America who wished to be deluded.

Henry Agard Wallace brought startling theories of scarcity into play to solve the nation's problems of overproduction and underconsumption—too much food and too little to eat. U. S. DEPT. OF AGRICULTURE PHOTOGRAPH

It was a novelty for the nation to have a woman Secretary of Labor. At first business and labor regarded Frances Perkins as a do-gooder, but even as these Pittsburgh steel workers, they were not long in learning that her friendliness covered a strong will. BROWN BROTHERS

Max Schmeling had said that no Negro could stand up to a white man. Two minutes and four seconds after the beginning of their second fight, Schmeling changed his mind. UNITED PRESS INTERNATIONAL PHOTO

WGN

CHAPTER NINE

ON THE DAY THAT HERBERT HOOVER was inaugurated as President of the United States in 1929, a tall, tweedy newspaper editor glanced over the report of the President's inaugural address on the desk before him. As he read, his face assumed an expression of intense disgust, and when he finished reading, he scribbled a note to his staff. This new man, the editor said, would not do at all.

In the election of 1932 that same editor was neutral, at least by his own standards, but four years later Colonel Robert Rutherford McCormick conducted one of the most virulent newspaper campaigns in American history against Hoover's successor and the editor's old schoolmate—Franklin Delano Roosevelt. In the election campaign of 1936 even the telephone operators of the *Chicago Tribune* were enlisted in Col. McCormick's campaign. The Colonel caused a warning to the nation to be printed on the front page of the *Tribune* every day during the 1936 campaign. One day the front page warning read: "Only 37 days to save your country—what are you going to do about it?" Then, and until the day of election, *Tribune* telephone operators responded to incoming calls with the warning that only a few days remained to save the nation from Franklin Roosevelt's re-election.

Colonel McCormick's opposition to Franklin Roosevelt and the New Deal at mid-passage did not set the Colonel on a lonely path. Most of the American press opposed Roosevelt in 1936, although few American newspapers were so outspoken in their criticism, so destructive, and so determined to find fault in every new policy of the federal government. The hatred and opposition of Colonel McCormick's *Tribune* was a measure of the degree of change wrought in American society by the events of the 1930's and the policies devised by government to deal with those happenings. The *Tribune*, standing in the splendid, isolated setting of mid-continent, was in a position to appraise those changes from the viewpoint of a newspaper whose proprietors had always stood firm for the right of the newspaper *proprietor* to speak his mind openly and fight what he saw as threats to the nation's welfare. Colonel McCormick was faithful to this tradition, he embellished it and strengthened it, and yet he failed. Newspaper criticism did not bring down the walls of the Roosevelt administration. The attitudes of American newspapers either changed, or the newspapers found their authority shrinking. The press was to emerge from the years of this decade expanded, tempered, and above all, changed in its relationship to the American public, or isolated intellectually as severely as Chicago was isolated physically as the center of the vast heartland of the Middle West.

In the middle-western states during the 1930's there was no mistaking the meaning of the initials WGN by anyone who followed public affairs or even listened to the radio. WGN was the call signal of a Chicago radio station, but more significant, it was the *Chicago Tribune*'s own symbol of its self-esteem.

WGN meant World's Greatest Newspaper before it meant anything else. Since the *Tribune* owned radio station WGN, and since call letters beginning with the initial W were assigned to the East and Middle West when radio had become a force in America in the 1920's, Colonel McCormick simply extended the usage of his wonderful claim.

WGN became the name of the radio station he bought in 1924 to add to the glory of the *Tribune*. WGN radio station functioned as an appendix to the newspaper during the 1930's. Colonel McCormick owned a radio station and a newspaper, but there was never any question as to where his real loyalties lay: radio, to the Colonel, was a plaything which became a necessary nuisance insofar as radio diverted advertising and attention from his newspaper.

What a newspaper it was! As the 1930's began Colonel McCormick's *Tribune* was one of a handful of immensely powerful daily newspapers in the land. The *Chicago Tribune*, in those years, maintained one of the largest and most talented news-gathering organizations in the world. Floyd Gibbons was a *Tribune* reporter, William L. Shirer covered Northern Europe for the *Tribune*, the newspaper maintained its own Paris edition, and no local or regional event of any importance passed unnoticed by the *Tribune*. The newspaper owned an airplane. The editors would not hesitate to charter others, to hire a fleet of cars or boats, or to send a bevy of reporters to cover an important news event. Yet at the end of the decade the *Tribune* had changed. The mighty foreign staff had melted away, the *Tribune*'s coverage of Washington affairs and even local affairs was no longer respected among newspapermen, as once had been true.

The newspaper's circulation had increased and it continued to increase after the end of the decade. Local and national news events were given as much attention as before. The great change was in emphasis. The *Tribune* had been boisterous, if conservative. It had become crabbed and reactionary. *Tribune* reporters covered the news, but too often with an "angle" that had been suggested from the proprietor's panelled office on the twenty-fourth floor of the Tribune Tower.

True, the handful of powerful American newspapers had lost much of the influence they had wielded in earlier years but most other newspapers accepted their changing role in American society and changed with the times. The *Tribune* did not change; it continued through the 1930's as a stronghold of personal journalism. The newspaper's proprietor, Colonel McCormick, had once been dubbed "Duke of Chicago" by waggish admirers. By the end of the decade he was also called "the greatest mind of the fourteenth century" by contemporaries of the twentieth.

Strictly speaking, the title proprietor was not fitting for Colonel McCormick's role on the *Tribune*, although he functioned as a sole proprietor in fact. The *Tribune* enterprise, its real estate holdings, its vast resources of pulp timber and land and money were held as a corporation. Colonel McCormick was not sole owner. Included in the ownership were two other publishing giants of the period, his cousins, Captain Joseph Patterson of the New York *Daily News* and his sister Eleanor Patterson, of the Washington *Times Herald*. These successful publishers traced their heritage to the marriage of Joseph Medill's daughters, one to a Patterson, one to a son of Medill's hated enemy, Cyrus McCormick, inventor of the reaping machine. These three were the grandchildren of Medill, who had come to Chicago in 1855 and had spent the next forty-four years building the *Tribune* and helping to build Chicago as the center of the Middle West.

Robert McCormick—Bertie to his intimates—was born on July 30, 1880, in Chicago. When he was nine years old his father was appointed Secretary to the U.S. Legation in London and the boy was promptly entered in an English public school at Lansdown. Here, his biographers have noted, McCormick apparently acquired a deep distaste for English society and the foundations of an Anglophobia that flourished in the 1930's. But Anglophobia was a cherished midwestern American heritage. The boy's grandfather, Editor Medill, had nursed a grudge against England since the days of the Civil War when British merchants bought Confederate cotton and helped the southerners run the Union blockade.

Young McCormick left England to enter Groton School in Massachusetts, where he was one form in advance of Franklin Delano Roosevelt. In 1899, McCormick entered Yale and graduated in 1903. He wanted to go on to Yale Law School, but his father insisted that he would live in Chicago, and thus must attend a college in that area, where he would be studying among the people with whom he would later live.

Bertie McCormick's first adult interest was not publishing, or law, although he passed the bar, but politics. When he was twenty-four years old, McCormick was elected to the Chicago board of aldermen. His most distinguished public service came later, when he was elected president of the city sanitary district at a time when Chicago was trying to cope with the serious problems its citizens had created for a growing city by dumping their sewage indiscriminately into Lake Michigan. Hard-bitten politicians laughed when McCormick took on this job. The idea of a foppish young aristocrat inspecting a sewer trench amused them. McCormick did just that; his lanky form became familiar to sewer workers as he tramped through the diggings in hip boots, watching progress and ordering changes in procedure and plan. Later, too, McCormick served on the Chicago Planning Commission.

In this period of his life McCormick formed lasting loyalties, including one to Chicago's Democratic political boss Ed Kelly, then a construction worker. Although in the thirties McCormick was to be the symbol of the ultraconservative wing of the Republican party, even in his most acidulous years his loyalties to these old friends did not waver. This aspect of McCormick's character was to surprise many men, but there was much about McCormick that was reminiscent of Franklin Roosevelt. Born to wealth, McCormick took a paternal and proprietary interest in the people who surrounded him. Had he not entered newspaper publishing, he might have entered national politics. In 1936, in fact, Colonel McCormick was eminently available for the Republican vice-presidential nomination, but by that time it was too late; he was already too alien to the American scene.

McCormick earned his military title of Colonel, as Joseph Patterson earned his as Captain, during the First World War. The cousins had entered the *Tribune* management in 1910, but in 1914 when World War I started both went off to war as correspondents. Bertie wore a tailored uniform. He lunched with Britain's Prime Minister in London, and visited Winston Churchill, then First Lord of the Admiralty. He went to France, and he visited the Czar. He made newsreels for Chicago's consumption, and he wrote a book.

When the United States sent a military expedition to the Mexican border, McCormick and Patterson went into service—McCormick as a Major of cavalry. When the United States entered the war in Europe in 1917, he was commissioned colonel and sent to France to join General Pershing's staff.

Joseph Patterson went to France, too, but Patterson enlisted in the ranks, and worked his way up to Captain. In France, one night, the idea of the New York *Daily News* was born. Patterson and McCormick met in a farmhouse near the front lines. They went outside, sat on a manure pile, drank Scotch whiskey, and settled their own postwar future. McCormick was to go back and run the *Tribune*; Patterson was to start a new tabloid newspaper, based on the London *Mirror*, which he had seen and admired.

Captain Patterson threw himself into the job of catering to a mass audience. His mind worked that way. Patterson had also graduated from Yale. He had served in the Illinois state legislature, toyed with Socialism, and had written two novels of Socialist cast. He had developed comic strips to bring reader interest to the *Tribune*, and he brought these strips, a sharp eye for pictorial journalism, and a formula of sex and sensation to the New York scene. The *News* struggled for a few months, but caught on, and then its rise was rapid.

The third member of this publishing family, Eleanor Patterson, was a director in both the *Tribune* and the *News*, but "Cissy" Patterson wanted to edit her own newspaper. She made her own place, persuading William Randolph Hearst to make her editor and publisher of his Washington *Herald*. By 1930, all these grandchildren of Joseph Medill were operating successful newspapers, all travelling different paths.

As early as 1930, when Franklin Roosevelt was running for a second term as governor of New York State, Colonel McCormick opposed Roosevelt on philosophical grounds, although the New York gubernatorial election was none of his business nor sufficiently important to him to raise his blood pressure. Captain Patterson was of different mind. In the early months of the depression he determined that America was suffering a great economic upheaval. The New York *Daily News* was to be friendly to Roosevelt's social experimentation in New York State and later to support him after he was elected to the Presidency in 1932. Cissy Patterson's *Herald*, a Hearst newspaper, followed the Hearst national policy. Hearst backed Franklin Roosevelt, too, although later Hearst and the Pattersons joined the anti-Roosevelt forces.

In 1932, Colonel McCormick's principal reaction to Franklin Roosevelt was suspicion that Roosevelt did not have sufficient character to stand up against the obstinacy of an obstructionist Congress. Otherwise, he was of the opinion that no one could do a worse job of running the country than had Herbert Hoover.

It did not take Colonel McCormick many months to change his mind.

On March 7, 1933 the *Tribune* praised Roosevelt's handling of the bank crisis. But Colonel McCormick disapproved of Roosevelt and the New Deal after the enactment of the National Industrial Recovery Act three months later. When that law was passed, Colonel McCormick was active in the committee of the American Newspaper Publishers Association which tried to draw up a voluntary code of fair practices within the industry. The law provided that any business which refused to adhere to the voluntary codes of its industry could be subjected to licensing by the President. Many publishers, Colonel McCormick leading them, took the position that this general provision, when applied to the newspaper business, abridged the freedom of the press.

When Roosevelt heard of this complaint he told a reporter to tell Bertie McCormick that he was seeing things under the bed.

McCormick replied that he agreed, and that if Roosevelt would look under the bed he would find the things were there. McCormick insisted, along with others, on a statement in the newspaper code which reiterated the constitutional guarantee of a free press. Roosevelt was exasperated, and let it be known. McCormick and other publishers were angry.

NRA brought another unwelcome change to the newspaper industry—the establishment of the American Newspaper Guild. Newspaper publishers had long resisted efforts to unionize their newsrooms. Some of them argued that newspaper reporters and editors were "professionals." Others did not argue, but firmly refused to countenance unionization. Still others found no objection to organization of editorial employees, but when the Guild organized as an industrial union, embracing elevator operators as well as reporters, publisher discontent was general.

Colonel McCormick settled the Guild threat to the *Tribune* in his own way, when the Guild began organizing in Chicago. He learned that the Guild was asking for a wage of seventy dollars a week, and immediately raised all his experienced reporters to that level. Neither then, nor at any other time, did loyal *Tribune* employees have cause to complain about the Colonel's treatment of them. His paternalism was sincere and effective. *Tribune* employees were better paid than most other newspaper people, they received more additional benefits, and their jobs were as secure as those of any people in the newspaper business. Elsewhere newspaper employees suffered serious paycuts in the early years of depression. The *New York Herald Tribune* cut salaries 10 per cent, and not long afterward cut them by 10 per cent again. The Portland *Oregonian* instituted similar cuts. The trouble, in Chicago, and elsewhere, was the fall in advertising revenue. Circulation of newspapers remained surprisingly stable throughout the depression years, but newspaper income was derived mostly from advertising, and advertising in newspapers slipped badly. In 1933, newspaper advertising had fallen by 45 per cent below the figure of 1929.

The rise of radio, and particularly of network radio, accounted for some part of the newspaper advertising deficit. The newspaper share of the advertising dollar dropped sharply during the thirties. National magazines maintained their position, but radio's share of advertising increased six times during the decade. Pressed by such competition, many publishers were inclined toward irascibility to an administration which seemed to increase their business problems as the years progressed, by encouraging labor organization, by pressing for higher national wage limits, and even by talking directly to the people through radio, as Franklin Roosevelt began to do in his fireside chats.

There is no serious indication that Colonel McCormick's growing antipathy for the Roosevelt administration stemmed from business concerns, however. The Colonel was an excellent businessman. He built his radio station, and he was an organizer and prime mover in the development of the Mutual Broadcasting System. For a number of years a *Tribune* official was head of the system. For a time, in 1931, McCormick took a strong stand against the incursions of radio on newspapers. He recommended against giving free advertising to radio station programs. He developed a radio version of the *Tribune* comic strip *Little Orphan Annie* to bring listeners into the *Tribune* reading fold. He followed a policy, for a time, of allowing only *Tribune* advertisers to sponsor programs on WGN.

Still, as the *Tribune* continued to prosper, the Colonel softened somewhat. In 1933 the *Tribune* was selling more newspapers every morning than any other daily in America except Captain Patterson's New York *News*. Colonel McCormick's circulation was healthy enough.

A French student of American affairs, Paul Alpert, attributed a much broader base to the opposition of Colonel McCormick and other conservatives to the New Deal. Alpert noted that Roosevelt affronted the powers of money. The world of big business, he said, grew unanimous in its hostility to the New Deal, and this was the origin of the campaign of calumny against Roosevelt, a campaign in which such opponents as McCormick accused F.D.R. of violating the Constitution and installing a collectivist dictatorship, and of leading America to ruin by his politics of high expense and persistent deficit.

In 1932 the *Tribune* had written editorially that "if the American people want more taxation, more bureaucracy, more regulation of their affairs by officials, more centralization of power at Washington, Franklin Roosevelt is their man." On July 2, 1934, the *Tribune* accused F.D.R. flatly of leading the nation toward totalitarianism.

From that point on there was no hope of reconciliation between the *Tribune* and the administration. Colonel McCormick had a long memory, and he was one of the most vigorous haters in the newspaper business. For his part, Roosevelt grew more and more exasperated with the *Tribune* and with all newspapers which criticized him, although he continued to read the *Tribune* every morning.

Roosevelt began his first administration with warm feelings towards the press and toward newspapermen. It did not take long for him to change, either. Clark Howell, the publisher of the Atlanta *Constitution*, had been an early backer of Roosevelt for the Presidency. Within a few years Roosevelt had broken with Howell, and in the later years of the decade he referred to the Atlanta publisher scathingly as a "mossback." Roosevelt broke with William Randolph Hearst, with Roy Howard of the Scripps-Howard newspapers, and, after eight years, with Joseph Patterson and the *Daily News*.

Long before that eight years had passed, however, Roosevelt's relations with the owners of the press had become execrable. William Allen White advised Roosevelt to ignore publisher criticism, but Roosevelt was a good hater, too, and he could not ignore it, even had he not been given more abuse by the press, according to historian Arthur Schlesinger, Jr., than any President since Andrew Jackson.

Generally speaking Roosevelt got on well with the working newspapermen—the reporters who covered the White House and who tagged along with him on inspection and campaign trips. He felt that most of these reporters were sympathetic to him. He knew, in some cases, that accurate reports of his activities were sent to the newspapers by correspondents, to be changed by the editors at home. Roosevelt, however, often used less than good sense in his approaches to newspaper publishers. He wrote to Adolph Ochs one time to complain about Arthur Krock, chief of *The New York Times* Washington bureau. Apparently he did not realize that Ochs had complete faith in Krock—that newspaper publishers did not maintain men in such key positions unless they felt they were trustworthy and accurate in their reporting. Like many men of action Roosevelt was so impatient with criticism as to be bull-headed on occasion.

Nonetheless, during Roosevelt's years in office, the White House and all the executive departments yielded more news than government had ever given out before. To be sure, government was growing, and becoming the largest employer by far in the land—in every department. But that was not all of it. Roosevelt also took the wraps off government as far as the press was concerned. He welcomed the opportunity to work and live in what Hugh Johnson called "a goldfish bowl."

There was more reason to this than might be readily apparent. Since most newspapers opposed Roosevelt, one way to overcome their harassments was to keep the administration on the front pages—which Roosevelt and his staff did quite successfully. The result was that government was better covered by the newspapers than ever before in history and that Americans learned more about the operations of government than they had ever before cared to know. Even the *Tribune* could not keep Roosevelt off page one of the newspaper all the time. Too much was happening every day in Washington.

The development of news also gave rise to a new kind of political column in Washington in the 1930's—the "inside dope" column, such as "The Washington Merry-Go-Round" conducted by Drew Pearson and Robert S. Allen. Roosevelt and his friends found this kind of column extremely valuable for "leaking" information they wanted to have out but were afraid for political reasons to state openly. Yet the columnists discovered that the sword cut both ways, and that Roosevelt's enemies could be valuable to them, too. The older type of political column, the wise words of the pundit, did not languish, although there were perhaps not so many practitioners of the art as there had been in the 1920's. Leading political columnists included Paul Mallon, Raymond Clapper, and Walter Lippmann, former editor of the New York *World*, who naturally gravitated to Washington once his newspaper was sold to Roy Howard's chain.

Columns, comics, and special features were in their heyday in the 1930's before television cut their audience. Color printing came gradually to the newspaper industry, and the comic pages, which had usually been printed on green or pink or yellow paper in black ink, came out in four colors, adding greatly to their liveliness and to the reading interest of the general public. A surprising number of the best comic strips were developed by the *Chicago Tribune* and by the New York *Daily News*. Captain Patterson had a genius for comic-strip development. He invented *Andy Gump*, one of the very first continuity strips. *Gasoline Alley, Moon Mullins,* as well as *Little Orphan Annie* were all *Tribune* and *News* inventions. In such matters, the cousins worked together, through the Chicago Tribune-New York News Syndicate. They sold the rights to use their comic strips and certain other materials in areas where they did not compete. But the *News* and particularly the *Tribune* used very little "canned" material. Hearst newspapers and others were filled with the writings of syndicated columnists and reporters. The *Tribune* preferred to send its own men to the scene, and to print its own brand of punditry from Washington.

One could read every and any brand of political thinking in the news columns of the newspapers and on the editorial pages. Eleanor Roosevelt started a column of her own—"My Day." In some newspapers it ran next to that of Westbrook Pegler, the professional debunker who became so soured on nearly everything by the end of the decade that his enemies wondered why he did not just melt and disappear after the manner of the wicked witches of Oz.

Perhaps the most significant development in political reporting in newspapers in the decade was the rise of the public opinion poll. Dr. George Gallup developed the poll, which came to prominence in the 1936 election. When the *Literary Digest* poll completely misread American public opinion, George Gallup's survey missed the final results by only 6 per cent. That was a high margin of error, but Gallup pruned his margin year after year.

During the last half of the 1930's there was much talk in Washington about the Hearst-McCormick-Patterson press. That hyphenated and tongue-twisting adjective became a term of derision. It referred, of course, to the unofficial liaison of the Hearst interests in Washington with the Patterson-McCormick interests, through Cissy Patterson's control of the Hearst *Herald*. More than that, after 1935 it referred to a point of view. In 1932 Hearst had supported Roosevelt, but in 1936 he deserted him and went to the support of Alf Landon, along with most of the other chain publishers. By this time some three hundred of the daily American newspapers belonged to chains, and nearly half of the total newspaper circulation in America was chain newspaper readership. But of all the chains, the Hearst chain was most powerful, and boasted four and a half million readers. The New York *Daily News* and the *Tribune* claimed another two million circulation. Among them, the Hearst-McCormick-Patterson press, then, claimed almost a sixth of the total reading public of America.

Hearst, in these days, was in trouble. His staggering personal expenses had eaten heavily into the Hearst fortune. No man can fill dozens of warehouses with works of art, purchased at any price, leave them to sit, and go on to purchase more works of art and castles to put them in, without denting a fortune. Hearst had so dented his fortune by 1930 that he had to sell $50,000,000 in preferred stock to support the warehouses full of artwork, and the barony at San Simeon, California. In 1937 matters became even more perilous, and he was forced to turn over 95 per cent of the stock, and business control into the hands of a banker trustee. In these days, some of Hearst's properties were not too healthy. He had bought or established forty-two different newspapers, but he was no longer particularly interested in running them (his political ambitions had gone sour) and his style of journalism had begun to pall on much of the public.

None of this was irrevocable, and yet Hearst's empire continued to decay. It almost seemed as though he did not care. Banker control never helped any newspaper survive, and it did not help the Hearst empire, which shrank steadily, from its high point until only seventeen newspapers remained. Cissy Patterson finally bought Hearst's *Herald* and his *Times*, and built the strongest paper in Washington with the combination—an all-day newspaper.

Colonel McCormick had some of the attributes of William Randolph Hearst, especially a liking for high living. McCormick maintained a town house near the Tribune Tower, but spent much of his free time at his thousand-acre estate near Wheaton, where he rode horses and walked the grounds with an ancient German shepherd dog at his heel.

The shepherd followed McCormick everywhere, from home to office, and even into the city room when McCormick left the sanctity of the floor he shared with his editorial writers to issue instructions to the news managers. Those instructions might cover any subject under the sun. When a reporter received an assignment on which it was noted that R.R.M. took a personal interest in the story he knew that the sky was the limit on expenses and time, and that he had better come back with the story the Colonel wanted, written as the Colonel wanted it written.

Usually, Colonel McCormick had his way in matters large and small for few men were brave enough to cross him. In 1935, when he had soured on Roosevelt and the Democrats to a point of rancidity, the voters of Rhode Island had the effrontery to turn out that state's Republican judges and replace them with Democratic judges. Wrathfully, Colonel McCormick ordered the star that represented the state of Rhode Island torn from the flag flown each day from the Tribune Tower. It was done. He proposed, then, to publicize his act across the country, and to fly the forty-seven-star flag from that day onward.

Fortunately for his personal escutcheon, a member of his staff warned that it might not be legal to do so, and the Colonel was restrained until he consulted the *Tribune*'s attorneys. Sure enough, it was a felony to deface the United States Flag, he discovered. The star of Rhode Island was quietly replaced in the *Tribune*'s Old Glory, proving that in his beloved republic there were certain restraints, even on the power of such a great man.

Angry as he was in 1935, the Colonel was even more angry in 1936, and he was convinced that the Democrats were committing acts of treason every day. After Roosevelt was nominated for reelection, the Colonel declared open warfare. "The unscrupulous organizing mind of Tammany, Jim Farley, is at work behind the smiling mask of Franklin Roosevelt to bring the end of self-government to the world," the Colonel charged. If no one else would stop this juggernaut, he and the *Tribune* would try.

That year, Colonel McCormick organized The Volunteers, a group of speakers for Landon. He gave heavily to the Landon campaign, and more important, he and the *Tribune* pushed Landon as hard as they could push him.

But Roosevelt, deprived of publisher support, had the new weapon of radio at his disposal, and in the field of radio, Landon's piping voice was best left unheard at all. In fact, after a first few attempts, Republican campaign managers decided that it was better that he not be heard.

Colonel McCormick's plumping for Landon in the campaign

took two forms. One method of support was to build Landon up, which McCormick did with all the means at his disposal. Cissy Patterson, his cousin, did so too, for on meeting Landon she had said she was reminded by the little Kansan of Abraham Lincoln.

McCormick's second method of supporting Landon was to snipe at Roosevelt and the Democrats in any and every way. Much of this was done by *Tribune* editors and headline writers. For example, a morality exposé which ran in the *Tribune* during the 1936 campaign was headlined: "Roosevelt Area in Wisconsin is a Hotbed of Vice." And although Roosevelt made it almost impossible for newspapers to ignore his speeches, because he created news in every single one of them—the *Tribune* managed the impossible. In one week of the campaign, the *Tribune* gave Roosevelt mention on a front page only once (while Landon was on the front page every day). One day the *Tribune* staff managed to keep Roosevelt's name out of the paper altogether—a neat trick to ignore the front-running candidate for President during an election year.

One of the Colonel's trusted foreign correspondents, Donald Day, reported one day that Moscow had ordered the Communists in the United States to back Roosevelt against Landon. Even if this were true, and it might well have been true, the *Tribune* story made it appear that Franklin Roosevelt was somehow in league with Joseph Stalin.

Chicagoans responded to Colonel McCormick's actions in kind. On election night, 1936, when it was apparent that Roosevelt had won, crowds of people gathered in State Street to watch a group of angry Roosevelt supporters grab piles of *Tribunes* and burn them. That same night other angry people threw rotten eggs at the great neo-Gothic Tribune Tower in defiance of the Colonel.

Undismayed, Colonel McCormick continued to go his own way, certain that Roosevelt was ruining the country and that it was up to the *Chicago Tribune* to trumpet that fact so all within circulating distance could hear. At the end of the decade McCormick was still going strong, but if he had cared to discover the facts, he would have learned that scarcely anyone was listening any more. Nearly a million people bought his *Tribune* every day, but not nearly so many read the Colonel's policy stories, and many of them had learned, over the years, to watch for the key words in the *Tribune*'s articles and to read around them to get the facts, for they had long since come to the conclusion that as institutions the Colonel and the *Tribune* were magnificent, but that they were best heard and read with healthy cynicism. The Colonel had fouled his own nest.

Other newspapers had changed with the times because their proprietors realized, to greater or lesser degrees, that the Roosevelt way had been embraced by the majority of the American people, and that the Roosevelt administration, more than any before it, was a compendium of pressure groups, each representing some legitimate portion of society. Colonel McCormick never accepted such a view. From almost the beginning, Roosevelt was, to him, dangerous. In the very beginning, when Roosevelt was governor of New York, McCormick saw his old schoolmate as an ineffectual country squire in politics. A few months later he found Roosevelt honest but misguided. By 1934 McCormick had convinced himself that Roosevelt was a traitor to the principles on which the American Republic had been founded. He remained convinced of that fact until his dying day. By the end of the decade nothing, it seemed, could change the Colonel's mind or ways.

ALONG FIFTH AVENUE

CHAPTER TEN

DURING THE ROARING TWENTIES when the nation still respected the wealth and exclusive social position of the leisure class the leading matron in the United States was Mrs. Cornelius Vanderbilt V. She was often called the Queen of American Society.

As the twenties ended, Grace Wilson Vanderbilt was in her mid-forties. Her husband, who had served as a General in the First World War, had also amassed a paper fortune in the stock market. Promptly he bought a $750,000 yacht. Aboard the ship Grace could entertain royalty, and when she was finished with her round of European entertainments and had gone on to the next stage of her schedule, the General could sail off into the Atlantic and drink. No one who knew the Vanderbilts wondered why the General drank. His son once asked him why he had never divorced Grace Wilson. The General looked at him sternly. People in their walk of life did not divorce, he said.

When the stock market of Wall Street crashed, General Vanderbilt's paper profits were wiped out. In the ensuing years, his moderate fortune barely sufficed to meet the requirements of his wife's entertainment, but the entertainment continued. The General sailed about on his yacht, and Mrs. Vanderbilt entertained thousands of people every year. She followed the way of life she had learned as a girl, and if she led all the other members of Society in her efforts, that was a matter of degree. No one looked askance on her way of life.

When Franklin Roosevelt ran for his first office—the New York state senate—he was regarded genially by the members of Society. By background and education Roosevelt was one of them.

Before Franklin Roosevelt ran for the Presidency, some of his actions had begun to cause unfavorable talk at the Piping Rock Club and on the gritty shore of Bailey's beach. In the bar of the New York Yacht Club, men who held investments in utilities did not like to hear the governor talk about "public power" on the St. Lawrence River. Like the ministers and the colored people, most of Society voted for Herbert Hoover in 1932. Roosevelt's acquaintances and country neighbors at Hyde Park, the Frederick William Vanderbilts, had so little loyalty that they, too, voted for Hoover.

As the bank crisis of 1933 overwhelmed the nation, most of these voters, including the gentlemen who held up the Union Club bar, took a new look at Hoover and found him almost entirely wanting in the quality of leadership. When Franklin Roosevelt resolved the bank crisis in a little more than a week, and then began to reorganize industry with his National Recovery Act, the self-styled upper class was lulled for a time. But the time was short, far shorter than it was for the businessmen and industrialists. Persons of inherited wealth learned within a few months that they would be hit hard by the Roosevelt philosophy of public welfare.

Roosevelt was damned, and invited, by innuendo, to resign from his various clubs. With an urbane smile F.D.R. passed off such minor insults, infuriating his erstwhile friends by not even deigning to recognize their hatred.

Neily Vanderbilt, the son of the General and the only Vanderbilt to support Roosevelt in 1932 or at any other time was called a traitor to his class. Neily not only supported Roosevelt, he worked for him, through Jim Farley and Louis Howe and Raymond Moley, in the 1932 campaign. Neily's adherence amused Roosevelt and it was valuable for Roosevelt to have a Vanderbilt on his side—even though it was a Vanderbilt whose father had all but disowned the boy and refused to see him when the younger man came to call.

Other Vanderbilts gathered with their peers at the well-worn bar of the Reading Room—the most exclusive of all clubs in Newport—and commiserated together over the misfortune of having been born into a century in which "that man" was turning the nation over to the Bolsheviks.

And what of Mrs. Vanderbilt?

Her attitude to politics was always one of disdain but she disliked Roosevelt because he had betrayed all that she held dear. One day, not long after Roosevelt had begun to infuriate her, he chanced to be travelling aboard Vincent Astor's yacht *Nourmahal*, when he discovered that General Vanderbilt's *Winchester* was anchored alongside. The President waved gaily at the Vanderbilts and invited them to come aboard the *Nourmahal*. The General, in his precise way, told the President of the United States that it was the prerogative of the owner of a yacht to invite guests aboard. Roosevelt blithely rejoined that he would waive the question. Mrs. Vanderbilt looked Roosevelt in the eye with the steely glance that had always made lesser persons shudder.

"I don't like you, Mr. President," she said. "I don't like you at all."

But here she was talking to a master of affairs—even social affairs.

"Well, Mrs. Vanderbilt," Roosevelt rejoined, "lots of people don't like me. You are in good company."

Roosevelt's disarming remark, might have humbled another. It only quieted Mrs. Vanderbilt. She *was* in expensive and exclusive company, if nothing else. When T. Suffern Tailer returned to Newport after competing in a number of amateur golf tournaments, the young man announced at a clambake that he favored Roosevelt, and that he proposed to vote for him in the next election. An older socialite took young Tailer aside and warned him in a friendly way that at Newport people did not make such remarks—even in jest.

Shortly after Roosevelt was elected, and had begun to change the face of America, the spry and sophisticated *New Yorker* magazine published a cartoon which showed an apoplectic old gentleman swelling visibly in rage, while his wife cried in distress: "Now you *know* the doctor told you not to discuss Roosevelt."

Although the rich were noticeably shaken by the Wall Street crash, they were shaken no more than the rich had been in the Panic of 1872 or that of 1907. The transfer of their hatred to Franklin Roosevelt as the cause of ruin is not entirely explained by the policies of the New Deal or by the refusal of Roosevelt to take his old Groton and Harvard classmates seriously. The revulsion of the rich against Roosevelt was an indication of their hatred for their own time. The wealthy felt themselves abused, members of a new "lost generation," and they lamented the hardships the era caused them.

This change in attitude crept slowly upon the leisure class. The depression began for the rest of the nation in 1930, but in 1930 a visitor to Newport would never have known that change had occurred, as long as he did not pry into the substrata of society.

The highpoint of that 1930 season at Newport had been the open-air extravaganza staged by Mrs. Moses Taylor at her country estate, The Glen. A few years before, Grace Wilson Vanderbilt had staggered Society by importing the entire cast of a Broadway play to Newport for an evening's performance, building a tent on her lawn to house the show, and then graciously allowing the performers to mingle with the guests for a little while.

This year, Mrs. Taylor staged an even more fabulous performance. She brought the three hundred members of Newport's top-drawer Society together to see a showing of Edmond Rostand's *Les Romanesques.*

It was performed in the gardens, which had been rearranged just for the evening to form a natural stage for the players. The next day the setting would be torn apart and the formal garden rebuilt. During the play, and throughout the evening, the guests were entertained by the Newport Casino Symphony Orchestra, which Mrs. Taylor had employed for the evening. Her entertainment, after the depression began, dwarfed even that of Mrs. Vanderbilt in good times.

Grace Vanderbilt entertained all the important visitors that season. Her dinners boasted more princes and counts and barons than those of any other hostess. The princes stayed with Mrs. Vanderbilt at Beaulieu, where their wants were met but their presence was generally unnoticed except at meals—so busy was Mrs. Vanderbilt directing her thirty-three servants and planning her social life for days and weeks ahead.

The most important days for General Vanderbilt every Newport season were those when the America's Cup Races were held, and 1930 was no exception. The *Winchester* had been damaged seriously in a fire at the New York Yacht Club landing in front of Bellevue Hospital. First there had been an explosion, which shook the ship from stem to stern, then the fire broke out, apparently in the owner's quarters, and burned fiercely until the New York City fire department's fireboats arrived on the scene and extinguished it.

General Vanderbilt had not been aboard during the fire, but in his town house at 640 Fifth Avenue. After the fire, the *Winchester* was laid up for repairs at the Todd Shipyard in Brooklyn for a month, repairs which cost the General $76,000. Then she had been fit for the season, as flagship for one of the crustiest commodores the New York Yacht Club ever boasted.

The America's Cup Races were postponed on September 16, because of fog and a windless sea. The General, or the Commodore as he preferred to be called at sea, decided to give a party. It was hard, in fact, to tell where one Vanderbilt party left off and another began. That day, partying began at lunch aboard the *Winchester*, then moved to Beaulieu, where the Vanderbilts welcomed their current guest of honor, Sir Ronald Lindsay, British Ambassador to the United States, who had come to be Vanderbilt's house guest during the cup races.

A year later, the world of Society was turned topsy-turvy. Weddings fell off. Among the lesser classes the drop in the marriage rate was notable in 1930. In 1931 the drop in Social Register weddings was noticeable too, from 1044 Society weddings in 1930, to 947 a year later.

Not only were there changes in alliances and slowdowns in the rate at which Society alliances were contracted, but the type of person who held wealth and position began to change. At Deauville, Mrs. Emily Baumann of New York and Paris gave a party at Ciro's for Tukoji Rao III, the former Maharajah of Indore and his wife, the Maharanee. The hostess stood at the top of the stairs to receive the royal pair, and curtsied as they came upstairs: thereby throwing all Deauville into a tailspin.

Mrs. Baumann's American guests also curtsied. Mrs. Baumann's British guests did not. After all, they knew that the Maharajah was no longer considered royalty, and that his bride, the former Miss Nancy Ann Miller, of Seattle, Washington, U.S.A., was not royalty at all. Besides, they remarked, for the benefit of Mrs. Baumann, if the hostess was really greeting royalty she should have descended to the bottom of the stairs to do her curtsying.

Mrs. Vanderbilt would never have made such a mistake, for she knew every nuance of the only tradition that mattered in the slightest to her—the British tradition of royalty and royal Society. She considered herself, if not equal to her beloved king and queen, at least to be on a par with the heir apparent to the throne.

With change all around her, Mrs. Vanderbilt did not change or relax her standards in the slightest. In the summer of 1931 she continued her round of entertainments, seating forty guests at a time at her summer palace in Newport, and even more in the grand dining room of the huge town house on Fifth Avenue.

She continued to spend more than $200,000 a year on her houses and entertainments: her expenditures for laundry and linen alone would have kept an average family in upper middle class comfort for a year. All the linens were imported. Her English butler believed that in a fashionable household the bedsheets should be changed every day, but Mrs. Vanderbilt's concession to economy was to reduce that change to twice a week. Three laundresses worked full time in the basement, washing and ironing two hundred sheets a week and all the towels, tablecloths, and personal linen of the family, their guests, and the servants.

Society, however, was crumbling beneath Mrs. Vanderbilt's feet.

Manners deteriorated. During the Thanksgiving holiday week of 1932 four college students "crashed" a debutante ball in Brooklyn. Even for Brooklyn Society this was unheard of, and would have been unpardonable a few months before. Now, no one seemed to mind the breach in etiquette.

The New York Social Register remained unchanged in 1933. It was published, as it had been since 1887, in a sombre red and black cover, using a typographical style that had been popular in the nineteenth century. But an examination of that Social Register for the winter season showed a marked increase in the number of prominent families which chose to remain in their country homes for the winter rather than open their town houses for the season. The reason was simple enough: these families could no longer afford the expense of maintaining two homes, and the demands on them in the country were far less than those of the rigorous social season of the city. Some Society families sold their town houses and moved into smaller quarters. Some deserted Fifth Avenue altogether for the less expensive side streets, or to live on Park Avenue, which heretofore had been a symbol of the *nouveau riche*. Some Society families even sent their children to public schools.

Retrenchment was common in all America but the industrial

depression was not the only cause of the woes of the rich. The undoing of inherited wealth came through taxation. And how? Well, in 1928, a man with an income of $500,000 paid a federal income tax of $115,000. The tax rate was 23 per cent. In 1932, under the Hoover administration, Congress revised the internal revenue laws to raise more money. A man who earned $500,000 that year paid a tax of $263,000. The rate of taxation was 52 per cent.

This increase in taxes in 1932 by the Hoover administration was the most important single factor in the breakdown of the upperclass structure, and while the change began before Franklin Roosevelt was elected, its first effects were felt by the wealthy families in March, 1933, just after Roosevelt was inaugurated. So, he was to be blamed for the destruction of his own class.

With the changes in living habits of the old Society, a new and very different Society developed, one dedicated to gaiety. Few families could afford to entertain lavishly at home, so they turned to restaurants and night clubs. The mark of social prominence in the new Society was not inclusion in the Social Register but "being seen" with the proper people in the proper night clubs.

The new Society was christened "Café Society" by the newspapers, and the name stuck. Among its marks, one of the favorite pastimes of members of the new "Society" was the scavenger hunt, an entertainment imported from the continent, where it was reportedly invented by the Prince of Wales.

Elsa Maxwell, a newspaper columnist, presided over the first scavenger hunt staged in America in the fall of 1933. Hundreds of couples came to the Waldorf-Astoria hotel to pay an admission charge of fifteen dollars for the benefit of the Maternity Centre Association of New York. Then they were sent out by a starter's gun to race around the city, securing a list of odds and ends which Elsa Maxwell had taxed her brain for a week to devise. The lists included one of Jimmy Durante's shoes, "the most beautiful woman in New York," a live goat, a red lantern, and a live monkey. When the laughing contestants straggled in, towing goats, kinkajous, parking signs, and stray bits of laundry, Miss Maxwell distributed prizes, and the party continued in the ballroom until dawn.

Mrs. Vanderbilt's Society did not countenance this new group, but many of the younger members of her set deserted the old ways for the new. Jock Whitney went so far as to ask that his name be removed from the Social Register, and Mr. and Mrs. George L. K. Morris showed their feelings by including in their listing the name of their four year old Pekingese dog.

Mrs. Vanderbilt was distressed by the breakdown of her Society, but she carried on. In 1934, after her mother-in-law died, Grace Wilson Vanderbilt assumed even further honor: she began to sign herself Mrs. Vanderbilt, on cards and stationery. But the honor was hollow, for already her world had grown very narrow.

In earlier years American socialites had observed a strict code. For example all her life Mrs. Vanderbilt looked down on the Rockefeller family as new rich without social standing—despite the fact that John D. Rockefeller paid income taxes of six million dollars one year late in the 1920's. Entertainers were never admitted into Society, no matter how wealthy or how prominent they might become. In 1909 Miss Maxine Elliott, a star of the British stage, had come to visit New York. She was an intimate friend of King Edward VII, and so was Mrs. Vanderbilt. But did Mrs. Vanderbilt give a party for Miss Elliott? She not only ignored the actress, but so did all of Society. Miss Elliott spent a few miserable weeks in New York, uninvited to the houses of Fifth Avenue or to Newport, and then she returned to the less stuffy atmosphere of England.

In the twenties Mrs. Vanderbilt was shocked when the Prince of Wales came to America and, instead of seeking her out, sought the company of families who were not even in the Social Register, and then spent most of one evening at a party sitting on the floor with the Duncan sisters, playing a ukelele. In the thirties matters grew worse for the old socialites.

During the last half of the 1930's the newspapers began to play an important regulating role in the New Society. Mrs. Harrison Williams became the best known woman in America because she was taken up by Hearst columnist "Cholly Knickerbocker," who made her important simply because he said she was important. The newspapers also vied with one another in the creation of "glamour girls," debutantes who haunted the night clubs with aging playboys and vied for the doubtful honor of becoming recognized as "Glamour Girl No. 1."

Elsa Maxwell achieved a position of considerable prominence by giving parties, many of them staged at the expense of catering houses and liquor salesmen. One of her favorite kinds of party was the "pet hate" party, in which habitués of Café Society came dressed as the person or type of person they admired the least. Miss Maxwell had only one rule to keep costumes under control: no one could come to her party dressed as Franklin or Eleanor Roosevelt.

In a sense, although she was unrecognized by Mrs. Vanderbilt, Elsa Maxwell became the arbiter of the New Society, a position she found amusing for a girl who had grown up in Keokuk, Iowa. Still Mrs. Vanderbilt never relinquished her own claim to leadership or recognized the existence of Café Society, but as the years passed the claims too grew hollow and her refusal to unbend seemed stubborn foolishness.

But there was no one to talk sense to Grace Vanderbilt about change and the need for change. Her husband, the General, moved his yacht to Florida, and spent most of his time living there. The Vanderbilt son, Cornelius VI, married and divorced a number of times, heedless of his father's dictum on the sanctity of marital appearances among the upper class.

In 1936 Mrs. Vanderbilt was mentioned in *The New York Times* only in a handful of social notes and in a feature article on the changes in Society. In 1937 and 1938 her name was high in the Social Register, but it was not listed at all in *The New York Times Index*.

When General Vanderbilt's uncle, Frederick William Vanderbilt, died in 1938, he left a fortune of seventy-six million dollars. State and federal governments took forty-one million dollars of this in taxes. Within a few years heirs closed Frederick William Vanderbilt's mansion overlooking the Hudson at Hyde Park, and the estate was given to the American people as a national shrine, to be maintained by the Park Service to show Americans of later years how the rich had once lived.

So, the arbiter of Society had indeed changed. It was no longer Grace Wilson Vanderbilt. As Elsa Maxwell remarked, it was the Collector of Internal Revenue.

MODERN TIMES

CHAPTER ELEVEN

IN THE FALL OF 1927 a movie called *The Jazz Singer* opened on Broadway. It was the first of the "talking pictures," the beginning of a revolution in the art of movie-making in America.

In *The Jazz Singer,* the throaty voice of Al Jolson captured the imagination of the American movie audience and drew thousands upon thousands of moviegoers into the handful of houses that had added sound projectors. The great success of the movie both frightened and intrigued the moviemakers of Hollywood, the film capital. It turned their world topsy-turvy.

Who knew, after that, how audiences would react to favorite silent-film stars once their voices were heard? In many cases the voices of the stars were no match for the public personalities constructed for them by publicity men. And in the three years that followed, the age of the heroic but silent matinee idol ended. The public demanded more sound. Burgeoning impresarios such as Louis B. Mayer were captivated by the promise of talking pictures. There was no turning back.

That was 1927. In 1929, Harold Lloyd, the comedy star, appeared in his first talking picture—*Welcome Danger.* The danger was real. Mordaunt Hall, movie critic of *The New York Times* was sympathetic, but Lloyd's voice was his undoing. From 1925 to 1928 Harold Lloyd had risen high, even to threaten the position of Charlie Chaplin as the foremost comedy star in American films. After *Welcome Danger* Harold Lloyd's career staggered, then ended. He was a victim of a new age and a new technology.

But the story of the great change in the American amusement industry during the 1930's is not Harold Lloyd's story or even the story of the new technology. The American nation underwent remarkable changes in this decade, changes that showed in American attitudes toward entertainment as in so much else. And those changes were illustrated in the dissimilar careers of two great figures: Charlie Chaplin and Robert Emmett Sherwood.

Chaplin was an anomaly. He had arrived in Hollywood almost

at the beginning of the growth of the film industry. He progressed from pie-throwing hero of Mack Sennett shorts to become producer, writer, director, musical arranger, and star of his own films. He was a genius, and one of the few movie stars to survive the initial flurry which killed off nearly all the silent film "greats."

Sherwood was a magazine writer who wanted to be a novelist, a quiet giant of a man who first earned reputation as a film critic for *Vanity Fair*.

In the decade that followed the great Wall Street crash Chaplin's career first fell, then rose again, indicating in a puzzling way the strange possessive attitude Americans developed toward the screen figures who meant so much to them. Sherwood's career did not falter, it developed with his character, along lines that paralleled, to a very great extent, the thinking of the "American people." For a moment the tiny, wistful Englishman who had become an internationalist and the hulking American stood side by side at a crossroads of history, but only for a moment, and that was to be much later in the decade.

In 1928 Charlie Chaplin released *The Circus*, and began to plan his next picture, *City Lights*. At that time he did consider making a sound movie—and rejected the idea. Part of the reason for rejection was artistic. Chaplin had always been a mime. He had never relied on sound effects even when on the music-hall stage. But equally important was the financial question. Chaplin's movies were truly international. He earned his production costs in Japan alone and his movies circulated all over the globe. If he were to intrude the English language into his films, universal acceptance would be lost.

With the release of *The Circus* and Chaplin's struggle against talking pictures, columnists and movie critics complained because Charlie Chaplin was so foolhardy as to ignore the wave of sound. Chaplin heard, and he proceeded silently to produce in *City Lights* the story of the Little Fellow in baggy clothes who befriended a blind girl in the big city, found the money for the operation that would restore her sight. The picture ended on a note of sadness. For when she saw her benefactor, the girl was appalled, yet still grateful.

Chaplin left his audience there, to imagine whether the girl would dismiss or encourage the little tramp.

City Lights opened on February 6, 1931, in New York City. Chaplin's one concession to talking pictures was to synchronize sound effects with the film and to add a musical score which he composed himself.

Chaplin *talked* about changing his style. He talked about appearing as Joseph Suss in a sound movie to be made from a successful play on Broadway, which in turn had been based on Lion Feuchtwanger's novel *Power*. This same year Robert Sherwood declared he would cast his literary lot with the novel.

Sherwood had written half a dozen plays by 1931. His first play, produced late in the twenties, was *The Road to Rome*, a historical drama which was written during "odd moments in two weeks." He had also written a novel, *The Virtuous Knight*, on which he had worked for two and a half years. In December, 1931, Sherwood's *Reunion in Vienna* was a Broadway hit, and Sherwood had just returned from Hollywood, where he had worked on three motion pictures.

Sherwood's flirtation with Hollywood was common enough in this period of change. When Wall Street "laid an egg" in 1929, as *Variety* put it, many of the successful people in show business were hurt. Broadway theaters began to go dark. The Shuberts failed. By 1931, some twenty-five thousand actors were out of work.

But as the legitimate theater and vaudeville languished the talking pictures prospered, along with radio since both were forms of cheap, mass entertainment. With the talkies, Hollywood producers turned to the stage for new talent—acting, directing, and writing talent, and for two years the move was westward, to the displeasure of the eastern entertainment kings. In 1930, Gary Cooper starred in *Seven Days Leave*. He had the voice and bearing suitable for a talking-picture star. Norma Shearer starred in *Their Own Desire* that same year. Hollywood changed so much that Abel Green and Joe Laurie, Jr. reported in their book *Show Biz* that in 1931 only three motion picture stars from the old days remained, but that twenty-six new stars had been made, coming from nowhere or from Broadway.

Some established playwrights stuck it out on Broadway. Elmer Rice was one of those. He had been awarded the Pulitzer Prize in

1929 for *Street Scene*. In the fall of 1931 he returned to Broadway, leased the Little Theater, and began to produce his own plays. But Robert Sherwood was not so well established, or so sure. He deplored the absence of interest in romance—*hokum* was another of his words for it—in the theater. He liked the personal freedom of the novel, and the hokum he certainly found in the movies. Sherwood's talent, like the literary and artistic worlds, was in ferment.

Not so with Charlie Chaplin.

With the production of *City Lights* Charlie Chaplin's career reached its zenith.

Chaplin attained the height of his career at the age of forty-two. In 1921 Chaplin had travelled to Europe and had been received with adulation in London and Paris. Now, a decade later, he decided to travel around the world to promote *City Lights*. The trip began as a personal triumph again, and yet also with some unpleasant overtones of bad publicity, even before the *Mauretania* had left New York harbor. Chaplin was popular so he was "good newspaper copy." As a Hollywood citizen he was expected to "cooperate" unfailingly. The rules called for him to be 100 per cent American in thought and action.

That was the problem. Charlie Chaplin loved Hollywood and enjoyed the Southern California climate, but he was not a citizen of the United States. He had said, several times, that he considered himself to be an American, rather than a citizen of his native England, but in recent years, particularly after observing the poverty of many of the people of the rest of the world, Chaplin began to think of himself as an internationalist, whose art transcended homage to any country.

Once asked if he would apply for citizenship in the United States, he replied jokingly that he could apply for citizenship only in Andorra, the smallest and weakest nation in the world. He had no interest in national boundaries and national problems. He was interested only in people, and in their betterment.

There had been unpleasant newspaper incidents before. But as the *Mauretania* pulled out from her pier that early spring day the cameramen aboard began staging their usual stock shots. One asked Chaplin to pose blowing a kiss to the Statue of Liberty. He refused to make an ass of himself and thus began the strengthening of the tale that Chaplin was anti-American.

Having broken one of the unwritten rules of the game, Chaplin continued to break others. He avoided everyone on the crossing and when he arrived in England to be greeted by another hero's-welcome, first he refused to see the press. When he did see reporters, his tongue began to wag.

It was unusual for Charlie Chaplin to talk too much. Through the years of increasing success he had steadfastly refused to talk in public. When asked to speak at banquets, Chaplin always confined himself to a bow and a smile, claiming, if pinned down, that he wanted to maintain the mystery of the character of "the Little Fellow."

But with the coming of talking pictures, Chaplin had been forced to defend his reasons for avoiding talking pictures. In the process of explaining, he began to talk a great deal for Charlie Chaplin.

After his arrival in London, Chaplin told interviewers a story about his creation of the character of the Little Fellow, or Charlie, or Charlot, as the diminutive tramp had become known all over the globe.

"My one object," he said, "was to create an entirely ridiculous figure. It was to be a satire on human habits. Big shoes—well, shoes are an impediment to humanity. The hat represents a convention and the cane gives the figure a mock respectability. The mustache is just a peculiar human vanity. And as for the trousers, they just make the figure utterly ridiculous."

All true, but as *The New York Times* replied editorially when its London correspondent cabled this information home, Charlie Chaplin was growing too large for those oversized breeches, which had, in fact, originally belonged to no less stuffed a personage than Charlie's friend Fatty Arbuckle.

Now *The Times* accused Chaplin of putting on airs. In an editorial addressed to the little graying comedian, *The Times* accused him of straying to the east and into the "mantraps and the vocabularies of the ultraviolet intellectuals and the infra-red aesthetes."

Charlie's words were nonsense, *The Times* said. He had become successful because he was the personification of Puck. He was a funny little man to whom Hottentots and Sorbonne professors could both feel superior. *The Times* reminded Chaplin of his custard pies and his duck waddle, and of the millions who had laughed at him long before he became the idol of the higher critics.

"Keep away from the highbrows," was *The Times*'s advice.

But Chaplin was intrigued by highbrows. They appealed to the ego of a man who had spent his boyhood in the poverty of London slums.

On his first trip home to Europe, Chaplin had met H. G. Wells, and a number of British notables. On the second trip, he met Bernard Shaw, whom he had been afraid to beard before. He showed a new turn of interest by spending the day with Ramsay MacDonald, Britain's Prime Minister, and trying unsuccessfully to engage the Prime Minister in political discourse.

Chaplin was becoming politically conscious in a way that he had never before shown the world and Americans did not like what he said. Then, as earlier, they preferred their clowns to be pure clowns. Fatty Arbuckle had been destroyed because he had a private life which did not fit his public part as funnyman. Rudolph Valentino died young, during the twenties, creating the archetype of Hollywood hero, who disappears romantically from the scene before he can tarnish his own suit of gold. Charlie Chaplin, in the twenties, was Golden Boy. In the early thirties, when he demanded the right to think, talk, and be heard on the condition of the world and his place in it, he found his American audience turning a little bit sour.

At first Charlie attributed this reluctance to accept him as a thinking person to "yellow journalism" and the caperings of a handful of reporters and photographers who would do anything for a story—sometimes even a story that might be more exaggeration than truth. Charlie's seriousness about political matters also stemmed from the respect with which he had begun to be treated abroad.

He was seen, not as a slapstick comic but as a master satirist in England and in France and even in Soviet Russia. Most foreign films were unwelcome in the Russia of the early thirties—but never Chaplin's. It was true that his later films were not being shown, but the Soviet attitude was changing. *Moskauer Rundschau*, the Soviet

German-language newspaper in Moscow, printed an article by Ann Bernfeld in 1930 calling on the Russian movie controllers to import all the recent Chaplin movies. Unlike *The New York Times*, Russia's *Moskauer Rundschau* saw a great social significance in Chaplin's work. The reviewer for that newspaper claimed that the "broad masses" were able to identify themselves with Chaplin's Little Fellow because here was a man using the mask of a great actor to bring change. Chaplin was showing social injustice, exploitation, and oppression of the poor, the starving, and the lowly. That was what gave him his great fame, said the Moscow journal.

If Charlie Chaplin had never before been conscious of this aspect of his films, he became conscious of it now. The idea that he was serving the cause of his own underprivileged boyhood appealed to him. If people outside America insisted on taking him seriously, then how could Americans expect Chaplin not to take himself seriously?

Undoubtedly, then, the 1931–32 world tour increased Charlie Chaplin's interest in politics.

Still, Chaplin responded to his lionization by the English in erratic ways. A Labor member of Parliament asked that Chaplin be given honors by the crown. Labor's *Daily Herald* backed the suggestion. He was a British citizen. It could have been done.

He dined with Viscountess Astor, with Winston Churchill, with Lloyd George. But a few days later, when he went to France, he refused to return to London for a command performance before King George V at a royal charity variety program. He sent a check for $1,000 instead, with the insulting statement that this represented "about as much as I earned in my last two years on the English stage."

Accused by British newspapermen of lack of patriotism, Chaplin remarked that "patriotism is the greatest form of insanity the world ever suffered." It was a telling remark, and it was told from the pulpits and press pits of America. A few days later Chaplin was under attack in New York churches.

At this same time, Chaplin's growingly internationalist political views began to become widely known in America. He talked about abandonment of the gold standard and inauguration of the thirty-hour week, as solutions to world unemployment. He was reported to have sent greetings to the Communist youth of Germany—a report he promptly denied. But Chaplin's denials were not respected. He had gained a reputation as a man who was uncooperative with the press, and had been caught in more than one gross exaggeration or outright untruth.

Most telling with the feminine population of America, however, was the stream of information about Chaplin's romantic life which began to spread to the United States. Already he had achieved a reputation as an incurable romantic, or an indefatigable satyr, depending on the viewer's background. This reputation made him a figure of interest to the sophisticated and to some of the star-struck, but to the ladies of the women's clubs it was disgusting and un-American.

In London Chaplin became interested in an actress named Sari Maritza. In Berlin the girl of the moment was Betty Amann, a German movie actress. He visited Frank Jay Gould, at Nice. Gould exploited the Chaplin visit to help build up his millionaire's playground. Chaplin became enamored of a girl named May Reeves and took her with him to dance the tango and play tennis daily in France, in Algiers, in Morocco, back to London, to St. Moritz, and to Rome.

Chaplin's publicity grew worse as he quarreled with employees about their salaries, failed to keep appointments with dignitaries, and refused to be discreet about his romances. Finally, he fired Carl Robinson, the public relations man who had been with him for sixteen years, and matters grew worse than ever. Chaplin left May Reeves on the dock in Italy, whereupon she contributed to the Chaplin legend by further publicizing the romance and finally writing a book about him.

From Naples, the reduced Chaplin entourage sailed for the Far East. In Japan, he was marked for assassination by the anti-foreign extremists who were then moving to seize control of the Japanese government. The plot was discovered after Premier Inukai was assassinated during Chaplin's visit and Chaplin thereafter received police protection. But this aspect of his trip was not made public until ten years later, although in 1932 it might have helped balance his bad publicity.

From Chaplin's financial standpoint the world tour was an immense success. He also developed an idea for a new movie about the ordinary people of the world, a movie he tentatively called *The Masses*.

Shortly after his return to the United States, Chaplin found a new leading lady, and a new love in the same girl. Aboard the yacht of Joseph Schenck, president of United Artists Corporation, he met Paulette Goddard, a young New York actress who had played a few small movie parts. Shortly afterward they were reported to be "engaged," since it was public information that Miss Goddard was living openly in Chaplin's Beverly Hills mansion. Reporters asked if they were married. Neither Chaplin nor Miss Goddard would give a flat reply.

Yet in spite of this apparent flouting of convention, Chaplin was respected as an artist and because he had made millions, and had kept his money when others had lost theirs. In 1932 the Los Angeles county assessor placed him at the top of the list of Hollywood millionaires, far ahead of the second-ranking Douglas Fairbanks. Kentucky Governor Ruby Laffoon gave him a colonel's commission. *Vanity Fair* called him one of the most important men of his time, ranking him with Edison, Ford, and Marconi. In Budapest a newspaper polled its readers to determine which of seven world figures they would risk their lives to save. Charlie Chaplin won overwhelmingly.

That was 1932.

In 1932 Robert Sherwood was becoming recognized as a major playwright albeit one who had not yet found himself. Brooks Atkinson of *The New York Times* noted that Sherwood's prefaces were often better than the plays they introduced, and far more revealing of the man.

In the preface to his first play, Sherwood had written of what Atkinson termed the "picnic years" of the twenties, in which Sherwood dedicated himself to enjoyment (personally falling $40,000 in debt). A few years later, Sherwood's preface to *The Queen's Husband* was a diatribe against theatrical critics, who pained Sherwood considerably. His preface to *Waterloo Bridge* had given a repertorial picture of London during World War I—what Atkinson called "the detailed sympathy of a fine soldier," culled from Sherwood's memories as a kilted Canadian of the Black Watch.

In the preface to *This Is New York,* Sherwood had attacked the common claim that New York is not America. In the preface to *Reunion in Vienna,* he had devoted himself to exploration of his own misgivings about the world. He found that the more knowledge men acquired, the less confidence he felt about the future of the race. He feared that reason had escaped, that scientific knowledge brought only the triumph of the "tyrannical average."

"Man is afraid of Communism," Sherwood said, "not because he thinks it will be a failure but because he suspects it will be too complete a success."

Atkinson found Sherwood's attitude a common enough one among intellectuals, but Atkinson was dubious of Sherwood's claim that the common man had never before enjoyed the dubious advantage of consciousness, for in the critic's eye the best that could be said in this spring of 1932 was that man had achieved a very muddled consciousness indeed.

Sherwood's reputation was enhanced that year when *Reunion in Vienna* won the Megrue prize of $500, given by the Dramatists' Guild. That year he worked on a new play, *Acropolis,* which opened in London in 1933 in a production by Marc Connelly. *Acropolis* was notable because it convinced the English that an American author could write "beautiful English," puncturing, if only temporarily, the English superiority complex about nearly all things American.

Sherwood returned to the United States in 1933, to work on a movie with George S. Kaufman, a comedy which would star Eddie Cantor, whose popularity was greater than ever. The market for motion-picture comedies was great in 1933—not only comedies, for Hollywood was turning to gangster films, and animated cartoons, too.

Examine this change in taste:

In 1930 the Academy of Motion Picture Arts and Sciences gave its best-picture award to the western, *Cimarron.* The following year the winner was *Grand Hotel,* with a special award for the rising Walt Disney's Mickey Mouse. In 1934 the best-picture award went to *It Happened One Night,* the bedroom comedy which starred Clark

Gable and Claudette Colbert. Comedy was leading, but it was talking comedy.

Charlie Chaplin was talking now, talking economics and politics in public, talking about what he was planning in movies. His tour of the world had sharpened his thinking, and neither the tour nor his troubles with the press had yet embittered him.

Chaplin approved of Franklin Roosevelt and the New Deal. In memoirs he wrote that year for the *Woman's Home Companion* Chaplin praised his adopted country. "In America," he wrote, "lies the hope of the whole world." Later he was to say that since Roosevelt there had not been any more forgotten little men, and that for this reason he eventually abandoned the Little Fellow. But in 1934 Chaplin was not ready to give up the character of the down-at-the-heels and gentle little man who was so sorely buffeted by a harsh society. He was determined to accomplish something new with the character.

For various reasons, the name *The Masses* was dropped and the film to be produced became *Modern Times,* the story of the gamin and the little tramp in a frightening impersonal world of industry from which they escaped finally, after he had been buffeted by an assembly line and forced into a mechanical feeding device.

Chaplin's talking, in Europe and America, had results. When the movie was released, the critics approached *Modern Times* with a view to its social significance. Critics of the right found Chaplin turning left, particularly in a scene in which the Little Fellow led a mob (by mistake) carrying the red flag of revolution (or danger, as this one was). Critics of the left were not aroused: when shown in Moscow, *Modern Times* provoked no social criticism.

The comment in America was based more on what the critics knew of Chaplin and his personal politics than on what they saw on the screen. Chaplin said he had no political aims, that his first consideration was to entertain, and that he had simply put his Charlie into the circumstances of the mid-1930's. The result, if viewed calmly, was a Chaplin protest against mechanization of the individual—which did not square at all with the growing feeling that Chaplin was a "parlor pink."

Modern Times was another box-office success. It earned nearly two million dollars in the United States, and more abroad. Yet its earnings did not please Charlie Chaplin, who had expected far more from the American market despite the depression and the recession that engulfed the nation. He grew resentful, because he believed the critics had damned him with faint praise.

One development in modern film-making seems completely to have escaped Chaplin. Although he was the idol of the 1920's, he made so few pictures in the late years of that decade and in the 1930's that he was largely forgotten by one generation of moviegoers and unknown to the next.

A few years later, Dr. George Gallup was to discover what some moviemakers had known instinctively and practiced during the 1930's —that a star's popularity grew with the number of pictures in which he appeared, and that the best and quickest road to oblivion was to remain off the screen. This was the antithesis of Chaplin's careful planning and selection of subject, but it was one of the great truths of the movie world. Clark Gable, Joan Crawford, Robert Montgomery, and Katharine Hepburn became great stars and remained stars because they were heavily exposed—over-exposed, Chaplin might say.

Hollywood learned some expensive lessons in the first four years that followed the Wall Street crash. The film-makers discovered that it was not enough to import talents wholesale from Broadway. Too often the talents were not readily convertible. The demands of the growing movie market were very great, but the differences in movie and stage techniques were such that Broadway could not supply the Hollywood demand.

Robert Sherwood was one of the few writers who seemed at home in many fields, in criticism, in playwrighting, in movie scenarios, and in serious fiction. His lights, like Broadway's, were brightening. Theater receipts had risen by 60 per cent over the near-disastrous 1933. Playwrights who were concerned with the social scene were welcomed by producers. Sherwood was one of these. He was finding that he had something to say, and that he wanted to say it beneath the proscenium arch.

In 1935, Sherwood's *Petrified Forest* was so great a success that it drove him back to Europe. On his departure, he told reporters, perhaps unwittingly, how much his attitude had changed in three years.

He was happy with his success, he said, but he had to get away from Broadway to write more plays. Not novels. Not movies. Plays.

A changed attitude was noticeable in America the following year. Robert Sherwood won the Pulitzer Prize of 1936 for drama, for *Idiot's Delight*, an attack on militaristic nationalism.

At least one dramatic critic, Clayton Hamilton, deplored the choice because the Pulitzer Prize was to be awarded to a play that dealt with American life. Hamilton saw no connection between Europe's troubles and America. *Idiot's Delight* was set in Italy, against a backdrop of European politics and war threats. Brooks Atkinson, however, continued to exhibit admiration for the growth of Sherwood as a playwright. In the absence of detailed prefaces to *Idiot's Delight* and *The Petrified Forest*, Atkinson noted that Sherwood was becoming more sure of his field and no longer needed to explain himself in another literary form—the prefatory essay.

That was 1936.

In 1936 it was also apparent that Sherwood had more to say than in the past, and if in saying much the same things that Charlie Chaplin was saying, Sherwood did not arouse the same degree of antagonism, the reasons lay in the great differences in personality.

Intensity—the word described Chaplin. While the tall, slow-speaking Sherwood expressed himself as intensely as Chaplin ever did, there was a difference. Sherwood was moving with the times. Chaplin was moving at his own pace, far ahead of America in some ways, far behind in others.

And—how was America moving?

In 1934 playwright Elmer Rice had attempted to set up as an independent producer. He had rented the Belasco Theater and had staged two plays—plays of protest, Burns Mantle termed them—one about Nazi Germany and the second about an affair between a young Russian Communist and a daughter of capitalism.

Both plays failed, the first because Rice's intense anti-Naziism permeated the play, and the second because few people seemed to care about the social conflicts between Communist and capitalist theory, at least as he portrayed them.

The year 1936 brought a major development in the world of theater: Harry Hopkins gave life to a WPA Federal Theater Project.

Congress appropriated $7,000,000 for theater performance, and soon nine thousand people in twenty states were employed in the Federal Theater.

Elmer Rice was aroused. His answer to an inner demand for positive action in a time of crisis was to accept a post as regional director in New York for the Federal Theater project. But even here he was to be frustrated.

The Federal Theater project introduced a new note: documentary plays which were enacted by a troupe called the *Living Newspaper*. Rice prepared enthusiastically for the first production in New York, a dramatization of the Ethiopian crisis and war. This idea, it seemed to WPA officers in Washington, held unpleasant overtones of meddling in foreign affairs, and Rice was squelched. He fought back, but was not satisfied. He quit the project.

Brooks Atkinson saw equal indignation fermenting in Robert Sherwood when he noted that "there is more to Robert Sherwood than *Idiot's Delight*." There was. Sherwood was observing world affairs, and becoming preoccupied with the New Deal and with the threat to freedom posed by the dictators.

One of Chaplin's troubles was that Hollywood was far slower than Broadway to respond to the pressures of world affairs. Foreign affairs to the Hollywood moguls meant the incursions of foreign pictures on the American market. The answer of the American studios was less to increase the intellectual content of their movies, and more to lavish huge sums of money on production of movies.

That was one trend Hollywood could be certain that Charlie Chaplin would not join. He was out of step with Hollywood.

And where was Chaplin heading in 1937? No one seemed to know. Chaplin announced that he would never again appear on the screen in the silent part of the Little Fellow. The press interpreted his feeling as irritation at the poor showing of *Modern Times*, but indicated that Chaplin finally had realized he could not back the tide of the "talkies." Also, they said, the trend in comedy had changed. It had—but only superficially. The Roosevelt Era was the heyday of the partnership comics. Stanley Laurel and Oliver Hardy, who had not achieved stardom as individuals, became stars when they teamed together and left audiences laughing across the country. The Marx

Brothers combined slapstick, vaudeville, and some old silent techniques to win fortune. Edmund Lowe and Victor McLaglen combined talents to play in a new kind of comedy, a boisterous combination of slapstick and derring-do. The Ritz Brothers and the Three Stooges brought comedy to new depths, proving once again Mack Sennett's contention of twenty years before that the American public loved pratfalls and pie-throwing, with or without sound.

So here, a bit past mid-decade the theater changed. The films changed. Sherwood changed. Chaplin changed, too. He stopped being a comedian. He became a bitter satirist.

Chaplin's immediate change was a change of method, not of conviction. *The New York Times* in 1937 had called him "a producer with certain politico-sociological messages to deliver," but it was not until 1939 that Chaplin was prepared to deliver such a message on the screen.

After Adolf Hitler conquered Germany, a number of people remarked on the similarity in appearance of Chaplin's Little Fellow —with the licorice-stick mustache—and the dictator of Germany. In 1937 a bit of nostalgia in a New York newspaper editorial column ended on the note that it was ironical that the mustached face of Hitler would be the only living reminder of the little clown. But in 1939, Chaplin made sure that this would not be the case. He began work on the script of an out-and-out satirical film, *The Great Dictator*.

Chaplin kept his plans locked up in the confines of his studio at Sunset Boulevard and La Brea Avenue in Los Angeles where he had been making pictures since 1918. But the secret was out before the script was begun. In December, 1938, the German press attacked Chaplin and, in the same breath, Secretary of the Interior Harold Ickes for allowing Chaplin to project a film that the Germans knew could not but be critical and derisive of the Third Reich. Germany's placement of responsibility on Ickes gave a clear picture of Nazi minds at work. In Germany the interior ministry's police held the power of life and death over the inmates.

There was other criticism, some of it from Hollywood itself, where controversial films were greeted with the enthusiasm usually reserved for an infectious disease.

Chaplin was also attacked by ardent American neutralists who

wanted no involvement in European affairs. In August, 1939, the Soviet Union and Hitler Germany signed their celebrated non-aggression
pact, which freed Hitler to go to war with Poland the next month.
The odor of war had been hanging in the air since the Munich default of the western democracies the year before. On La Brea Avenue
there was a moment of indecision, perhaps prompted by the realization that the international situation had made a spoof on dictators
far more dangerous than it would have been a year before. But when
war came (and the outright Soviet sympathizers in America shushed
their criticisms of Hitler) Chaplin moved ahead with his first truly
talking picture.

The Great Dictator was completed in the fall of 1940 and released almost immediately to linger hesitatingly before the public for
a time, and then to gain momentum as more Americans turned from
neutralism to active antipathy to the dictators. Other anti-Axis films
began to appear—but they came a year later than Chaplin's.

Chaplin played a dual role in this film—the part of the musta-
chioed dictator of Tomania, and the part of a little Jewish barber who
had many of the mannerisms of the Little Fellow, yet was not the
same. Paulette Goddard played the part of Hannah, the Jewish girl
the barber loved. And Jack Oakie delivered a supermaniac performance as Napaloni, dictator of Bacteria.

Charlie Chaplin retained as much of the old silent technique as
possible in his first talking picture. His Jewish barber spoke distinctly
and in short syllables, using words and gestures that could scarcely be
misunderstood anywhere. His dictator spoke mostly in shouts and
double-talk, which also could not be misunderstood even if it could
not be translated into any language.

The spoof of Hitler and Mussolini was understandable, if not
greeted warmly by those in America who still believed war could be
avoided without impairment of "the American way of life." But
Chaplin devoted the last six minutes of the film to a message. If he
had never before combined obvious propaganda and entertainment,
he offered this time an unalloyed statement of his beliefs. For a man
who had remained silent for so many years he seemed exceedingly
loquacious.

In the world, Chaplin said, there was room for everyone, and the world could provide for everyone, except that mankind had lost the way. Greed had poisoned men's souls. Machinery had given want, rather than abundance. Men thought too much and felt too little.

Charlie Chaplin then called on mankind to unite, to fight to free the world, to do away with national barriers, to do away with greed and hate and intolerance. He asked that men give jobs to youth and security to the old, that they fight for a world of science where progress would lead to the happiness of all. Above all, he called for the union of mankind.

This speech could scarcely be viewed as Communist propaganda, since Joseph Stalin at that point was allied with Adolf Hitler. Chaplin caused uneasiness, however, because his words were militant and because he presented facts and recalled ideals that pragmatic Americans did not at that moment want to consider or recall.

Hollywood columnist Sheilah Graham reported that Chaplin expected to win an Academy Award for *The Great Dictator,* and planned then to refuse it. Perhaps he did expect to win although he had never shown much regard for the system of awards in Hollywood. Perhaps Chaplin was eliminated from consideration because he was under a strange designation by the United States Department of State as "prematurely anti-Fascist"—which meant that he joined those who opposed Fascism before the United States government decided to do so.

In the ten years past, Charles Chaplin had reached the height of his movie career. He had seen that film career threatened by a peculiarly American custom of disallowing a public figure any private life. He had been involved in argument and litigation, much of it of his own choosing. And his actions and his attitudes were unique. He did not accept conventional morality, patriotism, or politics. For this he was not forgiven, particularly by the press.

And whither the rest of Hollywood? During the agonizing period in which Charles Chaplin staked his reputation and much of his fortune on *The Great Dictator,* how were the important film producers occupied?

For one thing the Three Stooges went to Europe in the summer of 1939. A critic promptly noted that Europe could now have something to worry about. *The Birth of a Nation,* D. W. Griffiths's three-hour epic on Reconstruction, produced in 1915, was banned in Milwaukee. It was "controversial."

Perhaps Milwaukee's action showed why Samuel Goldwyn was turning his efforts to movies like *Wuthering Heights*. That picture earned a fortune and sold more copies of Emily Bronte's book in the three weeks after the film was released than the book had sold in any five-year period since original English publication in 1846.

And one studio, which was preparing a series of short subjects based on the Ten Commandments, found itself stumped in 1939 about how to treat with the Seventh Commandment. A bright young studio executive suggested that they might solve the problem by showing the adulteration of foods. And for a day or two, the studio executives seriously considered the idea.

The change in Robert Sherwood was not as obvious. Critic Richard Watts was later to recall that one of the most interesting qualities he found in Sherwood was the playwright's way of rolling with the times, with complete sincerity. Occasionally, Watts said, Sherwood was a trifle ahead of his times, but more often right with them.

"The pacifism of *Idiot's Delight* changed to the belligerence of *There Shall Be No Night*, and, when the latter was done in London after the Nazi-Soviet split, he changed the scene from Finland to Greece."

Sherwood was notable, now, for the humanitarianism which had led him to give away most of the royalties from his plays to such causes as those of the Red Cross and Canadian veterans' relief.

In 1938 Sherwood joined with Elmer Rice, Maxwell Anderson, S. N. Behrman, and Sidney Howard to form the Playwrights' Producing Company. The next year, Sherwood and Anderson joined Rice in public condemnations of Adolf Hitler and Naziism. In curtain speeches at special performances of their two new plays, both spoke out.

Sherwood's play was *Abe Lincoln in Illinois*. Again it won him the Pulitzer Prize for drama. It also showed his deepening interest and sense of participation in public affairs.

Early in 1939, Sherwood wanted escape from the burden of the world. He wanted to write a romantic comedy. But so deeply did he feel about the state of the post-Munich world that he could not write comedy as long as he read the daily newspapers. He embarked on a cruise of the West Indies and Latin America, hoping, in a month's respite, to forget the cares of the world. He returned able to state only that he belonged to a species which "is hurtling toward self-destruction."

Would he write comedy? the reporters asked.

It seemed, Sherwood said, that there could be no better title for a current play than S. N. Behrman's *No Time for Comedy*.

In 1939 Sherwood was elected president of the American National Theater and Academy. It was a high honor. The next year, he presented his most stirring play—*There Shall Be No Night*. In this drama, Sherwood returned again to the preface, this time to detail his own political awakening. Once he had sympathized with Soviet Russia, as did Charlie Chaplin. But two events convinced Sherwood that he must take a stand against all totalitarian government: first, a speech in October, 1939, in which Colonel Charles A. Lindbergh convinced Sherwood that "Hitlerism was already powerfully and persuasively represented in our own midst"; second, the Soviet invasion of Finland.

The play, as it emerged from Sherwood's worryings, reflected a new philosophy, a disgust with the mechanistic defenses of man; with man's attempts to surround himself with Maginot lines and Mannerheim lines, or their equivalents in neutrality in the face of evil.

There Shall Be No Night was a classic piece of propaganda for intervention by the United States in the war in Europe. At first the play was greeted with the same outcries and outrage which had greeted Chaplin's film. The *Daily Worker* assailed Sherwood as an enemy of the people. The Christian Front, of the right wing, said Sherwood was a Communist. Raymond Clapper, the Scripps-Howard columnist, noted calmly enough that Sherwood's play was filled with rank inflammation, calculated to press America toward war.

Outside the theater Sherwood was as outspoken and more rasping than in. He spoke of a "conspiracy of silence" which kept Americans from learning the truths about the world. He expressed acute distaste for the "peace hysteria" which swept America, driving out concern for men of good will elsewhere, even concern for America's ultimate safety. He referred to Congress as a "mass of Chamberlains."

So there, for a moment at the end of the decade, Charles Chaplin and Robert Sherwood stood at the same crossroads. The tall Harvard graduate and the diminutive London slum boy had come to the same spot at almost the same time, having travelled along the most dissimilar paths. The nation was not far behind them.

DEATH IN A MARBLE HALL

CHAPTER TWELVE

DURING THE GREAT DEPRESSION in America in the 1930's the word dictator lost its frightening sound. The harsh word circulated freely in parlors and public halls because dictators had established power and prestige in Europe and in Latin America.

Always before in the United States the term had been greeted with distaste, when not with worry, contempt, and derision. It was to the point in the 1930's that many Americans truly believed American capitalism had failed. Some men, and women, too, after the winter of 1930–1931 began to believe that a dictator might solve our American problems. Those who wondered pointed first to the course of affairs in Italy, where the onetime socialist Benito Mussolini had brought a nation out of poverty by imposing totalitarianism. ("He made the trains run on time.")

After 1933 some began to point to Nazi Germany where Hitler, too, was "getting things done."

It was three long years before any significant number of Americans became sickened by Hitlerism and Fascism. It took far longer for the majority of people in the country to form a general opinion.

In 1933, one American made a flat public statement calling for totalitarianism.

"What this country needs is a dictator," said Huey Pierce Long, the junior United States senator from Louisiana, in a meeting with the press in the Hotel New Yorker on January 29, 1933. Anyone who doubted that he meant it did not know their man—the Kingfish of Louisiana.

Senator Long seemed to be in a position to know. He was and for three years had been absolute ruler of the sovereign state of Louisiana. His enemies were quelled, if not silenced. He collected 5 per cent of the pay of every appointee as tribute for the Long machine's political fund.

In January, 1932, Long had taken his seat as United States senator, but during that year he spent more than half his time in Baton

Rouge and in New Orleans, making sure that his hand-picked governor and his hand-picked legislators did his bidding.

Had the newly elected Franklin Delano Roosevelt chosen to seize power as a dictator in 1933, he most certainly would have received the support of Senator Huey Long—had he been willing to give Long sufficient promise and sufficient importance within the regime. In January, 1933, Huey Long, on a local scale, was a successful, functioning dictator in the United States of America. He could see no reason why what had worked in his state should not work for the rest of the nation.

It seemed strange to those trained in the democratic processes, but Huey Long's dictatorship had brought a veneer of prosperity to Louisiana which outshone the rest of the South. Other southern states were in serious trouble in 1932 and 1933. Louisiana was embarked on a mighty program of road-building and building construction. If, as Long's opponents charged, the senator was stealing the state blind, and was establishing a burden of debt which would eventually threaten the Louisiana economy, still the general public did not care.

Huey Long had brought free schoolbooks to Louisiana when children in other states still bought their own books. Children in Louisiana's parochial schools were treated just as those in public schools. The new roads and new buildings brought new trade and new businesses. Had Texas and other southern states seen fit to cooperate, Huey Long's unorthodox solution to the cotton program (a quota-support plan) might have solved a part of the southern agricultural problem. But the other southern states looked upon Huey as a clown and a scoundrel and would have no part of his brand of totalitarianism or economics.

Long had grown up in Winn Parish in northwestern Louisiana, a bare, poor land in which the Long family was comparatively well off. In his second decade Huey became a printer, and later he was to declare that the linotype machine had thrown him out of the newspaper printing business and into politics. Later he became a travelling salesman for a cottonseed cooking oil known as Cottolene. Then he decided to become a lawyer, and managed to squeeze his way into the University of Oklahoma, for a year.

He studied law for one year at Tulane University in New Orleans.

Then he passed the bar examination. He completed the display of character and brains often overlooked by later critics, who called Huey Long a stupid, bumbling clown.

He was a lawyer. He was twenty-one years old.

Long entered politics as an unpaid lobbyist for workmen seeking an increase in state funds for workmen's compensation. After World War I (in which he did not fight) he ran for elective office as a railroad commissioner. On the railroad commission he made his name by declaring war on the Standard Oil Company, then extending his war to all the big corporations which had for so many years kept Louisiana political control tucked in their pockets.

In 1924, Huey Long ran for governor, and was defeated. In 1928 he ran, and was elected. In 1929 and 1930 he accomplished a great deal by any standards. He tore down the governor's mansion, and built a new one modelled on the White House. He carried his war against the Standard Oil Company. He declared war on the city government of New Orleans, and called out the national guard so many times to enforce his will that guardsmen sometimes said guard barracks ought to be equipped with slide poles like those in firehouses.

He was accused of lobbying on the floor of the legislature (which he most certainly did) and of trying to hire a man to assassinate a legislator (which he probably did). The legislature voted to impeach him in 1929, on charges that included bribery, malfeasance, and misfeasance (although never nonfeasance), subornation of murder, carrying concealed weapons, theft of state funds, and other wrongs—which added up to absolute dictation of the affairs of Louisiana.

Huey Long was frightened enough by the proceedings that he persuaded fifteen senators to vote against conviction promising them rewards known only among themselves and to God. That was enough to block the impeachment. Then he set to work to eliminate his enemies from public office.

For a time he removed the governor's office to New Orleans. Then he moved it back to Baton Rouge. He acquired a reputation as a playboy. He received delegations of visitors in a flowered dressing gown. He received a Major General of the U.S. Army in his underwear. He received lesser dignitaries in nothing at all. He created an international incident by receiving the commander of the German cruiser

Emden in green silk pajamas. He was called thief, buffoon, brigand, demagogue, and outlaw by people who were willing to risk libel suits to prove their charges. He was challenged to duels and to fistfights—challenges he refused. His curly auburn hair, his bulbous, squashed nose, his red face and big ears and big grin became known across the whole of America as he fought with anyone and everyone who moved into his way.

Long was a clown. He inspired a war in the South; the subject was corn pone and potlikker, that famous juice of boiled vegetables which rouses emotion only in the American South. Governor Long claimed that corn pone was made to be dunked in potlikker, never to be crumbled into it and then spooned up. Other southerners, inside and outside Louisiana, took issue with him in what was probably the most lighthearted and insignificant debate in the history of America. Even New York Governor Franklin Roosevelt, a known crumbler, entered the fray by writing a letter to the editor of a Georgia newspaper during one of his stays at his Warm Springs hideaway.

Long also proposed to enact a federal law making it mandatory that the jew's harp be played with outward instead of inward strokes. By this time—1931—he had been elected senator although he hung onto his job as governor, and continued to serve as governor, leaving the senate seat vacant in Washington, until he could elect his own man to succeed him, because he was fearful that Lieutenant Governor Paul Cyr, a political enemy, would deprive him of control of the state.

It is doubtful if these antics and outright illegal moves could have been accomplished in any other state at that time—save perhaps Mississippi—but they were accomplished in Louisiana, by a man who understood the roots of power. He gave the white voters bread and circuses. If he was the circus himself, so much the better, for he had absolute control of the timing and the action.

He built a super-highway from New Orleans to Baton Rouge, at a time when other states could not be persuaded to build necessary roads. He secured a seven million dollar bond issue to build a highway and bridge across the Mississippi River, thus strengthening New Orleans' position as the foremost trading port of the South.

In 1931, Long was engaged in a bitter dispute with Governor Sterling and the Texas legislature over his cotton plan. Texans, thoroughly angry with some of the words which had been exchanged, called Long "a consummate liar" and dared him to come to Texas.

In all the fireworks, little attention was given to the action of President Hoover, who had proposed a solution to the cotton surplus that was not so much different from Huey Long's. Governor Long wanted all the southern cotton producing states to agree not to plant that coming year, a demand that grew insistent in the fall of 1931 when the price of cotton dropped to five cents a pound. Huey Long's plan was lost in the shouting that greeted it, but Herbert Hoover sent a proposal to the Federal Farm Board, providing that the government should buy eight million bales of cotton that year, and withhold it from the market for a year, if the farmers would agree to refrain from planting in 1932. The plan was supported by southern newspaper editors, bankers, and economists. But it, too, failed. There was too much misery, there were too many problems facing the nation at that time for much interest to be aroused outside the South.

In other states of the South, in 1931, visitors saw national guardsmen called out time and again. In Kentucky the guard was called into the coal fields to protect the mines from strikers. In Texas and Oklahoma guardsmen sat atop padlocked oil wells, protecting them. Even in Iowa, guardsmen were called out to enforce laws ordering inoculation of cattle against hoof and mouth disease. North, south, west, the nation's leaders were quick to call for military action to quell any suggestion of uprising or revolt. The fear of rebellion was general, if underlying, and in this atmosphere it was not hard for Huey Long's almost constant use of the national guard for his purposes to pass relatively unremarked, or for his dictatorial methods to arouse debate and interest rather than condemnation.

Huey Long noticed these signs, and in 1931 he was ready to move into the national political scene—waiting only until the following January when he was able to mousetrap Lieutenant Governor Cyr into vacating the lieutenant governorship by declaring himself governor. Huey Long then declared the lieutenant governorship open, put in his own man, and successfully removed Cyr from the field of political action.

When Huey Long moved to Washington, he took with him a program for the national economy. He called it Share the Wealth.

Essentially, Huey Long's program called for government seizure of most of the capital assets of the very rich, and division of those assets into shares for the poor. Over a period of time he developed several formulas. One called for a limit of a million dollars on the income of any individual, and a limit of five million dollars on assets held by any person. On the other side, he promised a minimum income of $2,500 to every poor person and the endowment of $5,000 in assets to everyone.

This was a revolutionary idea, and, of course, it frightened the wealthy citizens of America and, indeed, all the advocates of capitalism. Nonetheless, Huey Long's utterances were greeted with a great deal of sober consideration by a number of Americans for no one could say for sure what would replace the old economic system.

From the moment that Huey Long appeared to take his seat in the United States Senate he made of himself both a spectacle and a controversial national figure. He opened his Senate career by insulting the senior senator from Louisiana, and on his first day in the Senate he broke most of the rules, talking, waving his arms, and showing none of the humility new senators are supposed to display before their senior colleagues.

Huey Long called himself the Kingfish, long before he ever entered the United States Senate. He tried, briefly, to make a show of humility, in an interview with a reporter before he took his seat. But the Kingfish was not competent at displaying humility. He entered the Senate chamber smoking a cigar. After a few moments, he was embracing Senator Borah, jabbing his finger at Senator Watson of Indiana, and talking excitedly to Senator Robinson of Arkansas. A newspaperman predicted that "Huey would not remain a minnow long." He would become a shark or a whale in short order.

He became neither, but a barracuda, a fish who swam by himself in the treacherous seas of the Senate, swirling by his lesser contemporaries, snapping viciously at any who got in his way.

In the beginning, Huey Long thought Senator Robinson might be the next Presidential candidate of the Democratic party. By the time he reached Chicago in the summer of 1932, however, Senator Long had quarreled with Senator Robinson. Once Huey Long had dismissed Franklin Roosevelt with a wave of his hand, but in Chicago's heady atmosphere, he determined that he would support Roosevelt, and having done so, forever after took credit for Roosevelt's nomination.

The Roosevelt Democrats of the summer of 1932 were not inclined to take Huey Long very seriously. Before the nomination, Long called Roosevelt in Albany and advised him to come out for the soldier's bonus. Roosevelt refused. Huey made dire predictions, but offered to campaign for Roosevelt. James A. Farley, who underestimated Long, sent him to Nebraska and the Dakotas, firmly Republican areas where he could do little harm. Huey Long impressed the people of the Middle West, and when Nebraska and the Dakotas went Democratic in the election—who was to say how much of the credit should belong to the senator from Louisiana? He said it all belonged to him. And whether it did or not, the Roosevelt political machine then developed a healthy respect for Huey Long which it was never to lose.

When the Roosevelt administration came to Washington in March, 1933, Huey Long had aligned himself squarely with the new President. Within thirty days they had parted forever, some said over matters of policy, a view Huey Long encouraged; others said because Huey Long wanted to be Kingfish of all the land.

In the first few months of that year, Huey Long had announced to the world his plan for the salvation of America. It came about during the debate on the banking and currency bill sponsored by Senator Carter Glass, the grand old man of the Democratic side of the Senate. Huey Long filibustered—in all he talked for nearly a month against the Glass bill, which he said would do nothing but compound the nation's problems. What was needed, said the Kingfish, was a *real* program. And what was that? asked reporters.

Then the Kingfish grinned, wriggled his shoulders, and began to talk.

Inflate the currency, he said. Inflate it up to the point of 1926, so prices would hit that level again.

Stop industrial and agricultural production until all the surpluses were used up.

And how, then, would farmers and workers and white-collar people support themselves?

Put them to work on the public payroll, the Kingfish said. For that purpose he would demand a ten billion dollar bond issue, to build roads across the country—four-lane super-highways like his Baton Rouge road; to build bridges, like his auto and railroad bridge across the Mississippi; to build public buildings, like his new thirty-four-storey capitol at Baton Rouge.

"Decentralize the wealth," the Kingfish said. Cut inheritances down to a million dollars per person.

Carter Glass and a number of other conservatives in the Senate thought at first that Huey Long was crazy. Then they decided he was dangerous. Finally they came to the conclusion that he was both crazy and dangerous.

By the middle of March, 1933, Long's persistent efforts to destroy the Glass banking bill had so annoyed the old Virginia senator that he had to be restrained by Senator Robinson from striking Long during an altercation in the Senate cloakroom.

Long thrived on such opposition. Before the year was out, he had antagonized nearly every member of the Senate. The one senator who seemed to be able to exercize any influence at all on Huey Long was Senator Borah of Idaho, the maverick Republican, who shared Huey Long's isolationist views, and who had proved himself radical enough during the Progressive years to appeal to Senator Long. When Huey Long was obstructing the Senate's conduct of business to the point of absolute distraction and near chaos, Senator Borah would be called in by an embarrassed Democratic majority to try to talk sense into the Kingfishian head.

Yet even as he courted dislike and the gibes of others, Huey Long did not falter on his chosen route. In the fall of 1933, he brought forth his program for Share the Wealth in a book published in New Orleans: *Every Man a King*. The New York newspapers dismissed it quickly (the powerful *New York Times* book section included it in a column devoted to "miscellaneous brief reviews"). But others in the nation paid Huey Long's program greater heed. Unlike *The Times*'s book review they were not concerned that the senator broke nearly every rule of English grammar and good usage. They were concerned about the content, not the form of Senator Long's plan for prosperity.

When the American banking system faltered Huey Long had his

own method of shoring up the banks of Louisiana. George W. Healy, Jr., a later editor of the New Orleans *Times-Picayune*, recalled a widely circulated story that when one bank was threatened, Long walked into the lobby, flourished some large-denomination currency, walked to a teller's window, and deposited the cash. After the bank closed for the afternoon, Long returned by the back door and picked up his money.

Another story said that when one New Orleans bank seemed certain to fail, Huey Long appeared at the bank the first thing in the morning. One depositor, whom he knew, came in to withdraw several thousand dollars. Long announced that he was withdrawing $265,000 of the state's money if that were so. That would take all the bank's resources, the man's check would not be honored, the bank would fail, and the man would lose his money. How did he like that?

The depositor took his check and went away.

People listened when Huey Long spoke.

By far the most important of those who listened when Huey Long spoke and read what Huey Long wrote was Charles Edward Coughlin, a Catholic priest. Father Coughlin, priest at the Shrine of the Little Flower in Royal Oak on the outskirts of Detroit, was a zealot who had early espoused the cause of inflationism and social justice. Father Coughlin might have gone into political life had he not chosen the church. Indeed, in the early years of the 1930's it appeared that he was in political life although he had chosen to become a priest. Disgusted with the plight of the common man, particularly the status of the automotive workers who depended on prosperity for food and lodging in the one-industry city of Detroit, Father Coughlin had first lashed out from the pulpit. Then, given a chance to appear on radio, Father Coughlin soon became the most powerful commentator in the land, himself a subject of fierce debate in living room and newly opened beer parlor.

Father Coughlin began his career on radio as an ardent follower of Franklin Roosevelt's New Deal. But as he gained influence, the Radio Priest became independent. When he found the New Deal straying from the path he felt it must follow, Father Coughlin did not hesitate to criticize F.D.R. in sharp, and sometimes inflammatory terms.

In 1933, the New Deal enjoyed its brief honeymoon with nearly all voters and political forces. Then the Liberty League raised its head, that Liberty League of castoff Democrats, capitalists, and disgruntled Republicans, led by Al Smith and pushed by John J. Raskob, unfrocked chairman of the Democratic National Committee. At the end of December, 1933, an outraged, persuasive Father Coughlin told his radio audience that the League and other advocates of plutocracy were plotting against the social revolution brought about by Roosevelt's New Deal. But a few months later, Father Coughlin had decided that Roosevelt had deserted social justice and that the only way forward led through the forest of state capitalism.

Private capitalism, he said, was a Siamese twin, with socialism as its brother. State capitalism, said Father Coughlin early in 1934, was the only way forward. Capitalism was doomed, and further, it was not even worth trying to save, so badly had it failed the people.

These were harsh words, but the times were harsher. To judge the impact of leaders on the American scene, a radio commentator named Harlan Eugene Read of station WOR in New York City set out to discover which public figures were most important in America that winter. Read was wise enough to except Franklin Roosevelt from the start, as did Elsa Maxwell in her "pet-hate" costume parties, for it was obvious to all students of public as well as social affairs that if one man dominated this period it was the new, experimenting, cigarette-smoking, jaunty President of the United States.

Father Coughlin ran away with Harlan Eugene Read's poll. He polled 11,700 of 22,000 votes, more than 50 per cent, and he led his nearest opponent, General Hugh S. Johnson, head of the NRA, by 8,000 votes. They loved Father Coughlin in New York and in six hundred other cities in twenty-six states, for his attack on the bankers, for his support of Roosevelt, and for his defense of the New Deal.

Yet even as such results came in, Father Coughlin was deserting the New Deal fold. It was February, 1934. At that same time, another minister of the Gospel—the Rev. Gerald L. K. Smith—was engaged in actions which would have an impact on the American scene in the months to come. Smith, a heavy-set, handsome man, held a church in Shreveport, Louisiana, although he was not a southerner but a mid-westerner, a fifth-generation minister of a sect known as the

Disciples of Christ. After a trip to the 1932 Olympic Games, Smith had come into close contact with Huey Long, and had visited him in Washington a number of times. By 1934 his link with Long was public knowledge, his congregation did not like it, and he left Shreveport to undertake organization of the Share the Wealth movement which Huey Long was now prepared to launch as a national project.

The disgust and hatred of Huey Long exhibited by the press both in the big cities and in his native Louisiana was no indication of Long's true strength, nor did Huey Long worry about the press, except at one time to try to impose a tax on Louisiana newspapers, and to fight continually with the editors and publishers of the powerful press in New Orleans.

Sometimes, as in 1934, when he was struck in the face during an altercation at the fashionable Sands Point beach club in Long Island, the press tried to make Long seem to be a cowardly and disreputable figure. Disreputable he was, and always Huey Long eschewed physical combat. But he was more intelligent, more courageous, more dangerous than nearly any of his enemies gave him credit for being.

Among those enemies, the most dangerous to Long were those he had earned in the New Deal administration. For as 1934 began, Huey Long had struck out at the New Deal vigorously. Consequently, Harry Hopkins had ordered his WPA employees to keep hands out of Louisiana projects, and Harold Ickes had begun to hold up on PWA projects for the Bayou State. And worst of all, from Long's point of view, the federal government began a cautious, quiet, painstaking investigation of the tax facts of the life of Huey Long and his lieutenants. If they could find him in violation of the law, the federal authorities would do their very best to destroy this enemy of the New Deal, send him to prison, force him out of office—or at least bring him to his knees.

February, 1934, was the month in which Share the Wealth was launched as a national enterprise. The Rev. Smith undertook management of this campaign for Huey Long. "We're getting twenty thousand new members a day," he cried, when asked about the influence of the organization. When they were ready, Huey and his followers would act, Gerald Smith said.

Were those hollow words, or did Huey Long truly have hopes of taking power in the United States through a third-party movement? He had such hopes—none of his biographers have denied it and several of them have shown how even in his earliest days as governor of Louisiana he announced that he intended to take control of the United States, one day. When he left Baton Rouge for Washington, he said he was now going to "help the people of the rest of the nation." If the New York newspapers saw him acting "with all the effrontery of a holdup man" as one writer said, still in two short years on the national scene, Huey Long had made himself well known to millions.

Huey Long's vulgarity appealed to many Americans. In debate with Norman Thomas, on what was known as Huey Long's "seven point plan to soak the rich," Thomas held that capitalism was doomed. Huey Long drawled that under Socialism a man would not even own his garters. The public loved it.

The public also noted that Louisiana seemed very prosperous in 1934, compared to most of the rest of the nation. Part of the reason was the army air force construction of the huge Barksdale airfield outside Shreveport, a facility which occupied 22,000 acres and meant the construction of several hundred buildings. Besides, a new oil field had been discovered in East Texas, Shreveport's banks and stores were booming, and Huey Long's New Orleans-Mississippi bridge was paying off in prosperity for the whole state.

In the fall of 1934 two distinct forces began to converge on the political affairs of Huey Long. The intensive Treasury Department investigation of Louisiana politics and taxes bore its first results. State senator Jules G. Fisher and his nephew, Representative Joseph Fisher, were indicted for falsification of federal income-tax reports. The money involved had come from the sale of materials used in Louisiana's state highway program. Both Fishers were Long men. That net was closing in.

Huey Long grew nervous about his suzerainty in Louisiana, and took steps to protect himself. When a member of Congress in the dissident eastern parishes died in office, Huey delayed in filling the post, fearful that an anti-Long man would win a special election. At a meeting of the state Democratic committee he lashed his forces into action, to oust T. Sammes Walmsley of New Orleans as chairman of the state committee, and Huey Long then added that post to his own holdings. Even in trouble, he was capable of a huge, if ill-mannered joke. Knowing that he controlled, he cast his own vote for Walmsley, to make the total come out seventy votes for Long and fifteen for the New Orleans man.

Federal investigators and federal patronage brought new faces into the mainstream of Louisiana affairs. Huey Long saw the faces, and his nervousness increased. The investigators worked tirelessly, ruthlessly. They began turning up the edges of long-buried and Long-buried scandals. They went back to the impeachment charges registered by the Louisiana legislature. They dug into the charges made by Huey's brother Earl during a period in which they were at odds—a period in which Earl said he saw his brother take a handful of thousand dollar bills from a representative of one of the huge corporations Huey Long had said he was determined to bring under control.

James Farley refused to deal with Huey Long in patronage matters. Here he struck at Long's source of power, for if the federal government became important enough as a dispenser of money and privilege in Louisiana, Huey Long would be deposed as a federal machine was built.

Every day, Huey's perimeter grew smaller.

Yet it did not appear that way on the surface in 1934. In Louisiana Huey Long was more popular than ever. The Reverend Smith was producing results with his harangues and his efficient organization for Share the Wealth. Huey Long took five offices for his suite in the Senate office building, rather than the usual three—and many of the secretaries were fully occupied with the affairs of the Share the Wealth clubs which sprang up across the nation.

Huey Long began to attract a diverse following. He had come out for his own version of bi-metallism as early as 1932. That brought him an autographed picture of William Jennings Bryan from the silver-tongued orator's family, and the support of the mining interests in the mountain states of the West. Long's radical approach to agricultural problems and to the "vested interests" brought him the support of mid-westerners such as Milo Reno, the dissident farm leader.

Most important of all was the growing strength of Father

Coughlin. In November, 1934, the Radio Priest announced the formation of a National Union for Social Justice. It was to be a non-partisan
league, a pressure group above all pressure groups, not a party but a
surge from the grass roots of America. In essence, its principles were to
be these:

1. Government exists not for the welfare of any class.
2. Government regulates labor-management relations.
3. Property ownership does not imply unlimited control
   of the property.
4. The hourly wage should be abolished and replaced by
   a guaranteed annual wage.
5. Labor should have a voice in management.
6. Wages must not be allowed to rise so high that they
   drained working capital from industry.
7. The world of finance is nothing but an impediment,
   and so must eventually be destroyed.

Within twenty years all the portions of Father Coughlin's plan
that could be fitted within the capitalistic system were to become a
part of the American social scene. The last two provisions, however,
were so radical that they would have destroyed capitalism, by outlawing the whole capitalistic structure, which held the financial
market place to be the meeting ground for property, labor, and ideas.

Father Coughlin proposed a ten billion dollar program of road
building, to produce an eighteen thousand mile network of roads.
He wanted fifty million square miles of land brought under a reforestation program. He wanted the St. Lawrence River harnessed
for navigation and public power. He wanted to reclaim sixty million
acres of land, to replace slums by building nine hundred thousand
homes, to guarantee every man an annual wage of $1,500 a year.

From the point of view of Huey Long's Share the Wealth movement there was no incompatibility with the National Union. Senator
Long had never spelled out so specific a group of principles. It would
be easy enough for him to adapt himself to these, and then en-
compass the movement, and even five million adherents of Father
Coughlin—then swallow the entirety like an amoeba eating a particle.

Here, Huey Long saw, was a fitting companion for himself.

Coughlin was a northerner, a Catholic, an immoderate who had discovered, through radio, the importance and exhilaration of power.

Long, who was quick to descend upon those who disagreed with him, significantly did not declare war on Father Coughlin. The Father, for his part, alternated between exhorting and insulting the Roosevelt administration, as it moved ahead with its own program of reform, and Coughlin's power, like Long's, was reaching its zenith at the end of 1934. In December, he engaged in public dispute with William Cardinal O'Connell of Boston. He accused Cardinal O'Connell of failing in his duty—as prescribed by the monumental encyclical on social justice issued years before by Pope Leo XIII. The new pope, Pius XI, was not amused, but like the temporal powers in America's federal government, the Holy See moved more slowly than its demagogues.

Events seemed to draw Long and Coughlin together. In 1934 Huey Long had joined his ancient hero, Senator Borah, to struggle against American adherence to the World Court, although President Roosevelt favored at least this departure from isolationism. A large body of public sentiment in favor of the World Court existed in America. It did not include the isolationists of the Middle West, most of them Republican, the Hearst newspapers, Father Coughlin, or Huey Long. In the Senate, on January 16, 1935, Huey Long led the fight against the Court. On the airwaves, Father Coughlin led the fight. Both claimed credit for the defeat of the administration's proposal. Although the administration denied either the honor, National Democratic Chairman Farley was increasingly restless as he watched the growth of the radical movements of Coughlin and Long. Coughlin became more outspoken. Supported by his bishop, he denied the undeniable. When criticized by Osservatore Romano, the newspaper of the Vatican, the priest retorted that this did not represent the Holy Father's views.

Long grew more reckless. Tailed by reporters who could not resist his grins and colorful speech, he flowered publicly, travelled through Mississippi, Arkansas, Georgia to make speeches, and drew the greatest crowds ever seen at political rallies in the South. He was pictured under a Red flag by the cartoonist of Colonel McCormick's Chicago Tribune, but the Roosevelt administration paid him enough heed to pass his high inheritance-tax bill. His machine was defeated in local elections in Louisiana in 1934, but Huey moved confidently ahead into the national scene. In the winter of 1935 Gerald L. K. Smith claimed four and a half million members of the Share the Wealth clubs. In the summer of that year he claimed seven million members.

Huey Long was, as H. L. Mencken said, "a good show—expensive, perhaps, but also exhilarating." He was, as Raymond Moley's *Today* said, a dangerous man, who bought Louisiana legislators like sacks of potatoes, shuffled them like decks of cards, and bragged about it afterward.

Huey Long's formula for escape from depression was complete by 1935. He had raised Louisiana's debt from $11,000,000 in 1928 to $125,000,000. He had just loaded six new taxes on the state, including a fifty-cent-a-gallon tax on whiskey, a 2 per cent tax on advertising in newspapers (which was thrown out by the courts) and a new state income tax.

In the beginning of 1935, Huey Long was paunchy and liverish. Too much food and drink had bloated his clown's face. Sensing himself on the edge of an even more exciting career than in the past, he gave up drinking, to concentrate on the more heady wine of power, power over all America.

Huey Long's threat was real. The *Times* of London noted that Franklin Roosevelt's New Deal was bogged down, which indeed it was, in an overwhelmingly Democratic Congress which suddenly demanded that it be allowed to take responsibility for legislation on its own shoulders, and listened, but did not act, when the President demanded the passage of his administration's program. Unless the President were able to blast his way out of the impasse, the *Times* said gloomily, there was grave danger that Huey Long and Father Coughlin with their "quack remedies" might gain power in the Presidential and Congressional elections of 1936.

Feeling his power, in 1935 Huey Long declared open war on the Roosevelt administration. The issue was patronage, and his major enemy was James Farley, Postmaster-General and chief dispenser of patronage. Harold Ickes put an outright end to ten million dollars worth of PWA projects scheduled for Louisiana. In February, 1935,

Long demanded that Farley resign, charging illegal and improper activity. Farley refused to resign, but such was the power of Huey Long that the Postmaster-General sent a telegram to the Senate, denying the charges against him. Long then engaged in a radio debate with General Hugh Johnson. Johnson attacked Long, but Long used his time to present the case of Share the Wealth to the radio audience.

Senator Long was defeated in his attempt to force an investigation of the charges he made against Postmaster Farley. Still, he had displayed an unprecedented amount of power in standing against the administration. Postmaster Farley put on his national committee chairman's hat, and ordered a poll of the Louisiana senator's popularity within the states. He discovered, to his horror, that Huey Long could command three or four million votes in the 1936 Presidential election—and this was still only 1935, Huey Long had not really built a political machine, but the forces of Long, Coughlin, and Dr. Townsend, the old-age pension man, were converging. The position of the public was better than it had been three years before, as objective reporters from abroad observed. The agricultural sections of the country, in particular, had been helped by the farm mortgage and relief policies and loans of the Roosevelt Administration. But, as the London *Times* reporter saw in his survey of American affairs, "poverty and unemployment still exist on a colossal scale." H. G. Wells, asked to report in *Collier's* magazine on his impressions, predicted that Huey Long was to go a long way, despite his crudities, for Wells saw in Long many of the features of Adolf Hitler, and in America, many of the responses of Long that the Germans had given Hitler.

The intellectuals of America, like the loyal New Dealers, were lined up solidly against Huey Long and Father Coughlin's extremism. Long had taken one unforgivable step which put him at outs with the intellectuals. He had built Louisiana State University from an unimpressive college to a big school, but he had subverted the objective interests of education to his own purposes. He had installed an unknown educator as president, and an unknown doctor as head of his new charity hospital (and thus the most influential of medical posts) because they were his creatures, loyal to him.

In the spring of 1935 the state university planned a mammoth,

Long-inspired celebration of its seventy-fifth anniversary. President James Monroe Smith wrote to colleges far and near, asking that they send representatives to the ceremonies. But many colleges demurred. As the administrators of one school said, "the high purposes of the university had been subordinated to the political objectives of Huey Long."

When he heard of this, Huey Long snorted. The country hadn't seen anything yet.

The nation at large was becoming aware of that alarming fact. In Boston, columnist Walter Lippmann was asked by a Chamber of Commerce audience how much influence Father Coughlin really had. He said no one would ever know until Coughlin was willing to stake his influence on a question that was not bound to be decided his way. A few weeks later Socialist Norman Thomas called both Long and Coughlin "demogogues" who sought to subvert parliamentary democracy. In the Middle West, Milo Reno announced publicly for a Long-Coughlin union which would sweep the country in the elections of 1936. Huey responded to this talk with a humorous book—*My First Days in the White House*, written in the past tense, in which Huey Long told how he gave Franklin Roosevelt a job as Secretary of the Navy. It was a huge joke—or was it a joke? Anyone who knew the Kingfish was not quite sure.

The summer of 1935 was a period of excruciating anxiety for the New Deal. The Second New Deal had been declared—a program of broad social reform—but it was struggling in those areas where new legislation was needed. Agricultural resettlement had been begun under Rex Tugwell. Rural electrification had begun. The National Youth Administration came into being. The Wagner Labor Relations Act became law. Social Security was enacted (although Huey Long pointed out that it was not large enough or helpful enough), and Huey Long had won his fight for a heavy inheritance tax. But Congress was dragging its feet, and already the Supreme Court had begun to move against the administration, outlawing NRA and even the Federal Farm Bankruptcy Act of 1934 as unconstitutional.

Neither James Farley nor the other political leaders of the Democratic administration were seriously concerned about the Liberty League and the dissenters of the right. They were concerned about the dissenters of the left—the Longs, Coughlins, Townsends, and Renos.

Administration concern about the antics of Huey Long was heightened by his next move, after the Congress adjourned late in the summer. Long set out for Baton Rouge, determined to make the federal government pay for having defeated him in the battle to oust Postmaster Farley. Long went home to Baton Rouge armed with a punitive legislative program, one shaped to eliminate federal influence and federal interference in the affairs of Louisiana. The administration had held up patronage, and was feeding his enemies. when he had finished the federal government would be thrown out of Louisiana altogether.

It was the seventh special session of the Louisiana legislature that year. Huey Long called a special session whenever he felt like it, and the legislators trouped to Baton Rouge to do his bidding, some cheerfully, some reluctantly. It was a mark of his continuing power that they still came, after six previous sessions in the year, and that he felt no fear for his program—to throw the federal government out of Louisiana.

Huey Long was worried about his personal safety, and had been for a year. Five Louisiana representatives had demanded that Congress investigate Long's deprivation of Louisiana of the republican form of government. He was afraid someone was ready to take matters in their own hands, and he talked constantly of "plots" against his life.

On Sunday, September 8, he called a meeting of the state's house ways and means committee, and rammed through thirty-one bills. He did this himself, going to the floor and answering questions of his legislators—the unfriendly ones. Before lunch all the bills were passed by the committee and referred to the house. Then the committee and Huey Long took time off for lunch.

That same evening the house of representatives convened, to pass Huey Long's laws. Long came into the session, dressed in a linen suit which had become his trademark, talked for a while, and went out. All was proceeding according to plan. But in the marble hallway of the capitol building, despite the ring of guards, a young man named Dr. Carl Austin Weiss had entered and concealed himself.

He had a grudge against Senator Long. His father-in-law, Judge Benjamin Pavy, was being gerrymandered out of his judgeship by Long for having opposed the senator.

Huey Long walked into the governor's office, a trail of policemen and bodyguards behind him, then turned quickly, and headed out. Dr. Weiss stepped out of the shadows, to Huey Long's side, put a gun against Long's abdomen and fired.

Immediately, even as Huey Long staggered back, the bodyguards came to their senses. Dr. Weiss was dead in a moment, and in revenge his body was riddled with some sixty bullets.

Huey Long disappeared, almost beneath the eyes of his befuddled guardians. He was driven to a nearby sanitarium, and his favorite surgeon Dr. Arthur Vidrine, was called from Charity Hospital.

The bullet had nicked a kidney and had passed through three loops of intestine. Long was hemorrhaging.

It was apparent that surgery was necessary, as soon as possible. The best surgeons were in New Orleans. They were called, but their auto was wrecked on the way to Baton Rouge. Dr. Vidrine had to perform the surgery himself in the end. It was not successful. Thirty hours after he was shot, Huey Long died.

Long's death brought confusion to Louisiana, but an audible sigh of relief to the New Deal administration in Washington. Gerald L. K. Smith took over the leadership of the Share the Wealth clubs. All Long's other henchmen were Louisiana-oriented, and they struggled for the spoils within the state. Three days after Long's death, the anti-machine forces in Louisiana sought peace with the federal administration, and not long afterward, President Roosevelt visited New Orleans, dined at Antoine's restaurant with the anti-Long men, and the war between Louisiana and the Union was ended.

A few months later the new Governor Noe put an end to the requirement that state employees kick back 5 per cent of their salaries to the Long political machine. There was not much Long political machine left, in fact, and there would not be until it was recreated by the senator's brother a few years later.

The radicals who had hoped for an entente between Huey Long and Father Coughlin continued to hope. In the fall of 1935 and early

Café Society took over from the Fifth Avenue set during the 1930s. William Rhinelander Stewart, Jr. and Cole Porter were equal in the eyes of social arbiter Elsa Maxwell. UNITED PRESS INTERNATIONAL PHOTO

Robert Sherwood's plays changed drastically during these years. He entered the period as novelist and casual playwright but such works as *The Petrified Forest* established him as a social critic. Leslie Howard starred, but a new star named Bogart was born. VANDAMM COLLECTION OF THE THEATRE COLLECTION OF THE NEW YORK PUBLIC LIBRARY

Poor Charlie! What worker in what land could not grasp the meaning of scenes like this one? *Modern Times* earned millions, but Charlie Chaplin, too, became a social critic. THE MUSEUM OF MODERN ART FILM LIBRARY

Which road was the American worker to follow? Would he join Socialist Norman Thomas on the thoughtful path of "Democratic Socialism?" Or would he go with Communist Earl Browder? WIDE WORLD PHOTO

Colonel Robert R. McCormick went into the campaign of 1936 determined to save the nation from the grasp of Franklin Roosevelt. His chosen instrument was Governor Alf M. Landon. UNITED PRESS INTERNATIONAL PHOTO

in 1936 Gerald L. K. Smith, Father Coughlin, and Dr. Townsend did try to create a third-party movement. But the spark was gone. The Kingfish—the one man who could have amalgamated these diffuse groups—was no more.

In 1936, Father Coughlin called a convention of his National Union for Social Justice in Cleveland. The convention framed a platform designed to appeal to the followers of Smith and Townsend, too, and then voted to support a third-party candidate, William Lemke. Smith said that year that he would "take over" the government by combining forces with Townsend and others, but his plans did not seem very concrete, and indeed, so much had things changed in Louisiana that the Kingfish's right-hand man was arrested on November 3 in New Orleans for disturbance—something that could not have happened in the halcyon days without fear of instantaneous reprisal from Long.

During the heat of the campaign, Father Coughlin so far forgot himself as to assert that Franklin Roosevelt was "anti-God." Immediately, he was rebuked by Archbishop John T. McNicholas of Cincinnati, and while he was again backed by his Bishop Gallagher, and promised to keep right on saying what he wanted, the election changed Father Coughlin's mind.

It was not so much that Roosevelt won again in a landslide. More, it was the drubbing Father Coughlin took, and the sudden realization that he was far out on a limb in every way—again under fire from *Osservatore Romano* for radicalism and rash statement.

John J. O'Connor, the Democratic congressman from the sixteenth district of New York City, had offered to kick Father Coughlin from the Capitol to the White House and back again. With some relish, the Father announced his support for another candidate that year, and indicated that he expected his National Union to poll at least nine million votes in the Presidential campaign.

When the results of the election were in, Father Coughlin bravely admitted that his National Union had been "thoroughly discredited" by the voters. He warned that Roosevelt, in moving to a radicalism of his own had "suspended the American system," but Father Coughlin declared himself defeated, and promised thenceforth to pursue a "policy of silence." Well he might. Only 10 per cent of the nine million he had boasted actually supported Coughlin's candidate. The question asked of Walter Lippmann in Boston was answered. Father Coughlin had staked his influence on a candidate, and the results had shown how limited that influence really was. The Smith group showed itself to be equally fragile at the polls, and Dr. Townsend's ferocious fighters for $200 a month pensions began silently to melt away, even in their bastion of California.

There it was—the end of a third-party movement to share the wealth out among the poor, just a little over a year after the man who might have made it work had perished. Times had changed. Joe Messina, Huey Long's principal bodyguard, got a job watching watchmen on the docks at New Orleans. Murphy Roden, the man who pumped the first bullet into the unresisting Dr. Weiss, found himself a place on the state police force, and went off to the FBI school for law enforcement training. Father Coughlin announced his retirement from politics in a radio address on November 8, 1936, and Gerald L. K. Smith read the results of the election, then took his energies off to begin a crusade against the menace of Communism.

Huey Long, as *New York Times* reporter Raymond Daniell recalled two years later, had been the first home-grown American dictator. But two years after Huey Long's death, the American system which had seemed so shaky in 1935 had survived an administrative attack on the foundation of the Republic, and a recession that in any other period might have been called a major financial panic. If not stronger than ever, the Republic showed no signs of dying.

THE FARMER FROM FIR CONE

CHAPTER THIRTEEN

HAREBRAINED AS HUEY LONG'S PROPOSAL to stop planting cotton seemed to the Texas legislature in 1931, the Long plan was no more radical than many others. Indeed, the official plan established in 1933 by Secretary of Agriculture Henry Agard Wallace provided for the destruction of crops planted in the spring of that year, and the slaughtering of piglets which had been bred in desperation over the farmer's steadily declining income and his efforts to buttress himself by overproduction.

The city dwellers could not understand it but the agricultural problem of the United States in the 1930's was not basically a depression problem at all. It was more a cause of overall depression than an effect. For even in the boom years before 1929, while factory workers and entrepreneurs prospered, and so came to believe that all the nation prospered, the American farmer's position had grown steadily more shaky. Certainly these 1920's were years when wheat sold well above a dollar a bushel, but farm mortgages continued to grow heavier, the prices farmers had to pay for what they bought continued to rise faster than their income, and their market was overloaded because the nation's income was disproportionally allocated. There were hungry people in America and huge food surpluses existed. But the tragedy of America was the maldistribution of wealth—the hungry could not afford to buy the food, so it sat in warehouses, waiting for foreign buyers. When the millions of tons were sold, the glut tended to depress the world price of the product, whether it was wheat or cotton.

There was nothing new in this state of affairs. American farm overproduction was a product of the boom of World War I. In 1916, 1917, and 1918 farmers were encouraged to plant every bit of land in crops. The Allied governments needed every boll of cotton and every grain of wheat that could be raised. The weather was fine in those years, the land prospered and bloomed and the crops were fat and heavy. The farmers were encouraged enough to continue to plant. When the lean years came, and prices fell, the farmers tried to plant more, and thus sell more, to make up in volume what they were losing in unit price.

The cycle was vicious, but there seemed to be no way out.

No, farm depression was not a phenomenon of the 1930's. It had begun in 1920, an outgrowth of that lessening demand and of the high tariff to which the Republicans were committed. In two years in the early 1920's three hundred thousand farmers lost their land in mortgage foreclosures.

Following this debacle early in the 1920's a fruit grower from Oregon named Charles Linza McNary had tried to help the farmers through a bill which was to go down in history as the most important farm measure ever proposed but not enacted—the McNary-Haugen bill.

Senator Charles McNary at the time knew more about the problems of the farmer and was more sympathetic to the American farmer than any other man in the United States Senate. McNary had come to the Senate in 1917, fresh from his own fruit orchard at Fir Cone, near the Oregon state capital city of Salem. McNary shared some elements of background with Herbert Hoover. Both had spent formative years in the Willamette Valley of Oregon, and both had attended Stanford University. There, however, the similarities ended, for Hoover was rock-ribbed and conservative as a politician, compared with Charlie McNary, who had adopted many of the ideas of the old Progressive movement which left so deep an imprint on the Pacific Northwest. The ideals of progressivism, centered in the North and West, were to make Franklin Roosevelt's job easier than it might have been in the first two years of the New Deal, although the national politics of progressivism was long dead.

So the seeds of the farm legislation of the 1930's were planted, although they did not flourish, in the decade before. Along with the Republican high tariff of the 1920's came a movement designed to allow the farmer some benefits from it, by putting aside the surplus of agricultural products and offering it abroad at world price. The government then would make sure the farmer who sold abroad was paid most of the difference between the lower world price and the artificially held domestic price.

As C. E. Huff, a member of the Federal Farm Board, later put it, "The farmer would himself underwrite the loss on export sales but his average price would be on a parity with manufacturers."

McNary-Haugen had grown out of a demand that the tariff be made effective on farm crops. George N. Peek, then president of the Moline Plow Company, originated the proposals. Peek suggested that farmers do what implement manufacturers did. The manufacturers sold their surplus implements abroad, at competitive prices, relying on the tariff on foreign implements to give them a profitable edge in American sales. Even if some foreign sales were made at a loss, the average was profitable.

Peek's proposal to McNary was something like this:

U.S. wheat production equalled 800 million bushels. Domestic sales accounted for 650 million bushels. Export sales, then, should be 150 million bushels. Assume a world price of $1.00 per bushel and a domestic price, protected by the tariff at $1.40. Then when 650 million bushels were sold at $1.40 a bushel and 150 million were sold at $1.00, the loss on exports would equal a loss of 7½ cents a bushel on the entire crop. Another half cent would be added to that figure, to cover administration costs. The farmer, then, would sell his *entire* crop to the dealer at $1.32 a bushel. The government would police the market, and make sure that the exporters were reimbursed the difference of 32 cents a bushel between the "equalization price" and the world market price of $1.00.

McNary had put the Equalization Fee into the McNary-Haugen bill in January, 1924. The bill was defeated. He brought it up again in February, 1927. It was defeated again. In 1927 the bill passed, but President Coolidge vetoed it. And in 1928, once again Coolidge vetoed the bill.

When Herbert Hoover replaced Coolidge in the White House in 1929, the farmers saw some hope for a sympathetic attitude from the President, for had not Hoover been the great relief man of the period after World War I, and had he not, as Secretary of Commerce, delved into produce market problems throughout the country?

All this was true, but Hoover's exposure to farms and farmers had given him no greater understanding of the real farm problems of production and distribution than had Coolidge's boyhood exposure and Presidential visits to his father's farm given that President.

One problem was that Hoover really believed he knew more about farm problems than Senator McNary, and Hoover's ingrained distaste for any kind of government regulation caused him to veer sharply away from the McNary-Haugen approach.

It was not that Hoover failed to understand that there was a farm problem. In 1929 Hoover called a special session of Congress to revise the tariff and to bring farm relief—even before depression made relief a necessity for other groups in American society.

Congress created a Federal Farm Board of eight members in 1929 and gave great encouragement to the establishment of farm co-operatives. This, Hoover thought, was the ideal solution to farm problems. Earnest men, cooperating, would buy together, pack their products together, and sell their products together. Thus they would have the advantage of all the corner-cutting that could be accomplished by mass effort. They would not lose their individuality, because it was cooperative effort. There would be no coercion by government. Each man was free to choose.

The Federal Farm Board would regulate the price of farm products by buying up surpluses, and then holding them until the world market price was favorable. Thus, some optimists believed, the Farm Board could support agricultural prices temporarily and maybe even make a profit in the long run.

Neither the administration, the Farm Board, nor farmers were completely happy with the measure that established the Board. The administration did not like the law—particularly the provision for lending against products or buying them outright to support prices.

Farmers did not believe the law established enough machinery to solve their problems. The Farm Board found its position hazardous.

To see exactly what happened, examine the case of one of Senator McNary's constituents, a rancher in eastern Oregon named Jack DeVore.

Jack DeVore was not a businessman or an economist or an agronomist. He was a rancher with little formal education, who ran his ranch just as hundreds of others ran theirs, gambling every year on the weather and the market for his crops. DeVore's ranch was located a few miles outside the little town of Heppner, near Pendleton. Heppner was then a one-street village consisting of a few feed stores, a handful of saloons which had become speakeasies or halfhearted cafés during prohibition, and most important—a bank. DeVore lived with that bank in a state of intimacy. He borrowed in the winter and he paid off in the fall, after the crops were in.

In the war years, Jack DeVore prospered. Much of eastern Oregon was prairie grassland, covered with sagebrush and the tough long grass on which sheep and cattle could survive, even if they needed fattening with high protein grains for market. Grazing was the function of that land, but during World War I the price of wheat rose like a rocket. Three-dollar wheat brought out the avarice in Jack DeVore and most of the other ranchers around Heppner. They plowed up their grasslands and planted that three-dollar wheat. When the wheat sold, they bought more land and planted that.

At the end of the war, Jack DeVore was a wealthy man. He owned five thousand acres of land, he kept a few hands at the ranch year around, and hired crews to thresh his grain in the summer. Then, when the wheat market weakened Jack DeVore lost a great deal of money. He mortgaged his farm at the bank, and switched back to sheep. In those years of the 1920's sheep seemed a better gamble. The new tariff protected sheepmen, because it kept British woollens and Argentine and Australian wool out of the American textile markets. For a few years, DeVore prospered again, although markets for his wool and meat were spotty. The year 1929 saw Jack DeVore in trouble —not because of the stock market, but because he was unable to clear old debts. The following year, 1930, the bottom dropped out of the wool market, too, and in 1931 wool fell even further, as the depression cut domestic buying, and the high tariff on imports of industrial goods made it impossible for some foreign businessmen to sell successfully in the United States. There was less money, then, for foreign buyers of American agricultural products to spend in America. The American farmers and ranchers suffered.

Abroad, it was estimated that European markets could absorb twenty-five million bushels of wheat and a million bales of American cotton. But that was theoretical, not actual. The need was apparent in Europe. But where was the money? The normal resources of banking were not available for farm loans to Jack DeVore and others this year. The American government had refused to back its own farmers

by buttressing their prices and guaranteeing them the difference between the world price and the domestic price. That same government
made no moves to lend money to potential buyers abroad. And to top
its own actions, the American government exacted so high a price for
foreign manufactures, through the tariff, that the foreign consumer
could not afford American farm products.

Some efforts were made to persuade the Reconstruction Finance
Corporation to make loans to foreign companies and governments, so
they could buy American farm surpluses. The RFC, busy bailing out
American banks from immediate ruin, had not the time or the inclination to listen.

To Jack DeVore all this meant disaster. He lost his ranch and
nearly everything he owned. He was forced to go to work for another
rancher as a common hand.

Faced with such hardship, Senator McNary grew concerned.

By the middle of 1930, Charles McNary could have been recognized as the most important man in the Republican party—although
he was not so recognized. The Republicans, harassed from all sides,
had lived with the farm problem for nearly ten years. Most of them,
Hoover included, did not realize how serious the problem had become,
although the statistics were available. Wheat production had increased thirty-four million bushels over 1929—and that was typical of
most crops—but farm income had decreased by nine and a half billion
dollars, or 20 per cent. Farmers were ready for almost any kind of
rebellion.

Their rebellion took the form of desertion of the Republican
party. In 1931 and even in 1932 the Republicans continued to think
of the great farm belt as Republican country—but it was no longer
Republican country. Had Charles McNary been the Republican candidate for President in 1932 there would have been a chance of woo-
ing the farmers back, for McNary was one man the farmers knew to be
their friend. But had not his own party thrown him to the wolves,
killing his farm plan time after time?

McNary was not a serious candidate for the Presidency in 1932,
although his name was mentioned here and there. There was no
serious Republican candidate except the incumbent, Herbert Hoover.

For two years McNary had been doing his best to help the farmer, in the face of determined efforts by Republican representatives of manufacturing states to help industry, even if it meant helping business at the expense of the farmer. In the spring of 1930, a combination of senators from industrial states increased the duty on sugar and cement. It was a combination of southern Democrats and northern conservative Republicans, led by Senator Grundy of Pennsylvania, the chieftain of the Republican old guard.

In a misleading gesture to the farmers, the Grundy group raised the tariff on agricultural products to its highest point in history, thus making it certain in fact that foreign nations could not dump their farm produce in America (as if America was not the most overproduced nation of all). To those who believed in the high tariff this was a protection of sorts. How it worked out was quite another matter.

By the middle of the following year 1930, when the Farm Board ran out of money, the tariff policy was already proving disastrous, but such "experts" as the presidents of the various produce exchanges in the country were convinced that produce ought to be allowed to find its own market levels. They did not have to grow the farm products, or lose their livelihood in a 30 per cent price drop.

The farmers had been encouraged by government, as far back as President Harding's urges to keep up farm production. They planted even more in 1929 than in the past, trying to make up for those lean years in which many had mortgaged nearly all they possessed.

During 1930, the Federal Farm Board made loans of a $165,000,-000 to a number of cooperatives and corporations, which held grain and other products for future sale on what was hoped to be a rising world market. But man and the weather confounded the experts. Farmers planted. They refused to exercise the restraint and mutual helpfulness that Hoover had so wanted. And the weather remained bright, beautiful, and gentle; the rains came at the proper times, and not in harsh overabundance. It was as good a crop time as the 1920's. The fields shimmered in the fall under loads of heavy grain.

By the end of 1931, the Federal Farm Board's grain stabilization corporation held 157,000,000 bushels of wheat. The cotton corporation held 1,320,000 bales of cotton. The price of cotton had dropped so that while the Board had loaned money at sixteen cents a pound, the value of the cotton was now only seven cents a pound. The Farm

Board became dormant—and cotton fell again, and wheat dropped from a dollar a bushel to 57 cents a bushel. The farmer was worse off than ever—for by this time the depression had dried up normal farm markets, and had sent thousands of people back to the farms, where they tried to make a living. These new farmers added to the surplus, farm prices dropped steadily as the markets were glutted, and the race grew more intense.

Before it went out of existence, the Farm Board had made commitments of more than a billion dollars. Not all this represented losses; before the end of 1933 a total of $777,000,000 had been repaid to the federal Treasury. But the Farm Board had lost more than $350,-000,000. Even this was not the basic failure. The real failure lay in the fact that the Farm Board experiment had brought confusion. Having started a program, and stopped, the administration was blamed for making the situation of agriculture worse than ever.

From the beginning, Senator Charles McNary was leery of the Farm Board proposal. He knew his farmers, and he knew that they were not businessmen. He also knew the current problems of American agriculture.

In 1926, after nine years in the Senate, McNary had become chairman of the Senate Agriculture Committee, the highest honor to which he then aspired. He had worked with Henry Wallace, President Coolidge's Secretary of Agriculture, and with Wallace's son, Henry Agard Wallace, to develop the old McNary-Haugen bill. The McNary farm plan, in other words, was put together by farm experts.

Further, McNary was a successful orchardist in his own right. He developed the Imperial prune and sent pits all over the world to other orchardists. He spent many hours at home working with his managers, trying to improve crops and increase his unit yield per tree. The master of his local Grange organization in Salem once told writer Richard Neuberger that Charlie McNary knew more about farming than anyone else in the Willamette Valley. The Willamette is a long valley, filled with good and successful farmers, and that valley represented the limits of that Grange master's world. It was the highest compliment he could pay his senator.

In the election campaign of 1932, Senator McNary looked around him and noted that the two basic issues of the Presidential election would be farm problems and public power. Most of his Republican cohorts paid McNary's words little heed, but the Democrats, who seemed to have more respect for McNary than the Republicans, *made* these two issues the most important in the campaign. Governor Franklin Roosevelt spoke for public power in the St. Lawrence, at Muscle Shoals, in the Columbia basin, and particularly in the Columbia River itself.

Had Charles McNary not been so strong a Republican in his leanings in 1932, he would have joined some of his brothers in the Senate —Hiram Johnson, George Norris, Robert La Follette—to support Roosevelt. As it was, he confined himself to support of most of the policies Roosevelt believed in, because those were the beliefs of Charles L. McNary, too.

Before the close of Congress, he pushed through a Senate resolution which called on the RFC to make available a hundred million dollars to support agricultural buying. It was a stopgap measure, but in an election year, a stopgap measure was just what was needed. The RFC could hardly take lightly the advice of the United States Senate, and particularly that of the assistant floor leader of the Republicans.

In the end the RFC chiefs wrote a pleasant enough letter to the Senate, but the content was negative. That spring of 1932 a million fewer bales of cotton were sold abroad than the previous year. The wheat surplus was partly alleviated by the purchase of sixty-six shiploads of grain and flour by the Chinese Nationalist government at Nanking. Yet the total purchase was less than half a million tons— hardly enough to make any impact at all on the wheat market.

Once Congress adjourned in the spring of 1932, Senator McNary made his way home to the farm at Fir Cone, to tend his three hundred acres, and to travel about the state campaigning for himself and the programs in which he believed. Since coming to the Senate in 1917, the senator had been positive in his advocacy of federal government assistance to the people of his native state of Oregon. He wanted help for the farmers, for the miners, for the timbermen, and for the infant and growing industries. The Willamette Valley was a sleepy place, and Portland, the principal city of Oregon, was so quiet and so sedate that it was often known as the Victoria of the United States—so called after the British Columbia city which seemed to many to have been plucked straight out of the English countryside.

These were surface indications, and misleading. Oregon was also the home of a majority—Republican and Democrat—who were by nature progressives and even radical in their thinking. Oregon had been a testing ground for the initiative, the referendum, the recall, and other steps in the reform of state governments. Oregonians were also convinced—or most of them were—that the proper application of hydroelectric power to their natural resources would make of their state a manufacturing paradise as well as a happy home for farmers, sportsmen, and vacationers. They were joined in this by citizens of Washington State, of Senator William Borah's Idaho, and of Montana, the easternmost state in the Columbia basin. Oregon possessed a liberal tradition, beneath a solid Republican exterior. Both the exterior and the tradition were exemplified in Senator Charles McNary, whom Herbert Hoover regarded with growing distaste for his liberalism, and whom Franklin Roosevelt was to meet in Washington as his most effective, if one of his friendliest opponents.

In May, 1932, before the nominations of the major parties were settled, the country's interest was held by such events as Amelia Earhart's exploits in flying alone across the Atlantic. The horror of the Lindbergh kidnaping was not yet fully known, although the boy had been missing for several days and Colonel Lindbergh had offered a $25,000 reward for his return. These matters seized the public attention. Few people cared to read in the newspapers or hear on the radio tiresome stories of the efforts of a handful of high-tariff men to tinker once again with the Hawley-Smoot tariff law. (Who understood the tariff, anyhow?)

Such otherwise reasonable legislators as Senator Arthur Vandenberg of Michigan continued to believe that the high taxes on imports could somehow solve the nation's economic problems. By this time Herbert Hoover was not so sanguine about the tariff, and was desperately grasping for further straws of national cooperation.

On May 23, President Hoover invited thirty newspaper publishers to the White House for dinner and discussion. He hoped, obviously, to resolve the national economic problem by exhortation. He did not face the need to persuade American farmers, now thoroughly aroused and thoroughly radical, that they would be the first helped.

Two months later, in July, Governor Roosevelt published a small book of speeches. *Government—Not Politics* was the title, but that title was misleading. Roosevelt's proposals were thoroughly political, issued on the eve of the Democratic National Convention. Nonetheless they were understandable and persuasive.

A third of the population of the United States depended on wheat and cotton for its livelihood, Governor Roosevelt noted. (Most people did not know this.) Did it not make sense to take immediate steps to protect those crops—particularly the prices at which they were sold in the United States? The governor then went on to espouse Senator McNary's Equalization Fee plan, in which the exportable surplus of farm goods would be sold at the world market price, and the government would make up the amount of difference between that price and the tariff. He did not name the Republican senator, of course. But if Roosevelt was stealing Senator McNary's idea, the senator did not mind, for his concern was over the desperate situation of the farmers.

By the fall of 1932 that farm situation had become more serious than ever. The tariff had done it this time. The high tariffs exacted by Senator Grundy and his coalition might have saved a few industrial jobs in Pennsylvania and Alabama and Massachusetts. Those same rates wrecked the farmer and destroyed his last hopes. Even by overproducing, he could not make ends meet, because as the surplus grew, the market price for farm goods fell so rapidly that it took three bushels of wheat in 1932 to bring in as much money as one bushel had brought in 1929.

Following the Roosevelt victory, when the Seventy-third Congress assembled in Washington in March, 1933, there was little initial argument about the President's program. These were gloomy days, of course. The banks were closed. The entire country seemed on the edge of economic collapse. The Republicans in Congress were not inclined to argue with an Executive who at least gave signs of presenting a positive and novel approach.

There was another reason for Republican transigence. The Republican party had been decimated in the election of 1932. The old

Republican leader, Senator Watson of Indiana, was gone—defeated. So was Senator Moses, former president *pro tem*. So was Senator Smoot. So was Senator Jones.

Senators Norris, Johnson, and La Follette had supported Roosevelt, and there was serious doubt if they were still Republicans at all. Senator Johnson, at least, could not again run as a Republican under the election law in effect in California. Further, Senator Reed was trying to arouse enough emotion among the Republicans of the Senate to throw the three dissidents out of the Congressional Republican bloc. Senator Reed failed in his attempt, largely because there were so few Republicans left in Washington that differences which had loomed large in 1932 suddenly diminished in 1933.

In the head-counting in the Senate caucus room, it became apparent that Charles McNary, with only sixteen years' service, was the senior Republican senator. He was chosen Republican leader on March 7.

Senator McNary began to earn a reputation in conciliation. "All Republicans look alike to me," he said, thus effectively silencing the post mortem within his party in relation to Democratic leanings.

As the months wore on, Senator McNary proved himself to be one of the most popular senators ever to walk the Capitol halls, and, considering the position of the Republicans in that Congress, one of the most effective minority leaders of all time.

Senator Cutting had declared in favor of Roosevelt, too. Senators Nye and Frazier had not deserted their party, but they had made their pro-Roosevelt sentiment quite apparent in the months before the election. The annoyance of the conservatives of the party was apparent and immediate. Somehow, however, Charles McNary managed to weld together a Republican Senate group, even while he worked with the administration to solve the problems of agriculture and development of hydroelectric resources.

It might have seemed odd to some mid-westerners to contemplate the political coloration of the Secretary of Agriculture who came to office with Franklin Roosevelt, but Charles McNary welcomed this young man, Henry Agard Wallace, as a farm editor who knew what he was talking about. Whether or not Wallace would turn out to be a good administrator remained to be seen, but he was an excellent farm editor, and he had made some modest success in business, producing and marketing hybrid corn at a time when the corn crops were going begging like so much else.

Wallace had grown up in the Republican party, but by 1929, when the Republicans passed the Hawley-Smoot tariff, young Wallace declared that it "would do the farmers of the United States tens of millions of dollars of damage every year." Three years later his prophecies were proved accurate, and Wallace was thoroughly disgusted with the old. He was ready to embrace the new.

Rex Tugwell recommended Wallace. Wallace also knew Henry Morgenthau well, and they had spent some hours at one time discussing the problems of farm publications—since Morgenthau was also involved in farm papers. It was easy enough for Wallace to switch to the New Deal. It was politically sagacious of Roosevelt to have a middle-western man in his cabinet as Secretary of Agriculture.

Then, in the spring of 1933 began what columnist Walter Lippmann described as "the most daring economic experiment ever seriously proposed in the United States." Wallace, Tugwell, and M. L. Wilson reorganized the Department of Agriculture before Roosevelt took office—on paper at least. Few believed Wallace would become Secretary of Agriculture. There was much talk that Morgenthau wanted it for himself, and Tugwell was seriously mentioned. But in his forty-fifth year, Henry Wallace went to Washington in a post that immediately, at least, was second only to that of Franklin Roosevelt in its importance to the national welfare. By August, 1933, ten million acres of planted cotton had been plowed under, and by September, six million pigs had been slaughtered, the first farm act had been passed in the spring, the farm mortgage situation had been alleviated, and the Civil Works Agency was conducting a mapping program. For the first time, the Department of Agriculture would have accurate pictorial information as to the number and kind of acreage planted in the United States.

Even as 1933, the years 1934 and 1935 were years of experimentation on the land. The Agricultural Adjustment Act of 1933 attempted to establish a balance between the production and consumption of agricultural products. Even as Secretary Wallace, Undersecretary Tugwell, and their advisers framed the law, they were repelled by its consequences. It went against the grain of any farm-raised man to limit agricultural production when there were hungry people in the world. But they could see no other solution. Wallace was glum about it, but he accepted it. Tugwell, approaching the problem from a more intellectual level, felt sure crop limitation was absolutely necessary. And that became administration policy for the decade.

The farmers continued to have their ups and downs. An attempt was made to help tenant farmers and others who tried to work sick lands by moving them onto better lands. This program was the subject of much debate and criticism. Actually it was scarcely more than an experiment, involving only five million acres of land purchased by the federal government, and the movement of fewer than 4,500 families to that land. The experiment did nothing to eliminate sharecropping, and very little to aid the farmers.

But the rest of the Roosevelt administration farm policies did help the people who worked the land. By 1935, farm incomes were almost double those of 1933, and the farmer could see that administration policies were helping him. In the Tennessee Valley, where the government had taken over the construction and operation of power, irrigation, and flood-control facilities, the farmers were benefitted even more. On the Columbia and Missouri Rivers, great dams were built, too.

These were years of pulling and hauling, for even with the best of intent, men disagreed on solutions to the problems.

George Peek, an old associate of Henry Wallace's father in government, agreed in the beginning with the emergency moves, but Peek and the others fell out over the basic question of tariff. Peek stood steadfast against lowering of tariffs. Roosevelt and Wallace stood for the gradual development of reciprocal trade agreements. Peek left government.

In the early years of the Roosevelt administration, Senator McNary's position was that of a bystander. As Republican leader of the Senate, he was head of the loyal opposition, a post he was well-equipped to fill because he agreed in principle with much that was being attempted and so could not be accused of reactionary opposition. At the same time the position was difficult for him, personally, because of his importance to the Republican party. He favored rural electrification and betterment of the farmer. He did not like Franklin Roosevelt's efforts to secure tariff-making powers for himself, and as early as March, 1934, he said as much. He was critical of the inflation policy, which some of his western colleagues favored. But mostly, in these years, Charles McNary was the catalyst of the Republican party in Congress. From the Democratic viewpoint he was, as Arthur M. Schlesinger, Jr., has noted, "an urbane political professional who, in his weather-beaten and cynical way," tried to maintain the tradition of honest opposition in a Congress so thoroughly dominated by Democrats that the Republicans were in danger of becoming either shrill malcontents or—worse from their viewpoint—impotent critics of the party in power.

Between 1933 and 1936 there was not very much a Republican minority leader might do to stem the tide of the Democratic policies. The Democrats held 60 seats in the Senate, the Republicans 35; the Democrats held 310 seats in the House and the Republicans 117. In the Seventy-fourth Congress it was worse: 69 Democrats to 25 Republicans, plus two minority members; 319 Democrats in the House to 103 Republicans, seven Progressives and three Farmer Labor members.

And yet, by 1936, Franklin Roosevelt had been in power long enough that the Democrats were in disagreement among themselves. Here was opportunity for the agile McNary to make the Republican voices in the Senate far more important than their numbers would indicate. He was so skillful in his conduct that he took every such advantage, yet retained the friendship of his Democratic counterpart, Senator Robinson of Arkansas, and the respect of Franklin Roosevelt, who, when he signed the bill establishing the Bonneville Power Administration as part of the Columbia Basin Development, announced that he was giving Charlie McNary his dam.

Senator McNary's technique of minority leadership involved intricate maneuvering. A pair of skilled Washington reporters, Joseph Alsop and Robert Kintner, wrote admiringly of McNary's effectiveness in *The Saturday Evening Post*. His technique was to lie low when popular measures were on the agenda—especially when he was certain that the Democrats had all the votes they needed to pass the legislation. Some of these measures were embarrassing to the Republicans because they were reminiscent of liberal measures some Republicans had tried to force through during the Hoover and Coolidge days (such as farm legislation). In such cases, Senator McNary kept quiet, helped move the laws along as quickly as possible, and then allowed them to pass by a simple voice vote which would, he hoped, go relatively unnoticed.

In other matters, such as Social Security and other social legislation, it was McNary's practice to add on impractical liberal amendments. Then, when the Democrats, as responsible party in power, were forced to slice away these embellishments, Senator McNary and the Republicans could take credit for wanting even more for the people than the Democrats were willing to give.

One other technique, which was used in the Roosevelt Supreme Court fight, was to let the Democrats fight among themselves—then exert the Republican leverage to achieve as many Republican or regional aims as possible in exchange for support of one of the warring Democratic factions.

Lying low was the advisable Republican *modus operandi* in the first years. In 1935 when Huey Long filibustered for days, Senator McNary made only one speech as long as fifteen minutes on the Senate floor. It should be noted, however, that this did not represent quiescence on the part of the Republican leader. He preferred, during his entire career, to work by telephone and through committees.

In 1937, after the Supreme Court had outlawed the NRA and the original Agricultural Adjustment Act, and when the Democrats of Congress split so bitterly on the Supreme Court packing measure, Senator McNary's prestige and importance increased.

In some of these measures the senator from Oregon disagreed with his more conservative Republican colleagues. He favored, and helped the government secure, government transmission of power to carry hydroelectricity—for his farmers. His support of TVA, of government spending, of agricultural subsidy all brought him criticism within his own party. He opposed Democratic legislation, including Secretary Wallace's farm plans—but there were many among the Republican fold who thought some of Senator McNary's opposition had a hollow ring to it.

Never did he show any patience with the hidebound in his own party who wanted to return to the good old days, even after two Roosevelt elections. In 1937, Charles McNary laid down a new creed for Republicanism. "We must show a progressive front, deal generously with the farmer, modify our policies as to labor, and recognize that social legislation is here to stay," he said then. His Senate colleagues listened in 1937, for there were only sixteen Republicans in the Senate that year, compared to seventy-six Democrats and four minority Senators. But by 1938, the Republicans had increased their Senate representation by seven members, and they felt more cocky than before. They were not so inclined to listen to Charles McNary, because in the recession of 1937 and 1938 they saw signs of Democratic failure which should lead to a Republican resurgence.

That year, 1938, the Roosevelt administration pushed through Congress its most comprehensive agricultural law—the Agricultural Adjustment Act of 1938, which attacked the old problem of farm surpluses in a number of different ways. It encompassed many of the ideas for which Charles McNary had been working for years, and while he supported Republicans invariably, and opposed Democratic measures for the record, McNary could not help but be gratified, to a large extent, by the attention now given the farmers he had supported for so long.

"Parity" price support by loans, purchases, and direct payments, acreage limit, quotas, and referendums, soil conservation payments, and crop insurance were all debated hotly in the Senate, yet the act became law, giving American agriculture the most comprehensive support and protection (and potential regulation) in the history of the United States. By 1939 the American farmer had lost a great amount of the independence he had valued so highly in the past, but he had gained an economic security he had never before known. It was too late for Jack DeVore, the eastern Oregon rancher, but it was not too late for younger men, who began to subject themselves to the teachings of experts on contour plowing, crop rotation, and voluntary limitation of production.

In the spring of 1940 Senator McNary was touted in the West as a candidate for the Presidency. He was not the only pre-convention candidate, by far, nor was he more anxious to incur the responsibilities of a national campaign than he had been nearly a decade before when the wealthy Senator James Couzens offered to back him for the Presidency.

McNary's support did not come only from Oregon or from farm areas. The students of Oberlin College in Ohio chose him in one of the typical college polls. He did run in the Oregon Republican primary, and he outpolled the combined Roosevelt and Garner votes of the Democratic primary—but Oregon was still basically a Republican state, despite its swing to the Democratic columns in the Roosevelt years.

From time to time Senator McNary went home to the farm at Fir Cone to examine his political conscience and to tend the pot of beans visitors always found ready and waiting in front of the senator's spacious fireplace. On such a visit he talked fundamentals, and speaking fundamentally, he neither wanted the Republican Presidential nomination in 1940 nor did he suggest that he had any great hope of acquiring it, if he had wanted it.

It was a correct estimate. As the Republicans assembled in Philadelphia, the front-running candidates were Thomas E. Dewey and Senator Robert Taft of Ohio. Dewey had nearly won election to the traditionally President-making post of governor of New York in 1938. Senator Taft, an able conservative, occupied a very important position in the Republican senatorial bloc. If McNary was the spokesman for the old Theodore Roosevelt type of Republican, so Taft was the spokesman for the William Howard Taft type who had succeeded to power after T.R. split the Republican party in 1912, and the fact that Robert Taft was his father's son brought him much support from those who worshipped the old times.

The nomination was captured by neither man, but by a rumpled, open-faced corporation lawyer named Wendell Willkie, an Iowa farm boy who had grown up in the city, and now was president of Commonwealth and Southern, one of the largest privately owned electrical companies in the United States.

It was an odd nomination, carried out by a group of Young Turks, or rebellious young Republicans who had grown to maturity in the Roosevelt mold. But because Willkie was a city man, an eastern man by residence, and a former Democrat, the Republicans felt they needed some strong medicine. Senator George Norris and the liberal-to-insurgent wing of the party agreed. They insisted Charles McNary be the nominee for Vice-President. Thus, by putting in a farm man, a western man, a lifelong Republican, they might counteract criticism.

There was criticism aplenty. The conservatives of the Republican party had no use for Willkie and no more use for McNary, who was isolationist, protectionist, and a loyal party man, but who nonetheless was a liberal in domestic affairs. The candidates had very little use for one another, and during the election each went his own way, each speaking his mind on matters of public policy.

Charles McNary's friends claimed one great honor.

"Henry's our answer to Charlie McNary," one western delegate to that year's Democratic convention in Chicago shouted, when questioned about the reason for Henry Wallace's selection as Franklin Roosevelt's third-term running mate. There was something to the argument. If there was a man in Washington who exercised power without ever delivering an oration on the Senate floor, it was Senator Charles McNary. The Democrats had captured the Republican farm vote in 1932, and had held it in 1936. The presence of "the farmer's friend" on the Republican ticket offered a threat to Roosevelt which could not have been ignored even had he not been facing the unusual difficulty of running against tradition.

The election campaign of 1940 was a spirited campaign, in almost every way. The Willkie-McNary ticket was a strong one, and the Democrats knew it. Together, the Republican candidates gave an impression that the party had truly reformed its way, and was accepting social change with grace. John L. Lewis, having quarreled with Roosevelt, came out for the Republican candidates, splitting the CIO, shocking Henry Wallace into using bad language.

It was an election in which the Republicans had more outside, independent support than they had enjoyed in ten years. But they also had only lukewarm support from the old guard of conservative Republicans. Charles McNary had alienated Herbert Hoover—most recently in asking him to be quiet about the Democratic split over the Supreme Court plan so that the Republicans could maneuver effectively. Hoover's enmity did not help the Republican cause.

The campaign of 1940 was a close campaign, and sometimes it seemed closer than it actually turned out to be. At first the President indicated that he would not indulge in an active campaign since he had been "drafted" by popular appeals. In October he was deep in a personal campaign, as the professional politicians reported that he might be in trouble if he did not work for himself.

Franklin Roosevelt did work. Willkie worked too, speaking constantly at banquets and luncheons, until his voice threatened to give out, travelling aboard a special train the press christened the Squirrel Cage. Robert Montgomery, the Hollywood actor, made his first appearance in national politics, by bringing in a doctor who stayed with Wendell Willkie, working to keep his voice alive, until the very last.

In the end, Roosevelt won the election by five million votes. The result was apparent early in the evening, in both East and West—or at least it was apparent to that old professional, Charles McNary, who conceded early and went off to bed. Wendell Willkie did not concede. He stayed for hours in his New York hotel suite, watching the results on the newest instrument in communications—television. Finally, he too, was forced to admit that Roosevelt had won election once again.

The election finished, Willkie moved into that limbo which is the special dwelling place of the unsuccessful Presidential candidate. Charles McNary moved back onto the stage of Congress, to engage himself again in the political maneuvering he liked so well, and which he found as enjoyable as golf and far less expensive.

For a moment in history, the Republicans had done what Charles McNary called for in 1937. They had shown a progressive front. In offering McNary as a candidate, the party had promised to deal generously with the farmer. Willkie had indicated considerable modification of the old standoffishness of Republicans to labor. And both Willkie and McNary recognized that the social revolution of the past decade was installed as a permanent part of American life. Even the Republican party had been modified, even if it was not readily apparent in a nation whose basic and extra-political concern was suddenly the transcendental question of war or peace.

PUBLIC ENEMY NUMBER ONE

CHAPTER FOURTEEN

THE 1920's, the gay, bawdy years of the Prohibition era, are often characterized as the Lawless Years. In this third decade of the century, ordinary, law-abiding citizens poured millions of dollars into the coffers of organized crime, wittingly and unwittingly, but almost always without caring. Drink was forbidden, but drunkenness flourished, and with drink and drunkenness and the wild abandon of the years the lawless grew powerful.

The highest law of the land—the American Constitution—was honored on the highest levels in winking breach. Was it any surprise then, to anyone, when judges and legislators and high government executives broke the law openly—even bragged about their bootleggers —that the bootleggers would have small regard for any law?

New York's Mayor Jimmy Walker seemed to spend most of his evenings in speakeasies. Chicago's Mayor "Big Bill" Thompson campaigned for election successfully on a promise to keep Chicago a wide-open town. Lesser officials were disillusioned if not corrupted. Some metropolitan police forces across the nation *were* corrupted, from top to bottom. Even federal forces were untrustworthy. Prohibition enforcement agents paid forty dollars a week or less, were bought wholesale by the beer barons. One symbol stood out in this era. It was the pudgy, hirsute figure of "Scarface" Alphonse Capone, standing triumphantly astride a prostrate Chicago, beer stein in one hand and baseball bat in the other, a pearl-gray felt hat of the finest quality perched atop his head, and his mouth split in a malevolent, toothy grin.

Crime in the 1920's developed an organization all its own. The Unione Siciliane controlled many of the activities of the underworld in the eastern and midwestern cities, although there were independent gangs and many gangsters. New York had its Dutch Schultz, as well as its Frankie Uale, whose name was simplified to Yale before he was gunned down by orders of Al Capone in a dispute over rights of succession in the syndicate in Chicago. Capone, himself, had come to major, if not total ascendancy in Chicago after battering out the brains of other gang leaders with his famous baseball bats. Violent as gang life was, in a way there was an orderliness about the underworld of the cities. The gang leaders controlled their underworld and when they were not fighting among themselves, they kept their minions, adherents, and customers safe from most interference by small-time punks and penny-ante confidence sharpsters.

But, as the old decade closed in the roaring thunder of Wall Street's crash, the life and outlook of millions of Americans began to change subtly. Before, nearly everyone had been too busy trying to make money and whoopee at the same time. There was little occasion in the happy world of the 1920's for examination of either personal or national conscience. It took the violent tremors of depression to bring to Americans the remorse of woeful hangover.

The forces of change had begun to work late in the 1920's. Gangsters, and particularly the Capone gang of Chicago, had defiled the law so completely that even a complaisant federal government could not but take notice. Late in the 1920's a quiet U.S. Attorney named George E. Q. Johnson set to work to prepare a case against Capone for violation of the federal income-tax laws and prohibition laws. It was tedious work, for Johnson could not trust local enforcement officers to help him. Too many of them were involved with Capone or other segments of the underworld. In all, the job took four years.

While Johnson was working, others joined the struggle against lawlessness, in their own ways. In 1930, civic groups estimated the cost of crime and racketeering as $3,000,000,000 a year to the American people. The National Surety Company put it higher—$7,500,-000,000. The Department of Justice noted that crime had risen in 772 cities that year. President Hoover said he was declaring war on gangsters, but he did so in his usual fashion, offering the declaration and moral support but no weapons for the warriors. The war against crime, said the President of the United States, was a local matter and must be handled locally. He was applauded in these sentiments by the World Association of Detectives, which gave its guarantee of assistance in the struggle.

Such an approach was hardly geared to strike terror into the hearts of America's criminals, and they remained unterrified in these last years of Prohibition. In the fall of 1930, Jack (Legs) Diamond was

shot to death in another of the gang killings which had made newspaper headlines for so long. Newspaper readers looked over their
papers calmly, if with interest. More excited was the *Manchester
Guardian* of England, which chose the Diamond slaying as occasion
to remark on the breakdown of law in the United States. The
Guardian compared America to China, where rival bandit chiefs killed
one another openly, and the public shrugged.

But the *Guardian* was behind the times. The forces of law and
order were slowly showing some signs of regrouping. The later-cele-
brated Elliott Ness was proving a thorn in the side of the Capone
gang and others in the Midwest with his unique Prohibition enforcement and still-smashing techniques. G.E.Q. Johnson plugged away
at securing the information against the Capones.

And most important of all, in an obscure office at 14th and K
Streets in Washington, a slender thirty-five year old man named J.
Edgar Hoover, chief of the Department of Justice's small Bureau of
Investigation, was lecturing on the need for better weapons, including
centralized files on criminals and their activities, and was slowly as-
sembling three million fingerprints and the finest law-enforcement
laboratories in the nation. In 1929 President Herbert Hoover had
named a national commission to study law enforcement. With assistance from the other Hoover the students were discovering that
crime was not a local problem, but a national one.

Half a continent away, at Michigan City, Indiana, a slim, dark-
haired young native of the little town of Maywood was just complet-
ing six years of service at hard labor for the robbery of a grocery store
in 1924. This Indiana farm boy—John Dillinger, Jr.—and Hoover
were to share the honors of the decade as symbols of the public attitude toward law and order in the turbulent 1930's. Dillinger was to
become a rebel gangster, more of the school of Jesse James than that
of Al Capone, and he was to capture the public imagination.

Shortly after the ignoble gangland death of Jack Diamond, President Hoover stubbornly reiterated his claim that state laws were ample
to control lawlessness. To push the federal government into law enforcement across the nation, he said, would be a "reflection on the
sovereignty and the stamina of state government."

Hoover was not alone. Representative Bertrand Snell of New

York, responding to criticism of the President, remarked that "unless our civilization is in a process of decay, racketeering in New York, Chicago and other cities can and will be stopped by the citizens of those cities when they are aroused from their lethargy."

But could it be stopped, and were the citizens in process of being aroused from the torpor of the past?

Hardly. On the day that Representative Reed gave his vote of confidence to the current American system, charitable organizations noted that forty thousand meals were being served the poor of New York City in fifty-three breadlines, soup kitchens, and charity dining rooms. The New York Junior Board of Trade was preparing, that day, another in its series of advertisements urging people to "Stay Away from New York" lest they become public charges. Three hundred and seventy-five unemployed men each received three cartons of candy bars on credit. They bought the bars at sixty cents a carton, and were to sell them at $1.20—thus earning $1.80 a day if they were lucky enough to dispose of all the candy in a glutted market. St. Mark's Catholic Mission was planning a Thanksgiving dinner for a hundred unemployed of a new, but growing category, the business and professional people—the lawyers and stockbrokers and company presidents who no longer had companies. Each day, fewer of these people could summon large outbursts of righteous indignation at the state of American criminality. Law enforcement of *all kinds* was in serious danger of breaking down in the winter of 1930.

During the following year, law and order won an important victory in a strange way. The assiduous Mr. Johnson in Chicago had sent Jake (Greasy Thumb) Guzik and Ralph Capone to federal prison on charges of willfully overlooking their income taxes. Prohibition enforcement being as weak as it was, this was the best weapon in the federal government's slender arsenal. Mr. Johnson used it, too, against Scarface Al. He filed five thousand charges of violation of the Prohibition laws against Capone in 1931, but Capone was far more worried about a handful of evidence which involved failure to pay his income taxes.

Capone had truly come into the limelight as a national figure in 1931. The previous year, even as overlord of Chicago's underworld, he had managed to keep his name out of the papers, except in his adopted town. But in 1931, Capone was a celebrated figure: even *The New York Times*, which disliked criminal news, reported his activities on a hundred different days. And there was nothing Scarface Al could do about it.

The government charged that Capone had forgotten to pay six million dollars in taxes on the past four years' income. Capone had never signed a check or maintained a bank account in all his years of power, but unfortunately for him federal agents had raided two or three of his personal establishments, had broken open the safes, and had cracked the gang's secret code pertaining to fiscal matters.

Capone's attorneys quickly offered to settle for four million dollars. Federal Attorney Johnson took up the matter with Federal District Judge James H. Wilkerson, in the privacy of the judge's chambers. A deal was made, after that, under which Capone would pay up his taxes and fines, and would spend two-and-a-half years in federal prison. There was reason to believe that Capone was tired of the gang wars, and that he would welcome the prison term as a rest. Afterwards, it was said, he planned to retire to the Neapolitan life, and never to darken Chicago's Loop again. Strong indication of the truth of the claim lay in a one year jail term which Capone had just served in Pennsylvania without a whimper. In the old days of the 1920's, no gang leader would ever have gone to jail over the simple error of carrying a concealed weapon, but Capone had just done exactly so. This arrest was brought about by the FBI, although FBI agents did not then have the power to arrest. It was the beginning of the end for Capone, for while he was in jail the Treasury prepared its tax case.

The deal was made, but Scarface Al committed the most serious error of his career. Instead of keeping silent and taking his medicine, he felt it necessary to preserve his lordship. He announced to the press the exact terms of the arrangement with the federal government. When his tax case came up, Federal Judge Wilkerson had no choice but to deny any intent to "make a deal" on the part of the government, to the horror of Capone and his attorneys. But had the judge let the arrangement stand after Capone's thoughtless announcement that a "deal" had been made, federal justice would not thereafter have been worth a plugged nickel in Chicago, and Judge Wilkerson might have ended up unbenched.

Capone felt that he had been double-crossed when he was sentenced to eleven years in prison. Senator William Borah felt the same way, and did not conceal the belief. While Capone went to prison, finally, to serve his eleven years, and while District Attorney Johnson was rewarded by President Hoover with a federal judgeship, Judge Wilkerson could not be rewarded at all. The U.S. Senate disapproved of double-dealing, even with Scarface Al Capone.

The destruction of Al Capone did not put an end to the big gangs of the cities any more than the coming of Prohibition did. But the end of Scarface Al's career did inculcate in the gang lords a healthy respect for an aroused federal government and considerable care in the filing of federal tax returns.

But the following year, 1932, saw the rise of a new kind of criminal, the amateur kidnaper who held his victim for ransom.

There was nothing new in 1932 about kidnaping. It had been carried out for centuries with varying degrees of success. But usually the motive of monetary gain in kidnaping was coupled with revenge or with organized piracy. Spurred by the neediness of criminals and others during the harsh years of the depression, kidnaping became a crime of the amateurs as well as of the professionals early in the 1930's. Here, indeed, was a sign that law enforcement was truly breaking down.

The inefficacy of Herbert Hoover's *laissez faire* policy in law enforcement was shown to the public fully in the Lindbergh kidnap case, which began on March 1, 1932, when someone abducted the twenty-month-old son of Colonel and Mrs. Charles A. Lindbergh from their home near Hopewell, New Jersey. Within a matter of hours the entire nation was aroused by the crime against a national hero. Even Al Capone offered a reward for the return of the baby and the arrest of the kidnaper. Police officials from the entire eastern seaboard met, to try to cooperate in solving the case. From the federal government in Washington came J. Edgar Hoover, specially deputized for this job by Herbert Hoover.

In the beginning of the case there was little that J. Edgar Hoover could do. Federal laws gave him small excuse for concerning himself with a state problem, no matter how much the nation at large might feel involved. Kidnaping was an offense against the law, but not against federal law.

Three months after the crime, the Lindbergh baby was discovered, dead, just a few miles from the family home. The effect of the discovery was such that Congress passed the Lindbergh kidnap law, which came to assess the death penalty for transportation of a kidnaped person across a state line. Equally important, the Lindbergh law gave the federal government legal reason to enter kidnaping cases. In essence, it not only made kidnaping a federal offense, but placed the responsibility for these extremely delicate cases exactly where it belonged—in the hands of the best-trained and best-equipped investigative force in the nation: the FBI.

The Lindbergh law did not solve the problems of a growing crime rate, of course. Nor did FBI men have very much power or authority. They could not even carry weapons to protect themselves. Director Hoover sympathized, generally, with President Hoover's position that crime was a local and state problem, but the FBI chief also realized that crime was growing more rapidly than the demoralized local enforcement agencies could expand or clean up to counteract it.

When the Roosevelt administration took office in March, 1933, Presidential assistants Louis Howe and Raymond Moley brought new knowledge and new attitudes to bear upon the problems of enforcement of criminal justice. At the same time, the spectacular varieties of crime were on the increase. Despite the Lindbergh law, kidnapings continued. On an average two banks were robbed every day—and remarkably enough a gang of bank robbers could clean out the vaults and drive across a state line without violating a single federal law, unless they happened to be driving a stolen car.

The new administration saw need for a new approach to crime. There was evidence of the interstate nature of racketeering. J. Edgar Hoover noted, perhaps a bit ruefully, that the most effective weapons in federal hands against racketeering were the anti-trust laws. But even was there the time to move through this complicated machinery, it was not designed to control the new violent criminality and the new kind of criminal. The old Prohibition gangsters were on their way out.

The criminals changed with the times, moving from rumrunning and alcohol and beer manufacture into narcotics, numbers rackets, and labor extortion. Crime was big business. However, the crime that shocked the nation was of another type, in which innocent bystanders were killed and injured. The Capones and the Lucianos and the Schultzes and the Frankie Costellos looked with distaste on the new criminal class. Well they might be annoyed, too, for the new criminals brought the federal government into the greatest war against crime in American history.

The plans for the campaign against crime were slow to materialize in the beginning of the Roosevelt years. In March and for weeks thereafter, Roosevelt and his principal advisers were beleaguered by even more vital problems. But by summer, 1933, Franklin Roosevelt was able to take a breathing spell, even to spend a few weeks in the gentler atmosphere of his estate, Krum Elbow, at Hyde Park. And while he was there, an event occurred in Kansas City which so shocked the nation and the nation's lawmakers that the drive against crime was begun ahead of plan.

On June 16, at Hot Springs, Arkansas, agents of the Federal Bureau of Investigation had captured Frank Nash, an escaped convict who had managed to remain at large for three years. They took Nash to Fort Smith, to avoid complications. Such were the times that a gang associate of Nash's named Vern Miller had sworn that he would rescue Nash from the law, and the officers expected an ambush.

The next day, the officers arrived with Nash by train at Kansas City. Miller and two gunmen were waiting for them, apprised of the lawmen's intentions by the underground communications system. Early on the morning of June 17, when the officers were met by others and had entered an auto to move Nash to Leavenworth penitentiary, the gangsters attacked with pistols and submachine guns. Four officers were killed, Nash was killed, and two other officers were wounded. Miller, accompanied by gunmen "Pretty Boy" Floyd and Adam Richetti, escaped in a roaring auto.

A month later an Oklahoma oil man named Charles F. Urschel was kidnaped at his home by men armed with submachine guns and pistols.

These two crimes aroused the nation as it had not been aroused since the Lindbergh case. Within a week of the Urschel kidnaping J. Edgar Hoover was appointed to direct a full-scale war on crime in America. Any reluctance he might have felt about invasion of state's rights must have been dissipated in the agony of contemplating the death of unarmed officers in the Kansas City massacre, and the full realization that local law enforcement agencies were not equipped to deal with the new criminals.

The Federal Bureau of Investigation did not spring, full-blown, into battle, and overwhelm its enemies in the summer and fall of 1933. The newspapers talked about the "war," but in the early months there was little surcease in criminal activity or little added caution from the criminals who seemed to range the country at will. The total FBI force in the summer of 1933 numbered only 326 investigators. The force had to be expanded to cover the nation and the bureau's crime laboratories had to be expanded. Most of all, the FBI needed new federal laws to permit it to carry on the war against crime.

While these requirements were demanding the attention of the authorities, a new one-gang crime wave swept across the Middle West. John Dillinger, following his release from the Indiana state penitentiary, had continued to rob stores and even banks. Alone, he might not have attracted attention, but during his prison stay he had met a number of hardened gunmen, chief of them a forty-one-year-old former carpenter named John Hamilton.

In September, 1933, John Dillinger engineered an escape from Indiana penitentiary, in which Hamilton and nine others fled the walls successfully.

They were grateful men. Three weeks later, when Dillinger was arrested and held in the jail at Lima, Ohio, charged with bank robbery, John Hamilton and his friends shot their way into the jail, killed the sheriff, and brought Dillinger out. Then, the gang began a spree of bank robberies, which carried them through Ohio, Indiana, Illinois, and Wisconsin, killing and robbing. In all, their loot was estimated to be around $200,000, with the largest haul of all taken from the bank at Greencastle, Indiana—a sum of $144,000.

Yet even as the Dillinger gang terrorized bankers of the Middle West, the Federal Bureau of Investigation drive was gathering momentum. Two weeks after Dillinger's escape from the Lima jail, FBI agents and policemen in Memphis, Tennessee, completed the roundup of the Urschel kidnaping gang with the capture of "Machine Gun" Kelly, who emerged from hiding unarmed, frightened, and crying, "Don't shoot, G-Men." The FBI men thus acquired a nickname which was to remain for years, publicized in newspapers, radio and in a movie which starred the young James Cagney.

Neither the nickname nor the reputation of the G-Men seemed to frighten John Dillinger and his gang. His crimes were murder, bank robbery, and participation in a prison break. He did not, in 1933, come under the jurisdiction of the FBI.

Early in 1934, Dillinger was recognized in Tucson, Arizona, by local officers. He was arrested and taken back to Indiana to stand trial for the murder of an East Chicago policeman. He was placed in a modern jail in Crown Point, under the jurisdiction of Sheriff Lillian Holley, who claimed that her jail was escape-proof, and that the nation need not fear Dillinger any longer.

On March 3, 1934, however, John Dillinger pulled a gun from his pocket, frightened the jail guards into opening his cell, took the sheriff's car, and headed for Chicago. He claimed that the gun he used was fashioned with a razor blade from a piece of wood while he sat in his cell. Later, the guards claimed that gun was a real one which had been slipped in to him. Whatever the truth, Dillinger headed for a brief period of glory—and into trouble he could not possibly understand. For as he sat in the Crown Point jail, whittling, Congress had begun to act to strengthen the federal government's war against crime.

On February 20, 1934, administration supporters introduced a dozen bills to add teeth to federal law enforcement. One bill would regulate machine-gun sale and the sale of firearms. Another would make it a federal offense to move stolen property across state lines. Another said robbery of a national bank would be a federal offense. Still others strengthened the Lindbergh law, established protection of interstate trade against racketeers, made it a federal offense to take flight to avoid state prosecution, made extortion by telephone across state lines a federal offense. In the mass of legislation came some over-exuberance, too, such as laws to limit *habeas corpus*, the right of comment, and the protection of wives and husbands against testifying against one another.

f bombast and honeyed words
ould solve the problems of the
ountry, then Huey P. Long, the
Louisiana Kingfish, was the man
or the job. UNITED PRESS INTER-
NATIONAL PHOTO

There they were, three of a kind. At least Dr. Francis E. Townsend, the Reverend Gerald L. K. Smith, and Father Coughlin all thought they could run the country better than FDR. UNITED PRESS INTERNATIONAL PHOTO

This was the turning point and the place was Flint, Michigan. And these were the men who led the way. Richard Frankensteen (second from left), Homer Martin (second from right) and the young leader of Detroit's west side local, Walter Reuther. The target was Chevrolet. UNITED PRESS INTERNATIONAL PHOTO

When Alfred P. Sloan, Jr. talked to Senators or to anyone else, he expected them to listen to his words. UNITED PRESS INTERNATIONAL PHOTO

But from all the law-giving attempts, came stronger powers for the federal law enforcement agencies, and particularly the FBI, than ever before in history. When John Dillinger set out in his stolen car for the safety of anonymity in the big city of Chicago, he became a marked man. By transporting a stolen auto across state lines, for the first time he was fair game for the FBI.

For five months, John Dillinger was the most important man in the world of crime and punishment. He never became wealthy. He spent most of this time in hiding, or in acts of violence. He was a miserable, hunted creature. Yet in his daring escape from the Crown Point jail, John Dillinger attracted the attention of the children of America. J. Edgar Hoover and other lawmen were shocked to learn that boys who once played cowboys and Indians were playing cops and robbers—and that many of the youths wanted to play the part of John Dillinger in their childish game.

Partly because of the unfavorable public reaction—the sympathy that had developed toward this lawless man and his gang because the public found him "romantic," J. Edgar Hoover unfolded the resources of the bureau. The order to get Dillinger became the prime business of the FBI. He was Public Enemy Number One on the FBI's list. He was not a Robin Hood, said Director Hoover, but one of the "vermin" which must be stamped out of American society.

Following Dillinger's escape from Crown Point, the gangster leader headed for St. Paul, Minnesota—and why St. Paul? Because that lesser of the Twin Cities had earned a reputation during the wild years as a haven for criminals. It was a sort of Miami Beach of the machine-gun set.

The city fathers of St. Paul had some peculiar ideas about city management, and crime prevention in particular. Police Chief John J. O'Connor had begun the system years before in the theory of live and let live. He offered unofficial sanctuary to criminals as long as they did not "work" St. Paul. Since he was the brother of the head of the local Democratic machine, Police Chief O'Connor's word was the law. St. Paul was an ordinary city—and a rest for Director Hoover's vermin. At first Paddy Griffin, who ran a boardinghouse on Wabasha Street, was the unofficial interlocutor who maintained relations between officialdom and the underworld. When criminals travelled to

St. Paul, first of all they checked in with Paddy Griffin. Then they settled down, and perhaps even went to work. The system had proved satisfactory for St. Paul for a number of years—officials believed. When Paddy died, Danny Hogan took his place, and long after Chief O'Connor's time the system remained. Dillinger, Machine Gun Kelly, Terrible Roger Tuohy, and all the other infamous bank robbers and killers of the period had "connections" in St. Paul. Verne Sankey, who had kidnaped Denver's Charles Boettcher II in 1933 had headed for St. Paul like a homing pigeon the moment the $60,000 ransom was paid. Harvey Bailey, one of the Urschel kidnapers, had sent part of the $200,000 Urschel ransom to St. Paul to be "fenced." That horrid old woman Ma Barker, her gang of sons, and Alvin Karpis made St. Paul their playground.

In the wake of the federal war on crime, some citizens of St. Paul became aroused about the unsavory reputation their city had received. The St. Paul *News* opened an editorial campaign against lawlessness in January, 1934, but three months later a grand jury whitewashed the police department. The grand jury's claim to spotlessness came on March 30. St. Paul, said the grand jury, was not a haven for criminals, but a good clean town.

As those words were spoken John Dillinger and his paramour, Evelyn Frechette, the Indiana moll, were holed up in a St. Paul apartment house where they had set up temporary housekeeping under the friendly eye of a segment of the law. Officers discovered them and closed in, but one of the Dillinger gang spotted the lawmen. Dillinger reached for his machine gun, while Miss Frechette, the chauffeur, ran for the car. Homer Van Meter, a Dillinger gangster, covered the retreat with a revolver, duelling with the incoming police. Dillinger came out of the building, when the car appeared, spraying machine-gun bullets as a gardener sprays his hose. They escaped, although one lucky marksman put a bullet into Dillinger's leg.

Across the river, the pair drove into residential Minneapolis, where they stopped momentarily at the home of Eugene Green, a new Dillinger follower. Dr. Clayton May was persuaded to take the bullet out of Dillinger's leg and keep his mouth shut—for which he later paid heavily before the law. Dillinger moved to an apartment, for the law officers, led by the FBI, were on his trail. A few days later the new gangster, Green, was ambushed and killed. Dillinger and Miss Frechette fled to Indianapolis then, but the hot breath of the law was singeing them. She was captured there and Dillinger escaped narrowly, thence to make his way to Little Bohemia lodge in Wisconsin.

Since there were only five hundred FBI agents in the entire nation at this time, it was impossible for the agents to cover every hiding place. Bureau agents made extensive investigations to discover where Dillinger might go. As a result, a call was received in the Chicago office advising that the Dillinger gang was at Little Bohemia. Immediately, agents were dispatched to Little Bohemia.

Due to two automobile breakdowns the posse did not arrive near the Wisconsin resort until after dark. Then, three Civilian Conservation Corps youths who came out of the lodge in an old car were challenged by the officers. When the CCC boys refused to stop, officers opened fire, killing one of the misguided innocents, and also warning the Dillinger gang that trouble was upon them. In the confusion Dillinger, Baby Face Nelson, John Hamilton, Homer Van Meter, Tommy Carroll, and Patrick Reilly got away. The gang's new group of women were captured, and while the officers did not know it, John Hamilton of the gang was mortally shot in the liver. That same night, FBI Agent Carter Baum was slain by Baby Face Nelson in the gun battle.

When J. Edgar Hoover learned of the killing of one of his agents, he intensified the search for Dillinger. He assigned Special Agent Samuel P. Cowley to do nothing but get Dillinger, and Cowley moved into the Chicago area to work with Agent Purvis.

The capture of Dillinger was largely due to the slogging work of two East Chicago policemen. This pair, Captain Timothy O'Neill and Sergeant Martin Zarkovitch had never forgotten the murder of policeman William O'Malley in the robbery of the First National Bank of East Chicago, that January. This was the crime for which Dillinger had been brought to the Crown Point jail to await trial. The officers, friends of the dead O'Malley, believed that justice had been cheated. They did not forget Dillinger, and they kept lookout on the North Side of Chicago for him, week in and week out—for this was Dillinger's old stamping ground.

After the Little Bohemia incident, and a brush with the law near

St. Paul, where he had headed once again, Dillinger simply disappeared from sight. He and Baby Face Nelson and Van Meter held up a bank in South Bend on June 30, spraying the streets with machinegun fire in their fashion, and killing a traffic policeman. Dillinger, the outlaw, became "too hot" for his own gang. Soon, even the underworld's hand was turned against him, for he was bringing trouble and bad reputation to the less spectacular gangsmen. The price on Dillinger's head had risen to $15,000, so badly was he "wanted."

Dillinger decided that he would undergo plastic surgery, to change his features. He did so, and hid in Chicago somewhere for weeks, until the bandages could be removed.

Then, one day in July, Sergeant Zarkovitch learned from an informant in the underworld that Dillinger was in Chicago. He received that word from Ana Cumpanas, a Rumanian brothelkeeper in Gary, Indiana. Dillinger had taken up with one of her girls, Polly Hamilton. That very evening, Ana Cumpanas said, Dillinger was taking the pair of them out to the movies.

Sergeant Zarkovitch took Ana Cumpanas to the FBI headquarters where she repeated her story. She was turning Dillinger in, she indicated, not because she had anything against him, but because the price on his head was so great she could not overlook it. Ana Cumpanas was in trouble. She was about to be deported as an undesirable alien, and she needed money. She turned Dillinger in to the authorities hoping for leniency in the deportation case, and demanding money.

That night, Special Agent Purvis, Special Agent Cowley and others, police and FBI men, gathered around the Biograph theater on the North Side. Here Dillinger and the two women had gone to see Clark Gable playing in *Manhattan Melodrama*. Purvis had waited outside, and had seen Dillinger enter the theater. He had entered the theater, but he could not find the man. Then he had waited longer.

At ten-thirty in the evening, after he had waited nearly two hours, Dillinger and the women came out. Dillinger was coatless, smiling, chatting, and unworried, walking a pace ahead of the women, who had dropped back suddenly.

Purvis, who knew Dillinger, had stationed himself as lookout, and when he recognized his man, despite a straightened nose and a filled dimple, he lit a cigar, a signal that had been prearranged. Suddenly, someone shouted, and Dillinger was alert. He leapt into the alley entrance, to the left of Purvis, saw armed men, and whirled back into the street, realizing in one split second that he had been betrayed. As Dillinger's hand snaked toward his hip pocket (where he had holstered a .38 automatic pistol) three government men began firing. Two shots ricochetted off the walls and injured two women, but three of them struck Dillinger, killing him almost instantly. He did not speak a word.

Dillinger's death was greeted with sighs of relief by law enforcement officers and the law-abiding in America, yet so strained were attitudes toward the law in this time of trial that he was still regarded as a hero by many. The Dillinger funeral was held at Maywood, Indiana; the body was claimed by his sister, who kept it resting in state in her little bungalow on the day before the funeral, so he might be viewed one last time by his friends and admirers.

More than twenty-five hundred people came to the bungalow to see Dillinger on the day before the funeral. Dillinger's sister kept watch until 2 A.M., as a steady stream of visitors moved through her parlor. Thirty floral pieces appeared at the funeral, where the family minister preached a sermon in behalf of the "wayward boy" who had become America's Public Enemy Number One and had been shot to death at the age of thirty-one.

The funeral, and its implications, disturbed J. Edgar Hoover, who redoubled his war against crime, determined not only to wipe out the power of the gangs of desperadoes who roamed the country robbing and killing, but also to break the romantic hold they held on a sizeable segment of the American people.

Later that year, Baby Face Nelson became Public Enemy Number One, so designated for his killing of Agent Baum. In the fall of 1934, Nelson gunned down Special Agent Cowley and Special Agent H. E. Hollis, but was so badly wounded that he died shortly afterward. The tempo of the war increased. Pretty Boy Floyd, the killer of the Kansas City massacre, was shot down in Ohio. The Barrow boys and Bonnie Parker, another gang, were killed in Texas.

The remainder of the Dillinger gang fell, one by one. Hamilton was dead, although the authorities did not learn of this for months.

Homer Van Meter was killed in St. Paul, Tommy Carroll in Waterloo, Iowa, Jack Klutes in Chicago, and Harry Pierpont, the last of them, went to the electric chair in Ohio. Evelyn Frechette, Dillinger's most famous "moll," joined a sideshow and for months astounded gaping crowds by describing the habits of her paramour.

Once the Dillinger gang was wiped out, Doc Barker and Alvin Karpis succeeded one another as Public Enemy Number One. By the end of 1934, 75 kidnapers had been convicted, and 614 FBI agents were on the prowl, looking for 6,000 wanted men.

In 1935, after the solution of the Weyerhauser kidnap case, Hoover announced that the big gangs had been wiped out once and for all. In the sense that the desperadoes had been eliminated as a force in American society, he was correct. In 1936, after a smarting Director Hoover personally led in the capture of Alvin Karpis to assure his critics that he was capable as a law enforcement officer, the list of Public Enemies ceased to interest the public. That year Maurice Denning, a bank robber, became Public Enemy Number One, and who ever heard of him?

The FBI continued to strengthen its police facilities, to instruct and guide state and local police officers, and to better the enforcement of law throughout the land. But the emphasis in crime-fighting in these middle years, while publicly vested in the FBI, turned to another aspect of criminality: the control of post-Prohibition racketeering by new kinds of gangs, so tightly knit as to form big business associations. The middle 1930's marked the specialized organization of what was to become infamous as The Syndicate, an amorphous grouping of underworld captains who controlled crime in America's big cities.

The change in the thirties which brought legalized gambling to Nevada, gave the criminal element of the United States great hope, and also a base from which to work. But the important criminal operators did not need to take advantage of that haven immediately. Arthur Flegenheimer (Dutch Schultz) controlled the rackets in New York, until he was ambushed in New Jersey in 1935. The gangs then split up the take, and began to move around. Bugsy Siegal and Meyer Lansky moved into Philadelphia, Pittsburgh, and Cleveland, and finally to Los Angeles. Louis (Lepke) Buchalter controlled rackets in

New York, and Baltimore. Lucky Luciano ran dope and prostitution in New York, and Jacob (Gurrah) Shapiro and Joe Adonis completed the picture. Together they were known as The Big Six, and after Dutch Schultz's demise they controlled most of American racketeering. Harry (Dutch) Schomberg moved to Nevada to take over the legalized gambling connection. Frankie Costello moved into New Orleans when slot machines were barred in New York City in 1934. Costello took his five thousand machines down to put them at the service of Huey Long. He and Long established the Pelican Novelty Company, whose take was $800,000 a year, in a city a fourteenth as large as New York.

Following the death of Dutch Schultz, the city of New York became restless under the heel of the gangsters, and Thomas E. Dewey was appointed to a post as special prosecutor to try to clean up the city. This was before the Richard Whitney case, and Dewey was best known as a short but energetic young lawyer from Michigan who had secured a judgment of a million dollars against Charles Mitchell of the First National City Bank, when criminal income-tax charges had been dropped against Mitchell, after his spectacular speculations of the twenties became known.

In 1936 Dewey secured a conviction of Lucky Luciano on charges arising from his control of prostitution. Working from an office in a midtown New York office building, Dewey brought in prostitutes, pimps, and other underworld characters, yet made their evidence stand up in court.

A year later he ran for district attorney of New York City, and was elected, largely on the basis of his record and warnings that the crime syndicate lurked like an octopus just below the surface of American life. If Dewey was not personally responsible for the growing awareness of the American people that two worlds existed in their society, he was at least as important in bringing this knowledge as was J. Edgar Hoover. Like Hoover, Dewey brought awareness of the dangers of crime home to Americans, and like Hoover, Dewey brought new methods into play to counteract the growth of crime in a puzzled and often lawless society.

Elected district attorney, Dewey began bringing in more prosecutions, and his record of convictions was startling. In seventy cases,

Dewey convicted sixty-eight criminals, including four out of five of the men responsible for fixing prices and running a racket in the bakeries of New York. He broke rackets on the docks, in the Teamsters Union, and in the electrical unions.

Both Dewey and Hoover talked long and often on one subject: the relationship between organized crime and politicians. Both men were sincere, although their paths were so very different. Hoover, having dedicated himself to law enforcement at an early age, remained with the Federal Bureau of Investigation, despite all attempts by political groups and industry to woo him away. Dewey, a Republican of a political turn of mind, used the fame he acquired as a crime fighter to pull himself into the national political scene. By 1939, when Hoover distinguished himself by accepting the surrender of Louis (Lepke) Buchalter, Dewey had emerged as a potential candidate for the Presidency in 1940. Hoover's activities changed somewhat that year, too, for at President Roosevelt's request the FBI began a searching inquiry into Communist and Nazi organizations in the United States, seeking evidence that they might be planning subversive activities in the land. Hoover and the FBI had investigated Nazis and Communists before, beginning in 1933, but in 1939 President Roosevelt issued a special directive assigning the bureau a formal responsibility. Not long afterward the FBI was also given responsibility for collection of intelligence for the entire Western Hemisphere.

The FBI investigations of Communism and Naziism brought squeals of pain from the left and right sides of the political spectrum. An attempt was made, particularly by the Communists, to create an image of the FBI as a Gestapo-type organization, and of Hoover as an omnipotent secret police chief who had such power that even Presidents could not unseat him. All this was arrant nonsense, but in the 1930's, for reasons of his own, President Roosevelt chose to allow this myth to flourish.

As the 1930's ended, FBI Director Hoover was under bitter attack from the Communists and their allies, particularly after the FBI arrested a dozen people in the Middle West on charges of conspiring to recruit volunteers for the Spanish Loyalist Army. So far had the battle of pure crime been won that both the bureau and its enemies could turn to other affairs. That same spring, Thomas E.

Dewey, District Attorney of New York City, felt it important that he comment on President Roosevelt's "belligerency in international affairs." If these matters seemed far removed from the booze, dope, prostitution, and murder problems of the previous decade, it was only because after ten years of effort, first faltering, then gaining confidence and strength, the American people had learned that only through united, federal action could the criminal elements in American society be controlled.

THE BROTHERS REUTHER

CHAPTER FIFTEEN

IN RECENT YEARS the health of the American automotive industry has been accepted by economists almost everywhere as a significant indicator of the economic health of the United States. This indicator was not so generally recognized at the time of the Wall Street crash; still President Hoover in the late twenties talked of "two cars in every garage," which certainly showed how generally automobiles had been accepted as a barometer of national prosperity just during his ten years in national politics.

By the end of 1930 a foreigner could have known there was something seriously amiss in the American economy had he never heard of the stock market, nor ever visited the United States, but only had access in his homeland to figures which showed American automobile production in the years 1925 and 1930. In 1925 automotive manufacturers produced 3,735,000 passenger cars. In 1930 they produced 2,787,000 cars, although the population had increased by eight million people since 1925 and the country had more and better roads than ever before. Even those figures do not show the total depth of the American fall from an economic pinnacle. In 1929 the Detroit auto factories—and these were the most important in the industry—employed 470,000 men. Two years later the factories employed only 257,000 men, and most of these workers labored on a part-time "share-the-work" basis. Consequently, the industrial statistics of the depression years concealed almost as much human misery as they revealed.

Thousands of men lined up each day before the gates of the Ford Motor Company in River Rouge, and in the geographically small but economically huge industrial complex centered around East Jefferson Avenue on Detroit's East Side. At Chrysler, Briggs, and a handful of other plants the men clustered, looking for work. A few found the work, steadily. Most of these were friends of someone "on the inside." But for the vast majority, these early depression years meant countless hours of standing and waiting, from six in the morning, perhaps through two shifts for part-time work, for relief, for handouts of bread and soup.

There was no automobile workers' union in those days, nor did it seem likely that there ever would be one. There were some union men in the factories, members of the trade-organized American Federation of Labor. But they caused the auto manufacturers little concern. They had no interest in the industry as a whole. They were specialists—such as machinists, carpenters, or electricians. Some few radicals advocated industrial union and basic principles of labor organization, but they were seldom heeded, even by their co-workers.

At the beginning of the 1930's it appeared that the employers held all the trump cards. The very nature of the auto business gave employers a tremendous weapon. Each year the models were changed, which meant that production always slowed down beginning late in the spring. Then production came to an absolute stop during summer while the plants were retooled. Late in the summer the work force was brought back to its peak, for the new models. In early winter after sales figures began to become apparent, the industry slackened to its median employment levels.

In those spring and summer layoffs, the company decided who would work and who would not. Decisions were made in very basic human ways. Foremen chose the men they liked, the men who produced the most, and the men who caused them the least trouble. In radical terms, they chose the company stooges, the speed-up artists, and the toadies. Men who did not conform got the least work. And if there was no work in the automobile plants for these men there was no work at all. Detroit had grown as a one-industry city. Auto workers "went broke" in off-season or in bad times.

In this atmosphere unionization was to come to the automotive industry through two factors: the growing awareness of some labor leaders that industrial unionization offered the greatest potential membership and strength of all organized labor, and the dedication to principles of unionism by a handful of radicals who were also auto workers.

From the top, John L. Lewis was to lead the fight for the auto workers. From the bottom the fight was to be carried by men like the three Reuther brothers who went to Detroit in their youth to work in the factories.

The first of these brothers to descend on Detroit was Walter Reuther, who was a skilled tool-and-die maker before he was twenty-one years old. The second was Victor, his more intellectual, studious brother. The third was Roy, the extrovert of the family, who had briefly considered a career as athletic coach before their German-born father Valentine Reuther had brought him back to the ways of Marxian Socialism and unionism.

The Reuther brothers grew up in Wheeling, West Virginia, where their father worked in the local brewery, ran the local union, and served also as unpaid president of the Ohio Valley Trades and Labor Assembly of the American Federation of Labor.

All three boys were indoctrinated with the principles of their Social Democrat father. They engaged in household debate on carefully chosen subjects. They learned that labor has a dignity of its own, and were taught that the laboring class existed as a class. They became convinced that labor had political as well as economic responsibilities.

Walter Reuther left high school in his third year to learn the machinist's trade. Three years later, he was fired from his tool-making job for agitating against work on Sundays, and for carrying his agitation to the point of organizing his shop. Then Walter set out for Detroit, where opportunity seemed to beckon. Here, in 1926, the nineteen-year-old machinist found a job with the Briggs Company at eighty-five cents an hour. Shortly afterward he moved to the Coleman Tool and Die Company, and then to Ford Motor Company, when that manufacturer announced it was seeking specialists in the change-over from Model T to Model A production.

At Ford, Walter Reuther talked "union," but apparently he did not talk too loudly within earshot of Harry Bennett's company intelligence organization, for Walter Reuther prospered at Ford. He became a foreman with forty men under him, and he earned a dollar and ten cents an hour for his work.

When depression struck the automotive industry in 1930, Walter Reuther retained his job. He was able to continue a course of schooling he had begun. He completed high school in Detroit, and then enrolled at Wayne University. His brother Victor, who had completed high school in Wheeling, came to Detroit to share an apartment and also to register at Wayne.

The brothers were active on the campus in student political affairs. They fought and helped win a battle against establishment of a Reserve Officers' Training Corps unit on the campus. When Norman Thomas ran for the Presidency in 1932, Walter Reuther was an avowed Socialist who supported Thomas and campaigned for him in Detroit.

The election campaign of 1932 in Detroit was violent, although none of the Reuthers participated in the open warfare. Nearly a third of the city's industrial workers were unemployed, and thousands of families were without heat or water or light. The utilities companies— once bills had run for months unpaid—turned off even the necessities of life.

In this misery, it had not been too difficult for the Communist party, working through an underground union called the Auto, Aircraft and Vehicle Workers of America, to stage a mass meeting outside the Ford gates at River Rouge. William Z. Foster, the old syndicalist leader turned Communist, came to serve as principal speaker and to advance the cause of revolution. He believed Detroit was very near to revolution, and what happened that day of his speech quickened the pulse of William Foster and his fellow Communists.

Ostensibly, the meeting at Ford's gates was held to petition the Ford management for jobs and relief. The workers marched to the company's gates. Foster rallied them and urged them on, and then the violence began. Harry Bennett had risen to a position as one of Henry Ford's major assistants because he was an expert at strong-arm tactics. The workers were determined to come inside the gates. Bennett and his burly guards were equally determined that they would not enter. Bricks were thrown—one struck Bennett in the head and knocked him unconscious. Shots were fired, killing four demonstrators and injuring others. With the shooting, the demonstration broke up into a disorderly retreat.

When the dead were to be buried, the Communists took charge of the ceremonies, trying to create from this incident an unforgettable day of martyrdom. A crowd of ten thousand followed the coffins down Woodward Avenue, and then to Woodmere cemetery, carrying banners which denounced the company, urged workers to join the union, and urged equally a demand of freedom for the Scottsboro boys, those victims of circumstance and southern prejudice whose cause had become a Communist rallying point. At the gravesides, pallbearers in red berets slowly lowered the four caskets into the earth, while a band played the *Internationale*, and a file of mourners trudged by, dropping red roses onto the last refuge of their dead.

This tragedy preceded any truly organized labor action by several months, yet in a sense it marked the beginning of the struggle of the auto workers for a union. The struggle began at the gates of Ford, and it was to continue with Ford and end with Ford almost a decade later. Not until the Ford Motor Company could be brought to terms with organized labor could an auto workers' union claim success or the security it would need to bargain with the industry.

The Reuther brothers had nothing to do with the Ford incident of 1932, but one of the Reuthers was deeply involved in the Briggs strike which broke early the following year. Roy Reuther—the third of the brothers to come to Detroit, and a worker at Briggs—joined the strikers and worked in the kitchen which supplied the hungry of the picket lines. This strike, like the Ford demonstration, was engineered by the Communists, although that fact should not obscure the frightful conditions under which the Briggs Body Company worked its men. Some, in the Waterloo plant where the strike began, were working fourteen hours a day, at a rate of ten cents an hour. Five hundred of them there walked off their jobs one January day. Within two weeks, ten thousand workers at other plants struck. While this strike did not directly affect Ford or other finished auto manufacturers, Briggs made bodies for many of them, and within a few days a hundred thousand auto workers were idle, and their plants shut down.

Walter and Victor Reuther left Detroit before the end of the Briggs strike. Walter had saved money on his foreman's pay—until the last few weeks of 1932, when he was summarily discharged by Ford. He was given no reason for dismissal, just a pink slip in his pay envelope. But the reason was clear enough. He had become far too open in his espousal of Socialism and unionism. At Ford it was not sensible for a foreman to drive around in a coupe plastered with Norman Thomas stickers, or to talk openly in the shop of the need for union organization. Walter Reuther, convinced Socialist, would not stop his advocacy of the revolution. There was no place for him in the Ford Motor Company of 1932.

With what Murray Kempton has wryly described as Reuther's "customary knack for the act of good fortune" the ex-foreman withdrew his savings from his Detroit bank the day before the beginning of the series of runs on all that city's banks—runs which brought the Motor City to a scrip and barter basis weeks before the crisis numbed the rest of the country.

As left-wing Socialists, Walter and Victor Reuther at this juncture were enthusiastic and curious about the experiment in revolution which was in progress in Russia. They also had a normal interest in visiting industrial Germany, from which their father's ideas and thus their ideas about social justice had been derived.

Between them the Reuther brothers possessed nine hundred dollars, enough for a trip to Europe, if they did not stay too long, and if they travelled by bicycle and lived simply. Both young men were used to simple living. Walter neither drank nor smoked. It was easy enough to make the decision they wanted to make, too. Most of the auto plants were shut down because of the Briggs strike. Walter's discharge by Ford had certainly not made him one of the most desirable of foremen-applicants in the glutted job market.

There was no need for the young Reuthers to steal away from Detroit in order to leave unnoticed. Except among the élite of the intellectual left, and to a handful of friends, educators, and Harry Bennett's goons they were unknown. They travelled to New York, where they dined with a group of intellectuals from the *Nation* before sailing. In western Europe they tramped their way, sleeping in haystacks or in cheap rooms; walking and cycling or travelling by the cheapest class. They saw Germany in the transition from limping democracy to Naziism; they arrived there just before the Reichstag fire, and they examined the ruins of the parliament even as Adolf Hitler was castigating the Communists for the vicious act he had ordered done. A few months in Germany were spent waiting for Soviet visas, and the youths then set off for Soviet Russia.

As tourists anywhere, the Reuther brothers saw just what the governors wanted them to see. Yet on the basis of his Ford experience, but undoubtedly without recommendation from Ford, Walter found a job at the motor plant in the model industrial city of Gorki—a plant which had been assembled by Ford for the Soviets. There the brothers learned something of Russian society in a Communist state. At Gorki, Walter Reuther became a *stakhanovite*. In America for the same work habits he would have been called a victim or a stooge of the speed-up, but in Russia, working for a cause instead of money, the relationship of man to job was different. Victor Reuther learned fluent Russian and confined himself to more intellectual pursuits. The pair lived with other American workers at Gorki. Walter wrote articles on production methods for the newspapers, but his articles appeared originally in the Moscow *Daily News*, the relatively unimportant English language newspaper.

The Reuther brothers remained in Russia for sixteen months, and although they were insulated from the purges a tyrant Stalin was forcing upon the Russian nation, these Americans were not enough taken by the Russian system to stay longer. True, they wrote home glowingly of the Soviet experiment (one of their letters was to be resurrected to damn them as pro-Communist in later years) but they decided in 1935 to move along. They secured permission to travel through Soviet Asia, then returned to America by way of the Far East, visiting China, Japan, and India. They came back to Detroit near the end of 1935.

The brothers could not have chosen a more fortunate or significant time to return to the auto industry, given their passion for unionism. John L. Lewis had been agitating for industrial unionism within the AF of L for many months. In February, 1935, he had urged upon William Green and the AF of L Executive Council the formation of an industrial union in the auto industry, despite the objections of the craft unions, such as the machinists' union, which claimed jurisdiction over some twenty-five thousand jobs—but made no attempt to enforce its claim in most auto factories. Reluctantly, the AF of L acceded to Lewis's pressure, and that spring the United Automobile Workers union was organized as a probationary AF of L union, whose initial officers were appointed by the AF of L leaders.

The union which emerged was tiny, numbering only some 20,000 members of a potential work force of more than four hundred thousand. But the UAW was an industrial union, into which could be fitted, without argument, all the hundreds of skills that go into the production of a complicated piece of machinery, the automobile.

When the Reuther brothers returned to America, Walter found a job at the Ternstedt plant of General Motors under an assumed name, since he was blacklisted for his radical and union activity. Now, however, Walter Reuther's job was only a means to an end. The end was unionism.

The auto workers' union had little effective bargaining power. It could boast only sixteen written contracts with small-parts manufacturers. No large automobile manufacturer recognized the UAW as anything but a nuisance. The big companies did recognize it as a considerable nuisance, however, as attested by their willingness to spend money to avoid unionization. Between 1934 and 1936 General Motors spent nearly a million dollars on labor espionage, sometimes keeping two hundred spies on the company payroll. Later, Richard Frankensteen, a UAW organizer and official, related in embarrassment how he had been wined and dined time after time by the "rich uncle" of a fellow worker. He did not learn for months that the rich relative was really a company spy.

Even as a probationary union, the UAW found itself almost immediately engaged in several varieties of ideological struggle. John L. Lewis formed the Committee for Industrial Organization in November, 1935, and broke finally with the AF of L the following year. When the infant UAW was assembled for convention in April, 1936, in South Bend, Indiana, CIO organizers were in the crowd, but the new union was in no position to take a stand against its parent AF of L. At this convention, Homer Martin, a persuasive former Baptist minister, was elected president of the UAW, and Walter Reuther became, at twenty-nine, a member of the executive board. At first, when Reuther came to the convention with five dollars in his pocket he was greeted with suspicion. No one seemed to know anyone by the name of Walter Reuther, at least as an elected delegate from the Ternstedt local. The mystery was solved when Reuther admitted his double identity.

There was another kind of double identity at that early convention, and Reuther was a part of that, too. Most of the unionists were primarily interested in labor organization, but some of the most militant were Communists first of all. Even when the Communists were known, in these early days, the others accepted them without fear. Communism and the Soviet idea might have been hated, from the beginning, by factory owners and businessmen. In the 1930's industrial workers in America had neither so much at stake, enough sophistication, nor proof that the American system was working satisfactorily. Many of them kept open minds about Communism. Only later, when the Communists proved equally adept at union "busting" and at dog-in-the-manger techniques, were the moderates of the UAW to turn against them and throw them out.

But in 1936 there were few "moderates" in the union, and there was little place for them. The auto companies were as determined that there would be no union as this cadre of workers was determined that there would be a union. Open and bloody clashes, then, were inevitable from the beginning.

The weakness of the workers' position in the auto industry had been illustrated a few months before in a strike at the Motor Products Corporation plant, where jurisdiction was claimed by an independent union, the Associated Auto Workers of America. The men had walked out. The management had refused to negotiate. Mediators, a rabbi and a bishop, were called in, but found nothing to mediate. Father Coughlin, who took a personal interest in the auto workers, was called in too. He found nothing to mediate either, but said he would be glad to help form auto workers into a real union which would esablish an annual guaranteed wage for auto workers.

Here was an idea which struck immediate chords in the hearts of all the union men no matter which union they claimed, for insecurity was the single greatest driving force in unionization in this industry. The average income of an automobile worker was estimated at somewhere between $1,200 and $1,500—but this figure concealed huge variations, as author Walter Galenson noted in *The CIO Challenge to the AF of L.* An NRA study of four automobile plants showed that a fifth of the workers earned less than $600 a year, and nearly a half less than $1,000 a year. Still, the guaranteed annual wage was to be nothing more than a dream during the 1930's. The basic problem was organization, and four unions competed for the allegiance of the men.

The problem of scattering was partly resolved that spring. At a party during the UAW convention, Father Coughlin had reportedly declared himself in favor of one big union. His influence among auto workers was great in the spring of 1936. Further, the logic of a united front was unassailable to industrial unionists. Two of the opposing unions joined with the UAW, and only the Mechanics Educational Society was left on the outside.

John L. Lewis had finally broken with the AF of L in a speech to the rubber workers at Akron, Ohio, in January, and had declared in favor of outright organization of industrial unions. In midsummer, 1936, the UAW voted to join the CIO, and with Lewis's help, the organization drive began.

The three Reuther brothers were all active in union organization. Walter set up offices on Detroit's West Side, although there was no money in the union treasury to pay him, and began to work for union strength by amalgamating tiny locals into one large one—West Side Local 174. Roy went to Flint, as a paid union organizer to work with the men in the Chevrolet plants there. Victor helped Walter for a time, then became an organizer in Anderson, Indiana.

John L. Lewis had less than half a hand to turn to the assistance of the auto workers, since he was deeply engaged in the drive to organize the steel industry, and still faced a dissidence within his United Mine Workers which led opponents to call periodically for his resignation, or for the UMW conventions to displace him. Lewis managed, however, to maintain and strengthen control of his own union, while he continued the drive to build a massive labor organization on an industrial framework. He had been among the first—if not the very first—unionists to see in the National Labor Relations Act an invitation for industrial union—in the provision that exclusive bargaining rights should be granted to the majority union in a factory. While industrialists were as aware of the act as was Lewis, many of them believed the labor law would be declared unconstitutional, and in 1936 they were stalling for time.

The union could not stall. It must either succeed or die, and there was little enough time for success to be achieved. In the fall of 1936 the auto workers discovered the sit-down strike, which was to bring them strength if not solidarity.

The sit-down strike was not an invention of the UAW, or even an American innovation, for that matter. French workers were the first on record to seize control of company property and maintain themselves in safety if not in comfort, with the security that attempts to drive them from the property would surely damage corporate assets as well as men's skulls. But the sit-down strike was a weapon made for a union in the position of the UAW—a small union, representing only a handful of the potential workers, infiltrated by company spies whose reports would have done much to destroy the effectiveness of an ordinary strike. By calling a sit-down, union leaders could use a few trusted men, and bring them into action quickly to bring production to a halt.

Maintaining possession of the company property, legal or not, they forced the company to go through the ponderous legal processes of court appearance and injunction, while the strikers sat, gaining sympathy and costing the company money every minute.

The Rubber Workers were the first in America to make large scale use of the sit-down. In the spring of 1936 they carried out scores of sit-down strikes to enforce union demands. In Akron, at the Goodyear plant, union men sat down nineteen times in a little more than two months. And among the auto workers, the employees of the Bendix plant were the first to use this weapon. Rebuffed in attempts to achieve union recognition, they sat down and occupied the plant for nine days, winning their objective.

After the Bendix strike, the sit-down came to Detroit. In November employees at one small plant struck, and won union recognition. Then, Walter Reuther made his first important move as an aggressive union leader.

Reuther had built his Local 174 in a few months from a membership of less than a hundred to a membership of several thousand. With this strength behind him, he called on the management of the Kelsey-Hayes Wheel Company in Detroit, asking them to negotiate with him to settle some worker grievances. The company representatives told Reuther he did not represent their workers.

To prove that he did represent them, Walter called a strike. At an appointed hour a girl "fainted" on the assembly line. Union men shut off the power in the plant, shouted "Strike," and sat down. There they stayed, while Victor Reuther exhorted the workers from a truck-borne loudspeaker outside the plant, and Walter supervised the strategy of logistics to feed and care for his small but determined army. In a few days the company capitulated and recognized the union and Walter Reuther.

The Kelsey-Hayes strike established Reuther as a power in the UAW. Its success brought the membership of Local 174 to 30,000 workers. But Reuther's success was an intermediate victory. If the UAW was to become a force in industrial affairs, or even to survive, it must attack one of the big automotive manufacturers and force recognition of the union as the bargaining agent for *all* the workers. The logical corporation to attack was General Motors, which accounted for half the production of the industry.

The record does not indicate that the General Motors battle which was to begin in December, 1936, was the result of any long-range plan by the auto workers' union. Indeed, John L. Lewis had cautioned the UAW to go slow. He was now totally immersed in the delicate task of trying to organize the steel industry against great odds. The CIO was too young and not yet rich enough to do battle on more than one front. He wanted no part of a major showdown in Detroit at that period.

The General Motors UAW struggle began in November in Atlanta, where an employee of the Fisher Body plant was discharged for union activity. The men sat down. The following month, another worker was discharged at the Fisher Body plant in Kansas City. The union sat down again, but this time more successfully: within a few days the Chevrolet assembly plant in Kansas City was closed for shortage of parts.

Homer Martin, president of the UAW, went to see William S. Knudsen, executive vice-president of General Motors. He was granted an interview, grudgingly, but was informed that GM would not negotiate these matters. Mr. Martin could take them up with the various plant managers, if he wished. Homer Martin was not a good union president. He was not an executive. He was not a negotiator.

But neither he nor the union could accept such a rebuff and maintain strength. Action must be taken, or the union's 100,000 members would begin to drift away. If there was any doubt of that, or of the militancy of union members, it was resolved shortly by the spread of strikes. First the union members of the Fisher Body plant at Cleveland struck, when management postponed a conference with the union. Then the strike spread to the Fisher Body plant and one of the Chevrolet plants in Flint, the home of Chevrolet and the center of the General Motors empire. The strikes spread further, to Anderson, Indiana, to Ohio, to Wisconsin and Detroit. In a month GM auto production fell from 53,000 cars a week to 1,500.

Early in January, 1937, a county court judge granted General Motors an injunction against the strikers sitting in the Flint plant, upholding the company view that this was trespassing, but going further, and enjoining the union against picketing or in any way interfering with men who wanted to work. That judge held more than $200,000 in GM stock, it was discovered. The strikers refused to leave the plant. GM President Alfred P. Sloan, Jr., announced that General Motors would not recognize any union as sole bargaining agent for its workers. The strikers stayed on.

When the police and company guards tried to starve the strikers out at Fisher Body Plant No. 2, the strikers seized the gates. The police attacked, using tear gas and riot guns, but the strikers stood behind their barricades and heaved door hinges and splashed the police with jets of water from the company's fire hoses. Fourteen union men were wounded in this battle which they later called "the battle of the running bulls," but the word of it spread across the industrial Middle West, and within hours reinforcements of union men were on their way. But so were fifteen hundred national guardsmen, dispatched by Governor Frank Murphy, a Democrat, who had just come into office a few days before. Fortunately for the union and for public safety, the guardsmen were ordered to quell rioting, which threatened the safety of this city of 150,000 people, but to leave the strikers in their plant.

On January 15, union and company men met in Lansing, the state capital, where Governor Murphy arranged a truce. The union agreed to evacuate the plants in exchange for negotiations between company and union. But on the day in question, William Lawrence, then a reporter for the United Press Associations, learned that the company intended to negotiate with the Flint Alliance—a rump labor group which had sprung up in opposition to the UAW and had tried to break the strike. The strikers sat down again.

In this crisis, Victor and Roy Reuther conferred with Governor Murphy, who was trying desperately to bring peace, in the face of opposition from even the Flint city government, which was attempting to halt the movement of food in to the men in Fisher Body Plant No. 2. Other union men were still pouring into Flint, creating traffic jams and the atmosphere of a powder plant. Walter Reuther arrived with a flying squad of his roughest members of Local 174.

Victor manned his sound truck, deploying the union's forces around the plant.

This battle was not only being fought on the General Motors grounds at Flint, it extended even to Washington, where President Sloan of the company agreed to meet Secretary of Labor Frances Perkins, in a gesture which meant a considerable comedown for the company. He would allow this much recognizance of the interest of the government in the strike; he would not see John L. Lewis, who could control the strikers if any man outside Flint could do so.

In Flint, the sheriff ordered the UAW men to vacate the plants, and they replied that if the militia, armed thugs, and deputies entered the Fisher Body plant blood would be shed. Governor Murphy hesitated.

In Washington, John L. Lewis noted that the "economic royalists"—the people of General Motors and the Du Ponts—had contributed their money to the Republican campaign in 1936, while organized labor gave its help to Roosevelt. Lewis called on Roosevelt now "to help the strikers in every reasonable way." Lewis had, at the UAW convention of 1936, forced the infant union to pass a resolution supporting F.D.R., over much protest—or he would have withheld a donation to the union coffers from the CIO. The radical UAW men, many of them Socialist and others Communist, did not like the resolution, but they passed it as one of their last orders of business. Now it was called to Roosevelt's attention.

Sloan left Washington after conferring with Mrs. Perkins, unbending not in the slightest. When she wrote to him in New York to come back, he at first refused as long as the strikers held his company's plants, later capitulated to pressure.

The pressure? The President of the United States intervened in the dispute. Secretary Perkins condemned General Motors for refusing to negotiate while the question of the legality of sit-down strikes was pending. She recalled that once strikes were illegal, and that even later, picketing had been illegal. Roosevelt, softer, forced Sloan to agree that Vice-President Knudsen would meet with John L. Lewis. It was easy to condemn Sloan for his attitude. It was difficult for him to admit that an emergency of national proportions existed, and that there was a link between a group of angry men sitting down in one of GM's plants and the bushy-browed Mr. Lewis taking his ease in Washington. Sloan was being forced to admit that the strike was not just the lawless action of lawless men, but a move by organized labor to demand recognition. Once he admitted so much, the battle was lost by the company. From that moment on, it became simply a matter of how long the chief company officials would take to respond to the public pressure which would be placed upon them.

It did not come to that solution in that way, because the strikers forced Lewis's hand, and Lewis set out for the barricades at Flint, full knowing that although he had not willed it, the future of his Committee for Industrial Organization lay in the outcome of this strike. Were he to back down, or to show the slightest weakness, the CIO would be destroyed, not just the auto union, but his efforts in steel, and in rubber, and everywhere, and even the Ladies Garment Workers and the other strong unions which had entered into the industrial union experiment would be jeopardized.

Before Lewis left Washington, the strikers took further action. Roy Reuther saw that the tactics of his army were getting nowhere. He determined to seize Chevrolet Plant No. 4, but he decided to do it in the greatest of secrecy. Secrecy was needed, since before the strike the General Motors delegate to the UAW convention from Flint was a man who had long been a company spy, and the local union was heavily infiltrated. Roy Reuther decided to make a feint at Plant No. 9, then send a smaller task force to seize No. 4 when the guardians of that plant hastened to protect No. 9.

That is what happened. Roy led the men to No. 9. Walter brought his shock troops from Detroit to the gates. Victor went about in his sound truck stirring up a ruckus. And meanwhile, the tiny handful slipped in and took over Plant No. 4, the key plant in the Flint Chevrolet complex. They shut Chevrolet down.

When Lewis arrived on the scene, and Governor Murphy ordered him to get his men out of the plant before the governor sent the national guard in, Lewis told the governor to go ahead. He would leave the conference and he would join the strikers. The governor could shoot him out of the plant, too.

That was almost the end of it. Governor Murphy patiently struggled with the harsh minds and words of the two sides, and on February 11, 1937, arranged a truce. General Motors recognized the union as the bargaining agent for GM workers, if they belonged to the union. It was not a total victory, yet it was victory for the union, and GM was spared embarrassment through a formula which used Governor Murphy as a buffing board. The company agreed to bargain with no other union for six months without consulting with the governor.

Six months was all that the UAW needed. The prestige of the union was such, after the GM strike, that membership doubled. The AF of L tried to intervene in behalf of the crafts, even going to Roosevelt for support, but Roosevelt would not listen, and the AF of L, grumbling, left the field, defeated for the moment. A few weeks later, Chrysler Motor Company signed an agreement with John L. Lewis in behalf of the UAW. By fall, the UAW held contracts with four hundred different companies, and its future was not in doubt. The one major holdout was Ford.

After this victory in Flint, even the major defeat of the CIO organizing drive in the failure of the Little Steel strike in May could not sink John Lewis and the CIO. Backed and strengthened by the Roosevelt administration the industrial union complex grew, and continued to grow. But late in the 1930's the union of the CIO faced new problems, attendant to their growth and to the men who had worked so hard to help them. Once stability came to the unions, political differences became important, where they had been unimportant in the life or death struggle against the employers.

The UAW was split as early as 1937 by factional fights which involved the Communists, Reuther's Socialists, and the right wing of the union (which would be called moderate or mildly left wing anywhere else). President Homer Martin grew distrustful of the Reuther brothers. Roy was pushed out of Flint, Victor was demoted within the union, and only Walter was able to maintain his position because of his personal strength with his huge West Side Local. The factional fights were to be a part of another period. Even Ford was to hold out for nearly four more years against the organizers of the UAW. Richard Frankensteen, one of the militant organizers of the early days, was to break with the Communists and even the Socialists, and become a conservative. There were open Communists, Lovestoneites, Socialist Workers, Socialists, apostate Socialists such as Walter Reuther, and many others within the UAW group that was known as the Unity group.

Their unity was only in opposition to the policies of Martin and the leaders. Life became infinitely complicated for the union with the coming of the serious recession of 1937, when it was patently insensible to seek huge concessions or wage increases in a market where auto production had fallen by two-thirds, and where, by 1938, two-thirds of the three hundred thousand auto workers of Detroit were out of work. Passenger car production fell by half that year—from the nearly four million vehicles produced in 1937.

In the summer of 1938 the UAW international executive board split wide open in a fight that was basically caused by differences in ideologies, Communist and non-Communist, but which had become so enmeshed in union politics that the root causes were seemingly unimportant. Martin seized upon the Communist issue to try to retain his shrinking power. He managed to oust some of his enemies, and to retain control a little while longer, but by the fall of 1938 the union was all but in the hands of a CIO receivership, so low had it sunk and so deep were its schisms that membership had slipped badly. Many local unions refused to pay their international dues. Since its chartering by the AF of L, the auto workers' union had never been nearer dissolution than that summer.

In 1939, after strange dealings with Henry Ford—which other unionists saw as an outright attempt by Martin to take the UAW out of the CIO, to maintain his own power Martin called a separate special convention of the UAW from the UAW meeting. Martin's was called for March 4, 1939, and the CIO's convention for March 27. Each convention was held, and each group had its adherents or representation of local unions. Martin then took his smaller group into the AF of L, for a time, with Henry Ford's blessing, but the AF of L system and the AF of L support was never satisfactory for the auto workers, in spite of Mr. Ford. Within a few months the attempt failed, and Martin was finished as a union leader. Later he became a Ford pensioner, a sad end for a once-militant unionist.

At the convention called by the CIO, Walter Reuther proved himself one of the strongest and most canny leaders in the hall. He had personally broken with the Communists over their attempt to place politics above unionism, and while he spoke for the Socialist point of view in the convention, he was no longer even an active Socialist. Walter Reuther was now a trade unionist—and politics mattered less than unionism to him. Richard Frankensteen, the old romantic turned opportunist, moved into an alliance with the Communists, and while the CIO managed to have R. J. Thomas elected president, thus keeping the top leadership free from the ideological battle, the Frankensteen-Communist group won a majority of the national board.

This 1939 convention marked a new low point in the union's affairs—lower than 1938. Because of strife and recession—really depression again—the membership had fallen to 90,000. But with the return of more prosperous times in 1939, employment in the auto industry rose to nearly 400,000, and by July, 1940, the union became strong again. The auto workers' union that year claimed nearly 300,000 members and contracts with 647 plants. The United Auto Workers Union had come of age in 1939. The union was to continue as a center of an ideological struggle that would last well into the following decade, long after World War II had begun and ended. But of all the auto industry's employers of any importance, only Ford held out against the union by 1939, and even at Ford, despite the waning efforts of Homer Martin and Harry Bennett, the writing was clearly visible on the wall. Unionism had come to the auto industry to stay, and the auto industry was representative of the rest of the nation.

The change in the attitude of responsible employers towards unionism was remarkable, if sometimes slow in materializing. In the steel industry, for example, Tom Girdler of Republic Steel, leader of the Little Steel group which fought unionism so desperately, was opposed to unionism in principle. Thus on May 30, 1937, after a mass march by workers on the Republic plant near Chicago, police opened fire, killed ten of the marchers, and wounded eighty others. Seven of the ten dead were found to have been shot in the back, running from the police as the firing began. Temporarily, Little Steel won the battle against unionization.

But the real war for steel unionization was waged against the big steel companies, and here the struggle was won more easily and the issue was truly decided, months before. Little Steel resisted but Big Steel capitulated, and set the pace. Myron C. Taylor, chairman of the board of directors of U.S. Steel, signed an agreement with John L. Lewis, recognizing the steelworkers' union as the bargaining agent for its workers. Taylor adopted an unusual attitude for a mass employer. "The grave danger was in allowing events to proceed to a point where the ordinary rules of reason would not govern," he said. "I felt that it was my duty as a trustee for our stockholders and as a citizen to make any honorable settlement that would ensure a continuance of work, wages and profits."

It is impossible to give too much credit to John L. Lewis for this mass organization of the important industries of America. Lewis was *the* key figure. To do his organizing he was unafraid to use Communists, Socialists or anyone else who would work for him. He was confident of his own ability to maintain power in his own hands at the crucial moment. Lewis and the United Mine Workers financed the CIO. They financed the steel organizing committee. They financed other unions, including a large share of the beginning expense of the auto workers. In 1937, the UMW lent the CIO and its subsidiaries nearly a million and a half dollars from the union treasury. Without that money, the CIO could not have existed.

Lewis helped James Carey put together the United Electrical Workers union as an industrial union, too, and Lewis busied himself organizing textile workers, the maritime industry, lumber, meat, and petroleum. In all this ferment, the Communists managed to gain an important foothold in the CIO and its subsidiary unions. James Carey awoke to the issue in August, 1939, after the signing of the Nazi-Soviet pact. At that moment, as he said, the Communist officers of the union "laid off Hitler and started ranting about the imperialist war . . ." As the months passed, Carey discovered that the Communists had seized absolute control of his union, they operated the national office to their own ends, they dominated the executive committee, they ran the union newspaper, and they were entrenched in control of locals and districts. Every union organizer was a party-line man.

The United Electrical Workers union was an extreme case but it was not unique. Communism in industrial unions *was* a serious problem and a serious threat in the last two years of the 1930's. The problem was not solved in this decade, either, it was simply tabled in 1940 and 1941 by the emergence of more serious national problems, and by the return of prosperity. As the decade ended, unionism had advanced further than in any other ten year period in history. In 1933, before the organization of the CIO, union membership had totalled less than three million persons, or 5 per cent of the available work force. By 1940, nearly nine million men and women were enrolled with organized labor, 15 per cent of the work force of the nation; most important, employers in the nation had accepted, finally, the principle of unionism. The threat of anarchy or of a workers' state—very real in 1933—had been dissipated by the ultimate recognition of responsibility, reluctantly by such men as Alfred P. Sloan, Jr. and readily by such as Myron Taylor. In many cases the struggle had been bitter and bloody. No precedent was set in the fierceness or violence with which the captains of industry opposed social change. Always the possessors have opposed the strivings of those who seek a large share of the possessions. What was different, important, and unique was the attitude with which American capitalists and management approached labor problems, even in the thick of the struggle.

Elsewhere capitalists and labor men had always regarded themselves as lifelong enemies. Marxism was built in this enmity and thrived on it. But in America, as in few places, capitalists and labor men regarded themselves first as Americans, and none lost sight of the fact that many capitalists had come up quickly from the ranks of the laboring group. The existence of such opportunity continued and had widespread effect on development of American labor and American business.

In this decade industry and labor had come to terms.

CHAIRMAN OF THE BOARD—I

CHAPTER SIXTEEN

WHEN ALFRED P. SLOAN, JR., returned to New York after his successful business trip to Europe in the fall of 1929, for good reasons of his own he was not unduly disturbed by the collapse of the stock market. Sloan believed firmly in the resilience of the capitalistic system. For some time he had suspected that there was too much cream on the top of the market. It seemed only logical that the spiral of speculation should come to an end.

Alfred Sloan's confidence in capitalism was a product of the thirty-four years in which he had dedicated his life to American industry. In 1895, when young Sloan graduated from Massachusetts Institute of Technology, he went to work for the Hyatt Roller Bearing Company as a draftsman. Four years later he was general manager of the little company. Just at that time Hyatt Roller Bearing received a letter from a man named Elwood Haynes of Kokomo, Indiana. Mr. Haynes inquired if the Hyatt firm believed its roller bearings might be useful in the manufacture of horseless carriages. Thus, giving every credit to Sloan for diligence and foresight, was the fortune of Alfred P. Sloan, Jr. assured.

Sloan and Hyatt Roller Bearing grew up with the American automobile industry. The general manager of the Cadillac motorcar company taught him the importance of precision. From the beginning Cadillacs were built to last. Their parts must be interchangeable, too. And if they were to be changed, all the parts must be precisely the same size.

Cadillac officers demonstrated this fact to the public one day by taking three automobiles completely apart, piling up the parts, and then putting mechanics to work to assemble three cars from the pile. The mechanics did so, and the three automobiles ran. From Cadillac, Alfred Sloan had learned a lesson in quality control. He was not to forget.

From Henry Ford, Sloan learned that mass production demanded high standards and low prices for his bearings, and also that mass production of Fords meant huge increases in Hyatt's volume of sales and more profit from lower prices. He did not forget that lesson, either.

When William C. Durant formed United Motors, and eventually joined it to General Motors, Durant created a unified corporation which made automobiles from the ground up. Alfred P. Sloan sold Hyatt Roller Bearing to the combine for $13,500,000. His personal fortune was established. He might have retired then, during World War I. Instead, Sloan took half-payment in stock, then served first as president of United Motors, and later as vice-president of the greater General Motors.

William Durant was a gambler who lost, and was thus forced out of General Motors in favor of the Du Pont family. Had there not been a Du Pont family to shore up the company in the recession of 1920, General Motors might have failed. After this crisis, Alfred P. Sloan frowned on stock speculation. He paid little attention to the vagaries of the stock market.

Sloan's background indicates why it was perfectly logical for Alfred P. Sloan, Jr., to say (and believe) in 1929 that there was no relationship between the stock market and the American industrial plant.

It is not so easy to see why Alfred Sloan did not understand the relationship between falling farm prices, a low wage level in comparison to corporate profits, and other signs of trouble in the industrial sphere. And yet the automotive industry was paying the highest wages of any industry in the country. That might have been part of it. Nor did most other businessmen expect that the nation was heading for a crash. Alfred P. Sloan, Jr., was no more perspicacious, nor less so, than others in this regard.

Even during the early months of 1930 Sloan did not seem to understand what was happening to the business community. As president and chief executive officer of General Motors, he authorized the distribution of $13,000,000 in extra dividends, despite the fact that GM's 1929 earnings had decreased from $174,000,000 of 1929 by $8,000,000.

Sloan did take cognizance of a certain unsettled condition which had effected the business community in 1929. Generally speaking, however, he was pleased with the showing of his company. During

To look at him no one would believe that John L. Lewis would create the most important labor movement in the United States of America. FSA PHOTOGRAPH BY SHELDON DICK, LIBRARY OF CONGRESS

The technique of the sit-down strike was simple enough. The men simply stopped working and took over the company's plant. But the problems of bringing in food were a bit harder. UNITED PRESS INTERNATIONAL PHOTO

He was a much tougher specimen than it might appear on the surface. The pose of friendliness to Prosecutor Robert Estill was no more than a pose. A few weeks later, John Dillinger escaped from this jail in Crown Point, Indiana, and a national man-hunt was soon begun. WIDE WORLD PHOTO

After a dozen years of the Noble Experiment the nation was heartily sick of prohibition and most of the people waited only for the stroke of the clock that marked the end in 1933. WIDE WORLD PHOTO

1929 GM had bought into the Bendix and Fokker manufacturing companies and into Radio Corporation of America. GM's Frigidaire refrigerators had been brought into the market, and such diversification was working very well to strengthen the company and maintain a high profit level. Sloan was pleased because the number of shareholders of General Motors increased 71,000 that year, bringing the total holders to 200,000. Further, the greatest increase had come in the last sixty days of 1929. To Sloan, quite rightly, this trend indicated investors rather than speculators.

Like all American businessmen, big and small, Sloan was most concerned about the continuing slump of business in 1930. Still, in his own industry he saw one of the greatest stabilizers of all. By 1930 the world contained thirty million automobiles, all of them aging and wearing out.

As January came, and with it the national automobile show at the Grand Central Palace in New York City, Sloan and the other automotive manufacturers radiated confidence for the coming year. Sloan said he believed automotive production would be high in 1930, and that the production of the automotive industry would eventually be stabilized at something near five and a half million vehicles a year. While production of cars had dropped 25 per cent in the last quarter of 1929, Sloan and Walter Chrysler both expected a return to normal within three months. After all, as Chrysler said, relatively little purchasing power had been affected by the Wall Street crash. The establishment still seemed secure.

Confidence was not the exclusive property of the automotive manufacturers, either. The Wall Street firm of Lawrence Stern & Co. asked two thousand investment bankers for their predictions. Of these, 1,940 looked for improvement in 1930. Sears Roebuck and Company reported its sales up in 1929 by more than a quarter, and looked forward bravely. C. P. Tolman, a consulting engineer, told students at the Stevens Institute of Technology in Hoboken on January 2 that a new industrial era of unprecedented prosperity would begin that year.

And yet a careful reader of *The New York Times* that week would have noticed that manufacturers were edgy. The leading shirt manufacturers were holding closed meetings in New York. Their object was to form a trade association to fight against what they considered to be unfair practices and a flood of cheap shirts which was deluging the market. Hardware trade had fallen off all across the country. Wholesale trade was off in nearly every category. Building had decreased sharply. In White Plains, New York, the building department announced that construction was off 50 per cent.

More important, the business journal called *The Annalist* showed that business was in a more precarious condition in December, 1929, than in any month since August, 1924, and that the most dangerous threat of all was the drastic reduction in the rate of automobile production. On the basis of the estimated output of 125,000 cars in December, only 51 per cent had actually been built. That reduction had been felt in a cut in the use of electric power and in a drop in steel ingot production, so vital was the automobile industry to the health of the nation.

Those few men who pretended to understand the business cycle were mildly cheered by the optimism of the auto manufacturers for they realized the importance of Detroit in the national picture. Virgil Jordan, director of research of the McGraw-Hill Publishing Company said he expected to see a real revival materialize in February or March. He did caution, however, that Americans could not expect to see another boom like that of 1929 for a long, long time.

By fall, most of that undue optimism had evaporated. Business recognized a slump when it saw one. This slump was so serious it was no longer called a "temporary adjustment" or a "minor recession" but a "depression." Richard Whitney of the New York Stock Exchange so termed it in a speech.

By fall Alfred P. Sloan, Jr., had lost some of his optimism of the beginning of the year. He now estimated auto output at only four million vehicles, but added quickly that he hoped for a better year in 1931. Samuel Insull, the utilities magnate, still said he found little to disturb him, but by November, Sloan was affirming the depth of the depression in statements that General Motors hoped not to have to make deep pay cuts because he realized that prosperity in the United States was founded on a high wage rate.

In December, 1930, most pretense was gone, and there was little to be gained by anyone's hollering down the rain barrel any more. The depression had set in with a vengeance, and just about everyone in the land knew it. President Hoover's emergency employment committee issued its call to six million farmers to employ workers that industry was laying off, forgetting that the farmers had been in trouble for ten years.

And what of business as this first year of depression drew to a close?

Oil production was lowered, all across the country. Standard Oil Company cut prices of gasoline by three cents a gallon. In an effort to stimulate business, the bank rate of the Federal Reserve Bank had been cut to 2 per cent, the lowest rate in the world. But business was not interested in being stimulated. Businessmen were pulling in their horns. Instead of trying to promote their own brands of perfume for the Christmas trade, perfume manufacturers persuaded the federal Customs officers to enforce a ban on import of sixteen brands of perfume where the brand names had been trademarked in the United States. Alfred P. Sloan was opposed to such attempts to raise the wall of tariff against the outside world. He was sure it would hurt domestic prosperity in the long run, by reducing America's ability to produce— and thus by adding to unemployment. Over a period, he warned, exports could only be paid for by imports. America could not sell unless it bought.

The New York *Evening World* attacked such defeatism as that exhibited by the perfume manufacturers. "The most serious threat to our country today," said the *World*, "is in the businessman of little faith whose fears are played upon by the most silly gossip which poisons the air with absurd rumors and mean and malicious lies."

And although Mr. Hoover had said so much about the prospects for a better year on Christmas, when the nation needed cheering, he made no mention of the state of the nation, but lighted the big Christmas tree in Sherman Square across from the Treasury building in Washington and made only a fatuous thirty-seven-word statement.

Business entered 1931 with a sense of coming rejuvenation, although there was no factual basis for such optimism. Walter Chrysler said he was making intensive preparation for a business revival. William S. Knudsen, the president of GM's Chevrolet Company, talked of a three-year production cycle—a year of recession, a year of recovery, and a year of peak volume. The year 1931, he said, was to be as good as 1928, and 4,600,000 cars would be sold.

Alfred Sloan was more cautious now. He noted that prosperity depended on the progress of American industry, which in turn depended, he said, on the ability of Americans to create new sources of wealth.

The year 1931 was not a prosperous year in any sense. In the agony of depression, few industrial men were even thinking of expansion. State and federal agencies were moving, but oh, so slowly, to replace industrial jobs with jobs on public projects. But in 1930 only 40,000 miles of paved highway were constructed in America, and in 1931 only 50,000 miles were built. Of a total of 3,100,000 miles of road in the nation, only 680,000 miles were hard-surfaced—most of these east of the Mississippi. No transcontinental highway existed. In Wyoming and in the Dakotas there seemed to be practically no highways at all except on the outskirts of the cities.

Public works projects were not coming into being rapidly enough to help greatly. No new source of wealth was in creation. In the spring of 1931 Alfred Sloan stopped predicting when high prosperity might return, and instead turned his efforts to exhortation of the business world to show more pioneering spirit. Others were talking about wage cuts, five-day weeks, and the spreading of labor to do the limited job that was waiting. Sloan opposed this in every way. He opposed wage cuts, because they lowered each family's purchasing power. He opposed the five-day week, because he felt men should work hard, produce, and be paid for it. Only if the United States reached the point of a labor surplus—when problems of automation set in—should the work week be shortened to spread jobs, said Alfred Sloan. The idea of spreading the work appalled him.

What, then, was Alfred P. Sloan's answer to the problems of poverty, need, and starvation which arose day by day? Sloan and many other business leaders did not recognize these problems except to pay them lip-service. They were concerned about matters of theory and principle. What had caused the depression? By 1932 most of the auto industrialists had accepted Hoover's view that the economic troubles arose from World War I. How could the nation escape the disaster of depression? The industrialists could not answer that question any more than could Herbert Hoover. All of them were wedded to the theory of the "business cycle."

Auto sales were falling sharply, and to see what that meant to the rest of industry, one need only examine the consumption by the auto industry of finished industrial materials. In 1930 the auto industry used 15 per cent of all steel produced, 82 per cent of the rubber, 55 per cent of plate glass, 57 per cent of upholstery leather, 80 per cent of the gasoline, and 30 per cent of the aluminum. When auto sales dropped a million in 1931 every one of those industries suffered proportionally.

The general cutting of prices did not help affairs. In 1921 a buyer paid $1,595 for an Essex. In 1931 he paid $595. Nearly all the manufacturers cut their prices sharply, partly because they were able to do so by tightening production methods, but partly because they cut payroll costs to save the companies. What other attitude could the business world be expected to take?

In the spring of 1932 Alfred Sloan expressed serious concern about the fear psychology which had grasped the nation. Sloan's concern was real. By 1932 the importance of the auto industry was recognized everywhere, and Alfred Sloan's quarterly statements which accompanied reports to stockholders had an effect almost as important as statements by cabinet officials. General Motors was the key corporation in the American economy. The public accepted this premise and Alfred Sloan, to a point, accepted the responsibility which went with it. If economists might argue that steel and not automobiles was the key industry, the public found it much easier to see the direct connection between the auto industry and prosperity than the indirect link with steel.

That summer of 1932, as the nation neared the depth of the depression, Alfred Sloan had only one bit of advice to give. Let Congress cut expenditures, balance the national budget, and adjourn as quickly as possible. In other words, let the nation sweat out these last few months of the depression free from constant rumor and fear. Let there be less news about the economic situation, and thus less concern.

Other businessmen believed the bottom had been struck and that there was nowhere to go but up. (None of them publicly considered the possibility that hungry farmers and workers might rise up and destroy the whole capitalistic system.) Roger Babson, who had been so right about the crash in 1929, noted on October 6, 1932, that it really did not make much difference who was elected—Hoover or Roosevelt—because the depression was nearly over. While most of his friends thought recovery would be complete by 1935, Babson wrote, he was an optimist. He believed it would come much sooner.

As these speculations were being made by practicing businessmen, one of their former associates was indicted to stand trial for his business methods. Early in that October of 1932 Samuel Insull, his brother Martin, and his son were called by a Chicago court to account for the failure of their huge public utilities trust, in which the savings of thousands of ordinary Americans had been wiped out. After the failure the company had $27,000,000 in assets, but it owed $120,000,-000. Why? For one reason because $232,000,000 of the assets claimed at the peak of the boom in 1929 had been bought at the actual peak of speculation frenzy. When the market crashed, Insull's empire crashed with it. Until 1932 Samuel Insull was not regarded as a speculator, but as a magnate in the power industry. In 1932 he became, in the public eye, a manipulator who embodied all the evils of uncontrolled capitalism.

Late in the year, after Franklin Roosevelt had been elected, Alfred Sloan was disturbed enough about the economy to offer the incoming administration public advice. With the nation standing at the crossroads, GM's president said for the benefit of America's new President, the nation was faced with the question of attacking fundamental economic problems or using palliatives. The fundamental problems, Mr. Sloan said, were: an unbalanced budget, the disregard of war and postwar debt by European nations, and Congressional inaction on the lowering of the tariff.

As 1932 ended, *Dun's Review* saw an upturn in 1933. But before the upturn, if it was to come, the nation was to undergo its most searing experience of all—the bank crisis which occurred just as Franklin Roosevelt was coming to take power.

In Detroit, the bank crisis came weeks early, as noted. And what happened there could not have happened had the moguls of the automotive industry been as concerned with the broader aspects of industrial statesmanship as some of their public statements indicated.

Detroit banks fell into serious trouble just after the turn of 1933. President Hoover knew the trouble was coming. He tried to stall it off by seeking the cooperation of Senator James Couzens, of Michigan, Henry Ford, and the other automotive industrialists. This was ever Hoover's way, and even when it became apparent that Couzens and Ford, once partners and now deadly enemies, would not work together, Hoover persisted in the reasoned approach.

Ford's last word was that he welcomed the crash—it came on February 14, and Detroit's banks shut to remain so until all the nation's banks had shut and reopened during March. Then, Detroit was saved reluctantly by General Motors and Ford, each of which backed a new bank after strong pushing by Jesse Jones, head of the Reconstruction Finance Corporation.

That winter, Alfred P. Sloan, Jr., tried to find ways of spurring the business economy of the nation. He sent out a questionnaire of his own to 150 business leaders, asking how the national problem might best be solved. Research, invention, and labor saving would solve the problem, said such men as George Washington Hill of American Tobacco Company, Edward A. Filene of the Boston department store, George Horace Lorimer of *The Saturday Evening Post,* David Sarnoff of RCA, and Roger Babson.

Sloan then spoke of the importance of the automobile in the American way of life. The record did not back him up, for Detroit's sales in 1932 had been just half of those in 1930. Only a million and a quarter cars were sold that year, despite constant price reductions. General Motors stock had fallen to a low of 10 points. Sloan made no estimates about the future that winter, and when his assistant William Knudsen indicated that affairs must grow better the remark was greeted with general agreement since few businessmen could see how they could possibly grow any worse.

Both in and out of government in those dying weeks of the Hoover administration desperate attempts were made to use business as the force that might bring the economy back to stability. Earnest men searched for ways in which to take government out of competition. They asked the Post Office to stop making its own paste. They asked the War Department to stop manufacturing saddles. They asked the army engineers to stop dredging harbors, and to hire con-

tractors instead. They asked prison administrators to stop the manufacture of furniture, jute bags, or anything that might compete in any
way with industry. They asked the Coast Guard to refrain from salvaging any ships, so private salvage companies might profit. These were
indeed desperate measures, and had they all been immediately and
miraculously effective they would not have stayed the course of events
one whit. The problem was not government competition, it was
paralysis of the entire economy.

As Roosevelt's inauguration day came, many businessmen had
recognized the inability of business to salvage the American economy.
This group did not include the automotive manufacturers, as a group,
and most particularly it did not include Alfred P. Sloan, Jr. He was
dedicated to a strict capitalist economy. He could countenance none
other.

But less than a week after his inauguration, Franklin Roosevelt
had captured the imagination of a large segment of the business world.
To be sure, like the ministers of the gospel and other normally conservative groups, the businessmen of America had voted as overwhelmingly for Herbert Hoover in 1932 as the poor and the workers had
voted for F.D.R. After inauguration none the less, C. B. Dulcan, vice-
president of Washington's Hecht Company, wrote Roosevelt warmly,
thanking him for restoring a measure of confidence. The Hecht Company was having a sale and it was succeeding very well. A few days
later Adrian Joyce, president of the Glidden Paint Company, con-
gratulated F.D.R. on his magnificent leadership of the nation. Milton
S. Florsheim, the shoe manufacturer, wrote in praise and confidence.

This surge of confidence was about all the nation had to hold
onto at that moment. Incoming Secretary of Commerce Daniel Roper
circulated a confidential memorandum to government leaders shortly
after inauguration day. His figures showed that the national income
was 53 per cent below that of 1929. March, 1933, represented the
forty-first consecutive month of continued deflation. The banks were
closed, of course. Railroads and insurance companies were in serious
trouble. Business volume was at an all-time low. Taxes were high,
commercial failures were high. Unemployment was high and increasing every day. Secretary Roper's figures, as of March, showed 13,000,-
000 Americans out of work.

During the spring and summer the administration labored to restore confidence, to assist the business community with encouragement and cash. During the decade, the Reconstruction Finance Corporation alone was to lend ten and a half billion dollars of public funds to prime the pumps of industry. Industry, and particularly big businesses, responded positively to the National Industrial Recovery Act provisions. In the shirt industry, for example, the NRA code outlawed the price cutting practices that had so worried the major shirtmakers in 1930. In other industries, NRA codes acted to stabilize markets and fix prices. What business did not like about the NRA codes were the attempts to regulate wages, conditions of work, and even unionization of plants.

The return of confidence was encouraging. Early in July, Milton Florsheim reported that in response to Presidential request he had increased the number of employees by 11.3 per cent and the company payroll by 18.01 per cent. Myron Taylor advised Roosevelt that U.S. Steel had authorized production of three million extra tons of ore from the mines in the Great Lakes region. This meant that immediately twenty-seven more ore vessels would be put to work on the lakes, and that all mining and transportation activity would step up.

"Our motive," Taylor said, "is to further aid employment of idle men and make provision for possible increased output of products."

Du Pont's rayon and cellophane factories announced on July 6 that they would grant their second 5 per cent increase in wages scales in thirty days.

Elliott Springs, proprietor of Springs Cotton Mills, wrote endorsing the New Deal. In a radio address on May 15, Franklin Roosevelt called for business action. The next day Springs raised wages 10 per cent. A few days later he raised them 10 per cent more. He began building houses for his workers. He opened an idle plant, and bought $100,000 worth of new equipment to put it into operation.

Roosevelt received letters and telegrams and messages of praise and encouragement from businessmen both large and small, and few open complaints, until the fall of 1933. Then, suddenly, the brief period of overwhelming enthusiasm ended. To a large extent it ended because organized labor began to take advantage of the provision in the NRA law which called for collective bargaining.

In September, Alfred Sloan noted that many automobile manufacturers objected to the NRA collective bargaining provisions. As a
group, the auto men were anti-labor, although FERA investigator
Lincoln Colcord was to note that Walter Chrysler, William Knudsen,
and other important leaders of the industry were well-disposed toward
the working man. No matter, the companies as such were on
record for the open shop and against an industry-wide union. Alfred
Sloan had always favored company unions, hard work, and high pay
on an incentive basis (speedup, the unions called it). The federal
government had indicated its support of independent unionism,
shorter hours of work, and higher pay per hour as a social gesture.

Before the end of 1933 it was apparent that a large segment of
industry was flatly opposed to the course of the Roosevelt administration. After F.D.R. took the nation off the gold standard and began
the inflation of the dollar, industrialists began to protest. And why
not? Capitalists were the ones who had something to lose by inflation.
As the guardians of capital, such men as Alfred Sloan did protest, in
memorial and meeting.

Bernarr MacFadden, the magazine publisher, wired Roosevelt in
November, striving to persuade the President to follow the path of
business management. "Fear of dictation by the government and
labor," MacFadden warned, "is unquestionably greatly retarding business improvement." Thus in 1933 was enunciated the principle which
a great segment of the business community was to follow unquestion-
ingly during the remainder of the decade. Six months after Roosevelt
assumed office, business began war on the administration. Businessmen urged that Roosevelt accept the Swope plan, which would have
established business-government-of-business outside the federal framework, and when Roosevelt turned it down, as Hoover had rejected it
earlier, the business community saw reason to suspect the new President's motives.

THE STERN OLD MAN

CHAPTER SEVENTEEN

ONE OF THE PROCLIVITIES of newspapermen and politicians is to cate-
gorize public personalities as "liberal," "conservative," "radical," and
"reactionary" groups. This pigeonholing is not a phenomenon of the
second half of the twentieth century; it has been occurring since the
days when Thomas Jefferson suspected Aaron Burr of plotting against
the integrity of the Union, and even long before that. But in 1930 the
reckless practice of labelling brought confusion and national wrath
on the heels of what had been presumed to be a very popular appointment to the United States Supreme Court. If the upheaval did not
permanently scar the object of the furor, it was only because that
man, Charles Evans Hughes, was able to rise above politics to assume
without noticeable prejudice the role of highest jurist in the land.

As had nearly always been the case in changes in the Supreme
Court, the Hughes appointment mirrored tragedy for a family and
for the nation. By the end of 1929 the huge, amiable William
Howard Taft had been ill for months and had found it increasingly
difficult to maintain the clear head necessary for conduct of the awe-
some business of the court. In the winter of 1930 Taft travelled south
for a rest. He was only seventy-two years old, not really old by judicial
standards, but the disease that would kill him a month later was so
serious by February, 1930, that Taft knew he could not go on. He
resigned from the court on February 3.

On the following day President Hoover announced Taft's successor as Chief Justice. It would be Charles Evans Hughes, judge of the
Permanent Court of International Justice at the Hague, onetime
governor of New York State, onetime Associate Justice of the United
States Supreme Court, who had resigned from the bench in 1916 to
run for the Presidency against Woodrow Wilson in Wilson's victorious campaign for a second term.

At first announcement the appointment of Hughes to the post
seemed to be greeted with general good will. Certainly the newspapers
acclaimed Hoover for appointing a man of stature. The sixty-eight-
year-old Hughes was regarded as more liberal than Taft, the "intel-

ligent conservative," but Hughes was a Republican leader who in the past had stood firm for conservative Republican principles. The appointment fell well within the accepted practice in those years of replacing a retiring conservative justice with a conservative, and a liberal with a liberal. This hangover from the past was accepted by the country at large as the best protection of justice. Men realized, as Hughes had said himself years before, that while the nation was ruled by its Constitution, the Constitution was interpreted by judges. The practice of balancing the political leanings of the men on the court had long borne the seal of precedent.

The court in 1930 was almost evenly divided between men who espoused conservative and liberal views. Justices Oliver Wendell Holmes, Louis D. Brandeis, Harlan F. Stone, and to a lesser degree, Owen J. Roberts were regarded as men of the more liberal cast of mind. Justices J. C. McReynolds, George Sutherland, Willis Van Devanter, and Pierce Butler exhibited more conservative views. The Chief Justice, it appeared, would serve as a balance, bringing about more of the 5-4 decisions which irritated many members of the bar and left many high questions open to public argument if not to immediate legal reinterpretation. A 5-4 decision in the Cleveland administration had outlawed the federal income tax, much to the delight of the rich, and 5-4 decisions had often bedevilled others in the ensuing thirty years.

This was not an issue, however, as the Hughes appointment came up for consideration by the U.S. Senate. Judicial affairs in America had been conducted in an atmosphere of calm even when economic affairs were in turmoil. No President since Wilson had offered the judiciary any serious constitutional challenges. Congress had not kicked up its heels to pass questionable legislation. President Hoover made no attempt to move outside the normal framework of government even to cope with the growingly desperate depression. In fact, as noted elsewhere, neither Hoover nor many others seemed to realize in this raw February of 1930 that a depression had settled in. So the Hughes appointment was received in an air of general approval.

But the serenity did not last long.

The fireworks began in the Senate when the insurgent progressive Republicans (who had been battling with Hoover for two years) decided to oppose the Hughes appointment. They were joined immediately by a number of Democrats, who had their own obvious reasons for opposing any Republican appointment, in addition to an announced concern about Hughes's activity since he had left the bench in 1916.

A certain amount of indignation was expressed in the hearings. Hughes had resigned a lifetime post and great honor as an Associate Justice to seek the Presidency. Some moralists in the Senate, harking back to their puritan ancestry, felt it improper that Hughes should now be accorded the honor of leading the most dignified of the three branches of government. Some of the other senators were worried because Hughes had become a highly successful and wealthy corporation lawyer after his bid for the Presidency. The memories of trusts and corporation "steals" were yet much too recent for anyone closely connected with huge corporate enterprise to be completely free from suspicion of evil design on the public purse.

Senator La Follette opposed the Hughes appointment. So did Senator Borah, and so did many of the other insurgent Republicans. Among the Democrats, Senator Tom Connally of Texas called Hughes unfit, but for a different reason. The country was faced with great economic questions. Were the powers of the federal and state governments adequate to control and regulate the aggregated masses of wealth which had seized and controlled the necessities of life? Senator Connally reflected the concern of Democrats when he stated that the Supreme Court's construction of the law of the land would be all important, for the Supreme Court was the final authority and the most powerful of all branches of the federal government in the final analysis.

The question, said Senator Connally, was whether the government was to control the great corporations and trusts or whether the great corporations and trusts were to control the nation.

Here was more than a bare hint by one of the Democratic party's shrewdest men of the issues that would be important in the 1932 election. Politics, then, entered the Hughes confirmation vote, and although the Republican press characterized Hughes as a statesman and his detractors as guttersnipes, the issue was not so simple.

Hughes was confirmed on February 13 by a vote of 52-26. During the following year little arose to change the stream of judicial history. In the spring of 1931 a shrewd observer, R. L. Duffus, of *The New York Times* noted that Hughes had always shown a tendency to liberal interpretation of the Constitution and to liberalism, except as Secretary of State in the Harding and Coolidge administrations. Senator La Follette, however, announced in his clear Wisconsin accents that Herbert Hoover had successfully "packed" the Supreme Court with capitalist judges. And yet, that year, one decision written by Chief Justice Hughes showed the highest kind of liberalism in interpretation of the Constitution. California authorities had arrested a young woman named Yetta Stromberg for waving a Red flag in public demonstration. Hughes held that people had a right to express their opposition to organized government, as long as they expressed it in legal manner. In other words, Mr. Chief Justice Hughes stood for individual liberty against the encroachments of government. This was the old-fashioned liberalism.

The court was divided on specific lines even then, lines which made sense to men who studied the law but not to laymen. The basic line of division was over the question of the Constitution—whether it was a document to be interpreted literally, or figuratively, and if in between, just how much in between? The court here was separated into strict constructionists and liberal constructionists, with wavering back and forth across the line.

In January, 1932, a tottering but still sharp-eyed Mr. Justice Holmes resigned from the court at the age of ninety, and Hoover, as expected, replaced him with a well-known jurist of very liberal political views and liberal interpretation of constitutional law. Even crusty Senator La Follette did not complain in the appointment of New York judge Benjamin N. Cardozo to the high bench. President Hoover was playing the game as it was to be played. La Follette was pleased. So were Senator Reed and Senator Couzens of the regular Republican organization. So was Governor Franklin Delano Roosevelt.

Through 1932 the court lay quiescent in a sense. The nine justices did their duty; indeed, they worked as hard as they ever had worked, but the cases that came before them did not demand their action as the supreme constitutional authority of the land on the affairs of government. The justices decided the celebrated Scottsboro Boys case by granting a new trial to the seven Negro youths who had been sentenced to death for attacking two white girls. The court disposed of a great number of cases that year, but in these cases they did not deal with the relations and powers between federal and state governments or between branches of government.

In January, 1933, after Franklin Roosevelt's election to the Presidency an observant reader of *The New York Times* wrote that the nation could expect some jolting changes in interpretation of legal matters with the liberal appointments Roosevelt was certain to make. The reader, Mark Hesner, of New York City, foresaw the transcendental legal issue of the decade:

"A body of fundamental law," he wrote, "which cannot tolerate within its limits the recognition of the inescapable changes wrought by social and economic evolution would soon lose the confidence of the people." He expressed himself as serene, welcoming the changes he knew were coming, and confident of the ability of the Constitution and its interpreters to adjust to the changes.

In 1933, while the court had as yet little cause to be concerned with the vast social and economic changes brought about by the New Deal, it did seem to be showing itself favorably disposed to the experimentation of the New Deal. Writer Mildred Adams noted that Chief Justice Hughes, in the Minnesota Mortgage Moratorium and the New York Milk cases, had shown a surprising liberal turn of mind. It was noted in 1934, however, that the court would come squarely against the New Deal laws soon, and particularly it was believed that the issue of interpretation would be decided in a case brought to determine whether or not President Roosevelt had the constitutional authority to suspend the payment of federal debts in gold.

Fireworks were coming, that much was apparent, for the lower courts were backing up a huge number of cases which would be referred to the Supreme Court for constitutional interpretation.

The lower court backlog, and the crowding of calendars had started some talk about need for judicial reorganization even in 1934. With some New Dealers this was simply a blind, for they were uneasy about the attitude of what *Harper's* magazine had already entitled "the nine old men" towards the New Deal. To be sure, since the Civil War, the Supreme Court had declared invalid only fifty-three acts of Congress, but not since the Civil War had there been such upheaval in the United States. Even in 1934 law students among the ranks of the New Dealers were concerned because of the court's recent record of close decisions. They talked about enlarging the court by appointment of two known liberals.

It had long been held that the Supreme Court was extremely responsive to political currents. Finley Peter Dunne's fictional Mr. Dooley had wryly told his friend Mr. Hennessy years before that the Justices read the election returns. But the Justices also read the Law Reviews and the proceedings of Bar Association meetings, and by 1935 those normally conservative reports had become extremely critical of some peripheral court decisions about New Deal affairs—especially the Minnesota and New York Milk cases. Like most business-men, many lawyers were certain that Roosevelt was breaking every rule in the book. They gave little thought now to what might have happened had Roosevelt feared to tread on old constitutional interpretation in 1933. Their oxen being gored, they wanted retribution and relief.

Early in 1935 it was apparent that the administration shared the general concern about the course of the Supreme Court's decisions on the all-embracing New Deal. Secretary of Agriculture Henry Wallace proposed on January 24 a referendum in which the people would pass on measures suggested by a National Council of Economic Counsellors. He went so far as to suggest that Article V of the Constitution be amended to allow for this procedure. No major decision about the New Deal had yet been made by the Supreme Court, but even Roosevelt was uneasy about the constitutionality of some of the laws he had pushed through Congress in the terrible emergency of 1933.

Newspapermen speculated. The history of the court was written in the newspapers, week after week. This was unusual, for during normal times the Supreme Court commanded awe, but not much attention from the people. Now they read with interest of the five great historic periods of the court: the first in which the court had defined its own powers and clarified the relations between the states and the federal government; the second in which the court had dealt repeatedly with the slavery issue; the third in which the court had passed on issues of the Civil War and Reconstruction; the fourth which had dealt with the burgeoning of industry and finance into trusts and combines; and now the fifth, in which the federal government had surged far past old boundaries in directing the life of the American people.

By April, some four hundred cases in which New Deal agencies were involved were pending in the nation's higher courts. It had become obvious to even the least interested among the people that a broad decision would soon be made, although on what particular case was a matter in which opinions varied widely.

Dean Dinwoodey, editor of *United States Law Week*, suggested that the most important issue was the gold clause, but he also realized that other issues involved the NRA, TVA, AAA, and other agencies. Literally hundreds of angry businessmen were seeking ways to bring test cases into the courts to try the new laws. The gold issue was resolved in favor of the New Deal. The court found no violation of the Constitution.

During May, the administration was occupied in driving Congress to do its bidding. Before the Congress pended the Social Security Bill, Senator Wagner's Labor Dispute Bill, and amendments of considerable importance to both the AAA and TVA laws. Unfortunately, the legislation had been dragging although there was a push in progress to enact Roosevelt's legislation and then adjourn as close to the end of May as possible. Of all laws pending, the most important was a two-year extension of the National Industrial Recovery Act. Roosevelt insisted that this law be put through without delay, for on it hinged his entire federal program. If, as critics said, the NRA had already begun to collapse of its own weight, the nation at large was not aware of it. Many industries and businesses had adjusted to living within the confines of the industrial codes, and the industrial code system had become the backbone of a large segment of business.

On May 27, the Senate had already passed the extension of the NRA, and it was the subject of the day's business for the House of Representatives.

But that Monday, too, was decision day at the Supreme Court. Solicitor General Reed and NRA administrator Richberg were in the forefront of the crowd which assembled in the court hearing room. They expected the court to rule on three important cases. Richberg was particularly concerned, because so many cases in the lower courts involved NRA rulings that it was important that the validity of the NRA law be tested. In a move that some Roosevelt partisans regarded as precipitate, the administration had sought a test of the validity of the law.

The test came in what in itself was an unimportant case, involving a poultry dealer in New York City named Joseph Schechter.

The Schechters maintained a small wholesale business in chickens in the borough of Brooklyn. It was true that the chickens they sold came from New Jersey, by and large, but otherwise their business seemed to be peculiarly local, and yet they were subject to regulation by the NRA code enforcement administration. Schechter was accused of selling a sick chicken to a Brooklyn butcher. He decided to fight the case, and it went to the Supreme Court to determine whether or not the NRA had any jurisdiction over the Schechter business.

Immediately, long before it reached the high court, the case became known as the "sick chicken case," since "sick chicken" could also refer to the NRA itself. (Huey Long called the NRA eagle a mangy buzzard and other less genteel names.)

The other two matters to be determined that Monday involved the Frazer-Lemke Farm Mortgage Moratorium Law and the firing of a Federal Trade Commission member named William E. Humphrey whom Roosevelt had removed because he did not like Humphrey's approach to FTC matters.

When the hour came, the judges assembled in the robing room, then emerged into the public hearing room, one by one. The tall, distinguished Hughes led the way, and the others followed, seating themselves to his right and left in order of their seniority in office, with Cardozo, youngest member of the court in service, on one end.

The courtroom was silent, but tense as the decisions were read. Then the room erupted, and indeed, the entire nation erupted, so widespread was the effect of the decisions on daily life in America.

In the Humphrey decision, the court held that the President could not remove members of independent government agencies on caprice but only for causes specified by Congress. This was a blow at the power of the Executive, or at least at power he had assumed.

The Frazer-Lemke law had been brought to issue by the Louisville Joint Stock Land Bank in a case against William R. Radford, Sr., a Kentucky farmer. Radford had mortgaged his lands for $9,000, then had filed bankruptcy. Under the law he could have redeemed his property for $4,445, but when he sought to do so, the bank went to court. Justice Brandeis prepared the decision for the court which invalidated the law as unconstitutional, since it took away the right to property of the bank.

But the Schechter case was the main event of the day. Chief Justice Hughes prepared that opinion, although it reflected the views of all nine Justices of the court. The importance of the court's declaration that Joseph Schechter was not subject to federal regulation in his sale of chickens was the question it raised, not just about the invalid NRA law, but about the entire Roosevelt program.

A vast change came over the United States with the court's action. More than seven hundred and fifty codes were voided that day, and for each code in each state and each city there was an administrative organization, large or small. Hundreds, thousands, tens of thousands of federal employees were suddenly out of work. The whole of the New Deal was thrown into confusion, as the newspapers announced in their headlines the next day. The chief recovery weapons of the New Deal were suddenly demolished. As Justice Cardozo said in his concurring opinion "the roving commission" to make laws in the form of codes which Congress had granted Roosevelt was dishonored by the court.

That Monday Donald Richberg came down the steps of the Capitol a beaten man. When the news reached Attorney-General Homer Cummings in his office at the Justice Department, he dropped the ham sandwich he was munching. Within a matter of hours Richberg, Cummings, and Solicitor General Reed were meeting at the White House with Roosevelt to see what might be done to salvage the NRA program.

Nothing could be done, actually. Richberg issued a call to industry to maintain the fair labor practices and fair standards of competition set up by the codes, but industry responded according to its own individual standards. Within a week scores of businesses had abandoned wage and hour codes. Some businessmen tried to adhere to them, but the honor system had never been effective in control of business, and it was not then.

The New Deal now became fair game for business, and businessmen attacked. AAA officials prepared themselves for the outlawing of the agricultural administration. Businessmen, led by the Liberty League, prepared to assault every controlling phase of government and to return to the *laissez faire* policies under which business had managed the national economy in the past.

Washington landlords and restaurant proprietors worried publicly in those first few days. They had regained a measure of prosperity simply by the influx of government workers to Washington to administer the new alphabetical agencies. Now they feared the agencies would die, and so would their incomes.

Senator Borah welcomed the decision. Senator King thanked God publicly for the Supreme Court. William Green and the rest of organized labor were both shocked and worried. Their immediate reaction was to rally behind the Wagner Act and demand its immediate passage in protection of labor. Senator Hugo Black of Alabama announced that his thirty-hour-week bill was the only thing left to prevent wholesale, widespread, devastating unemployment from sweeping the land.

The court action was so final and so unexpected that it left the House of Representatives literally in midair. The House had nothing to do that Monday. It had scheduled the NRA extension bill as its sole piece of business, and now there was no business. House Parliamentarian Lewis Deschler examined the calendar to find something to keep the House occupied. Tentatively, that day he decided to bring up the McCormack antismuggling bill.

The nation's press, largely conservative and Republican in sentiment, crowed loudly. The Philadelphia *Inquirer* called the New Dealers a "wrecking crew." The Pittsburgh *Post-Gazette* predicted (and quite accurately) failure of the AAA. The Indianapolis *Star* chortled that the whole foundation of the New Deal had been undermined. The Portland *Oregonian* said righteously that there was no room for "centralized government" under the Constitution. The Denver *Post* cheered the news that the "bureaucratic brakes" had been removed from business. The Los Angeles *Times*, usually a little more anti-administration than most others, cheered because the "days of virtually uncontrolled one-man dictatorship in the U.S. are at an end."

Among businessmen, perhaps the most unhappy was Joseph Schechter, who had fought the battle of the big corporations and won. It had cost Schechter $60,000 for the fight, and now he was all but bankrupt. He had paid $22,000 of his legal bill, but had no money to pay more, and his business was in such bad repair that he had been forced to close down his branch store. Once he had done $20,000 a week in business. Now he was doing $2,000 a week.

But the NRA decision was not greeted so widely with pleasure as might be expected. The rest of the live poultry industry expressed shock at the decision. A month before, the members of the industry had voted 3-1 to continue the code system. Other businesses had adjusted themselves to living under it too.

The most violent reaction came from labor. A few days before the decision had been handed down, William Green had threatened the nation with a general strike if Congress did not pass the NRA extension. Now David Dubinsky of the International Ladies Garment Workers Union threatened to strike the whole garment industry if its members tried to cut wages or lengthen hours. Sweatshops began to do just that, however. The answer, labor said, must be immediate enactment of protective laws.

A few days after the NRA had been outlawed, the nation began to settle down. *The New York Times* noted philosophically that NRA had done its job. On June 1, Franklin Roosevelt told his press conference that the death of NRA had put the question of control of the economy squarely up to the people. Government had been stripped of the right to regulate the national economy and social conditions, he said. He now expressed doubts about the legality of his entire social and economic program.

Roosevelt was indulging himself in a bit of self-pity and recrimination that day. In reality, while he might have had such doubts, he was not beaten.

The key in the NRA decision was the unanimity with which the court had acted. The Justices, in other words, were convinced that the Congress had gone too far in delegating power to the executive department to act in time of crisis. While Raymond Moley and others suggested a Constitutional amendment passed to make NRA legal, this was not Roosevelt's final approach to the problem.

He decided against seeking a Constitutional amendment. He decided, instead, to work within the existing framework of law. What was needed, he said, was not new law, but liberal interpretation of the existing law by an enlightened court.

If an enlightened court meant a Supreme Court that would look with favor on the economic and social planning the administration had undertaken, Roosevelt seemed to be doomed to serious disappointment that year and in the succeeding year. The court continued to outlaw New Deal legislation. It almost seemed that the court had determined that it would govern the country and not allow the executive and legislative branches to make any changes at all in the old manner of doing business. AAA was outlawed. The Municipal Bankruptcy Act of 1934 was outlawed. The Guffey Act—passed to bring regulation to the coal industry after NRA—was outlawed by a majority. The court, with power suddenly thrust into the hands of the conservative members, seemed to be running wild.

Chief Justice Hughes was concerned and more, deeply troubled, as his biographer, Merlo J. Pusey has said. The court had turned to what Pusey called "standpattism." Apparently, no matter how much the liberals on the court might struggle, change in the court itself must come before either of the two other branches of government might make social or economic changes in America.

Within a few months, the court had upset twelve major New Deal laws (only six of them by unanimous decision). As Pusey noted, no court could have accepted all the hasty legislation of the New Deal without abdicating its function. But at the same time, no court could show the world a face so stern and so reactionary as the court was now showing its total face to be without stirring activity.

The activity was talk about changing the nature of the court—"packing" it with enough liberals to assure a new viewpoint towards the changes the administration felt were needed in America. The adverse decisions of the court had raised the level of anti-administration activity by business to new heights. Anti-administration vituperation was more open and more vicious than ever before. Mrs. Eugene

Meyer, wife of the publisher of the Washington *Post*, one day made a statement typical of the business community:

"If we do not soon get rid of WPA, including the National Youth Administration, and turn back relief to local control and local administration, God help America."

This ostrich attitude, this flat refusal to admit that local controls and local administration had failed the nation utterly and miserably was growing again. The Liberty League was growing in strength, too. At a banquet in Washington in the spring of 1936 two thousand loyal Leaguers assembled to see such leaders as Al Smith, a full dozen Du Ponts, Morgans, Whitneys and others. Cissy Patterson, Washington anchor man of the McCormick-Patterson axis, was there.

So was Dean Acheson, and so was James P. Warburg, once a Roosevelt treasury adviser, and Silliman Evans, former assistant Postmaster General.

As the election of 1936 neared, sentiment for a Constitutional amendment to protect Roosevelt's social legislation program grew stronger. Yet Roosevelt did not act. He was awaiting the verdict of the electorate. He felt that the need was not for amendments, but for means to adapt American legal forms and judicial interpretation to the actual needs of "the largest progressive democracy in the modern world."

Once the election was over, and won so overwhelmingly, the President did not hesitate to chart an aggressive course to assure this action. After all, before the end of 1936 even Alf Landon had come forth publicly to call for a federal child-labor law to protect children from exploitation, and to protect adult workers from the unfair competition of child labor. When a Republican leader *asked for* federal jurisdiction in social problems that was a drastic change in thinking.

Roosevelt maintained and much of the public agreed that it was impossible to expect decent and adequate legislation to be passed simultaneously by forty-eight different state legislatures to protect labor, to assure decent wages and working conditions, and to curb monopoly, unfair trade practices, stock market speculation, or any other evil of national scope. If the Supreme Court were to continue with its extremely narrow interpretations of the scope of federal government, something would have to give. Roosevelt felt that the best and simplest method of change, barring an emotional change in the court, was to pack the court with men of his own choosing.

The actual proposal was made by Attorney-General Cummings, and it was based on a recommendation made by Supreme Court Justice McReynolds years before. McReynolds had once suggested that if judges refused to retire when they reached retirement age, that substitute judges be appointed to serve with them. This suggestion appealed to Roosevelt for several reasons. McReynolds was one of the oldest and most reactionary judges on the court, and the irony of this appealed to Roosevelt's sense of humor and history. Further, this was a precedent, and Roosevelt loved precedents, no matter how far-fetched, particularly for his most outrageous proposals.

Just after the first of January, 1937, Roosevelt entertained the Supreme Court Justices, their wives, and some sixty other guests at the White House in an evening that was gay and seemed carefree. Two days later he sent to Congress a recommendation for legislation which outraged the court and its adherents. He asked power to appoint Justices up to a total of fifteen, provided the incumbents did not retire at retirement age.

This provision was half-heartedly concealed in a total bill calling for reorganization of the judiciary. But Herbert Hoover immediately charged that Roosevelt was trying to pack the court, since six of the judges were of retirement age, and none planned to retire.

The court plan was not well received in Congress. George Norris, an almost consistent Roosevelt supporter, turned against this idea. The Bar Associations were rebellious and sulky. Irving Fisher, now emeritus professor of economics at Yale, declared his opposition. John Hamilton, chairman of the Republican party, assigned a role of loyal opposition to the Republican Congressional contingent. Luckily for the Republicans, however, Senator Charles McNary was more intelligent on this question than Mr. Hamilton, and he chose to lie low and let rebellious Democrats carry the battle, rather than making a partisan issue of so serious a national problem. And it was regarded as a serious problem. Raymond Moley had been more devastated than many other New Dealers to learn of the overthrow of NRA, but Moley now said of the court-packing plan, "this comes perilously near to a proposal to abandon constitutional government."

The reaction was much the same all across the country. Roosevelt was surprised, puzzled, and finally nettled by it. He reacted with curiosity, determination, pique, but finally with resignation as the opposition grew steadily stronger until it forced the defeat of the measure by Congress.

Charles Evans Hughes learned of the bill almost as soon as it was presented to the Congressional leadership of the Democratic party, and before most of Congress knew of it. He opposed it, as did every judge on the court, but he never allowed his deep seated opposition to show, except to write one letter to Senator Burton K. Wheeler in opposition to the bill. The letter was produced in the hearings on the bill, and its reasoned arguments were convincing enough that the legislation failed to pass. Hughes had been certain that if the bill did pass, it would mean an end to the court as an institution.

Roosevelt had felt that the people were behind him in his demand for social change. In that he was proved correct, but the people were far more wise than he in foreseeing what consequences might arise from the abandonment of the system of checks and balances that had been established by the men who founded the Republic.

Public opposition to the court plan was not engendered by the Liberty League or any other group. Hundreds, even thousands of telegrams and letters poured into Congress from plain, ordinary people. More hundreds and thousands poured into the Supreme Court, too. Even Norman Thomas objected to the measure as a "clever but unsatisfactory way to deal with the constitutional problem." Earl Browder, of course, thought it was a "typical middle of the road" measure, but he supported it because the Liberty League opposed it (and perhaps because he saw in it a chance to break the strength of the American system).

The court plan failed in the spring of 1937, leaving Roosevelt embittered against a number of members of Congress, whom he tried to unseat in the Congressional elections of 1938. He learned then, that he could not unseat them, for he was almost uniformly defeated in his efforts. Roosevelt emerged from the court campaign and the 1938 election campaign a sadder but wiser Executive.

By 1939 the court problem had resolved itself. Actually, even in 1936, as Roosevelt was striving to change the court's composition, the tenor of decision had changed. Hughes moved more and more to the side of the liberal constructionists. Wages and hours laws, which had been outlawed earlier, were held legal and proper in the West Coast Hotel case, and here Justice Roberts, who had gone over to the stand-patters, changed his position and helped the court reverse itself. Thenceforth, the pattern was for a more amiable look upon the actions of the New Deal by the court—which truly did seem to be "reading the election returns."

Other decisions of importance included the acceptance of a new Frazer-Lemke law, acceptance of collective bargaining principles in the Railway Labor Act, and, in the spring of 1937, New Dealers called one court day, White Monday—to celebrate the changed attitude of the court since that Black Monday of 1935.

By 1939 Roosevelt had no call to argue about the court. He had appointed four men to office. Justice Van Devanter, one of the die-hard conservatives, had retired in June, 1937, during the court-packing fight. Roosevelt had appointed Hugo Black. Black's appointment was contested, partly because he was an extreme liberal, when it was learned that he had been a member of the Ku Klux Klan. But Black's appointment stood.

Justice Sutherland, another standpatter, retired in January, 1938, to be replaced by Stanley Reed, another New Dealer.

To the shock of all, the liberal Cardozo died in July, 1939, to be replaced by Professor Felix Frankfurter of Yale Law School, an archi-tect of many New Deal laws, and one of the few who had cautioned Roosevelt against trying to test the NRA act in the courts before amendment.

When Brandeis retired in February, 1939, William O. Douglas, the fire-eating chairman of the SEC, was appointed to the post. By this time the emphasis was clearly on the liberal side, and Roosevelt had no worry about the constitutionality of his approach to social and economic affairs. It was not that Roosevelt had succeeded in packing the court despite his loss in the Congressional fight. The court could interpret law as it saw fit. Hughes had said this years before, and Roosevelt had recognized it when he discarded suggestions of amend-ing the Constitution to achieve his ends. What had happened was that the court had become tempered, had decided to accept the philosophy of liberal construction of the Constitution, and had seen the need for increased regulation of business and personal affairs in a nation whose life was daily becoming more complex.

In time, before his retirement, Chief Justice Hughes had moved to grounds of mutual respect with Franklin Roosevelt. In 1939, after four years of turmoil, the court was in harmony, and that year on October 2, all members of the court but the recalcitrant Justices Butler and McReynolds went to the White House for tea.

Hughes perhaps had wavered from his liberalism at times during the first of those tempestuous years, but he had found himself quickly enough, and had moved on to become the balancing force in the court. He had voted to uphold the National Labor Relations Act, the second AAA, Social Security, the second Guffey Coal Law and much other legislation that the strict constructionists would have declared to be unconstitutional. But Hughes understood the days in which he lived, and the place of the judiciary in a changing, moving government. In his NLRA decision he stated the case for liberal construction of the Constitution. It was a close decision, won 5-4 in the period when the court was in turmoil. Hughes's opinion noted that the argument against the interstate commerce aspect of the case in hand was specious indeed. The stoppage of work in large industrial plants would have a most serious effect on interstate commerce, both immediate and catastrophic, he said. There was no room for an intellectual vacuum in which the Supreme Court might make its decisions. The court was a living, breathing arm of the American government, chosen to interpret living law.

It was indeed a change from the days before 1930.

CHAIRMAN OF THE BOARD—II

CHAPTER EIGHTEEN

THE PERIOD OF GOOD FEELING by business—and here the word might better be capital—for the frankly experimental New Deal ended at the close of 1933 after the National Recovery Act was passed. Such a turn of events might have been foreseen since businessmen are naturally conservative to the extent that they want to maintain the fixed conditions of business from year to year. Since the earliest days of the Republic the men who led the business community resented changes in taxation, regulation of business conditions, and any attempts by governing bodies to interfere with the businessman's day-to-day conduct of affairs or his command over the men and women who worked for him.

In 1934, Alfred P. Sloan, Jr., led the fight in the automotive industry to keep the American Federation of Labor from organizing the workers despite NRA. William Green and the AF of L were not completely convinced that industrial organization was in the American labor tradition, as noted earlier. The automotive industrialists were certain it was un-American. They organized company unions, they spent millions of dollars on labor spies and on anti-labor propaganda. They circulated petitions within the industry against unions.

The atmosphere was not one of open enmity in 1934, but on all sides the hostility was growing. George Berkenstein, president of the National Association of Waste Material Dealers, was one of the first to question Roosevelt's attitudes toward business. His questions came as he laid off half his own work force.

But questions came elsewhere, too. In 1934 blue-collar workers and white-collar workers, farmers and the unemployed showed a growing resentment against business. In Maine, for example, capital seemed to have deserted the state, leaving merchants and working people to shift for themselves. Lorena Hickok, chief investigator for Harry Hopkins, surveyed the town of Rockland a few months after federal relief began. She found that quarrying had been the biggest industry, but that now the quarries were still. New York was doing no paving or building, and so Rockland's once-prosperous lime quarry

was in the hands of the receivers. Hundreds of workmen were unemployed. Rockland's second industry had been a shipyard, but it had
built no ships of consequence since the end of World War I. The
town's third industry was a cannery, and it, too, was closed. Why not?
There was no money to be made in 1933 and 1934 in fish canning.

Miss Hickok told of two fishermen who arose before dawn and
went out to sea at 4:00 A.M. one day. They returned at 5:00 P.M.
They had burned eight gallons of gas at nineteen cents a gallon. They
had used a hundred pounds of bait at two cents a pound. They caught
eighty pounds of haddock and two hundred pounds of hake for
their day's work. They were paid four cents a pound for the haddock
and one cent a pound for the hake. At the end of the day each
fisherman was twenty cents richer than he had been on the day before.
They earned less than two cents an hour for their work.

The automotive workers in Detroit were not earning a great
deal more. Some were still being paid a living wage in 1934, but the
vast majority were unemployed or working part time. Yet profits of
some companies, General Motors among them, were increasing this
year.

By the end of the year, business had begun to show definite
signs of recovery. Then did Alfred P. Sloan, Jr., give any credit for this
to the federal government? He did not. Rather, he worried publicly
over the expansion of government into the industrial field, he returned from a jaunt on his million-dollar yacht, the *René*, to endorse
the activities of the anti-administration Liberty League, he fought
against the thirty-hour week and wage and hours laws. Sloan still
believed in increasing working hours and increased productivity before
wages could rise.

As 1935 began it was apparent that in 1934 business had enjoyed
its best year since the crash. Unemployment was still far too high:
the AF of L estimated the figure at 10,600,000. Not enough men were
working, but the average wage for those who were working had risen
to 59.3 cents an hour, the same figure as that of the boom year 1929,
and the conditions under which men worked now were far better
than before. Ground had been laid, in other words, for more favorable
conditions for the workers.

Franklin Roosevelt continued to call on industry to display confidence and thus help recovery. Here he agreed with Alfred Sloan, who devoted the General Motors exhibit at the Chicago World's Fair in 1934 to the theme of industrial progress. Roosevelt and Sloan agreed on another point that year, that tariffs were too high and that the President ought to be given discretionary power to adjust tariffs in the national interest. Here Sloan stepped outside the normal conservative ranks, for General Motors was deeply involved in international trade. It was to his interest to be on the "liberal" side in this regard.

When the figures were compiled for the auto industry in 1934, they showed sales of 2,885,000 units—double the sales of 1932—and as the motor show opened in New York in January, the leaders of the industry exhibited confidence that the wheels of all industry were getting under way. The industry stopped for a moment to take stock of the good things that had come of the depression.

As the president of Pontiac noted, the industry had made more technical progress, through necessity, than in the ten years previous to 1930. To bolster the economy the government had made huge increases in spending for roads. Highways to Alaska and to Panama were planned, and a million dollars had already been spent on the Inter-American highway survey.

This progress did not make for better feeling between industrialists and government. The year 1935 was the year in which the United Auto Workers began to win victories. Union progress certainly accounted for much anti-administration feeling in the industry.

Alfred Sloan declared that he was not anti-New Deal, and yet nearly every action belied it. In the Liberty League he sat down with such men as E. T. Weir, the Pittsburgh steel manufacturer who opposed the labor boards and collective bargaining of the NRA codes, W. L. Clayton, the Houston cotton man who opposed AAA, and John J. Raskob, Al Smith, and John W. Davis, all of whom opposed Roosevelt solidly.

In April, 1935, Alfred Sloan talked openly of the "experimental errors" of the Roosevelt administration, and referred cynically to the new fashion in government to "discredit every instrumentality of production." He had not changed his views, he had simply dressed them up. He favored the highest possible wage scale, he said, but as a corollary of prosperity. He was concerned lest the government establish a foundation for industrial welfare.

Men like Sloan, said the White House, put property rights ahead of human rights. Not so, said Sloan's Liberty League. The rights of property and humanity were equal rights. It was an equation that was to be bitterly disputed in the months to come.

After all industry's complaint about the wage and bargaining provisions of NRA one might suspect that businessmen would be pleased to throw off all the shackles. Some businessmen were entirely pleased, but much of big business wanted to retain, on a voluntary basis, the cooperative or cartel aspects of NRA while abandoning the aspects they did not like. For one, the National Electric Manufacturers Association asked its members to keep the code on a voluntary basis, and apparently that philosophy directed the industry for another quarter of a century.

The American Iron and Steel Institute, which had also been the code authority for the steel industry, mapped a program to keep much of the code, including the open price system which had ended the evil of secret discounts and rebates in the steel industry.

Nevertheless, the overthrow of NRA precipitated enough back-sliding by industry to create crisis. Mrs. Anna M. Rosenberg, New York State NRA Compliance Director, said that the Supreme Court decision brought on several full-scale price wars in her area. In Brooklyn, cigarettes dropped from fifteen cents straight for the popular brands to two packages for twenty-three cents. Yet this was temporary and pettifogging. The real danger lay in outright jettison of NRA principles, as when a Philadelphia manufacturing concern raised working hours from forty to fifty without notice.

After NRA, the National Chamber of Commerce called for retention of wage and hour provisions on a "voluntary" basis. William Green of the AF of L snorted.

Textile manufacturers in the South raised hours. Restaurants in Honolulu promptly returned to the four dollar wage for the seven-day week. The National Child Labor Committee gloomily predicted an immediate return to the child labor system.

The most pleased people in the world with this trend were the Soviet Union's Communist leaders who had been watching Roosevelt's peaceful revolution with dismay for two years.

"The skyscraper of capitalist planning which attracted the attention of half-baked reformers in all countries has collapsed like a house of cards," crowed *Za Industrializatsiu*, the industrial workers' newspaper in Moscow when NRA died. *Izvestia* assailed the Supreme Court as an instrument of capital, and indicated that the bloody revolution was not far off.

Wall Street's first reaction to the administration's defeat was unrestrained joy. So was Sloan's, and Sloan again took this occasion to attack the "theory of scarcity" on which the entire recovery program was based. The American problem was not over-production, he said, but maladjustment. Now, he saw recovery proceeding normally, if government would only retreat to its previous position and stop obstructing his kind of progress. He was grateful to the Supreme Court for eliminating Rooseveltian obstructions.

Here was a basic difference between Sloan, the spokesman for big business, and the administration. Big business truly believed it would be possible to return to the old way of doing things. Once the crisis of 1933 was past, the lords of business promptly forgot that their system had collapsed and had been rebuilt only through the efforts of federal government with public money. Having rebuilt, they now demanded that government return to the back seat and stay quiet. Having done the rebuilding, the men of government were determined to navigate the road ahead and remain close to the wheel of control. And in the Supreme Court decision on NRA both business and government saw the real crisis of the Roosevelt administration: Roosevelt was determined that his reforms of capitalism would not be overthrown; business was determined to return to the ways of the past.

The issue between business and government was well stated publicly that fall of 1935 in debate at the New York Herald Tribune Forum.

The debaters were governor George Earle of Pennsylvania, a Democrat, and Ogden Mills, former Secretary of the Treasury under Hoover. Earle warned that since the Supreme Court had outlawed

In 1935 the old Supreme Court justices balked and they nearly swamped the New Deal. L. to r., Justices Brandeis, Van Devanter, Chief Justice Hughes, McReynolds, Sutherland, Roberts, Butler, Stone, Cardozo. The new faces were Brandeis, Roberts, Stone, Cardozo. BROWN BROTHERS

One of Senator McNary's strongest attributes was his ability to get along with the opposition in the Senate. He made it a rule never to quarrel openly with Majority Leader Alben Barkley's steamroller. UNITED PRESS INTERNATIONAL PHOTO

By 1939 nearly all the news that Cordell Hull brought to the White House was bad news. UNITED PRESS INTERNATIONAL PHOTO

NRA as unconstitutional, the Constitution must be amended, lest the nation be unprotected against wage slavery and the evils of capitalism. Even then, Earle said, the miners of southwest Pennsylvania were in more desperate straits than the chattel slaves of the South before the Civil War.

Ogden Mills warned that in Constitutional amendment or in permitting the Roosevelt administration to continue to usurp the powers of Congress and to continue to interfere with business the country was heading toward dictatorship.

Alfred Sloan, of course, sided with Ogden Mills. By 1936 he was openly attacking the Roosevelt administration, opposing the forty hour week. Speaking for the Liberty League, Sloan said government was of no use to big business.

Harold Ickes, stung by this attack, began to talk back. He retorted that Detroit, the motor city, had been hardest hit of all American cities in 1932 and 1933. Of course, government was of no use to big business, Ickes said, when business did not need help for survival.

Spurred by such attacks, spokesmen of business became vitriolic, and Ickes became unfair in his attacks on business. So did F.D.R. He took an extreme view on productivity in May, 1936, stating that new machinery and new techniques would simply put more men out of work. Sloan and other industrialists contended that there was no end to the standard of living and the amount of goods that could be sold, in America and abroad, if only government would keep its hands off. Roosevelt said that if government kept hands off, business would exploit the workers and the national welfare, as business always had done in the past.

Here, then, lay the essence of the campaign of 1936, between Franklin Roosevelt's New Deal and the rugged individualism Landon allowed the Republican leaders to espouse in his behalf. As the year and the campaign progressed even some of Roosevelt's staunch supporters noted the growth of class feeling and hatred in the industrial areas. Employers felt it too, and blamed Roosevelt alone.

Roosevelt's attitudes toward business were the product of the information he received. In the spring of 1936, in Youngstown, Ohio, the Chamber of Commerce reported that steel production was up to 1929 levels, but that ten thousand fewer men were employed in producing the steel than had been needed in 1929. In the Mahoning Valley lived a million and a half industrial workers, all of them afraid of losing their jobs. They responded to Roosevelt's charge that big business would desert the people without a qualm, because they had already seen business doing just that. Lorena Hickok reported that a friend walked down Euclid Avenue in Cleveland one day during the campaign and asked the first twenty-five people she met who was going to be elected. All but six said Roosevelt would win, and three of the others were undecided. The other three were Roosevelt-haters.

When the election was won by Roosevelt in the famous landslide, the nation took the victory to be a repudiation of big business. The administration and Congress both began to move against many business practices. Not the least of these government actions and by far the most stinging, involved taxation of great wealth. Early in 1937, Congress began to investigate the personal habits of a number of industrialists. It was hardly an impartial investigation, noted Representative Hamilton Fish of New York. Of sixty men called before the House committee as "tax avoiders," twenty-seven were contributors to the Republican campaign of 1936 and only one was a Democratic supporter.

The committee looked into Myron Taylor's incorporation of his several residences. Taylor claimed a loss on running them, and thus cut his income tax. The investigators examined John Hay Whitney's incorporation of race horses, Alfred Du Pont's incorporation of his real estate, Fritz Kreisler's incorporation of his talents, and Alfred P. Sloan, Jr.'s incorporation of his yacht.

Sloan was outraged when the question of his yacht was raised. He fired back a response. He had paid $1,725,790 in income taxes in 1936, he said, and he had split the remainder of his income squarely between charity and himself. He had incorporated the yacht simply to avoid personal liability. Nonetheless, the public noted that he paid several thousand dollars less in income tax by incorporating the yacht. And the revelation of his income set some to wondering whether any man's abilities in industry were worth pay of $2,876,310 a year.

Alfred Sloan responded again. He was elected chairman of the board of directors of General Motors in 1937, and he announced that he was withdrawing himself from the bonus arrangement, which had contributed the greater share of his income in the previous year.

That year, something happened to the national economy once again, as the stock market showed, and it was not just a stock market slump, but a general recession which threatened to become renewed depression. Alfred Sloan said that recovery had been reversed by government policies which were inimical to business. Businessmen would not spend money, they would not try to expand in the face of punitive government action. What kind of action? Government encouragement of unions and their demands, the businessmen complained, and interference in industrial and business management policies, pricing, and methods of distribution. Heavy personal and corporate taxation, especially the tax on undistributed corporate profits was another. Sloan particularly detested the tax on undistributed profits, for it was through holding profits of General Motors and using earned income as surplus to buy and build that GM was becoming the largest industrial complex in the world.

Sloan was not the only businessman who blamed Roosevelt's anti-business policies for the recession. A. O. Overell, president of the Modern Furniture Store in Los Angeles wrote the President, asking him to destroy unions and above all to let business alone. All the Rooseveltian policies had backfired, Overell said. It was time to start over.

In Congress the Republican contingent prepared to campaign in 1938 on the issue of government interference in business. The New Dealers took the view with which Alfred P. Sloan quarrelled so vigorously. Representative Jerry Voorhis of California introduced an Industrial Expansion Act in the spring of 1938 when it was apparent to all that business was faltering. His theory was that the nation could not expect a business revival to re-employ more than a fraction of the men now out of work. He called for subsidies and broad government regulation of business.

The response was a deluge of protest from businessmen all across the country. Sheldon Cary, president of the Browning Crane and Shovel Company, pleaded with the President to reduce regulation of business for a time—to give business what Raymond Moley had characterized as a "breathing spell" in earlier days. In Portland,

Oregon, the *News-Telegram,* a Scripps league newspaper, printed a four-point program for relief of business-government relations. More than four thousand *News-Telegram* readers signed and returned coupons to the newspaper, which backed its program with a letter and a list of five thousand reader-sponsors to Roosevelt.

Such general dissatisfaction, translated into a political level, helped turn the tide. Business was picking up in late 1937, perhaps, but events of the first few weeks of 1938 brought about renewal of confidence.

Roosevelt decided to try to compromise with the business community. He called in Alfred Sloan, E. T. Weir, of Weirton Steel Company, C. M. Chester, Jr., of General Foods, and Lewis H. Brown, president of Johns Manville. They offered a proposal: to eliminate the tax on capital gains, to repeal the tax on corporate profits withheld, to hold back on wages and hours laws, to raise rail freight rates, to amend the Wagner Act in favor of business, to get government out of power production and plans for distribution, to lower prices and wages, and to eliminate rule by administrative bureau.

Of course Roosevelt would not and could not accept such demands, but he did meet with the four on January 11, and the news of the meeting helped bolster the nation's confidence.

R. E. Wood, president of Sears, Roebuck and Company, wrote James Farley that business would be much better in 1938 than it had been in 1937. Wood added, however, that he expected another recession in 1939 unless the government undertook a huge spending program or the President and business could arrive at some common ground less uneasy than that reached in the meeting of January with Sloan's group.

Sloan was encouraged in 1938 by one move, at least. He approved completely of the most-favored nation approach to tariff policies which was Secretary of State Hull's favorite dream. General Motors, which had cut executive and employee pay from 10 to 30 per cent at the height of the recession, restored those pay cuts and rehired 35,000 workers in October, adding $55,000,000 to its payrolls, and cutting the relief load remarkably in Michigan.

Actually recovery had not shown itself so heavily in General Motors, although the management's vote of confidence caused the stock of the company to rise to the year's high of 51 ¾. What was occurring was a manifestation of a new attitude on the part of General Motors management. Following the Flint strike, and the meeting with Roosevelt, the management had shown a much greater recognition of business responsibility and its place in the business-government scheme than seemed apparent before. Perhaps Roosevelt made this possible by convincing Sloan that while he might differ with GM on what was best for the country, the administration was not planning to bear down further on business.

In the Congressional elections of 1938, Sloan found some cause for encouragement, too. He noted what appeared to be a trend of rejection of the "extravagant experimentation" of the administration. He foresaw a return to "economic sanity." What he really seemed to see was the defeat of the Democrats in 1940, and he was cheered immensely.

Whatever the specific reasons for it, the business outlook and the outlook of business were vastly improved by the end of 1938. The course of steel production through the period indicated what had happened everywhere: Steel production had dropped in 1932 to a low of 15 million tons. Then, raggedly it began to climb back after Roosevelt was inaugurated. In 1936 it had come far, to 50 million tons. But in 1937 and 1938 it dropped to 30 million tons, showing how truly serious was the recession of those years. At the end of 1938 the graph was moving upward once again, and steel industrialists looked forward to better years.

In the spring of 1939 there occurred a single incident which seemed to epitomize the character and status of business. On April 19, Alfred P. Sloan, Jr., went to the New York World's Fair grounds at Flushing Meadows, Long Island, to unveil the General Motors exhibit—Highways and Horizons. He had polled 107 American industries to learn what was happening in research and product development.

Sloan felt he must contradict the view held so widely among the men of the New Deal that industrial frontiers had disappeared. GM prepared a film (*On to Jupiter*) and a 62-page booklet devoted to significant industrial developments. All this was to be unveiled as part of a pageant.

But on the day of the opening, the electricians' union and the stagehands' union argued over jurisdiction of the lighting work for the evening pageant. The electricians won the dispute. The stagehands reported the dispute to their old friends of the musicians' union, and the musicians refused to play that night. The pageant was cancelled, because the mighty General Motors could not buck the power of organized labor even when it was power misused. How could such incidents help but annoy a business firm caught squarely in the middle of a foolish jurisdictional squabble?

Still, the coming of war to Europe in the summer of 1939 found business and the Roosevelt administration in an uneasy truce, held together partly by the growing realization in industry as well as in government that America might be threatened and that some measures must be taken to strengthen national defenses. Even in 1939 there occurred important changes in attitude. In the face of greater potential danger, the strife between government and business did not seem to loom quite so large, and as the months crept on and defense spending increased, the improvement of business conditions occupied businessmen with their own affairs so fully that they had less time to spend in argument.

That year, Henry Ford had made the brash statement that his plants alone could produce a thousand planes a day for American defense, but Alfred Sloan knew better. The problem—and Sloan considered it to be very serious—was time. Certainly America could gear up for defense, but Mr. Ford could not produce those one thousand planes a day with the equipment in the factories he now operated for automobiles. An entire new industrial plant had to be built.

Sloan was to have more days of revulsion against the Roosevelt administration, and they were to be among his most ignoble. On September 24, at Pittsburgh, he spoke publicly on the issues of defense and government. That day, also, Alfred P. Sloan disclosed his support of Wendell Willkie, although in 1936 he had avowed that General Motors should not take political sides. Now Sloan reiterated all his old arguments against Roosevelt policies, and showed that no matter what had happened to the nation, he had not changed his ideas one single bit. He accused the administration of interfering with the normal processes of the American economy—intimating that otherwise the depression would have blown away by itself and the recession would never have come. He called Franklin Roosevelt a demagogue. He made the remarkable statement, obviously comparing Democracy and Fascism, that in recent years other forms of economy, "perhaps more aggressive and dynamic in action," had raised the question as to "which approach offers the greater efficiency and effectiveness." Always the industrialist, Sloan was true to form that day.

That year, despite the opposition of Alfred Sloan and most of the representatives of major business, Franklin Roosevelt was elected once again. In the fall of 1941, General Motors was working on $250,000,000 in defense contracts, and General Motors was simply blazing a trail which most of the rest of American business would soon follow. GM was too busy for politics. The battle between business and government was put aside in the face of the greater danger.

THE WIDE WORLD UNFOLDS

CHAPTER NINETEEN

IN 1931, after President Hoover declared a one-year moratorium on the European war debts, Americans looked up from their national preoccupations to note that Europe still existed. Some had not looked across the Atlantic for a dozen years.

Charles Merz of *The New York Times* wrote in the spring of 1931 that Americans had discovered Europe again for the second time in thirty years. But Mr. Merz was premature. The look Americans took across the Atlantic was brief, intense, and unfriendly. To be sure the *Times* displayed considerable interest in world affairs, but the interest of the *Times* and a handful of other newspapers did not add up to general concern. Most Americans wanted no further meddling in the affairs of Europeans.

Since the days of President McKinley American attitudes toward Europe had undergone several changes. In McKinley's time just before the turn of the century the nation had enjoyed a brief fling of imperialist sentiment.

The First World War forced Americans to consider Europe seriously. They did so cautiously at first from the safe distance of three thousand miles. In 1914 Americans faced the war with mixed emotions. Grace Wilson Vanderbilt, for example, adored both England's King George V and his cousin Germany's Kaiser Wilhelm. She found it hard to take sides, and so did millions of others. But Germany, exhibiting the singleness of purpose and the almost unbelievable lack of national tact for which Germans are so justly infamous, managed by 1917 to pit the vast majority of Americans against the Triple Alliance. Americans went to war as to a Holy Crusade, convincing themselves that theirs was a vital mission.

Two years after the war a casual visitor would have found it difficult to make sense of the American attitude toward Europe. It was first a reaction against war, and a distaste for the constant quarrelling of Europeans. By 1920, if anyone asked an American if he had "made the world safe for democracy" he was liable to receive a short answer.

In 1924, the Democrats campaigned for recognition of the existence of the world again, but they fought without heart, for they had blunted all the arsenal of their weapons in the struggle between William Gibbs McAdoo and Al Smith for the nomination.

In the end, when the compromisers settled on John W. Davis they had a candidate few Americans knew and few Americans wanted. The nation returned to its preoccupations with internal affairs. And foreign investment remained a minor factor in American business. There was too much to be done at home.

After the depression began there was talk in Congress and in Wall Street about foreign investment, but there was precious little to invest, too. So in 1931, while Americans may have rediscovered Europe their interest was almost purely negative. Senators began to talk about "cooperation" with other nations. Manufacturers began to take a good long look at the no-credit policy they had followed. Industrialists began to wonder if *all* the high tariffs were necessary. But they came to no fast conclusions.

But the measure of the new administration's attitude toward foreign affairs was in Franklin Roosevelt's appointment of the man to be Secretary of State in his cabinet. He chose Cordell Hull, senator from Tennessee, for the job.

Why Hull?

Hull was a confirmed internationalist in economic affairs. He had made his mark and dedicated his years of political service, most of them in the House of Representatives, to two propositions: the income tax and the lowering of trade barriers throughout the world.

By 1933 the income tax was as settled on the nation as a mother-in-law in her darling daughter's guest room. Hull could turn his full efforts to the tariff. The new administration, it seemed, would be thoroughly internationalist in approach. But those who so believed did not count on the intensely political nature of Franklin Roosevelt. He appointed an internationalist to the foreign affairs post, but he made it quite clear from the beginning that he would overrule Hull in matters of national and international policy as he chose. Hull, in fact, debated acceptance of the post when several officials, including Raymond Moley, were given harbor in his office although he had no say about the appointments.

Cordell Hull was an intense contradiction among men. He was

thoroughly dedicated to the cause of economic interdependence among nations. He was also stubborn as a Tennessee mule and as good a hater as had sat in Washington since the days of Thaddeus Stephens and Charles Sumner. He was, in short, the product of his background, which included birth in a log cabin, family feuds, and service in Cuba in the Spanish-American War, as well as his years in Washington.

At the time of his appointment Cordell Hull was sixty-one years old, one of the eldest among the cabinet. Even among those who did not know him by reputation, Hull was an impressive man. He wore high, stiff collars, but casual well-cut suits. His white hair and pleasant eyes were belied by his stiff upper lip, tight mouth, and forthright jaw. He was not a New Dealer, but a conservative whose appointment pleased the southern wing of the party. Among the conservatives, as indeed he was also among the nation at large, Cordell Hull could be counted among the most knowledgeable of politicians on international affairs. Yet what were the benchmarks he set for himself in surveying the field of foreign affairs and projecting American participation? He said his task would be to "increase and cement" American relations with other nations and, in the same breath, "to protect the interests of the United States abroad." General statements of policy, these, but even a casual observer from outside the United States would have noted how limited they were. In America they went unchallenged.

Coming into office in that spring of 1933, Cordell Hull saw no hope for immediate recovery for the world, even after the frightening bank crisis of March had been resolved. He did see an ultimate answer: international trade should involve exchanges of some fifty-five billion dollars a year. High tariffs had cut that to twelve billions, which, in turn had brought on panics and depressions.

Hull, that spring, looked ahead to the London Economic Conference as the beginning of the solutions of the problems of world trade and world recovery. World peace did not seem to be a problem that spring, although Japan was moving steadily ahead in China, having stolen Manchuria and having sent troops into the northeastern provinces in force. The Russians were quarreling with Japan about historic trade concessions and arming their Siberian bases. And yet no war seemed to threaten.

In Europe the problem, as Hull saw it, was to rebuild business and markets, a job to be done only if all nations would make broad trade concessions. "Economic disarmament and military disarmament" were the two most important factors in international recovery, including that at home, he said. War debts, which many Americans wanted paid immediately, were not the crux of the problem.

If the problem was to be solved, London was the place to go to solve it. For London was the financial capital of the world and Americans still turned to London before Roosevelt, to learn the value of the dollar every day in terms of gold. Later that first year Raymond Moley was to note hopefully that "in a financial way we are becoming more independent of England every day," a statement which indicates how very dependent on England was the United States in the spring of 1933 on the eve of the conference.

Hull held great hopes for the London meeting, even after he discovered how mixed a bag of delegates he had been handed by Roosevelt. From inauguration day very little else was on Hull's mind; his first major speech two months later was dedicated to the problem of international economic rehabilitation.

As Robert Bendiner of *The Nation* was to write in a survey of the State Department nearly a decade later, had Hull been appointed to his post ten years before he might have had a chance of doing what he foresaw as necessary. But in 1933, while Roosevelt was broadly internationalist in outlook, he was not so concerned with world affairs that he would let them interfere in the slightest with the development of his domestic program. The domestic program was being built, one brick at a time. Even as Hull sailed for England early in June, domestic affairs were moving rapidly. One crisis followed another. Even if he had wanted to do so, Roosevelt could not make any promises one minute that he could be sure of keeping the next.

Hull and his five-man delegation took with them a memorandum of policy. Roosevelt wanted these problems discussed:

1. a tariff truce for the duration of the conference.
2. general agreement on a coordinated money and fiscal policy.
3. removal of restrictions on foreign exchange.
4. establishment of an international monetary standard.

5. general agreement on gradual abolition of trade barriers.
6. agreement for control of production and distribution
   of basic commodities.

Had such agreement been reached in London the world might
have been changed. But much depended on the American indications
of good will. Hull had prepared a reciprocal trade bill and it had
been sent to Congress. As he sailed, he left with the hope that it
would pass before he reached England. But Roosevelt had already
decided to let the bill die, for the situation was becoming desperate
in Congress. Roosevelt wanted Congress to adjourn before the legislators pressed demand for bonuses, inflation, and other kinds of immediate relief of pressure groups which would ultimately hurt the
whole recovery program.

So, as previously noted, the London Economic Conference
failed, and Cordell Hull came home, reciprocal trade still on his mind,
but pushed far back in the American scheme of affairs.

The years 1933 and 1934 brought many harbingers of the future
to the halls of the old gingerbreaded State Department building,
even though they brought little but talk about economic cooperation
among nations.

In the summer of 1933 a uniformed Nazi in Berlin attacked
Dr. Daniel Mulvehill of Long Island College Hospital, during a Nazi
parade.

The brown-shirted Nazis had begun to march along Unter den
Linden, through the Brandenburg gate, singing their *Horst Wessel*
song. Dr. Mulvehill had come to Germany to study under a famous
professor of medicine at Berlin Charité Hospital, and the thirty-year-
old doctor was on the street that day, so he stopped to watch the
paraders. On the sidelines, thousands of Berliners raised their right
arms in the Nazi salute. When Dr. Mulvehill did not, a Nazi stepped
out of the line of march and slugged him behind the right ear, knock-
ing him down.

It was a portent.

Japan had withdrawn from the League of Nations after condemnation in the League for her actions in Manchuria, and she now

exhibited her interest in establishing a sphere of influence for herself which included the entire Far East. In 1933 and 1934 the Japanese tried to persuade Hull and Roosevelt to accept such a "Monroe Doctrine" for Japan—but Hull was outraged when the Japanese tried to equate their own swallowing of much of Asia with America's hemispheric policy. And Hull's annoyance was all the more pointed because America had begun the Good Neighbor Policy which was enunciated by Roosevelt in his first inaugural address. Hull had gone to Montevideo to declare that "no state has the right to intervene in the internal or external affairs of another" and Roosevelt had agreed that there would be no more armed intervention anywhere. Japan's suggestions came as cold water on a hot griddle.

Before the London Conference, Hull had persuaded Roosevelt to appeal for military and economic disarmament to all the powers in the world—fifty-four of them, including the Union of Soviet Socialist Republics, thus establishing an official relationship with the USSR. Hull stoutly denied that this was recognition, but at least it was a step above the personal relationship Senator Borah had conducted with the Russians a few months before. It emphasized the strange, peculiarly American, approach to recognition of foreign governments which had persisted for many years and was to persist for many more.

In the fall, however, fifteen years after the Bolsheviks took control of the Russian state, the United States government did decide to recognize Soviet Russia, and following Foreign Commissar Maxim Litvinoff's visit to Washington, ambassadors were exchanged.

By 1934 it had become apparent, even in Washington, that there was less to be feared, for the moment at least, from Moscow than from the upheavals occurring in Middle Europe and the Far East. These upheavals were important for they were shaping the future.

Adolf Hitler had made his ultimate ambitions totally apparent in scores of ways. The reader of *Mein Kampf*, of course, could claim later that he had been exposed to the whole German plan. But one need not even have read *Mein Kampf* to ascertain Hitler's intent. In April, 1934, Hitler barred the work of the Carnegie Endowment for International Peace in Berlin. The Carnegie fund had been working through the *Deutsche Hochschule für Politik*. Why was it banned? Because all its work was based on free discussion of international relations.

That same season, as Easter approached, the Nazis staged strange pagan ceremonies in Garmisch-Parternkirchen and other towns and villages. They hoped to revive the ancient Teuton celebrations to take the place of Easter.

In America a number of pro-German and German-American organizations sprang up, most of them innocent enough, if dedicated to German jingoism. German-Americans, and particularly the youth, were encouraged to see their mother country rising from the ashes, and such was the despair of youth in America in this period that many of these hyphenated citizens thought affairs might be better had we adopted dictatorship here.

From all these groups was formed the German-American Bund, ostensibly a cultural and physical training society, but actually a copy of the Nazi movement in Germany.

One of the first to expose the German-American Nazis was editor Raymond Moley in *Today*, but the nation was strangely apathetic to this ultra-radical group, just as it was to Communism. Or was it apathy? Perhaps it was the forbearance of a period in which values were in question.

At any rate, in the middle 1930's, as the strength and prestige of Nazi Germany and Soviet Russia grew, so did their organizations of sympathizers in the United States. In 1935 the American Nazis—the Bundists—were honored at the Nazi Congress at Nuremberg. That same year a Nazi parade was banned in Newark, and wherever the Nazis demonstrated, in Detroit, in Chicago, in New York, police gathered to protect them from anti-Nazis who stormed their meetings and their parades.

The Communists were less inclined to parades, except on May Day, for their strength did not lie in appeals to those who liked to dress up in uniforms and wear Sam Browne belts.

The year 1935 was important because it marked the end of pretense on the part of the dictators. Benito Mussolini sent his troops marching into Ethiopia, then admitted that his aim was conquest and re-establishment of an Italian empire. Italy, said the *Giornale d'Italia* in a frank statement, sought "a place in the sun." By fall, before the weather was suitable for conquest, Mussolini had mobilized 300,000 men for service in Africa. Not only were the trains in Italy running on time, but this year marked the virtual end of unemployment in Italy. War had brought her prosperity.

Secretary Hull's hope, even now, was peace through reciprocal trade. He said he saw no other way of lessening tensions. The American Federation of Labor did not agree. William Green called for mediation to avert Italian aggression in Ethiopia.

Mediation? How was one to mediate with the hungry lion in search of food? Certainly not without a proper arsenal, and America, which might have served as a mediator had she been strong enough, was physically far too weak.

As the Italians moved into Ethiopia, Secretary Hull talked about economic sanctions, but far more space in the newspapers was devoted to a half-dozen Americans who held winning tickets in the Irish sweepstakes in late October. It was the end of trade with Italy, but Adolph Nartowich, of the Bronx, New York, was going to give up his job as a gravedigger at Flushing Cemetery and live happily ever after on the $147,000 gift from a horse.

With Europe, and even America engrossed in the Ethiopian problem, Japan decided it would be a good time to move in North China.

"Cactus Jack" Garner and a Congressional delegation were touring the Far East. They stopped off in Japan to be "deeply impressed" with the hospitality of the Japanese.

As they were wined and dined in best Japanese fashion, the Emperor's general staff was making plans.

No homegrown groups of any size or strength represented Japanese foreign policy in this country. (The Nisei were overwhelmingly loyal to America.) Japan's movement was almost steely in its open hardness. The Japanese set out to conquer China, piecemeal, and it seemed that no one dared to stop them.

December 7, even then, was an important day in the Japanese scheme. On December 7, 1935, the Japanese established the North China Political Affairs Council, and virtually annexed Hopeh and Chahar provinces, which meant also the important cities of Peiping and Tientsin. The forty-seven-year-old Chiang Kai-shek became virtual dictator of what was left of China. He became vice-chairman of the Kuomintang council, a standing committee which controlled the nation when the party congress was not in session. He also became vice-chairman of the Central Political Council, and continued in his key post, chairman of the military affairs committee. Since he controlled the army, Chiang controlled all that the Japanese did not control, save the western and southern lands where warlords held sway.

The Japanese continued to play at respecting Chinese sovereignty, in a fashion. They were not yet ready to risk war with the Western world, or with Soviet Russia. They still needed six years for preparation. But they paid scant lip service to the normal conventions of international affairs. General Ho Ying-Ching, war minister of the Nanking government, went to Peiping during the days when the Japanese were setting up their puppet regime in North China. He was ordered out of Peiping by Colonel Tan Takahashi.

And what attitude did we take, as a nation? Secretary Hull warned the world that Japan was trying to establish a special sphere of interest in North China. America did not like it, but was not, so Americans thought, in position to do anything about it. And in truth, America was not, either physically or morally. The American army and navy had been all but disbanded at the end of World War I, and in the several disarmament conferences held since. Americans wanted no risk of sending soldiers or sailors overseas. The American navy, to be sure, looked strong on paper after the Washington Naval Conference. It would be three years before Congress would vote a billion-dollar naval building program, and then only after failure of the London Naval Conference and the sure knowledge that Japan could not be stopped from increasing naval strength.

In the following year, the condemnation of dictatorship became more open and more voluble. Norman Thomas assailed the Nazis, and so did the American Federation of Labor. But the American policy remained based on isolationism.

In the middle of 1935, Cordell Hull was certain that war involving at least one military power was coming on. It was not a guess; Italy had moved against Ethiopia in May. Only the weather held back a major military operation.

Hull was aware of the worsening European and Asiatic situations, but he was unable to act because isolationism was changing from a passive to an active force in the United States. The change came that year, as the international situation grew more strained.

Secretary Hull noted that the first serious blow of the isolationists was the investigation by the Nye Committee in 1934 and 1935 into munitions profits in World War I. The investigation unfortunately turned into a three-ring circus in which Senator Nye tried to prove that Americans had been forced into the war by profiteers. The nation was prepared to believe such charges for it had been primed by the Pecora investigation into Wall Street practices and the manipulations of banker J. P. Morgan and others.

In 1935, then, Congress determined that *it* would take the responsibility for keeping the nation out of foreign wars in the future and that it would do so by passing specific legislation to keep the nation at peace with everyone. So the Neutrality Law of 1935 was enacted, to be followed by neutrality acts passed in each of the two succeeding years, as war erupted in Spain and China.

After 1935 the tempo of aggression increased. Cordell Hull was certain that the United States would have to cast its lot with France and Britain and against Japan in the Far East, but he was not a seer. He could not tell when.

The march of events was steady and sure. In 1936 Hull opened the Third World Power Conference at Constitution Hall and told three thousand delegates from fifty nations that total war threatened. A few days later he characterized American policy as "willingness to be friends but not allies."

He continued to work for freer trade everywhere, hampered now by neutrality laws that enforced embargoes and restrictions on belligerent nations. Recognizing the overwhelming sentiment in Congress and the nation against foreign involvement, he worked to strengthen ties with Latin America, and did so. But as to the Far East, as Nathaniel Peffer wrote in 1937, "there is no policy; there is no program; there is no stated ambition. But there is an unvarying tendency." That tendency was for strained relations as Japan forged ahead in her drive to control all Asia.

One incident in 1937, however, forced a number of Americans to realize that there were situations in which determined neutrality became embarrassing. That fall, sailing up the Yangtze River, the American gunboat *Panay* was bombed and sunk by Japanese aircraft. Hull and Roosevelt demanded and received a Japanese apology and promises of reparations. But the taking of American lives and the strike against the American flag in China brought sober realization to many that war was coming.

Sentiment in the eastern section of the United States was rising in 1937 against Hitler and his excesses, too. The fiery Fiorello La Guardia referred in a public address to Hitler as a "brown-shirted fanatic." The German embassy protested and Hull delivered an official apology. He did not like that task. In fact, later in life, when writing his memoirs, he did not mention La Guardia. But in 1937, America was unprepared in every way, morally, physically, economically, for the dangerous years which lay ahead. Harry Woodring, the Secretary of War, was an isolationist. His one claim about the American army was that it was more efficient than ever before.

Efficient? Perhaps. But efficiency meant little when it involved a tiny armed force. Germany, Italy, and Japan had millions of men under arms. They were building submarines, capital warships, planes, and tanks as fast as humanly possible. America had less than half a million men under arms in all the armed forces. The American navy was old fashioned and outgunned. American air power did not exist. One could not call that handful of obsolescent aircraft "air power" in any sense of the word. When Colonel George C. Marshall held war games on the grounds of the Vancouver barracks across the Columbia River from Portland, Oregon, he was hard put to find enough old-fashioned biplanes to lay smoke screens for his forces. And that was the basic concept of American air power—for tactical use with troops.

By 1938 the intentions of the European dictators were unmistakeable except to the most myopic of Americans. Austria was seized and annexed. Hull showed his displeasure as best he could. That year, in fact, he kept in running battle with German Ambassador

Hans Dieckhoff. The isolationists were still extremely strong, especially in Congress. There Senator Hiram Johnson of California pressed for commitment against the use of American forces to support any alliance anywhere, anytime. Representative Louis Ludlow tried to push through a proposal for a popular referendum before war could be declared, thus effectively hamstringing the American defense.

Roosevelt and Hull won one important battle that year, however. They managed to secure a billion-dollar building program for the navy. It would not make the navy strong. It would make our two-ocean navy less weak.

The Nazis had stopped all pretense in 1938. In Austria, two months after the annexation, fifteen thousand people watched as Nazis burned books in a carnival atmosphere in Residenz Square in Salsburg. That May evening, the Nazis called on all Austrians to surrender their objectionable reading matter to the party. "We do not want to search homes," was the outrageous announcement, "but we appeal to your sense of decency." The bright-eyed young Nazis then proceeded to burn books by Emil Ludwig, Vicki Baum, Stefan Zweig, and even burned former Chancellor Kurt Schuschnigg's *Three Times Austria*—for Austria was now part of the glorious everlasting Third Reich. In a few days thirty thousand volumes had been collected from the university and other local libraries and burned.

As it developed, 1938 became an important formative year in the American attitude toward Europe. Unfortunately for public understanding, the Spanish Civil War never was a clearcut issue. Too much other than politics was intermixed, especially the emotionally charged questions of religion.

On November 22 that year social science professor Joseph F. Thorning of the Mount St. Mary's College defended Franco and his program as "essentially Democratic" in its aims in a symposium at New York City's Murray Hill hotel. Dr. Thorning had just returned from the Franco lines. Franco was not to win his civil war until the following year, but with German and Italian tanks and planes and fighting men he was wearing down the tired Republican army, whose help from Soviet Russia was far more limited.

Dr. Thorning not only defended Franco's social policy, he

denied a current charge that the Catholic Church was in alliance with Fascism in Spain, Italy, and Germany, and indiscreetly recommended that those who protested religious persecution in Germany "pay the same attention to that in Mexico and Soviet Russia." Franco, he said, had guaranteed religious freedom to all, including the Jews, while the Loyalists in Spain had suppressed all religious groups.

Jay Allen, a former foreign correspondent for the *Chicago Tribune* disputed nearly all that Dr. Thorning said. Allen went to the heart of the matter. A concentrated effort was being made, he said, to blur the real issues of the Spanish Civil War; the issue was the march of totalitarianism. It was moving rapidly, Allen said, even into the Western Hemisphere to threaten in Latin America.

Cordell Hull was not unaware of this danger in 1938, and he made it his personal responsibility to try to strengthen our ties and democratic institutions in Latin America.

Munich came that fall, and settled nothing, as Hull saw and knew. Yet such was his caution in discussing such matters before the press that many Americans had the wrong impression of the State Department's acuity. On the day after the Munich appeasement, Hull issued a brief statement:

"As to immediate peace results, it is unnecessary to say that they afford a universal sense of relief.

"I am not undertaking to pass on the merits of the differences to which the Four-Power pact signed at Munich yesterday related." He then said it was to be hoped that the forces of order would not relax.

Relax? He might better have said let the forces of order organize, for disorganization was the problem of the democracies in these years, and it was nowhere more noticeable than in the United States.

Belatedly, in 1939, both America and its government began to awaken to the threat to the American nation posed by the pincering movements of Japan and Germany. Even Herbert Hoover was speaking out against totalitarianism and mentioning Germany, Japan, Italy, Spain, although, of course he was mentioning Russia too, and coupling his remarks with lament for the loss of a sense of individual responsibility in the world. There was, he said, too much worry about public conscience and too little about private conscience.

As guardians of the public conscience, Franklin Roosevelt and Cordell Hull began to take a harder tone, even though they were well aware of the heavy layer of opposition and isolationism that still lay on the land. Actually, at this time, many private consciences were worrying about the problems of freedom and war, and the strength of isolationism was diminishing. But it would have been hard to note that early in 1939, for as matters changed the isolationists became more vocal and more active.

In March Hull was tired from the constant wearing of his difficult job, and he went to Florida for a rest. While he was there, Hitler marched into Czechoslovakia. By telephone Hull dictated a strong statement on this aggression. It was taken by Undersecretary Sumner Welles to the White House, where Welles and Roosevelt tinkered with it a bit, then issued it to the public.

This year Roosevelt saw the necessity of preparing the nation to make war, no matter how much opposition there might be from the isolationist bloc. His concern was that far too many Americans would not understand the need for what was later called "lead time" in production. In January, 1937, Roosevelt had wondered aloud if democracy would be able to arm itself to face the events of his time. In 1939 he felt he could wait no longer for mobilization, and he began to move, circuitously to be sure, but still to move.

In January, Roosevelt told Congress he proposed to help the democracies arm themselves, using every method short of war. Cordell Hull heard that speech aboard ship, as he returned from the inter-American conference at Lima, where he had achieved a greater degree of solidarity among the American republics than ever before. On his return, Hull put his abilities and his long experience in Congress to work to help Roosevelt persuade Congress to unfetter the fists of the administration.

One necessity was the subversion of the authority of Harry Woodring, whose isolationist tendencies made him totally unsympathetic to mobilization. As reported by Eliot Janeway in *The Struggle for Survival*, Roosevelt took desperate and heroic measures to work through Assistant Secretary of War Louis Johnson rather than Woodring. He worked to stockpile vital materials, to rebuild the armed might of America, and to obviate the Neutrality Act which forbade the supply of belligerents, whether basically friend or foe.

In this latter attempt Hull proved an invaluable adviser and go-between with Congress. Hull emphasized one point: aggressors and other nations knew in advance all and the exact plans of nations which were inflexibly neutral. This was not a brilliant deduction, but it was typical of the stern simplicity and common sense of Cordell Hull, in a period when the emotions of so many Americans blinded them to the inexorable march of events. Hull began to work whole-heartedly for mobilization.

The program Roosevelt managed to secure was pitifully small, and was contradicted by Congressional refusal to remove the fetters of neutralism. In July, 1939, Ambassador William Bullitt cabled from Paris that because Congress refused to act, Hitler would probably move to make war in August. British Foreign Secretary Vansittart was betting two to one that war would come that month.

Vansittart was wrong, by a few days. Hitler did not march into Poland until the morning of September 1, 1939.

Was America shocked? Some Americans were, but those who had been following foreign affairs could not be surprised, at least, because the march of events had been foretold. The remarkable truth was that the war itself, initially, did not change American opinion very much. A poll taken by Elmo Roper in September showed that more than 80 per cent of the American people wanted to stay out of the war, and moreover, that they believed it was possible. Here was the result of the soft-pedaling of information by the State Department and other arms of government for so many years.

Roosevelt declared publicly his intention of helping the democracies all he could and privately warned England and France that they must give him time to change opinions. The isolationists became shrill at this point in history. At Yale University a group of youngsters gathered together from time to time to discuss international alternatives. Their aim was to see America protected first— and their discussion group was to be shrewdly manipulated by professional publicists to become the nucleus of the America First movement.

'l'he isolationists were already in motion. Colonel Charles A. Lindbergh, national hero that he was, gave Americans much to ponder when he came out flatly for continued neutrality. One trouble with Lindbergh's attitude, however, was its extreme pragmatic inclination. He felt that Germany and Italy represented the tide of the future. He felt that Naziism was strong, and that it could not be defeated, so it should be joined, in a sense, or at least let alone.

This attitude aroused the resentment of idealists, and after Lindbergh's two radio addresses on neutralism in the fall of 1939, he became far less of a national hero than before. He removed himself from active duty with the army before he spoke out. He did not return to active duty, but neither did he return the medal given him by the Nazis in 1938.

As 1939 drew to an end, the forces that would push America into war were in motion. Secretary Hull and Franklin Roosevelt both knew that America was totally unprepared for war. Nor was there a preponderance of war sentiment yet developed in the United States. But idealism was beginning to develop more rapidly than some might suspect, an awakened idealism such as that displayed by Robert Sherwood.

After war broke out, Cordell Hull found time to reassess his stewardship of American's interests *vis à vis* the world. It was six years and six months after he had come to the State Department. In those six years he had made the position of America plain to the dictators, time and again. He and Roosevelt had argued unceasingly with the isolationists in Congress and in the administration itself. Without Congressional approval, and in the face of what would have been most certain national disapproval, Hull and Roosevelt had worked quietly to do what they could to strengthen America's hand for the coming battle. They had consolidated the Western Hemisphere. They had begun a tiny program of mobilization. They had established, falteringly, a nucleus of defense. Now they were to embark on the road of preparation in earnest.

THE TEMPERING YEARS

CHAPTER TWENTY

AN ARTIST ASKED to draw the outstanding symbol of the 1930's might sketch a picture of a pince-nez, a crushed felt hat, a long cigarette holder, a smiling patrician profile, or a set of initials. In any event the artist would be drawing a symbol of Franklin Delano Roosevelt, and rightly. The 1930's were the Roosevelt years, a period in which he dominated American history as George Washington dominated the first twenty years of American nationhood, or as Abraham Lincoln dominated the nation during the Civil War.

These comparisons are meaningful because the crisis faced by America in the 1930's was truly one of the three decisive periods of American history until that time. Had Washington failed, the United States would not exist as we know it. Had Lincoln failed, the United States would most certainly not have continued to exist as the dominant force on the North American continent. Had there not emerged in 1932 a drastic new approach to the problem of salvation of a faltering capitalism, the United States would most certainly not today be able to boast of the free-est economy of all among the world's major powers.

If it ever did, the United States has not enjoyed pure capitalism since the 1930's, but through the reform of the capitalist system it has retained more of the positive attributes of capitalism than any other society. Franklin Roosevelt brought that reform to a nation which was beginning to listen to the shouts and condemnations of the extremists of right and left totalitarianism and to the proponents of that great experiment in euphoria—Democratic Socialism. The tragedy in the life of Socialist leader Norman Thomas was that Franklin Roosevelt stole the revolution away from the Socialists.

Early in the 1930's Herbert Hoover claimed that the United States was going through a period of readjustment after the excesses of the capitalistic system's joyous, abandoned 1920's. He always claimed that the depth of the depression came in 1932, and that by the summer of 1933 the nation was showing signs of recovery. The inference is clear enough: that Franklin Roosevelt had nothing to do with recovery from the depression, that instead his New Deal delayed the recovery that might have been expected under the normal business cycle.

Figures compiled by federal agencies in the middle 1930's lend much credence to the Hoover view—outwardly. But to accept the Hoover view of American affairs—as most of American business did in 1935 and 1936—is to deny that society exists on any basis other than economic determinism.

The simple fact is that in 1932 capitalism was finished in America—"washed up" to use a phrase of the period. No less observant and no less conservative a seer than Walter Lippmann declared that to be truth. In 1932 the American systems of production and distribution had failed thoroughly. A visitor that year to Detroit, to Pittsburgh, to the coal fields of West Virginia, or to the American wheat belt could not but have felt the same distress at human suffering and disgust at government management that Herbert Hoover had expressed in 1919 during his visit to a starving and mismanaged Russia, where another system had broken down.

The granaries of Illinois were bursting with wheat. West Virginia miners' children starved to death. The sea was full of fish. Children starved also in New England factory towns. Skilled auto workmen in Detroit grovelled in the cold of their miserable houses as privately owned utility companies turned off the heat and the lights. The men could get no work. Local and state authorities could not supply the demands of relief. Yet the demands of the capitalist system were inexorable. If the bill could not be paid, the service was cut off. This was not the fault of the clerk who reported the delinquency. It was not the fault of the supervisor who made the decision, the worker who turned off the connection or even the president or the chairman of the board which made the policy. The company— no matter that it was a public utility—belonged to capital, to those who had given the company their money with the promise that it would return them a share of property and an income from the work their money bought. It was the fault of the system that thousands of men like Joe Louis and his family sat in cold rooms which could have been warmed by the turn of a screw.

The recovery began in 1933, said the Republicans—but what

else happened in 1933? The new President Franklin Delano Roosevelt took office on March 4, as was customary. But it was not customary for the entire banking system and the treasury system of the nation to have broken down completely. It had done exactly that.

Every bank in the nation was closed on the day Roosevelt took office. Here was the *total* failure of the capitalist system. The strongest nation in the world was reduced for a moment to a system of barter— a system which had been abandoned as unworkable by the people of the Fertile Crescent seven thousand years before.

On the weekend, as Roosevelt labored to resolve the nation's monetary crisis, bank-note companies printed and prepared to issue billions of dollars worth of "funny money" or scrip. And what were these? Pieces of paper—promises of various companies to pay. To pay in what? To pay in good money at some time in the future.

Had this extreme been reached, it is doubtful if the monetary and banking systems could have been salvaged. It is doubtful if the form of government could have been saved. This aspect of the depression crisis is by far the most important. The closing of America's banks was proof that the economic system had failed. Since the economic system then controlled the political system by mutual consent of all parties, the American system can be said to have died then and there, on the operating table. Franklin Roosevelt's first function was that of the skilled surgeon, to bring the system back to life.

Roosevelt was called many names during the 1930's, not the least of which was "dictator." Yet always he was the politician. His most undemocratic piece of legislation—the National Industrial Recovery Act—was widely hailed when it was enacted during the remarkable "one hundred days." When the NRA was invalidated in 1935, businessmen whooped with joy only because they detested the wages and hours and collective bargaining clauses of the codes established. Business had no objection to the truly undemocratic feature: the virtual fixing of all prices and marketing practices. It was all right, said big business, for government and business to conspire to fix prices of goods. It was not all right for government and labor to conspire to fix prices for the hire of labor.

Yet even in this most undemocratic movement of the NRA

Roosevelt acted without malice or a thought of establishing "dictator-ship."

Roosevelt was also soundly damned for "establishing" a class system in America. Had his critics damned him for creating an aware-ness of the class system that existed in America they would have edged nearer the truth. Roosevelt was a product of that class system, of the upper class of landed gentry who were welcome in the luxurious cot-tages of Newport and whose scions were expected to be exposed to education at such schools as Groton and Harvard. It was the very rich, Mrs. Vanderbilt and her peers, who first recognized in Roosevelt a rebel against this class system. Rather than building it, Roosevelt in bringing it into the open, and in his use of the great tax equalizer, did more than any previous President to *destroy* the rigid growth of a class system which was beginning to paralyze America. One difference was the variance in attitudes of businessmen and Roosevelt toward property rights. Businessmen went into the American depression of 1930 believing in the superiority of the rights of property. They con-ceded before they were through that property rights and human rights were equal. Roosevelt never agreed to that. It was part of his deeply ingrained philosophy that property rights are subordinate to human rights. He had always held that property existed for the service of humanity. Here was a part of the *noblesse oblige* of Roosevelt's coun-try seat upbringing in the home of one of the squires of the Hudson River Valley.

Still that is not to say that the Roosevelt who entered the 1930's was the same man who emerged from that decade. Roosevelt in 1930 was an internationalist in principle, although in practice, as governor of New York he had little occasion to consider such problems. He was to change, twice, in his approach to world affairs in the next ten years, but in 1930 Roosevelt was still rueful about America's refusal to ac-cept world leadership after the First World War. In 1925 he had won-dered aloud if Americans really believed they were doing their full duty to mankind. In 1928 he lamented the loss by America of leadership of the moral forces of mankind and the failure of Americans to con-tribute to the settlement of international problems.

As governor, perhaps Roosevelt did fail to control the New York stock markets as well as possible—as Herbert Hoover claimed. Yet Roosevelt in 1930 was showing elements of what were to be the basic policies of the New Deal. His state program for farm relief included a demand for cheaper light and power rates for farmers. He also demanded a reduction in the spread between farm prices and consumer prices.

Roosevelt urged municipal economy—particularly in a speech on June 11 that year. No government, he said, could long survive without a balanced budget. That attitude toward budget and expenditure was inherent with Roosevelt. His continued deficit financing a few years later was not a result of planning—he was accepting temporary deficit financing as the lesser of evils he foresaw. But it was only through change in character that he was to accept deficit financing at all.

Even in 1930 Roosevelt's policies were approved generally by organized labor. He adopted the position, shortly after the depression began, that social welfare was the responsibility of government. In this, because he was concerned with the state, he meant the state. As he grew, his ideas were to change.

And if it sometimes seemed to Franklin Roosevelt's friends and peers that he was going too far in his attempts to cater to the people of New York State, how much more askance they must have looked at New York's first lady, Anna Eleanor Roosevelt.

Eleanor, "Babs" as F.D.R. called her, was an indefatigable do-gooder. She taught school, ran a furniture factory, taught home crafts to the girls of Hyde Park and edited a baby magazine for the health faddist publisher Bernarr MacFadden. If that was not distressing enough Eleanor also in 1930 urged household servants to unionize and demand regulated hours of work, backed the dressmakers of the exclusive Fifth Avenue shops when they went on strike, and planned to extend her home-crafts teaching to other rural schools in the state. She scandalized her neighbors.

As far as Franklin Roosevelt was concerned, some of his attitudes toward public power, farming, stock regulation, and conservation far transcended the public policy requirements for a governor of New York and yet his enemies liked to forget that before he had been an important state politician he had been a national politician. In World

War I, Roosevelt had gained experience in foreign affairs and defense matters as Assistant Secretary of the Navy. In 1920 he had faced national political issues as the Democratic candidate for Vice-President of the United States. Roosevelt the governor of New York could not be separated from this earlier Roosevelt. F.D.R. had gained in experience, certainly; he had gained in the patience and humility brought on by his long illness; but he was the same man.

Two years later in 1932, Roosevelt the governor was suddenly thrust into national politics again as candidate for the Democratic Presidential nomination. Thrust, perhaps, is not the proper word, for Roosevelt had been aware of his own national potential as a politician since 1928 at least. Then he truly was dragooned into running for governor to strengthen the Democratic ticket in New York. But after 1930 he was almost certain to run, the politicians knew, for he was the strongest vote getter among the Democrats and he wanted to be President.

Raymond Moley and other advisers have told in so much detail of their participation in policy making and other aspects of Roosevelt's political life that they have given a picture of a composite Roosevelt who was all things to all men and something of a manipulated character besides. Such implications—not intentional—are inevitable because of the mass of detail written about Roosevelt. But if there is one point that biographers and historians have made clear it is that Roosevelt was his own man even as much as T.R. or Grover Cleveland.

The policies that began to take shape that year were partly the result of Roosevelt's long background in politics and government, partly the result of the experience of his advisers, partly a product of courageous foresight, partly a product of political and national desperation.

Roosevelt in 1932 opposed the dole as such and said so. He wanted a balanced budget and warned against federal deficit financing. He advocated, as he had for a long time, unemployment insurance. He wanted tariff revision, free trade, and greater American participation in world affairs. Roosevelt indicted the Hoover administration for failing to insist on European repayment of war debts. He insisted that farmers could be helped immeasurably by making it possible for them to sell to foreign markets. He did not then envisage any controlled production of agriculture for any long period of time.

Above all, said Roosevelt early in the campaign, "capital must not be made timid or progress will be slowed." Overproduction might have existed in industry in 1929. The problem in 1932 was underproduction, he said.

As the campaign continued Roosevelt espoused reforestation and public power. He was taken to task for these "Socialistic" ideas. Yet they were not new ideas for Roosevelt. He had uttered them first in 1928—and had recognized then the kind of reception they would receive from Republican-oriented businessmen. "We often hear it said that government operation of anything under the sun is Socialistic," he wrote.

In 1932 Roosevelt wanted to pay little attention to his critics. But again his innate sensitivity as a politician kept Roosevelt from enunciating many programs that were open to Republican attack in the conservative days of Republican ascendancy.

Roosevelt's advisers, particularly Raymond Moley, were much relieved when Roosevelt decided to make a general expository address on the relations of government and business before San Francisco's Commonwealth Club. The speech was delivered at the peak of Roosevelt's western trip, on September 23, 1932, and, although not fully appreciated at the time—because of its prophetic and sweeping nature—it was later called by biographer Basil Rauch "the most important statement of political philosophy Roosevelt ever made." Here Roosevelt traced the history of American government in terms of its service to the people at large and its protection of the basic contract made by the founding fathers in the Declaration of Independence and the Constitution. The problem, Roosevelt said, was that America had encompassed the geographic frontiers which had always proved a safety valve in the past. Men of property had formed huge combinations which were slowly driving the small, independent farmer and businessman to the wall. Laboring men had become totally dependent on daily employment for survival.

The solutions—the protection of American freedom—lay in cooperation between "the responsible heads of finance and industry" and government. And government, Roosevelt said, must stand always ready to protect the public interest should these forces try to use their power contrary to the public welfare. The government shall assume the function of economic regulation only as a last resort—when business has failed.

No matter how many turns might be made down how many devious alleys in the next few years, this remained Roosevelt's basic policy. His peculiar genius was to recognize the demand for such policy by the majority of the American people—who were not wealthy, not businessmen, who were more dependent on business than ever before in their history. Roosevelt recognized that in the final analysis the people held the roots of power in their hands. If government did not protect the basic welfare of the majority against the incursions of the wealthy minority the people would eventually rise, one way or another, to take control of this nation's wealth. By regulating the uses of great wealth, Roosevelt proposed to end the abuses of business by bringing peaceful change.

As noted previously, at the beginning of the depression, 13 per cent of the American people owned 92 per cent of the total wealth of America. It was not a question of dollars but of comparisons. The nation had reached the point when the rich grew richer, by doing nothing at all; while the poor grew poorer, no matter how hard they labored. The time was growing ripe for revolution.

To bring that revolution the nation needed men of courage, imagination, flexibility, and even brutality. Roosevelt had all these qualities. The brilliant men he brought into the campaign and into his administration shared these qualities, but not one of them claimed to be a Rasputin. There never was a Rasputin in the Roosevelt administration, although the charge was levied against Louis Howe, Raymond Moley, Thomas Corcoran, and Harry Hopkins in turn.

From the days when he had opposed the Niagara Hudson Power Corporation's attempts to increase its diversion of Niagara River water, Roosevelt had exhibited a new philosophy about the responsibility of government. He was to change, to be tempered by the years and events, but rather than to lessen his "equalizing" the tempering was to strengthen his belief in the need for public welfare activities of the federal government. He was to bring to fruition policies of public power, banking regulation, securities regulation, wages and hours laws, Social Security. All these and more regulation supported the common citizen's efforts to protect life, liberty, and the pursuit of happiness.

Roosevelt made many errors during the 1932 campaign. His speeches were vague, overstated, and often contradictory. Yet he offered the nation hope at a time when the only others to make such offers—the Socialists and the Communists—brought visions of a collective society foreign to American ways. Both the true contradictions and tempering began after the election.

Hoover wanted Roosevelt's concurrence in settling international problems. Roosevelt was so unsure of his ground that he refused to cooperate with the outgoing administration.

Roosevelt did want to conduct talks with other nations to reach international economic agreements. So did Cordell Hull. Hull, in fact, saw in the London Economic Conference an opportunity to re-establish prosperity and to establish world peace through reciprocal trade. Yet in the spring of 1933, pressed by his domestic advisers, Roosevelt jettisoned plans for international economic cooperation. Effectively, he walled the nation against foreign trade. His intent was to raise prices and wages through NRA and AAA. He could not afford to have that attempt undercut by cheaper foreign products—or he believed he could not.

That same year, Roosevelt reluctantly abandoned hope for a balanced budget and for government economy. He was convinced that he could not prime the pump of the national economy and do it within the current federal income. Sound money—money based on gold—also died that year.

By the end of that first year it was apparent that the key to Roosevelt's San Francisco speech had lain in his statement that government should assume the function of economic regulation as a last resort. Perhaps he had not anticipated when he spoke that the banks of all America would be in actual bankruptcy by March, 1933—that the economic system would fail even before his inauguration.

His strong policies offended many, quite aside from active businessmen. By the end of the year many old friends were out of Roosevelt's councils or removed to the fringes. The stars of Ickes, Tugwell, Wallace, and Hopkins were in the ascendance. The stars of Moley,

Hugh Johnson, Lewis Douglas, Will Woodin, and many others of basically conservative cast of mind were setting.

In those early years, as F.D.R. took on more executive power than any President before his time, he tempered this assumption of power with a new sense of accountability to the public. He inaugurated the regular, open press conference and the fireside chat. Eleanor Roosevelt did as much for women. She began her own press conferences. She also brought about a New Deal of her own for women, crusading constantly for equality of women, as she crusaded for so many causes.

Eleanor Roosevelt amused some New Dealers and annoyed others, especially Harold Ickes. Many of her pet projects and subjects of complaint, it seemed, fell within his Department of Interior. Yet the impact of Eleanor Roosevelt is best illustrated by her influence in securing the appointment of Frances Perkins as Secretary of Labor. Louis Howe used Eleanor Roosevelt to quiet the second bonus marchers. She toured hospitals, depressed areas, farm country, and the big cities indefatigably. To F.D.R. she was as important as the corps of investigators proved to be to Harry Hopkins. Mrs. Roosevelt had a far more panoramic view of America during the New Deal years than nearly any of her critics if for no other reason than that she travelled more than nearly anyone else in the nation and mixed at more social levels.

Roosevelt's struggle with business is often believed to have begun after the collapse of NRA in 1935. Actually it was not so simple: a large segment of business resisted the New Deal from the beginning, turning the NRA into an instrument of monopoly, and still trying to fight the growth of labor organization. Unlike business, labor threw its weight to Roosevelt. So by 1934, both personal and political considerations were turning Roosevelt toward labor, and where labor and business were in conflict, against business. That turning led to the "second New Deal," directed to benefit labor and the poor—the less well-to-do Americans. This was accompanied by levelling legislation of 1935— the heavy taxes on high incomes and inherited wealth.

In 1936, when he ran for a second term, it was generally conceded that conservatives had left the administration and that Roosevelt had "turned left." Still, much of his turning could be foreseen in the projection of his famous San Francisco speech. The Rooseveltian end was the same, but faced with the inflexible demand of business to return to the ways of the past, Roosevelt sought new methods of assuring maximum opportunity to life, liberty, and pursuit of happiness to the entire population.

In his speech accepting the Democratic nomination in 1936 Roosevelt spoke of "royalists of the economic order." He talked of the "war against want and destitution and economic demoralization" and of "survival of democracy" in the same sentence. Business then chose to believe that Roosevelt had declared war on business, and acted accordingly.

So it became true—so true that when in 1937 the recession destroyed many of the gains of the New Deal, Roosevelt was sure that the recession was caused by business working through the stock market to depress prices artificially. SEC chairman William O. Douglas assured the President that this was not so, yet the war was real, and it continued.

And why should it not continue? No privileged class ever gave up privilege without a struggle. The wonder of it was that the privilege of business and entrenched wealth was being tempered so easily, and with no more physical violence than that exhibited in the bloody strikes of steel workers and auto workers.

The middle period of the 1930's was a time of confusion, in words and deeds. The words dictator, undemocratic, economic royalist, big labor, bureaucrat, New Dealer—these and many others became epithets. Take the word "dictator." Roosevelt referred to "industrial dictators" of business. Business referred to the "dictatorship of Roosevelt." Soon businessmen called him "Franklin-the-first." Both sides exaggerated, of course. Had Roosevelt wanted dictatorial powers, he might have sought them through a Constitutional amendment which would have made NRA a part of the basic law of the nation. He did not. And Roosevelt's court-packing plan, which brought him the most criticism of all, was conceived in Roosevelt's belief that what the nation needed was more liberal social interpretation of law than change in the law.

Roosevelt's attitude had been to show faith in the flexibility of the Constitution—far more faith than his detractors. Roosevelt was tempered too, however, for when his Supreme Court plan had been thoroughly aired, condemned, and dropped, he in turn dropped attempts to change interpretation in this fashion.

The year 1937 was critical in many ways, but the end of it marked attempts by both business and government to reach a mode of living peacefully together. Irving Fisher, the emeritus professor of economics at Yale, announced in January of that year that Roosevelt ought to stifle fears of "dictatorship" by saying he would not seek a third term —and Professor Fisher represented the enlightened business view.

That year Roosevelt was assailed by the Du Ponts as "dictator," by Al Smith as "undemocratic," by the Republican National Committee as a "tyrant." More cutting, perhaps, was General Hugh Johnson's attack. Johnson, too, claimed that Roosevelt was seeking dictatorship. Even Walter Lippmann, slow to make strong charges, said Roosevelt aimed to impose personal government on the nation.

Whatever Roosevelt's personal aims at the beginning of 1937, by 1938 international events had taken a stronger role in determination of American policy than at any time since 1920.

The growing threat of the dictators in Europe caused the administration *and* business to make agonized reappraisal of national affairs. Roosevelt was accused then of "business appeasement" as he had earlier been accused of "labor appeasement." In the same sense both charges were true. He had turned to labor for support of what were essentially its own interests. Now he turned to business for support of its own interest. Labor's interest, earlier, was support of social legislation. The prime interest of business after 1938, was defense and survival of the relatively free economies of Europe and America.

In the eight years of the 1930's first Hoover and then Roosevelt had taken action to mix free enterprise with government more than ever before in U.S. history. Hoover's major contribution to the mixed economy was the Reconstruction Finance Corporation. Roosevelt's contributors were to bring business under intensive regulation, and in areas where business had defaulted most seriously, such as the power industry, to bring government into the industry as a control and a competitor.

The tempering years closed in 1939 with the attack on Poland by Hitler. They had been turbulent years in the United States. In a sense the emergence on the Atlantic horizon of the spectre of war exerted a leavening force in America. As always with the greater threat, the threat of war brought the diverse elements of American society closer together. After 1939 the basic struggles for control of the economy and society between business and government were not forgotten, but they were submerged for the duration of what would soon become a national emergency.

For twenty years the United States had stood aside in silent isolation while the seeds of war sprouted and grew in Europe and in Asia. Franklin Roosevelt's wife had worried at him from time to time during the last six years, trying to persuade F.D.R. to take a greater personal interest in international affairs. But the truth of it was that Roosevelt's interest in international affairs had never flagged. He had grown up in the internationalist tradition and in that tradition he remained.

The growing interest in the world around America was a result of the tempering of the nation, not of Roosevelt. By 1938 he had begun to convince Americans that their future lay with the Western World, but his beginnings were very slow indeed, and even in 1939 the nation was not ready for real involvement in Europe affairs. Such acceptance would not come really until it was forced on America by outright attack. But by 1939 the forces that would guide America were forged. Despite all the disagreement and tribulation of past years, in 1939 pollsters discovered that Franklin Delano Roosevelt was the most popular man in all America. America had been dedicated to self-satisfaction ten years before. Now it was tempered.

ACKNOWLEDGMENTS AND NOTES

The idea for this book came out of conversations with Gerald Simons and I am indebted to him for his help in this. Herman Kahn of the Franklin D. Roosevelt Library at Hyde Park, N.Y., was most patient in steering me to materials in the library and in suggesting various sources. I am also grateful to the librarians and archivists at the F.D.R. Library for assistance.

Librarians at the New York Public Library were very helpful, particularly those in the microfilm and newspaper divisions. I must also thank librarians at the New York Historical Society, and Stanley Ransom and the staff of the Huntington Public Library and Kirk L. Pressing and the staff of the Northport Public Library for many favors. The interlibrary loan service provided by the state of New York saved me countless hours of search for books.

Dr. George W. Adams, professor of history at Southern Illinois University read all the manuscript. I am grateful to him for this labor and his succinct and helpful comments.

A number of persons read portions of the manuscript in the course of preparation. I am particularly indebted to Justice William O. Douglas of the United States Supreme Court, Raymond Moley, Barnet Nover, my father, Palmer Hoyt, Frank Pace, Jr., Marquis W. Childs, Charles F. Brannan, C. E. Huff, Louis B. Nichols, George W. Healy, Jr., Richard Watts, A. H. Raskin, James Wechsler, and Edward W. Barrett.

Conversations with a number of people who participated and helped form the events of these years have also gone into the making of this book although many of these talks came before the book idea was formed. Some of these are detailed in the chapter notes. I am indebted to Mr. and Mrs. Harold Cash for suggestions about small town life, and to La Rue Applegate for material about the financial world.

CHAPTER ONE

The day-to-day account of life in America during 1929 and the 1930's came largely from the files of *The New York Times*, the *New York Herald Tribune*, the *Wall Street Journal*, the *Times* of London and the *Chicago Tribune*, although I found other newspapers, and particularly the *Daily Worker* informed on special views. The collection of Richard Whitney's addresses in the New York Public Library proved most instructive. A number of books not listed in the bibliography were consulted to establish minor points. The files of all the popular magazines of news and comment were useful.

CHAPTER TWO

A particularly useful article on Richard Whitney and the New York Stock Exchange was that written by Joseph Alsop and Robert Kintner which appeared in *The Saturday Evening Post* on January 25, 1938. All the magazines and newspapers of the period contained useful information about the market crash and the subsequent depression. The book *Democracy and Finance,* a collection of the SEC papers of William O. Douglas, edited by James Allen, lucidly and briefly gives the chronology of change. Justice Douglas kindly read this portion of the book in draft, and suggested a number of helpful changes. A detailed account of the financial affairs of Richard Whitney is contained in *United States of America before the SEC in the matter of Richard Whitney et al.,* published November 1, 1938.

CHAPTER THREE

Raymond Moley, now a close friend to Herbert Hoover, although a political enemy in 1932, was kind enough to read this chapter for emphasis. The principal sources for material about Hoover were his own writings, particularly his memoirs and authorized biographies. A number of pamplets, flyers, and political analyses gave the flavor of the times in 1932. Particularly notable was "Why Hoover Faces Defeat," by Robert S. Allen, which made the case against Herbert Hoover with great vigor, in its most negative form, as Hoover's own writings best make the case in his favor. The strange phenomenon of suicide in the 1930's is dealt with in detail in the book *To Be or Not To Be,* by L. I. Dublin and B. Bunzel.

CHAPTER FOUR

The best picture of life in America in the first years of the depression comes from the pages of the newspapers. Nearly every news story and advertisement in some way reflected the huge change in the lives of Americans, far more than any individual account. The statistical studies, such as *Work Relief in New York State,* 1931–35, by Alexander Radowski, give another aspect of the picture. Harry Hopkins's own book, *Spending to Save,* is far less interesting than his own reports and those of his staff, available in the Franklin D. Roosevelt Library in the collection of Hopkins papers.

Robert Sherwood's admirable *Roosevelt and Hopkins* gives an excellent picture of the younger Hopkins, perhaps not so much as an individual, but certainly excellent as a picture of Hopkins as a social worker.

CHAPTER FIVE

The intimate view of life among the poor of America in the depression is given in the "state of the nation reports" written for Hopkins by a team of excellent reporters. Lorena Hickok, Martha Gellhorn, Lincoln Colcord, and others, were dispatched by Hopkins to serve as his eyes and ears. From them he heard stories that were never printed, and learned of the near-despair of the poor in America. Those "state of the nation" reports deserve to be printed someday for there is no other record to match them in showing the grimness of life for the underprivileged and unlucky. Accounts of the activities of Hopkins, as Walter Davenport's May 13, 1939, and various issues of *Collier's*, *The Saturday Evening Post*, *Fortune* and *Today*, were particularly useful plus special newspaper features, such as that of R. L. Duffus in the November 19, 1933, issue of *The New York Times*. Various WPA publications yielded statistics and information of considerable importance, but again, the telling, compact account of Sherwood in *Roosevelt and Hopkins* was of great value.

CHAPTER SIX

Raymond Moley was frank and helpful in the preparation of this chapter. The basic document for it, of course, is his own *After Seven Years*. Interesting views on the matter of Presidential advisers can be found in Louis Koenig's *The Invisible Presidency*. Since Moley's role in the Roosevelt administration remains a controversial subject, perhaps the most balanced view is a foreign one—such as that of D. W. Brogan, the English historian, in *The Era of Franklin D. Roosevelt*. James Mac-Gregor Burns's *The Lion and the Fox* was consulted often in this chapter, as were the first two volumes of Arthur Schlesinger, Jr.'s *The Age of Roosevelt*. The files of *Today* were most revealing of Moley's defense of the administration in the first few months after he had broken with Roosevelt, and the gradualness of his slip away from the New Deal.

CHAPTER SEVEN

For information about the Negro in America I am most indebted to the excellent Schomburg collection in the New York Public Library's Harlem branch. Here I found material from the *Amsterdam News*, Chicago *Defender*, Pittsburgh *Courier*, Washington *Tribune*, Baltimore

Afro-American and other Negro publications. The Schomburg collection also contains voluminous material about Joe Louis, culled from the white press, which gives a clear picture of the evolution of Louis and of the attitude of sports writers on the race question.

The various biographies of Louis were less informative, on the whole, than newspaper and magazine material. Saunders Redding's account of the Negro in a white society (*The Lonesome Road*) was very useful for background.

CHAPTER EIGHT

Some of the material and background for the chapter on radicalism in America came from a study made late in 1956 for *Collier's* magazine. Howard Fast told me much. So did John Gates, then editor of the *Daily Worker*, the late Eugene Dennis, the secretary of the Communist party, USA, and Earl Browder, then living quietly in Yonkers. I am grateful to Norman Thomas for several talks over the years and drew heavily on his writings in books and newspaper columns. David Shannon gave me some information about radicalism, and his excellent books on Socialism and radicalism gave a great deal more. William Z. Foster's writings gave a clear picture of the Communist view of the years of the 1930's, particularly his *Toward a Soviet America*, and *Pages from a Worker's Life*. Reports of various debates between Communist and Socialist leaders helped sharpen the picture of differences between the groupings. Dexter Perkins's *The American Way* gives a useful account of the penetration of American life by the Communist movement. James Wechsler read this chapter in manuscript and offered a number of helpful suggestions.

CHAPTER NINE

John Tebbel's biography of Colonel McCormick was basic source material for this chapter, as were reminiscences of a number of former *Tribune* employees. The Tribune's own *A Century of Tribune Editorials* gives a view of the newspaper's broad policies over the years. A 1938 profile of Colonel McCormick in *The New Yorker* magazine was also useful, as were articles in *Harper's*, *The Atlantic Monthly*, and Jack Alexander's "The Duke of Chicago," which appeared in *The Saturday Evening Post* of July 19, 1941. Palmer Hoyt and Dean Edward Barrett of Columbia University offered valuable advice on this section of the manuscript.

CHAPTER TEN

Cleveland Amory's *The Last Resorts* gives a good picture of life among the self-proclaimed aristocracy of America during the period, and Gerald Johnson's *Roosevelt: Dictator or Democrat* is replete with social commentary on the subject. My own *The Vanderbilts and Their Fortunes* was useful for background. The files of various blue books and social registers gave some information, and reports on the registers in the newspapers gave more. Elsa Maxwell's amusing account, "Society—What's Left of It" in *The Ladies' Home Journal* in February, 1939, gives an excellent picture of the rise of Café Society.

CHAPTER ELEVEN

Richard Watts, drama critic for the New York *Post*, was kind enough to read the chapter and to offer some pointed suggestions about it. The newspapers and magazines dealt with the life and works of Charlie Chaplin exhaustively during this period—and in every editorial department, from the news pages of newspapers to the editorial pages. Sherwood's career was much less flamboyant, and reports were much more concerned with his work than with the man. By far the best book on Chaplin is Theodore Huff's *Charlie Chaplin*. Informative articles were those in *Collier's* by Kyle Crichton and H. G. Wells.

The New Yorker profile of Sherwood by his friend S. N. Behrman gives a good picture of the man. Brooks Atkinson's frequent comments about Sherwood in *The New York Times* give a picture of the dramatist. A most complete factual biographical sketch appeared in *Current Biography*, 1940. The state of the theater is given in columns by Ward Morehouse of the New York *Sun*, Atkinson, and the other critics of the press and magazines during the period.

CHAPTER TWELVE

Some of the information about Huey Long and Louisiana came from trips to New Orleans, most recently in 1956. George W. Healy, Jr., editor of the New Orleans *Times-Picayune*, is the source of much information. He was also kind enough to read the chapter in draft and indicate errors. Some of the material about Father Coughlin came from conversations and visits to Detroit over an extended period.

Herman B. Deutsch's article in the September 7, 1935, *Saturday Evening Post* was very useful in preparation of this chapter. So were articles in *Today, The New York Times,* the *Times* of London. H. G.

Wells took an interesting British view of Long in *Collier's* of May 25, 1935. F. Raymond Daniell, a *New York Times* reporter who followed Long closely, wrote an interesting sketch of him in *The Saturday Evening Post* on February 12, 1938. There were more references to Long in *The New York Times* index in 1935 than there were to Mrs. Eleanor Roosevelt.

The careers of Gerald L. K. Smith and Father Coughlin were discussed in various magazine articles and in the newspapers of the period. *Today, Time* and *Newsweek* were particularly useful here.

CHAPTER THIRTEEN

Charles F. Brannan, Secretary of Agriculture in the Truman administration and long-time public servant graciously read the chapter on Senator McNary and farm problems and offered several suggestions. C. E. Huff, a member of the Federal Farm Board during the Hoover administration, offered several specific corrections and much information. I found the late Richard Neuberger's articles on Senator McNary in *Life* and elsewhere to be most revealing of a man the late Senator Neuberger understood thoroughly. No biography of Senator McNary exists, and relatively few magazine articles were written about him, except during the campaign of 1940. Much information, then, was culled from newspapers and other sources, including peripheral references in many of the books listed in the bibliography. *The Wallaces of Iowa* gives an excellent background for understanding the complicated farm problems and plans of the 1930's.

CHAPTER FOURTEEN

Louis B. Nichols, who was J. Edgar Hoover's associate for many years, read the chapter to help eliminate error and also offered new information on several points. The best sources of information on the evolution of law enforcement are in the writings of Hoover himself, in the *American* magazine and other publications. His book *Persons in Hiding* tells a great deal about the attitudes of officers and criminals. An excellent study of criminality in America, particularly in St. Paul, is contained in the pages of *Today* beginning June 23, 1934. Another excellent article on Dillinger appeared in *Today*, August 11, 1934. Rupert Hughes's book *Attorney for the People* tells the story of Thomas Dewey's racket-busting and rise to fame. Minute-by-minute accounts of the killing of Dillinger and several other wanted men are contained in various newspapers, particularly the *Chicago Tribune* and *The New York Times*.

CHAPTER FIFTEEN

Murray Kempton's *Part of Our Time* contains as fine and sensitive a sketch of Walter Reuther and the UAW as I have ever seen. Some of the material in this chapter came from a conversation with Victor Reuther in Washington in 1956, some from newspaper reports of strikes and labor activities during the 1930's, some from magazines, and some from books listed in the bibliography. A. H. Raskin of *The New York Times* editorial board helped greatly by reading this chapter in manuscript.

CHAPTER SIXTEEN

The New York Times and the *Herald Tribune* were basic sources for the report on the activities of Alfred P. Sloan, Jr., and business. Sloan's speeches were particularly interesting, and outstanding among them was a speech to the Boston Chamber of Commerce on November 3, 1938, which outlined his philosophy of business and government. Sloan's biography, *Reminiscences of a White Collar Man,* did not prove particularly helpful either in book form or as it appeared earlier in the pages of *The Saturday Evening Post.* Several histories of the automobile industry were consulted, among the best of them Merrill Denison's *The Power to Go.*

CHAPTER SEVENTEEN

Various biographies of Charles Evans Hughes, newspaper accounts and magazine articles were used in preparing this chapter, including the section on Hughes from my own *Lost Statesman.* By far the most thorough and useful of these was Merlo Pusey's biography. An excellent feature on the judiciary appeared in *The New York Times* of January 20, 1935, and an excellent article on the Supreme Court in *Harper's* magazine in November, 1933. Mildred Adams, whose writings appeared in magazines and *The New York Times* during this period, was an acute observer of the legal scene, as was R. L. Duffus of *The New York Times.* Raymond Moley's columns in *Today* and *Newsweek* were useful. Marquis Childs, columnist for the St. Louis *Post-Dispatch* and many other newspapers, read draft material on this chapter and offered corrections and suggestions.

CHAPTER EIGHTEEN

This chapter, like Chapter Sixteen, was based largely on the tracing of the activities of Alfred P. Sloan, Jr., and the sources were largely the same. Also used were the papers relative to business in the private files of Franklin D. Roosevelt at the Hyde Park library and the Hopkins papers. Frank Pace, Jr., former chairman of the General Dynamics Corporation, was kind enough to look over the material for tone.

CHAPTER NINETEEN

Cordell Hull's *Memoirs* seem to conceal almost as much as they reveal about Hull's conduct of his important cabinet post, but they are important nonetheless to anyone trying to write about foreign affairs in this period. Raymond Moley's account of certain early frictions is at variance with that of Hull, but actually Hull leaves much unspoken. Robert Bendiner wrote a discerning article on the State Department in the July 25, 1942, issue of *The Nation*.

Articles by John Roy Carlson and Nathaniel Peffer showed interesting reactions to aspects of foreign policy. Charles Merz wrote a discerning article, although premature, about the sources of isolationism in *The New York Times* on June 28, 1931. The files of *Today* and the speeches of Cordell Hull were valuable. Reminiscences of Jay Allen, former foreign correspondent of the *Chicago Tribune*, and others came over a long period of years.

CHAPTER TWENTY

Many of the sources for the final chapter on Franklin Roosevelt are listed in the bibliography, and they include many papers at the Roosevelt Library in Hyde Park. But basically this chapter is analytical, and the opinions are the author's own, culled and formed during the period and in the twenty years since its ending.

BIBLIOGRAPHY

ACHESON, PATRICIA C. *The Supreme Court, America's Judicial Heritage*. Dodd, Mead and Co., New York, 1961.

ADAMIC, LOUIS. *Dinner at the White House*. Harper and Bros., New York, 1946.

ALLEN, FREDERICK LEWIS. *The Big Change*. Harper and Bros., New York, 1952.

ALLEN, FREDERICK LEWIS. *Since Yesterday*. Harper and Bros., New York, 1939.

ALLEN, ROBERT S. *Why Hoover Faces Defeat*. Brewer, Warren, and Putnam, New York, 1932.

ALPERT, PAUL. *L'Amerique de Roosevelt*. Nouvelles Editions Latines, Paris, 1936.

American Mercury.

American Heritage.

AMORY, CLEVELAND. *The Last Resorts*. Harper and Bros., New York, 1948.

AMORY, CLEVELAND. *Who Killed Society?* Harper and Bros., New York, 1960.

BANK OF MANHATTAN TRUST COMPANY. *Five Chapters in Finance*, published by the Bank of Manhattan Trust Co., New York, 1930.

BEALS, CARLETON, *The Story of Huey P. Long*. J. B. Lippincott Co., Philadelphia, 1935.

BERGER, MEYER. *The Story of* The New York Times. Simon and Schuster, New York, 1940.

BLUM, JOHN MORTON. *From the Morgenthau Diaries, Years of Crisis, 1928–1938*. Houghton Mifflin Co., Boston, 1959.

BOWMAN, W. DODGSON. *Charlie Chaplin, His Life and Art*. The John Day Co., New York, 1931.

BROGAN, D. W. *The Era of Franklin D. Roosevelt*. Yale University Press, New Haven, 1950.

BURNS, JAMES MACGREGOR. *The Lion and the Fox*. Harcourt, Brace and Co., New York, 1956.

BYRNES, JAMES F. *All in One Lifetime*. Harper and Bros., New York, 1958.

CARMICHAEL, DONALD SCOTT. *F.D.R.-Columnist*. Pellegrini and Cudahy, Chicago, 1947.

CHAFEE, ZACARIAH, JR. *Government and Mass Communications*. University of Chicago Press, Chicago, 1947.

COLLINS, HENRY HILL, JR. *America's Own Refugees*. Princeton University Press, 1941.

COREY, HERBERT. *The Truth About Hoover*. Houghton Mifflin Co., Boston, 1932.

CROWTHER, BOSLEY. *Hollywood Rajah*. Holt, Rinehart and Winston, New York, 1960.

DANIEL, DANIEL M. *The Mike Jacobs Story.* The Ring Book Shop, Inc., New York, 1950.

DAVIE, MAURICE R. *Negroes in American Society.* McGraw-Hill Book Co., New York, 1949.

DAYTON, ELDOROUS L. *Walter Reuther, Autocrat of the Bargaining Table.* Devin-Adair Co., New York, 1958.

DE MILLE, CECIL B. *Autobiography.* Prentice-Hall, Inc., Englewood Cliffs, New Jersey, 1959.

DEXTER, W. F. *Herbert Hoover and American Individualism.* The Macmillan Co., New York, 1932.

DRAPER, THEODORE. *The Roots of American Communism.* The Viking Press, New York, 1957.

EASTMAN, MAX. *Great Companions.* Farrar, Straus and Cudahy, New York, 1942.

EINAUDI, MARIO. *The Roosevelt Revolution.* Harcourt, Brace and Co., New York, 1959.

ELLIS, DAVID M. *A Short History of New York State.* Cornell University Press, Ithaca, 1957.

EMERSON, EDWIN. *Hoover and His Times.* Garden City Publishing Co., Garden City, New York, 1932.

Five Years of Rural Relief, WPA Division of Social Research, Washington, D.C., 1938.

FLYNN, JOHN T. *The Roosevelt Myth.* Devin-Adair Co., New York, 1956.

FOSTER, WILLIAM Z. *Pages from a Worker's Life.* International Publishers, New York, 1939.

FRANK, JOHN P. *Marble Palace. The Supreme Court in American Life.* Alfred A. Knopf, Inc., 1958.

FREIDEL, FRANK. *Franklin D. Roosevelt: The Triumph.* Little, Brown and Co., Boston, 1956.

FURNAS, J. C. *Goodbye to Uncle Tom.* Wm. Sloane Assoc., New York, 1956.

FUSFIELD, DANIEL R. *The Economic Thought of F.D.R. and the Origins of the New Deal.* Columbia University Press, New York, 1956.

GALENSON, WALTER. *The CIO Challenge to the AFL.* Harvard University Press, Cambridge. 1960.

GOODMAN, EZRA. *The Fifty Year Decline and Fall of Hollywood.* Simon and Schuster, New York, 1961.

GREEN, ABEL and LAURIE, JOE, JR. *Show Biz from Vaude to Video.* Henry Holt and Co., New York, 1951.

HAMILTON, THOMAS J. *Appeasement's Child, The Franco Regime.* Alfred A. Knopf, Inc., New York, 1943.

HEATON, JOHN L. *Tough Luck, Hoover Again*. Vanguard Press, New York, 1932.

HICKS, GRANVILLE. *Where We Came Out*. The Viking Press, New York, 1954.

HOOVER, HERBERT. *American Individualism*. Doubleday, Page and Co., Garden City, New York, 1922.

HOOVER, HERBERT. *The Challenge to Liberty*. Charles Scribner's Sons, New York, 1934.

HOOVER, HERBERT. *Memoirs*. The Macmillan Co., New York, 1952.

HOOVER, HERBERT. Memoirs, 3 vols. The Macmillan Co., New York, 1951.

HOOVER, J. EDGAR. *Persons in Hiding*. Little, Brown and Co., Boston, 1938.

HOPKINS, HARRY L. *Spending to Save*. W. W. Norton and Co., New York, 1936.

HOWE, IRVING and WIDICK, B. J. *The UAW and Walter Reuther*. Random House, New York, 1949.

HOWE, QUINCY. *News and How to Understand It*. Simon and Schuster, New York, 1940.

HOYT, EDWIN P. *The Vanderbilts and Their Fortunes*. Doubleday and Co., 1962.

HUFF, THEODORE. *Charlie Chaplin*. Henry Schuman, New York, 1951.

HUGHES, RUPERT. *Attorney for the People*. Houghton Mifflin Co., Boston, 1940.

HULL, CORDELL. *Memoirs*. The Macmillan Co., New York, 1948.

ICKES, HAROLD. *The Secret Diary of Harold L. Ickes*. Simon and Schuster, New York, 1954.

JANEWAY, ELLIOT. *The Struggle for Survival*. Yale University Press, New Haven, 1951.

JOHNSON, GERALD W. *Roosevelt: Dictator or Democrat?* Harper and Bros., New York, 1941.

JOSLIN, T. G. *Hoover Off the Record*. Doubleday-Doran, New York, 1934.

KANE, HARNETT T. *Louisiana Hayride*. William Morrow and Co., New York, 1941.

KEMPTON, MURRAY. *Part of Our Time*. Simon and Schuster, New York, 1955.

KENNEDY, H. A. A. *Hoover in 1932*. The Forallon Press, San Francisco, 1931.

KNIGHT, ARTHUR. *The Liveliest Art*. The Macmillan Co., New York, 1957.

KNOX, JOHN. *The Great Mistake*. National Foundation Press, Inc., Washington, D.C., 1930.

KOENIG, LOUIS. *The Invisible Presidency*. Rinehart and Co., New York, 1960.

LAIDLER, HARRY W. "Socialism in the U.S." (Pamphlet) League for Industrial Democracy, New York, 1952.

LAWRENCE, DAVID. *Nine Honest Men*. D. Appleton-Century Co., New York, 1936.

LORD, RUSSELL. *The Wallaces of Iowa*. Houghton Mifflin Co., Boston, 1947.

LOUIS, JOE. *My Life Story*. Duell, Sloan and Pearce, New York, 1959.

LUNDBERG, FERDINAND. *Who Controls Industry?* Vanguard Press, New York, 1938.

MADISON, CHARLES A. *Leaders and Liberals in 20th Century America.* Frederick Ungar Publishing Co., New York, 1961.

MICHELSON, CHARLES. *The Ghost Talks.* G. P. Putnam's Sons, New York, 1944.

MILLER, MARGERY. *Joe Louis, American.* A. A. Wyn, New York, 1945.

MOLEY, RAYMOND. *After Seven Years.* Harper and Bros., New York, 1939.

MOLEY, RAYMOND. *27 Masters of Politics.* Funk and Wagnalls, New York, 1949.

MORRIS, RICHARD B. *Encyclopedia of American History.* Harper and Bros., New York, 1953.

MOTT, FRANK LUTHER. *American Journalism.* The Macmillan Co., New York, 1959.

MYERS, WILLIAM STARR. *The Foreign Policies of Herbert Hoover.* Charles Scribner's Sons, New York, 1940.

MYERS, WILLIAM STARR and NEWTON, WALTER H. *The Hoover Administration—A Documented Narrative.* Charles Scribner's Sons, New York, 1936.

MYRDAL, GUNNAR. *An American Dilemma.* Harper and Bros., New York, 1944.

NESS, ELLIOTT. *The Untouchables.* Julian Messner, Inc., New York, 1957.

OPOTOWSKY, STAN. *The Longs of Louisiana.* E. P. Dutton and Co., New York, 1960.

PAYNE, ROBERT. *The Great Charlie.* Andre Deutsch, London, 1952.

PERKINS, D. W. *Wall Street Panics 1813–1930.* Published by the Author. Waterville, New York, 1931.

PERKINS, DEXTER. *The American Way.* Cornell University Press, Ithaca, 1957.

PERKINS, DEXTER. *The New Age of Franklin Roosevelt.* University of Chicago Press, Chicago, 1957.

Pittsburgh Courier.

Popular Interest Series Publishing Company. "Which Offers More for the Future?" (Pamphlet) Chicago, 1932.

PUSEY, MERLO. J. *Charles Evans Hughes.* The Macmillan Co., New York, 1951.

RAUCH, BASIL. *The History of the New Deal.* Creative Age Press, Inc., New York, 1944.

RAUCH, BASIL. *The Roosevelt Reader.* Rinehart and Co., New York, 1957.

REDDING, SAUNDERS. *The Lonesome Road.* Doubleday and Co., New York, 1958.

Review of Reviews.

ROBINSON, EDGAR EUGENE. *The Roosevelt Leadership 1935–1945.* J. B. Lippincott Co., Philadelphia, 1955.

ROOSEVELT, ELEANOR. *This Is My Story.*

ROOSEVELT, FRANKLIN D. *F.D.R.—His Personal Letters*, 4 vols. Duell, Sloan and Pearce, New York, 1947.

ROOSEVELT, FRANKLIN D. *Government—Not Politics.* Covici Friede, Publishers, New York, 1932.

ROOSEVELT, JAMES and SHALETT, SIDNEY. *Affectionately, F.D.R.* Harcourt, Brace and Co., New York, 1959.

ROSENMAN, SAMUEL I. *Working with Roosevelt.* Harper and Bros., New York, 1952.

ST. JAMES, WARREN D. *The National Association for the Advancement of Colored People: A Case Study in Pressure Groups.* Exposition Press, New York, 1958.

SALOMAN, LEON I. (editor) *The Supreme Court.* H. W. Wilson Co., New York, 1961.

SANN, PAUL. *The Lawless Decade.* Crown Publishers, New York, 1957.

SCHLESINGER, ARTHUR M., JR. *The Coming of the New Deal.* Houghton Mifflin Co., Boston. (Year?)

SCHLESINGER, ARTHUR M., JR. *The Crisis of the Old Order.* Houghton Mifflin Co., Boston, 1959.

SCHLESINGER, ARTHUR M., JR. *The Politics of Upheaval.* Houghton Mifflin Co., Boston, 1960.

SHANNON, DAVID A. (editor) *The Great Depression.* Prentice-Hall, Inc., Englewood Cliffs, New Jersey, 1960.

SHANNON, DAVID. *The Socialist Party of America*, The Macmillan Co., New York, 1955.

SHANNON, FRED ALBERT, *America's Economic Growth.* The Macmillan Co., New York, 1951.

SHERWIN, MARK and MARKMANN, CHARLES LAM. *One Week in March.* G. P. Putnam's Sons, New York, 1961.

SHERWOOD, ROBERT E. *Roosevelt and Hopkins.* Harper and Bros., New York, 1948.

SHERWOOD, ROBERT E. *There Shall Be No Night.* Charles Scribner's Sons, New York, 1940.

SMITH, ALSON J. *Chicago's Left Bank.* Henry Regnery, Chicago, 1953.

SMITH, RIXEY and BEASLEY, NORMAN. *Carter Glass.* Longmans, Green and Co., New York, 1939.

STACKPOLE, J. LEWIS. *Rosie in Squanderland, or Billions for Votes.* The Paisley Press, Inc. New York, 1936.

Statistical Abstract of the United States.

STEINBERG, ALFRED. *The Life of Eleanor Roosevelt.* G. P. Putnam's Sons, New York, 1958.

STEWART, KENNETH. *News Is What We Make It.* Houghton Mifflin Co., Boston, 1943.

STEWART, KENNETH and TEBBEL, JOHN. *Makers of Modern Journalism*. Prentice-Hall, Inc., Englewood Cliffs, New Jersey, 1952.

STUDENSKI, PAUL and KROOS, HERMAN E. *Financial History of the United States*. McGraw-Hill, New York, 1952.

Survey Graphic.

TEBBEL, JOHN. *An American Dynasty*. Doubleday and Co., New York, 1947.

THOMAS, NORMAN. *As I See It*. The Macmillan Co., 1932.

THOMAS, NORMAN. *Democracy vs. Dictatorship*. League for Industrial Democracy, New York, 1937.

THORNING, JOSEPH F. "Communism in the U.S.A.?" (Pamphlet) The American Press, New York, 1933.

TUGWELL, REXFORD G. *The Democratic Roosevelt*, Doubleday and Co., 1957.

TULLY, GRACE. *F.D.R.—My Boss*. Charles Scribner's Sons, New York, 1949.

TUOHY, ROGER. *The Stolen Years*. Pennington Press, Cleveland, 1959.

UNTERMEYER, LOUIS. *Makers of the Modern World*. Simon and Schuster, 1955.

WARREN, HARRIS GAYLORD. *Herbert Hoover and the Great Depression*. Oxford University Press, New York, 1959.

WEHLE, LOUIS B. *Hidden Threads of History*. The Macmillan Co., New York, 1953.

WHITEHEAD, DON. *The FBI Story*. Random House, New York, 1956.

WOLFE, HAROLD. *Herbert Hoover. Public Servant and Leader of the Loyal Opposition*. Exposition Press, New York, 1956.

WOODS, JOHN A. *Roosevelt and Modern America*. The Macmillan Co., New York, 1959.

Yale Review.

INDEX

INDEX